Modern Agricultural Management

A Systems Approach to Farming
Second Edition

Modern
Agricultural
Management

A Systems Approach to Farming
Second Edition

Donald D. Osburn
Kenneth C. Schneeberger
The University of Missouri

Reston Publishing Company, Inc.
A Prentice-Hall Company
Reston, Virginia

Library of Congress Cataloging in Publication Data

Osburn, Donald D.
    Modern agricultural management.

    Includes bibliographies and index.
    1. Farm management.   I. Schneeberger, Kenneth C.
II. Title.
S561.O73 1982   630'.68   82-7650
ISBN 0-8359-4550-2   AACR2

© 1983 by Reston Publishing Company, Inc.
A Prentice-Hall Company
Reston, Virginia 22090

10 9 8 7 6 5 4 3 2

Printed in the United States of America

16041

Contents

Preface to the Second Edition

The trend to larger commercial farms has accentuated the need for capable, educated farm operators and managers. The first edition was developed to help students hone their decisionmaking skills in farm and financial management. With this edition we have modified and improved some sections of the first edition and updated other sections. The Economic Recovery Tax Act of 1981, for example, required some major adjustments in the discussion of costs and taxes.

The first edition was committed to helping students understand the variety of tools and principles available for managers to use in solving today's complex farm/ranch problems. The focus of the first edition was apparently "on target," as nearly 100 colleges and universities—and numerous vocational programs—adopted the text.

We were gratified by the response to the first edition. We have tried to make improvements in this edition which will make Modern Agricultural Management even more useful in preparing U.S. agriculture's future managers.

Modern Agricultural Management

A Systems Approach to Farming
Second Edition

Part 1

Introduction to Agricultural Management

Management

- Management defined
- Scope of management
- Management as job, resource, and procedure
- Problem-solving steps
  Setting goals
  Defining the problems
  Gathering information
  Analyzing alternatives
  Making decisions
  Implementing decisions
  Accepting responsibility
  Evaluating outcomes

1

The manager is the "nerve center" of the modern agricultural business. Once the owners have determined the goals of the business, the manager is charged with facilitating the attainment of those goals. In the case of many family farms/ranches, the business's goals are totally intertwined with family goals.

An appreciation for the scope of management responsibilities and familiarity with tools and principles of analysis are preconditions for effective management. A manager must develop the ability to take information from many sources, analyze it, and make decisions on a variety of problems. Decisions are often complicated by incomplete information, complex interrelationships, and uncertainty about the future. Yet decisions have to be made and implemented if today's agricultural units are to be in operation tomorrow.

The organization and control of farms, ranches, and farm-related businesses are becoming more and more complex. Firms are getting larger. Capital requirements are increasing. Labor is becoming more scarce. Markets are truly international in dimension. Amid such complexities, how can a manager be most effective? This book relates economic and management principles to real-world problems in an attempt to provide models or approaches for meeting the infinite variety of problems and opportunities of a dynamic, modern agriculture.

To the question, What is management? this text takes a broad view. *Management is viewed as those activities relating to the organization and operation of a firm for the attainment of specific ends. It directs resource use after interpreting the goals of those controlling the firm.* Management's responsibilities include *organizational* decisions about (1) what to produce, (2) how much to produce, and (3) when to produce it, along with the day-to-day, month-to-month *operational* tasks of (1) determining methods of production, (2) timing jobs, (3) selecting equipment or techniques, and (4) choosing personnel. Operational tasks vary from choosing among alternative ways of accomplishing a particular organizational goal (such as clearing 200 acres of timbered land and putting it to improved pasture) to making sure the cows are fed on a regular basis during the winter months.

THE SCOPE OF THE MANAGER

In general, agriculture continues to be dominated by many owner-operator, or family, units, although the family may include sons and daughters and their families in addition to the parents in a partnership or corporate arrangement. As such, the management and worker functions are simultaneously lodged in one or a few persons. Further, as contrasted with large corporate businesses, agriculture managers are generally responsible for all areas of management. These areas have been variously subdivided. One such breakdown is:

1. *Technical activities:* Include responsibility for all production know-how, seeing that production is accomplished on time, and adapting production processes to changing economic and technical conditions.

2. *Commercial activities:* Include all buying and selling. This area involves procurement of inputs in the quantities and combinations necessary for efficient production, plus orderly storage, handling, and marketing of commodities produced. It also includes the tasks of market forecasting and contracting for services of others.

3. *Financial activities:* Involve the acquisition and use of capital, pre-

sumably in an optimal manner. This requires forecasting future investment needs and arranging for their financing.

4. *Accounting activities:* Include physical, human, business, and tax records. This area may involve setting standards for certain enterprises or segments of the business.

In addition to directing these activities, the manager may be the goal setter, the planner, the motivator, and the public relations person for the agricultural firm. In Exhibit 1–1 the scope of the modern agriculture manager is highlighted.

Exhibit 1–1. Scope of management activities

Technical Activities	Deciding what to produce and how	Enterprise choice and combination Input levels and combinations Quality of output
	Using land	Capability–fertility Tillage practices–conservation Regulations–constraints
	Determining level of mechanization	Capital requirements Availability of services Labor implications
	Determining scale of production	Economies in production or buying Shape of cost curves Degree of specialization Capabilities of management
Commercial Activities	Acquiring inputs	Own Rent/lease Hire From whom When/how long Quality and quantity Financing
	Marketing products	Open market? Contract? Hedge? Direct to buyer or store Delivery point Quality Integration
	Forecasting price	Inputs Products

Exhibit 1–1. (cont'd.)

Financial Activities	Acquiring funds	Quantity and terms Sources Lender services Equity position-liquidity position
	Using funds	Relative profitability of alternatives Time horizon and payback Cash flows
	Forecasting future needs	Depreciation of assets Expansion/contraction Changing technology
Accounting Activities	Keeping production records	Enterprise Ownership units
	Recording business transactions	Accounting method Choice of accounts Periodic summary Cash flow forecasting
	Tax reporting	Income taxes and other taxes Wages Social Security Depreciation
	Filing documents with governmental and regulatory agencies	

VIEWS OF MANAGEMENT

Three basic views of management have evolved over time. These are:

1. Management = Job
2. Management = Resource
3. Management = Procedure

Job

The concept of management as a job derives from the idea of being paid for performing the tasks of running a business. This is vividly portrayed in the general business area where persons who may have little direct ownership of the business are employed to perform certain functions. These functions generally include planning, organizing, controlling, motivating, staffing, and communicating, but may include others.

All the functions are within the purview of modern agriculture management; however, managers of farms and farm-related businesses do not generally control the number of employees and variety of enterprises that business managers outside of agriculture do. Consequently, there is often less specialization in specific functions in agriculture.

Resource

The concept of management as a resource relates to an increasing awareness that the human factor is important in agricultural businesses. It is not uncommon to see two individuals with very similar land and other resources show very different results after the same period of time. The "key" factor often noted is the difference in management, what has been called "the intangible part of production expressed in the lives of persons." It might be visualized as a difference in human-related output or an output performance gap due to different managers. This difference is illustrated in Exhibit 1–2 as the difference between curves A, B, and C. Managers A, B, and C are assumed to control/operate the same set of physical resources (capital), but the output would be different depending on the manager. It is this "gap" which distinguishes why some agricultural businesses have grown and prospered, while other similar ones have failed and gone out of business. Chance and windfall gains may play a role; but since agricultural businesses are run by men and women, it is logical that the long-term success (or failure) depends in large part on the manager's efforts and abilities. Although practically impossible to quantify, some persons seem to have an "art" of applying business and scientific information in a way that allows their businesses to outperform other similar businesses.

Problem-Solving Steps

The concept of management as procedure relates to the scientific method of problem solving associated with John Dewey and others. It involves the following steps:

1. Clearly define the problem.
2. Gather objective facts and arrange them in relevant order.
3. Evaluate and analyze the data.
4. Draw conclusions or make decisions based upon the analysis.
5. Take appropriate action.

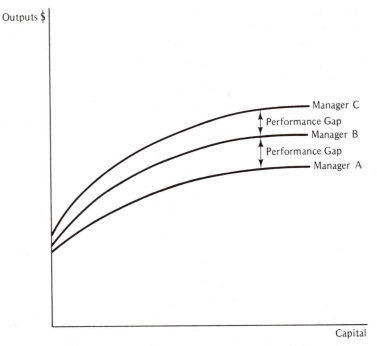

Exhibit 1–2. Differences in management shown as a difference in production with other factors equal.

Some have said the performance gap discussed above can be explained in part by differences in managers' ability to think problems through, make decisions, and then to execute those decisions.

Because modern agricultural management involves a whole complex of interacting forces and activities, it may be useful to expand the steps given above. The steps are:

1. Formulation of goals and objectives of the firm
2. Recognition and definition of problems or opportunities
3. Gathering and organization of facts
4. Analysis of alternative courses of action
5. Decision making based on sound criteria
6. Implementation: acting on the decision
7. Acceptance of responsibility for the decision regardless of the outcome
8. Evaluation of the outcome of the decision

Goals: It would make little sense to start out on a trip without a pretty firm idea of where you are going. Yet agriculture business owners and managers are frequently criticized for just that.

The establishment of goals and objectives appears to be one of the most neglected phases of management. Several reasons have been offered:

1. It takes time to decide on goals. A manager will frequently respond, "I'm too busy for that."

2. Coming to grips with the many, and often conflicting, goals and selecting the more important ones is a demanding task. Some managers don't have the preparation or experience. Others lack confidence or ability.

3. As the ramifications of problems become more numerous, goals become more difficult to define.

4. Some managers have never thought about the need to set or the means to arrive at goals. They see their major goal as surviving for another year and fail to recognize that survival is but one of many goals. But, other goals are contingent upon survival.

Recognition of conflicting goals is particularly relevant for family farms. It is often difficult to distinguish between farm and family goals. Further, choosing a particular farm goal may preclude the choice of a family goal or vice versa.

Goals give purpose and direction to decisions and actions. They must be defined so as to serve as a measure of success or failure.

Among suggestions that have been made for goal setting are:

1. Choose practical goals. This means set realistic, attainable goals. It is well to aim high, rather than too low, but a manager who never attains some of the established goals can become very frustrated.

2. Have some specific goals. These may range from realizing $100 per acre above cash costs to making certain purchases for the farm home. Specific objectives provide definite ends toward which to strive and can give a manager an effective basis for his actions. The resources to use and the risks to take are easier to determine when the objectives are specific.

3. Have a hierarchy of goals. Goals have different weights. There are $10 goals and $10,000 goals. They should be treated accordingly.

4. Recognize the multiple and shifting nature of goals. This ties in to the previous comment. Managers have not one, but a multiplicity

of goals. Maximization of earnings may be one. But there are likely many others, such as security, prestige, and leisure. Some of these may be competing goals. Further, because change is a fact of life, goals may need to be altered. Goals may shift due to economic conditions, changing family circumstances, or new knowledge.

5. Recognize the time dimensions of goals. Some goals are readily attainable in the short run. Others are long-term, ultimate, and more difficult to obtain. Long-range objectives related to planning are useful in forecasting (a) the direction in which a business should move or (b) forthcoming investment needs.

Opportunity recognition: There has been much conjecture about why one person recognizes an opportunity or problem and another does not. Basic findings suggest a preparedness or frame of mind able to recognize and define new conditions or problems. Consider the case of the fellow who went to an auto mechanic because his car was making a "bumping" sound. He couldn't locate the problem, but thought it was in the rear end. The mechanic drove the car and came back to tell the fellow he had a bad tire. The fellow with the car recognized he had a problem, but was unable to define it adequately because his level of preparation and/or experience did not provide the framework to do so.

Several factors have been identified as being associated with competence in opportunity/problem recognition. Included are (1) experience (growing up on a farm or having farming experience), (2) level of schooling (exposure to a broad range of ideas and approaches to problem solving), (3) motivation by accomplishing a goal, and (4) willingness to take risk.

Some managers say defining the problem is equal to achieving one-half the solution. Nebulous or unclear problem definition can lead to wasted time and motion, collection of inappropriate data, and use of incorrect or inadequate analytical techniques. Sometimes wasted motion means a missed opportunity. Recognizing that the cattle enterprise is not making money is only the beginning. The problem must be brought into sharper focus by looking at more specific reasons, such as calving percentage, rate of gain, selling price, cost per hundredweight, pounds of beef sold, and so on.

The problems and/or opportunities in most agriculture businesses are practically limitless. Wise managers select problems which, when solved, promise a high payoff in terms of a goal of the business. The payoff may be financial profit or a nonpecuniary return that has high psychic value, like being named the outstanding farm family by the local bank.

Successful managers also tend to recognize the organizational demands of problems, to see the relationship of problems to each other, and to understand their relative importance and urgency. This ability to see the big picture and focus on the critical relationships requires considerable managerial skill. It is also a characteristic that may be impossible to learn from a book or in a classroom.

Distinguishing between *major* and *minor* problems, although seemingly obvious, is often a problem for managers. To spend time researching and analyzing situations that will have minor impact on the business is unwise if the time could be more profitably spent on a major problem or in seeing that jobs get done on time. One should frequently step back and ask, "Is this a significant problem I am worrying about?"

Gathering of data: Data act as the fuel for decision making and must be of good quality if the process is to run smoothly. All succeeding steps in decision making rely on data collection. No other step can compensate for poor information. Thus, care should be given to defining the problem in such a way that reliable quantitative data can be collected if they exist.

Serious obstacles may be encountered in data collection. First, some important decisions do not lend themselves well to quantification (e.g., problems relating to human relations, attitudes, or family goals). Further, fact gathering costs time and money. In most cases the operator or manager will be forced to decide when enough information has been obtained. In information gathering, as with other productive activities, there exists a point of diminishing returns. Obviously, data need not be collected if they add less to profits than it costs to obtain them.

Common sense is important in data gathering. There may be many means to the solution of a problem, and thus many sets of data. Determining the more important information minimizes wasted time and speeds up the data collection process. By concentrating on the essential or limiting facts (and accumulating the lesser ones in progress), a manager can be sure of maximum information should a decision be forced sooner than desired, which is the usual case.

Sources will depend upon the data needed. Are the factors technical, economic, regulatory, human, or even intangible? The list of potential sources includes neighbors, firms providing services, newspapers and magazines (the most often mentioned source of new information by farmers), market reports, professional agriculturalists, and the many services of governmental and university agencies. One's own business records may be the most valuable data source.

Analysis: Additional discussion of the basic data needs in decision making is a major focus of several later sections in this book (e.g., enterprise analysis, records, selection of coefficients for budgeting, and linear programming). Tools and procedures for objective analysis of the operating firm or for projecting effects of proposed organizational changes are also extensively treated. However, it seems useful at this point to make some general points regarding the analytical stage.

1. Analysis means looking at two or more potential solutions in a systematic fashion. It compels the problem solver to prepare a logical approach, using the relevant data, for suggesting or forecasting a probable result from an alternative course of action.

2. The logical analysis, or analytic model, must include the important technical or economic relationships. It can then serve as a test of the feasibility of the alternative in meeting some specified end or goal.

3. A logical analysis has the benefit of replication. It is possible to retrace or reconstruct the analytical procedure. Analyzing the question "Should I place calves on wheat pasture?" should be much different from making the decision based on a hunch or on custom.

4. It is reasonable to assume that systematic analysis, based upon good data, is more reliable than hunch or intuition simply because it forces the problem solver to get down all the relevant facts. The chances of overlooking something important are minimized.

5. Although objective data are desired for analysis, there are likely to be intangibles. It is often unwise, and probably impossible, to try to quantify all factors that influence a problem. But intangible, or qualitative, factors can be incorporated by (a) recognizing their existence, (b) ranking them in terms of importance, and (c) trying to assess their probable effect on the proposed course of action.

6. Because of data limitations or the complexity of some problems, analysis may have to be supplemented with intuition and tempered with judgment based upon experience. This gets into the "art" of management. But the problem solver should not give up analysis simply because it is difficult or incomplete.

Decision: To make a decision is to select a course of action. It requires coming to a conclusion, although that conclusion may be either (1) to do something, i.e., launch a new activity, (2) to do nothing, or (3) to go back and reformulate the problem, gather more information, or do further analysis.

At the decision point, the manager must consider the consequences of the alternatives developed by the analysis. He must select the alternative that appears most desirable and consistent with (1) the goals of the business, (2) the resources that the business has or can marshal to implement the proposed action, (3) the strengths and weaknesses of the business, and (4) the risks or opportunities that appear to be associated with that course of action.

Decision making is a creative event when many factors are brought together for action. Since it generally involves the future, it also involves uncertainty.

Implementation: A decision without implementation is like going into a candy store without money. Although creative thinking and decision making are good experiences, they have no payoff unless some action is taken. How many times have you heard a person say, "If I had only . . ."?

To implement a decision means to put that decision into operation. The decision may be to try a new variety of crop or to construct a new building. However, the new variety must be ordered and planted, or financing and a builder must be lined up for the building if the decision is going to take effect.

The implementation stage is difficult for some people. There is risk in taking action. You may have been incorrect or incomplete in your analysis. Or, conditions may change. A person can be worse off after implementing a decision.

A good "implementor" will be better off a majority of the times if he or she has done a good job in the prior problem-solving steps.

Acceptance of responsibility: Most actions can give multiple outcomes, depending on the events and conditions that actually occur once a decision is implemented. Despite careful analysis, most decisions must be put in motion before a manager can find out exactly what will happen.

The responsibility for decisions and their results ultimately has to rest with some person or group. The "buck" has to stop somewhere. That "somewhere" is management, even if an unfavorable or unprofitable outcome is the result of a subordinate's actions. A manager is responsible for the supervision and direction of employees under him; a manager of a farm business that loses money is the one held accountable, not some hired employee.

Evaluation: Evaluation is plagued by some of the same problems as goal setting. Managers are often so busy they don't take time to assess the impact or effects of decisions made previously. Further, knowing when to evaluate is sometimes difficult, although that is less often the case with actions that show results, such as trying a new crop variety or production practice (e.g., crossbreeding livestock or planting narrow-row soybeans).

Sometimes an unwillingness to evaluate is a means to put off or avoid confronting the outcome of a particular decision.

Of the several approaches to evaluation, one that makes sense for agriculture is to ask a series of questions. (1) What did I think would happen (that is, what were my expectations) when I made the decision? (2) Did the outcome approximate or approach my expectations? Were my expectations consistent with the realities of the situation? If not, what factors might explain the difference between what I had predicted and what actually happened? (3) Did I include those factors in my analysis? Are they sufficiently important that I should include them the next time I come to a similar decision? (4) Am I satisfied, or is a new activity called for?

Intertwined problems: It is obvious that problems do not come to the manager one at a time. Seldom can the problem solver cope with one problem until it is resolved, then move to problem number two until it is resolved, then number three, and so on. Typically one must stop in the middle of one problem to tackle a new and more urgent one that has unexpectedly presented itself, and then go back to the first. Farm management problems cover a wide variety of fields. One minute the manager is getting things in order for a loan application and the next, adjusting the spray rig for applying herbicide. Meanwhile, he confers with his wife about a domestic matter over the two-way radio and assists a first-calf heifer in delivery. The competent manager must have a multiple-track mind; he must be a decision-making "juggler."

It is also obvious that some situations do not require all, maybe not any, of the eight problem-solving steps. Managers can make some decisions out of habit without serious consequences. For example, a dairyman may not need to decide which cow to milk first each day, or a crop farmer may not need to decide which field to till first after a big rain. Neither will a cattle feeder tediously weigh the costs and returns of vaccinating a new load of incoming feeder calves.

Managerial Success

The ability to define a problem, evaluate it, and make an informed decision is a characteristic shared by top managers. However, a major management consulting firm has identified seven other common traits of top managers. Such managers:

1. Have motivation, or drive.
2. Set goals for themselves, as well as for the businesses they direct.
3. Stress their strengths.

4. Put emphasis on improving productivity.
5. Concentrate on one key area at a time.
6. Are willing to take calculated risks.
7. Keep in touch with buyers and suppliers.

Motivation: Successful managers tend to have a lot of ambition. They want to succeed and spend long hours managing the businesses they operate. The attitude of these managers is often "Make as good a decision as you can, then adjust it." They do not wait for an overall perfect plan.

Set goals for themselves: Top managers are more than motivated—they are motivated with a purpose. They have set goals for themselves. They want to be a major executive in their company, the leading farmer in their community, or they want to achieve a certain income level. They probably want to be recognized as a top manager by those who know them, and they often have community leadership goals. As was mentioned earlier in this chapter, they have some goals for the short run and some that may take several years to attain.

Stress their strengths: A top manager knows her or his strong points. One person may be best at farrowing hogs while another is a very good cotton producer. Someone else may understand the futures markets and be a really good marketer. We all have a comparative advantage in some area. Successful managers define their strengths and build on them. They are slow to jump into enterprises for which they have poor preparation unless they are sure someone else in their business is qualified. They prefer to be tinkerers rather than inventors, making small but consistent steps of progress rather than adopting every new idea that comes down the road.

Improve productivity: Even though a top manager stresses her/his strengths, he or she should not close out the option of improving their performance. This may mean doing your current job better or expanding into a new area.

One way to get productivity increases is to install new or more modern capital improvements. But another method is often overlooked. Productivity can be improved by (1) improving your knowledge (or an employee's knowledge) in an area and (2) realizing a financial gain as a result of improved knowledge. Thus, participation in short courses, young farmer groups, and special seminars may have a payoff in increased productivity. A day or two spent visiting with another farmer or rancher who is recognized for her/his expertise in an area may allow you to achieve productivity gains.

Almost all businesses, farm and nonfarm, use some method to recognize employees for productivity gains. This usually includes a monetary gain but may include something else like a certificate, a special dinner paid for by the boss, or an extra day off.

One key variable at a time: A manager must deal with a multitude of different problems and opportunities each week. However, they also find one key area of the business that gets their special attention. For example, economic conditions may be such that machinery prices are low this year relative to past years. That may mean that this is the year to make adjustments in the line of machinery being used. Or, pounds of pork produced per sow may be lower than your goal—or the cost per pound of gain is too high. Then, the manager may devote extra time and effort to that particular key problem.

Take calculated risks: Few actions a manager takes are risk-free. That is the reason an earlier section of this chapter emphasized the decision-making steps. A problem that is carefully evaluated and analyzed is more likely to be correctly resolved. However, being a manager means taking well–thought-out risks.

Keep in touch: A really successful manager must stay in contact with the key people that affect his business. In a larger business the key people are probably the employees and the customers. In agriculture, it may again be employees and customers. But it includes key sources of inputs. Thus, a manager should keep the lender informed on the performance of the business and on plans for the future. Contact with the feed and fertilizer dealers and a machinery dealer or two is essential. Being able to call these suppliers and get instant help can be the difference between profit and loss. Knowing and being known by suppliers can help you understand their perspective as well as their capacity for helping you in your business.

SUMMARY

This chapter has pointed out that:

- Firms operate in a complex and changing environment.
- Because of the complexities and uncertainties, there is a need for managers.
- Management can be viewed as either (a) a job, (b) a productive input/resource like land and labor, or (c) a scientific approach to problem solving.

• Decision making is a primary function of managers and should be based on a knowledge of firm goals, a clear definition of the problem about which the decision is being made, sound data, and a complete, well-reasoned analysis.

• The procedure or "step" approach for dealing with problems or new situations can insure that important factors are considered, researched, and weighed.

• Management must accept the responsibility for the performance of a business or part of that business in terms of the achievement of that firm's goals.

• In agriculture-related firms, particularly farms and ranches, the range of management activities is usually lodged in one or a very few individuals.

The next chapter begins to illustrate how facts and principles can be combined to provide the manager with sound bases for choosing among alternative courses of action.

APPLYING THE PRINCIPLES OF CHAPTER 1

1. Develop an alternate definition of farm management.

2. Is there any similarity in the executive skills needed by a farm manager and the manager of a large corporation? Which manager has the greater breadth of responsibility? Which has the greater responsibility for specific activities within the business?

3. What are four major decisions facing farm managers in your area this year?

4. Why do we need managers anyway?

5. What do you see as the first task of a new farm or ranch manager?

6. Some decisions are unique; they occur only once. How would you propose to resolve or decide a unique problematic situation?

REFERENCES

Bradford, L. A. and G. L. Johnson. *Farm Management Analysis.* New York: John Wiley & Sons, Inc., 1953.

Castle, Emery N., Manning H. Becker and Fredrick J. Smith. *Farm Business Management*, 2nd ed. New York: The Macmillan Co., 1972.

Eisgruber, L. and J. Nielson. "Decision-Making Models in Farm Management," *Canadian Journal of Agricultural Economics,* Vol. XI, No. 1, 1963, pp. 60–70.

Headley, J. C. "Evaluating Farm Management Performance and the Challenge to Farm Management Research," *Illinois Agricultural Economist,* January 1967, pp. 11–16.

Hedges, Trimble R. *Farm Management Decisions.* Englewood Cliffs, N.J.: Prentice-Hall, Inc., 1963.

Hilkert, Robert N. *The Art of Management: and Other Talks.* Federal Reserve Bank of Philadelphia, 1970.

Justus, Fred and J. C. Headley, eds. *The Management Factor in Farming—An Evaluation and Summary of Research,* Minnesota Agricultural Experiment Station Technical Bulletin 258, 1967.

Kay, Ronald D. *Farm Management.* New York: McGraw-Hill Book Co., 1981, pp. 3–17.

Krause, K. R. and P. L. Williams. *Personality Characteristics Related to Managerial Success,* South Dakota Agricultural Experiment Station Technical Bulletin 30, 1971.

Peters, T. J. "Putting Excellence into Management," *Business Week,* July 21, 1980.

Riggs, James L. *Economic Decision Models for Engineers and Managers.* New York: McGraw-Hill Book Co., 1968.

Rushton, Willard T. and E. T. Shaydys. "A Systematic Conceptualization of Farm Management," *Journal of Farm Economics,* February 1967, pp. 53–63.

Suter, Robert C. "The Management Process," *Journal of the American Society of Farm Managers and Rural Appraisers,* October 1963, pp. 5–14.

Part 2

Applying Economic Principles

Marginal Analysis in Short-Run Planning

2

- Diminishing returns
- The production function
- Profit maximization
  One input and one output
  One input and multiple outputs
- Least-cost combinations of inputs

There are many management decisions which, although repetitive, cannot be made out of habit or custom. Some important variables (e.g., price of an input, price of an output) may change and call for a different decision than was made the last time a similar situation was faced. For example, a cattle feeder may find it more profitable to feed steers one time, but heifers the next. It may return more to feed a predominately forage ration this year, when a high energy–high concentrate ration was more profitable last year.

There are many short-run decisions that require a manager to use both physical production data and economic information in making decisions and taking actions for attaining business goals. Some economic principles useful in analysis are presented in this chapter.

Economic principles are viewed as economic hocus-pocus by some who are unfamiliar with these useful tools. Yet some of these same people are unable to answer complex questions like "Why am I not making more money?" Such questions can only be dealt with in parts; principles can assist in evaluating the parts. Principles give the practical decision maker a filing system within which to arrange and systematize facts and extract the maximum use from them.

Principles are generalizations having wide application. They describe universal relationships that may exist among certain factors and permit a quick and concise explanation of those relationships. The application of principles to problem solving facilitates efforts to make logical, practical, and profitable judgments. Knowledge of principles can help a person:

1. Identify the alternatives involved in an economic decision

2. Improve the estimates of the results that may be expected with certain changes

3. Develop a framework within which a sound economic decision can be made

INPUT-OUTPUT RELATIONSHIPS

A manager combines input/resources, sometimes referred to as factors of production, to produce some output/product. He may vary the quantity of one or more inputs while holding other inputs constant. The crop farmer may have a fixed amount of land, fertilizer, and seed, but vary the amount of irrigation water. The addition of more and more water to an acre of growing crops alters the proportion of water to the other factors. The livestock operator with yearlings on grass can feed varying amounts of grain to induce higher levels of average daily gain per animal.

Diminishing Physical Returns

The tendencies for the ratios of output to input to vary along with the proportions among input factors is called the law of variable proportions, or the principle of diminishing physical returns.

The diminishing returns phenomenon is observable in all productive activity. The principle may be stated in this way: *As a variable input is added to fixed resources, added output increases at a decreasing rate immediately or after an initial stage of increasing at an increasing rate.* This assumes all inputs are fixed except one, the one being varied.

The diminishing physical returns principle is illustrated for corn and fertilizer, other things constant. Exhibit 2–1 summarizes the basic input-output relationship. The variable input is nitrogen fertilizer. Fixed resources are labor, tillage practices, phosphorus and potassium fertilizers, seed, and land. The first 15-pound increment of nitrogen increases corn yield by 17 bushels. However, the second 15 pounds adds more to yield than the first 15 pounds did. That is an example of output increasing at an increasing rate.

The more common response observed in agriculture is illustrated by the range from 30 to 150 pounds of N (units 2–9) in the example. Additional increments of N increase production, but the increases get smaller and smaller; hence, the concept of diminishing marginal physical returns, or output increasing but at a decreasing rate.

The Production Function: One Variable Input Case

The general input-output relationship may be illustrated graphically as in Exhibit 2–2. The curve labeled TPP (total physical product) is commonly referred to as a production function. It illustrates all possible combinations between the variable input and the output being produced when other inputs are held constant for the given unit of time to which the production function applies (e.g., a crop season, cattle feeding period, etc.).

Because it is not possible to discuss all production functions, the

Exhibit 2–1. Corn response to nitrogen fertilization: an input-output relationship

Input units (one unit = 15 lb. of N)	Output (bu. of corn)	Added output (bu.)
0	70	—
1	87	17
2	105	18
3	115	10
4	123	8
5	128	5
6	132	4
7	134	2
8	136	2
9	137	1
10	134	−3

general case will be described. The shape of the production function indicates what happens to output, Y, as increasing amounts of the variable input, X, are added to the set of fixed inputs. Exhibit 2–2 output is zero when no units of the variable input are applied. (This is in contrast to the 70 bushels of corn assumed produced in Exhibit 2–1 even though no nitrogen was applied.) Output increases at an increasing rate as the first few units of input are added; it continues to increase, but at a decreasing rate, at higher input levels until maximum output is attained at X_n units of X.

Two physical measures are commonly derived from the TPP curve, namely average physical product and marginal physical produce (see Exhibit 2–3). These measures are basic to certain economic analyses, but are useful decision variables in and of themselves as they help define the logical stages of production. Average physical product, APP, is determined by dividing output, Y, by a particular level of X (e.g., X_i). It is determined from the formula

$$APP = \frac{Y}{X}$$

where Y is total product and X is the number of units of the variable input required to produce that output. Thus, if three units of fertilizer are combined with fixed inputs to produce 115 bushels of corn, the APP of fertilizer is 38.3 units of corn per unit of fertilizer. The term physical means that the average product is measured in physical units like tons, pounds, or bushels, rather than in dollar terms. The APP curve will have both a positive and negative slope when derived from the general production function.

Marginal physical product, MPP, gives the rate of increase (or decrease) in TPP as more and more units of the variable input are used. MPP increases if TPP is increasing at an increasing rate. MPP is decreasing, but is greater than zero if TPP is increasing at a decreasing rate (see Exhibit 2–3). MPP is exactly zero when TPP is a maximum and less than zero when TPP turns down. MPP is the change in or additional output resulting from a unit increase in the variable input. It is computed by dividing the change in output by the causal amount of input, that is, by the increment in input that caused the change in output. The formula for the marginal product of a variable input is

$$MPP = \frac{\Delta Y}{\Delta X}$$

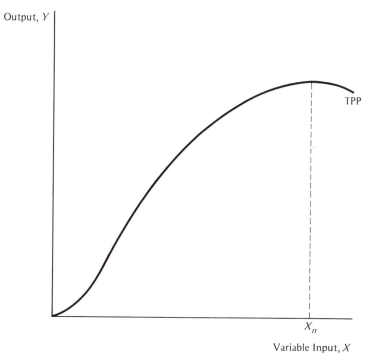

Exhibit 2–2. **A general production function.**

where ΔY refers to the change in total product and ΔX refers to a one-unit change in the variable input. Column 3 in Exhibit 2–1 is a schedule of MPPs. The change in output associated with the first unit of inputs was $17 \div 1 = 17$. The change in input going from one unit to two units is 1; the change in output is 18. Thus MPP for unit 2 is 18.

Stages of Production

The general production function can be divided into three parts, or stages. Each is important from the standpoint of efficient resource use. The stages are shown in Exhibit 2–3. In Stage I, MPP is greater than APP but APP is increasing, indicating that the efficiency of the variable input is increasing in this stage. Each additional unit of the variable input pays better than the one before it. It pays at least to use a variable input to the level where APP is a maximum, if it pays to use any of the input at all.

Stage II or production occurs where MPP is declining and less than

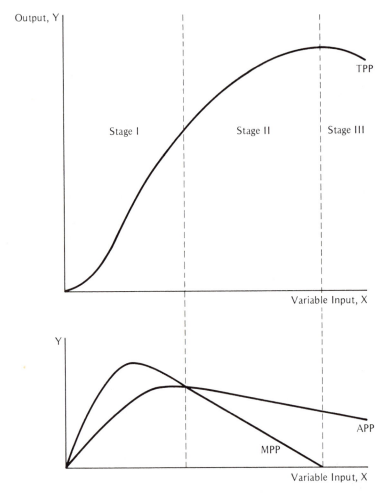

Exhibit 2–3. Average physical product, marginal physical product, and stages of production.

APP, but greater than zero. Most practical farm input-output problems relate to Stage II. It is the rational stage of production because the efficiency of the variable input is declining but marginal productivity of the input is still positive. The most profitable level of use of the variable input lies within Stage II, but cannot be determined without a knowledge of input and output prices.

Stage III is an area of declining TPP. Any output level in Stage III is inferior to some level in Stage II because equal or greater amounts of product could be produced with fewer inputs. Stage III occurs when excessive quantities of the variable input are applied to the set of fixed inputs.

The Maximum Profit Point

It is not uncommon to hear agriculturalists speak in terms of maximizing production. In most cases, pursuing such a goal will yield a profit. However, in few cases does production maximization also give maximum profit. The fact that inputs have a cost means that a production level other than output maximization usually is the point of maximum profit. The principle of maximum profit says: *To maximize profits, add increments of a variable input as long as the value of the added output resulting from the last unit of input is greater than or equal to the cost of that last unit of input.* This is the point where either an increase or decrease in the variable input will decrease net returns.

The corn response example of Exhibit 2–1 can be used to illustrate the application of this principle. The example requires adding economic information in the form of input and output (product) prices to the physical input-output data. Exhibit 2–4 is an expanded version of Exhibit 2–1. It incorporates price data of $2.50 per bushel for corn and 20¢ per pound for nitrogen. Total variable input cost is obtained by multiplying pounds of nitrogen used by nitrogen price per pound (column 4). Total value product is yield times price per bushel. Marginal input cost (MIC) and marginal value product (MVP) are the added costs and added returns associated with each incremental unit of nitrogen fertilizer.

The technique of comparing added costs with added returns as prescribed in the principle of the maximum profit point is called marginal analysis. (The word margin refers to the last increment.) In the corn example, the relevant economic variables are marginal input cost and marginal value product. (Other terms used for MIC are added cost or marginal factor cost and for MVP, added returns or marginal returns.) The marginal input cost of the first unit of nitrogen is $3, value of marginal product is $42.50, and the increase in profit is $39.50. The second 15-pound increment of nitrogen gives added returns of $45 and adds $3 to costs for an increase in profit of $42.

Each of the first eight units of nitrogen gives added returns greater than added costs. Net returns (profit) per acre increase over the entire range. For example, if only one unit of fertilizer were used, the difference

Exhibit 2-4. Response of corn to nitrogen: application of the profit maximization principle

(1) Variable input (in 15 lb. units of N)	(2) Output (TPP)	(3) Additional output (MPP)	(4) Total variable input cost (N @ 20¢/lb.)	(5) Total value product (corn @ $2.50/bu.)	(6) Marginal input cost (MIC)	(7) Marginal value product (MVP)
0	70 bu.	—	—	$175.00	—	—
1	87	17 bu.	$3.00	217.50	3.00	42.50
2	105	18	6.00	262.50	3.00	45.00
3	115	10	9.00	287.50	3.00	25.00
4	123	8	12.00	307.50	3.00	20.00
5	128	5	15.00	320.00	3.00	12.50
6	132	4	18.00	330.00	3.00	10.00
7	134	2	21.00	335.00	3.00	5.00
8	136	2	24.00	340.00	3.00	5.00
9	137	1	27.00	342.50	3.00	2.50
10	134	-3	30.00	335.00	3.00	-7.50

between added cost and added returns would be $39.50. At eight units of fertilizer the return to added fertilizer is $141 (total value product = $340, minus $175 possible with no fertilizer, minus $24 fertilizer cost).

Many good managers normally think in terms of added cost versus added returns. The operator who says "I don't believe it will pay to cultivate this crop again because the added yield from weed control will not pay for the fuel and labor" is using a crude form of the maximum profit principle. The farmer who decides to feed hogs another week because the added gain will pay for feed and holding costs is also thinking along these lines.

The Equi-Marginal Principle

In the previous section we discussed profit maximization as though there were no limit to dollars, land, or labor. The criterion for the economic decision was simple: "Is added return greater than or equal to added cost?" Most managers, however, are faced with a scarcity of some resource, particularly dollars.

The farmer whose dollars are scarce must ask more than whether added returns are greater than added costs. He must ask, "Are scarce resources (e.g., dollars) most economically allocated to the alternative uses?" The equi-marginal principle is useful in determining how to allocate limited resources among two or more alternatives. The principle says: *If a scarce resource is to be distributed among two or more uses, the highest total return is obtained when the return per unit of the resource is equal in all alternative uses.* For example, if capital is limited and $100 spent buying protein feed will return more than the same $100 spent on fertilizer, additional feed should be purchased. If there are diminishing returns from both feed and fertilizer, the capital should be allocated so that the last dollar spent on feed will return exactly the same as the last dollar spent on fertilizer (assuming sufficient capital is available to reach that point).

An analysis using the equi-marginal principle can be illustrated using (1) a barley alternative, (2) a steer fattening alternative, and (3) the opportunity to invest off-farm. The problem concerns a farmer who must determine the most profitable allocation of $1,800 among fertilizing 100 acres of barley, fattening steers, and putting money in government bonds at 9 percent. The farmer knows what added returns can be expected from successive $200 capital outlays. These added returns are given in columns 2, 3, and 4 of Exhibit 2–5.

The equi-marginal principle can be used to determine the most profitable allocation of the $1,800. The logic of the principle is: When re-

Exhibit 2–5. **Hypothetical example of additional returns from investing operating capital**

Units of capital (in $200 units)	Barley	Fattening steers	Government bonds
		Added returns from $200 invested in	
1st	$1,400	$470	$218
2nd	900	490	218
3rd	700	460	218
4th	400	425	218
5th	300	410	218
6th	200	370	218
7th	100	315	218
8th	− 200	240	218

sources are limited, distribute them among different production activities beginning with the one giving the highest net return. Continue distributing the inputs progressively to the next highest paying activity until the input is exhausted. It is understood that in no case will resources be used past the "point of maximum profit" for any individual production activity.

In the tradition of good management, the manager looks first for the most profitable allocation and observes that one $200 unit of capital expended to fertilize barley will return $1,400. Spending a second $200 unit on barley will return $900, and a third will return $700. From knowledge of the maximum profit principle the farmer knows it would be profitable to spend up to six capital units on barley.

But wait! The farmer sees from the estimates of return that, although the fourth capital unit will return $400 from barley, it will return $470 if invested in fattening steers. Thus, the farmer observes that units 4 through 8 will return more when spent on steers than they would if spent on barley fertilization. The ninth capital unit would be spent on barley because $400 would be expected from barley whereas the next capital unit would return only $370 if invested in fattening cattle.

The scarcity of capital prevents the farmer from realizing the maximum possible profit from barley, steers, and off-farm investments. However, by using the equi-marginal principle to determine the allocation of four capital units to barley and five units to steers, the farmer realizes the largest possible return from the nine capital units. There is no other way of allocating the nine capital input units that will give greater total returns.

If the farmer had been fortunate enough to have 19 capital units rather than 9, he could have realized even greater returns. The most profitable allocation of 19 capital units would be 5 units in barley, 8 units in steers, and 6 units in off-farm investments.

The equi-marginal principle makes it clear that a manager should not view each economic decision as an isolated event. Rather, it indicates that each adjustment should be measured in comparison with alternative adjustments.

Opportunity Costs

Closely allied to the equi-marginal returns principle is the concept of opportunity cost. This concept says: *The cost of using a resource in one way is the return that could be obtained from using it in an alternative way.* Opportunity cost refers to the *return foregone* because resources were used for alternative A rather than alternative B. A farmer who grows sorghum on a tract of land cannot grow corn there. If sorghum returns $12,000 and corn $13,000, the opportunity cost of growing $12,000 worth of sorghum is $13,000 in corn. In the previous section, the opportunity cost of investing the ninth $200 unit in steers is the $400 that could have been returned had that $200 been invested in barley (see Exhibit 2–5).

Consider again the allocation of nine capital units discussed in the previous section. One allocation would be to use six units of capital to attain the maximum profit level for barley and to use the remaining three units in off-farm investments. The total returns from this allocation would be $4,554. Total returns from equi-marginal allocation are $5,655. The opportunity cost of investing six units in barley and three units off-farm would be $5,655, a net difference of $1,101 ($5,655–$4,554). This is the "lost profit" resulting from an allocation not determined using the equi-marginal principle.

Money is not the only resource that has an opportunity cost. When a farmer has to spend time with a livestock enterprise at the same time that crops need to be planted, something will probably end up being sacrificed. If the livestock enterprise gets all the labor it needs, then the crop may not get planted in the most timely manner. That may result in lower crop yields than would have been possible if the crop had gone in at the "right" time. The farmer has to decide where to spend his time. What does he give up in crop income if he spends too much time with livestock? Conversely, what does he give up in livestock income if he spends too much time on crops?

The opportunity cost concept is also applicable when allocating limited capital to the machinery purchase decision. Most farmers or ranchers would prefer to have relatively new machinery. However, some items have a pretty big price tag. Used machinery can be purchased for less, but the repairs and "down time" due to breakdowns also have a cost. So, the farmer-manager must look at machinery decisions both in terms of "What can I afford?" and "What is the added income or lost income of using my money on machine A vs. machine B?"

INPUT-INPUT RELATIONSHIPS

A manager with a high profit objective does not face a simple situation where he can use the maximum profit principle at the first of each year and then settle back and wait for the money to roll in. Economic conditions change, sometimes rather abruptly, as they did during the energy crisis of the 1970s. In the other cases, current-year decisions are influenced by decisions made in the past. For example, a cattle feeder who invested $80,000 or more in facilities is not likely to let those facilities stand idle if he can at least cover production costs and realize some "profit" to yield a return to the facilities. In fact, he is likely to feed cattle regularly even though there is some alternative enterprise that looks more profitable on the surface. Thus, the cattle feeder's decision is not so much "Which enterprise is most profitable?" as "How much feed should I put into an animal?" and "What combination of feeds should I choose?"

The Substitution Principle

The principle of substitution applies to those situations in which choices must be made between input combinations. The principle states: *When two (or more) inputs can be combined in varying amounts to produce a given output, it is economical to substitute input A for input B if the additional cost of A is less than the amount saved on B.* For example, if 100 bushels per acre of corn are being produced with $15 machinery cost and $25 fertilizer cost but could be produced with $10 machinery cost and $28 fertilizer cost, it would lower costs to change to the latter combination of inputs.

Rarely is there only one means for accomplishing a given production objective. The following are examples of input combination decisions faced by managers.

1. A crop farmer must decide between different combinations of seed and fertilizer that will give a particular level of grain production.

2. A feeder pig producer can choose from feeding systems ranging from the highly automated to one with high labor requirements.

3. A cotton producer can substitute herbicides for cultivation.

4. A dairy farmer can choose among a multitude of ingredients in formulating his ration. A variety of choices also faces the hog and cattle feeder.

5. A crop farmer can choose between monoculture with often substantial fertilizer requirements and alternatives which include livestock manure, green manure, and/or crop rotation.

The significance of the substitution principle can be illustrated with a true example of a midwest cattle feeder. The feeder was not large. He finished about 1,600 head per year. Using the least cost principle in ration formulation (along with the assistance of a computer), the feeder was able to save an estimated 1.6 cents per pound of gain in one recent year. That was a savings of $10,240 (1,600 head × 400 pound gain per head × 1.6¢ saving per pound gain). The only thing the feeder did differently was change the composition of the ration, substituting a grain he had not been feeding for some he had. Although not all applications of the substitution principle are this profitable, many opportunities occur to apply the principle in farming and business.

The cattle feeder example illustrates why the substitution principle is sometimes referred to as the least-cost principle. The least-cost method of achieving a given level of production is the prime application of the principle. The mechanics of using the principle are fairly straightforward.

1. First estimate the rate at which inputs substitute for each other (e.g., rock phosphate for superphosphate, barley for corn, diesel for gasoline). This ratio is sometimes referred to as the marginal rate of substitution (MRS) and can be written:

$$\frac{\text{Number of units of ``saved'' input}}{\text{Number of units of ``added'' input}}$$

2. Prices of the substitutable inputs must be obtained. This is essential to determining the value of inputs saved and added so a comparison can be made. These are sometimes put into a price ratio that is "inverse" to the substitution ratio, that is:

$$\frac{\text{Price of the ``added'' input per unit}}{\text{Price of the ``saved'' input per unit}}$$

3. Once the substitution and price ratios have been determined (or estimated), the values of each should be compared to determine if substitution should take place. It can be verified that if the substitution ratio is greater than the price ratio, the cost of producing the given output can be reduced by increasing the units of the "added" input, i.e., substituting more of the "added" for the "saved" input.

An Application of the Substitution Principle

Recent feeding tests with steer calves examined animal performance when various proportions of corn and corn silage were fed. The rations had corn to silage ratios ranging from 30:70 to 80:20. All rations were formulated to contain approximately 12 percent crude protein and meet minimum vitamin and mineral requirements.

Exhibit 2–6 reports the various combinations of corn and corn silage (on a dry matter basis) which gave 500, 600, and 700 pounds of gain. The calves averaged 460 pounds each at the start of the experiment.

Let us consider the silage and grain columns in Exhibit 2–6. Columns 1 and 2 indicate the various rations that gave 500 pounds of gain. One possibility is 800 pounds of silage and 2,316 pounds of corn grain. Another possibility is 1,000 pounds of silage and 2,124 pounds of corn. In this case the marginal rate of substitution was .96 (192 ÷ 200). The addition of 200 pounds of silage "saved" 192 pounds of corn. The next 200 pounds of silage saved 171 pounds of corn, and so on. Each added 200 pound increment of silage replaced less and less corn.

The economic decision becomes one of choosing between the various combinations of silage and corn. Suppose the going price for corn was $3.30 per bushel and the going price for silage was $20 per harvested ton. On a dry matter basis, that would translate into 6.0 cents per pound of corn and 3.0 cents per pound of silage. That is a price ratio of 3:6 or 1:2. The least-cost ration for 500 pounds of gain, other things constant,

Exhibit 2–6.   Feed substitution trial using 460
pounds choice grade Hereford steers;
crude protein at 12% +
diethystilbestrol

	Corn* to get—pounds gain		
*Silage**	*500 lb.*	*600 lb.*	*700 lb.*
800	2316	3128	
1000	2124	2904	
1200	1953	2698	3598
1400	1792	2510	3365
1600	1642	2338	3155
1800	1502	2179	2965
2000	1373	2032	2791
2200	1252	1896	2632
2400	1141	1771	2487
2600		1656	2355
2800		1549	2233
3000		1451	2121

SOURCE: G. B. Thompson and R. M. Finley, "Substitution
Ratios for Corn and Corn Silage," 1973.

*Both corn and silage are on a dry matter basis.

would be 2,400 pounds silage and 1,141 pounds corn. Moving to a ration
composed of 2,000 pounds silage and 1,373 pounds corn would cost an
added $13.92, but save only $12.00.

Exhibit 2–7 graphically represents the equal product curves for the
500-pound, 600-pound, and 700-pound gain conditions.[1] The fact that the
curves are not straight lines indicates that silage does not substitute for
corn grain at a constant ratio over the range of possible combinations that
give equal output. This contrasts to situations where the inputs substitute
at a constant rate (e.g., diesel for gasoline, wheat for barley, and anhydrous ammonia for ammonium nitrate). It should be obvious that, if inputs substitute at a constant rate, the choice will be one or the other,
whichever is the least costly per unit.

---

[1]The reader is referred to an economics text for an explanation of the determination
of least-cost via graphs which have equal product and equal cost curves.

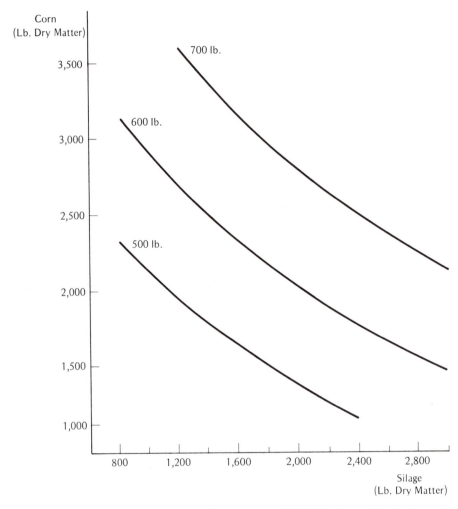

Exhibit 2–7. Equal output curves derived from Exhibit 2–6—an illustration of diminishing marginal rate of substitution of silage for corn.

SUMMARY

This chapter has illustrated four important economic decision principles: (1) the maximum profit point; (2) equi-marginal analysis; (3) opportunity cost and (4) the substitution principle. It is hoped the reader will grasp the relevance of balancing added returns (or savings) against added costs in many decision problems, particularly as they relate to production.

Sometimes the analysis will simply require adding more of a particular input. In other cases many alternatives must be considered simultaneously and the decision maker may want to rely on a computer for the data processing phase of the analysis.

APPLYING THE PRINCIPLES OF CHAPTER 2

1. A manager makes (production, consumption) decisions when he chooses the methods he will use to produce a given commodity. The thing he is producing is an (output, input), and the things he uses in the production process are (outputs, inputs). The basic relationship between inputs and output can be characterized as (a production function, profit maximization).

2. A basic characteristic of all productive activities that have at least some inputs fixed is (they are physical phenomena; at some point output will increase at a decreasing rate as a variable input is added to the fixed inputs).

3. An example of diminishing returns is (A, B).

A		B	
Lb. N	*Corn yield*	*Lb. N*	*Corn yield*
0	65 bu.	0	30
63	101	63	40
94	114	94	60
125	122	125	90
156	129	156	130
187	130	187	180

4. In question 3, nitrogen was the (fixed, variable) input. Other inputs like labor, seed, tillage, and land were assumed (fixed, variable).

5. A young farmer is concerned about applying the "right" amount of nitrogen to his corn. He has obtained the following graph for a seven-year yield test on Seymour Silt Loam, a soil which predominates on his farm.

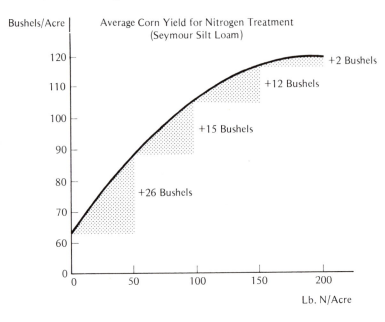

(a) Can the young farmer estimate the maximum yield he can achieve from applying nitrogen to corn from this graph? Why or why not?

(b) Based upon the study, the highest yield was obtained at _____ pounds of nitrogen.

(c) The marginal (added) product was the highest for which 50-pound increment of N?

(d) How many stages of production are illustrated in the graph?

(e) Suppose nitrogen were free. How many pounds should be applied?

6. Another farm operator, a small dairyman, is concerned with the level of production he has been getting from his dairy cows. He has average or better stock, but has only been averaging 9,500 pounds of milk per cow. He is short on cropland and has been feeding limited concentrates to his cows. A USDA bulletin reports the following relationship between milk production and total digestible nutrients (TDN).

Lb. of TDN	Production of 4% milk	MPP	APP
1,000	1,300		
2,000	3,500		
3,000	5,800		
4,000	7,200		
5,000	8,200		
6,000	8,800		
7,000	9,400		
8,000	9,900		
9,000	10,400		
10,000	10,600		
11,000	10,500		

(a) What is the MPP from the fifth unit of TDN (4,000 to 5,000 pounds of TDN)? From the tenth unit?

(b) What can you say about the marginal increase in production that can be expected from successive increases in TDN?

(c) Compute the MPP and APP schedules and put them in the above table.

(d) How many stages of production are illustrated in the feed response data?

7. The following feed-grain data for hogs gives output in equal units and illustrates the increased feed required to attain heavier weights. That is, the efficiency of gain decreases as hogs get heavier.

Feed requirements for 50 pounds of gain at five weight intervals

Weight of hogs (lb.)	Feed required for each 50 lb. gain	Feed per lb. of gain
75 to 124	167	
125 to 174	190	
175 to 224	206	
225 to 274	223	
275 to 324	252	

(a) Determine the pounds of feed required per pound of gain for each 50-pounds gain and put your results in the table. Compare the efficiencies at the various weight levels.

(b) The statement "the efficiency of gain decreases" is the same as saying what about APP?

8. A (total physical product [TPP], total value product [TVP]) curve shows the relation between various levels of a variable input and the commodity being produced. The (TPP, TVP) curve is obtained by multiplying the units of output by price per unit at each point on the (TPP, TVP) curve.

9. Suppose the production response of corn to nitrogen was that given in 3(a)

Lb. N:	0	63	94	125	156	187
Corn yield:	65 bu.	101	114	122	129	130

and price of N was 20¢ per pound and corn was $2 per bushel. The TVP values corresponding to the levels of N would be (A, B).

A: 0 $ 12.60, $ 18.80, $ 25.00, $ 31.20, $ 37.40
B: $130., $202.00,   228.00, $244.00, $258.00, $260.00

10. Marginal value product, MVP, refers to (the change in TVP for a unit change in the variable input, the average value of production resulting from use of the variable input).

11. Suppose a hog farmer thought the feed-gain data from question 7 was appropriate for his situation.

Feed production response of butcher hogs to fattening ration

Weight of hog (lb.)	Added feed per 50 lb. gain	Added gain	Value of added gain (MVP)	Cost of added feed (MIC)
75	XXX			
125	167			
175	190			
225	206			
275	223			
325	252			

(a) Suppose the price of the mixed fattening ration is $140 per ton (7¢ per pound) and expected selling price for hogs is $35 per cwt. What is the profit maximizing level of production (assuming all other costs constant)?

(b) What is the profit maximizing level if hog prices of $35 are expected, but feed costs are 8¢ per pound? How much profit would the manager forego if he fed to the next heavier weight? The next lighter weight?

(c) Suppose nonfeed costs of fattening hogs are $2 for each 50 pounds of gain. What is the profit maximization level for $35 hogs and $140 per ton feed?

(d) Experiment with other price ratios and see where the profit maximizing level is. What if hogs are docked $2 per hundred when they get over 240 pounds?

REFERENCES

Castle, Emery N., Manning H. Becker and Frederick J. Smith. *Farm Business Analyses,* 2nd ed. New York: The Macmillan Co., 1972.

Doll, John P. and Frank Orazem. *Production Economics.* Columbus, Ohio: Grid, Inc., 1978.

Goodwin, John W. *Agricultural Economics.* Reston, Va.: Reston Publishing Co., 1977.

Ohio State University Department of Agricultural Education. *Profit-Maximizing Principles.* Columbus, Ohio: Agricultural Education Service, 1970.

Thompson, G. B. and R. M. Finley. "Substitution Ratios for Corn and Corn Silage," Department of Agricultural Economics Paper 1973–4, Columbia, Mo., 1973.

University of Missouri Agricultural Economics Extension Farm Management Staff. *Outline of Farm Management,* Miscellaneous Extension Publication. Columbia, Mo., 1964.

Cost Concepts in Decision Making

3

- Cost versus cash outlay
- Fixed costs and variable costs
- Total cost and average cost
- Cost curves related to production
- Average variable costs and efficiency of input use
- Economies of scale

Costs are the manifestation of the basic economic fact of scarcity. The planning or analysis situation faced by the manager will determine the type of cost information that is needed. Frequently he will be concerned with the proportion of or relationships between fixed and variable costs. In some cases total costs will be the primary concern, while in others cost per unit will be more informative. This chapter builds on the production economics principles discussed in Chapter 2. The role and importance of time in terms of cost analysis and in terms of planning and operational decision making are discussed. The influences of costs on production decisions in the short run and on the size of the firm in the long run are also presented.

In his business dealings, a manager encounters many different terms that include the word *cost*. There are production costs, out-of-pocket costs, fixed costs, overhead costs, operating costs, cash costs, non-cash costs, accounting costs, and on and on. Many of these terms have similar or identical meanings.

Most of the confusion over the various kinds of costs evaporates once it is realized that cost information is needed for different kinds of problems and the particular cost information required varies from one situation to another.

This book defines costs as *expenses incurred in organizing and carrying out the production process in a business*. Alternatively, a cost may be defined as a charge that should be made for an item used in the production of goods and services. In agricultural production, the goods and services are food and fiber. In industrial production, the goods and services could be machines, chemicals, petroleum products, bakery products, or clothing. Managers should be familiar with all of the costs and their classifications and understand which costs are important in decision making at a particular time.

Although it may seem elementary to define cost, we must understand that when we say it "costs" so much per acre to produce corn, we are including in this figure not just one but a large number of individual cost items. A partial list would include seed, fertilizer, taxes, depreciation, and interest. The composition of cost items that go into the production of a commodity is known as the *cost structure* of that commodity. Each commodity has a different cost structure.

CLASSIFYING COSTS

The economic implications of a business decision cannot be analyzed unless costs are considered. For short-run decisions, cash costs may be the only relevant costs. However, basing long-run decisions on cash costs alone could lead to economic disaster.

Cash versus Non-Cash Costs

The definition of costs emphasized a charge that should be made. It makes no reference to an actual cash transaction. Costs may or may not involve a cash transfer during a given time period. Money outlay is not a prerequisite for a cost.

Cash costs are incurred when inputs are purchased for production. The cost of the input is explicitly determined as the direct money outlay required to obtain it. Cash expenditures for fuel, fertilizer, repairs, wages, and utilities are easily recognized as cash production costs. (Accountants sometimes refer to these as explicit costs.)

Non-cash, or implicit, *costs* are more difficult to handle because they represent items like unpaid family labor, interest on owners' equity, and depreciation.[1] However, they also are costs of production and must be charged to the business (or preferably individual enterprises in the business) if a true costing of output is to be made.

The difficulty of charging non-cash costs to the proper enterprise becomes apparent when one considers a business with several enterprises, each producing a different product. The question of how to allocate items like building and machinery depreciation becomes difficult when a farmer raises corn, soybeans, wheat, cows, and hogs.

To an economist, the total of cash and non-cash costs constitutes the total costs of a business enterprise. Unless both types of costs are fully included, the costs of the enterprise will be understated.

Fixed versus Variable Costs

Most readers already know that *fixed costs* are unrelated to output volume and *variable costs* vary directly with output. *Fixed*, or ownership, *costs* are those obligations like interest on real estate, real estate taxes, and depreciation, which are incurred just because you are in business. The fixed costs of a business are constant for a specified time period (e.g., year, growing season, feeding turn). They are not changed by the productivity of the farm. They are the same whether there is a bumper crop or no crop at all. (Per unit, or average, fixed costs are affected by quantity of production. They are discussed later in the chapter.)

The terms *overhead costs* and *ownership costs*[2] are sometimes used in referring to fixed costs. This use of terms is derived from the nature of the components of fixed costs (e.g., depreciation, taxes, interest, etc.). These are cost items normally associated with ownership. Similarly, they are sometimes viewed as overhead costs because of the difficulty of allocating items like taxes to specific products or production enterprises.

---

[1]The term *deferred cost* is sometimes used in reference to certain costs associated with capital expenditures. A farmer constructs an $8,000 grain storage and handling facility one year and pays cash at the time of construction. The $8,000 is really an investment.

Because the structure will be used for a number of years, it would be illogical to charge the entire $8,000 against the business during the year of construction, even though cash was expended at that time.

[2]The mechanism used to charge this cost over a period of years is called *depreciation*. It is a bookkeeping charge against the business and rightly called a deferred cost. In the year the charge is made, it is a non-cash cost.

It is important to note that a manager cannot control fixed costs in the short run. Fixed costs are incurred regardless of how much or how little fixed resources are used. A firm might have the potential for producing $100,000 in products, but because of unfavorable conditions produce only $20,000. The lower production will not reduce fixed costs.

Variable, or operating, *costs* are normally defined as those costs that change as production (hence, output) varies over a specified period. Variable costs are generally associated with volume of business and with inputs that are transformed or used up in the production of an output. Thus, operating costs are avoidable in the sense that they vary with the level of output. For example, the fuel cost in drying grain would be incurred only if grain is dried. In contrast, a fixed cost associated with obsolescence, such as depreciation on the dryer, would be incurred even if no grain is dried in a given production period.

Variable costs refer to those outlays that we normally think of as farm production expenses. Seed, fuel, fertilizer, pesticides, feed, feeder animals to go in the feedlot, veterinary supplies, and similar items represent variable costs. Expenses for custom work, hourly labor, and electricity are also variable costs. In the short run it is variable costs that are important in determining whether to produce, and how much to produce. If you cannot at least cover variable costs, then you should not produce at all.

Making a distinction between fixed and variable costs is sometimes difficult. Depreciation, for example, is generally influenced by both use (wear and tear) and obsolescence because of time. Should depreciation associated with wear and tear be a variable cost? Probably not, since we can assume the repair costs to keep an asset operational would be treated as a variable cost. Fixed costs are discussed in more detail in the next chapter.

Sunk Costs

Once an item has been used in production the cost of that item becomes "sunk." The concept of sunk cost is very nearly that of fixed cost; that is, costs become sunk once they have been incurred, and they cannot be affected by any current decision. Once seed is planted, fertilizer is applied, or gasoline is used, the cost is sunk even though the input item is generally considered a variable input.

In the context of farm management, it is useful for a manager to recognize when a cost becomes a sunk cost. He or she no longer has managerial control over that cost item. He/she must now live with the decision (bear the responsibility) that caused the input to be used. A good manager will not dwell on sunk costs, but direct his or her energies to those new cost decisions over which he/she has some control.

Necessary versus Postponable Costs

Some costs are for items employed because they perform an essential function. Seedbed preparation, weed control, and harvesting are necessary functions in crop production. Feed handling, sanitation, and disease control are necessary functions in livestock production.

It is the responsibility of the manager to weigh costs and benefits in selecting methods of getting the job done and simultaneously economizing on costs. For example, the profit-conscious cattle feeder will be interested in feeding at a low cost per hundredweight of beef produced, but several alternative means may be about equally as economical. Some management approaches for choosing among alternative means are discussed in later sections of this chapter and under the enterprise and investment analysis sections of other chapters.

A cost is postponable if the decision frees the enterprise from an outflow of funds. Costs that can be put off include maintenance expenses on some buildings and machinery. As other examples, feeder calves might be put on pasture and grazed rather than put directly in the feedlot; the purchase of concentrates may be postponed; or fertilizer rates on high fertility soils might be reduced below usual levels for a year or two.

SHORT-RUN AND LONG-RUN COSTS

Two basic cost functions are used in managerial decision making. Short-run cost functions relate primarily to regular operating decisions. Long-run cost functions, more typically used for long-run planning, are sometimes referred to as planning curves.

The *short run* is defined as a period during which certain inputs are fixed. Such inputs as breeding livestock, land, buildings, and equipment are fixed in the short run. Short-run variable inputs are items like livestock medicine, feed ingredients, herbicides, and purchased services, such as custom grinding-mixing, custom hauling, and harvesting. In the short run, decisions are limited by prior investment decisions and other commitments (e.g., 5-year lease, contract with full-time hired employee).

The *long run* refers to the cost structure of a firm over a period of time long enough so that no resource need be considered fixed. It is a period of time sufficient for all the firm's costs to be variable.

For a feed mill, the short-run output might be increased by working a crew twelve hours rather than eight hours or running two shifts rather than one. In the long run the size of the feed mill might be altered or an entirely new mill constructed.

The next section looks at cost concepts that relate to the short run. Later sections deal with cost analysis relating to durable investments like machinery and land.

SHORT-RUN COST CURVES

When fixed and variable costs were discussed earlier, it was noted that deciding how an individual cost item should be classified is not always easy. In general, *fixed costs* are invariant with respect to output. The firm is committed to pay them one way or another on a regular basis over an extended period of time. *Variable costs* change with output; they are a function of the output level.

Total Costs

Total cost (TC) for any output level is the sum of total fixed cost (a constant) and total variable cost. The TC curve is "built" by adding together the total fixed cost (TFC) and total variable cost (TVC) curves. The TC curve has the same general shape as the TVC curve, but is above the TVC curve by the amount TFC is above the horizontal axis (see Exhibit 3–1).

The *total fixed cost* curve is a horizontal line because fixed costs remain constant regardless of the level of output in a given period. The firm has some obligation for the resources whether they are used in producing an output or not. The fixed cost of an upright silo is an example. The firm must bear certain depreciation and interest costs whether the silo is filled once, twice, only half filled, or not filled at all during a year. The same applies to an expensive mechanical cotton-picker. There are certain fixed commitments whether the picker is used to harvest 300 bales or 1,500 bales.

Total variable cost is related to input use in a specific production period. Thus the manager has some control over it. TVC must necessarily rise as a firm's output increases, since larger output requires larger quantities of a variable input(s) and, thus, larger cost obligations.

Cost Curves Related to Production Function

As indicated above, costs are related to production. They are expressed in terms of expenditures for given levels of output. In fact, the S-shaped cost curve is a mirror image of the production function (flipped over and rotated 90°). For the general production function (i.e., all three

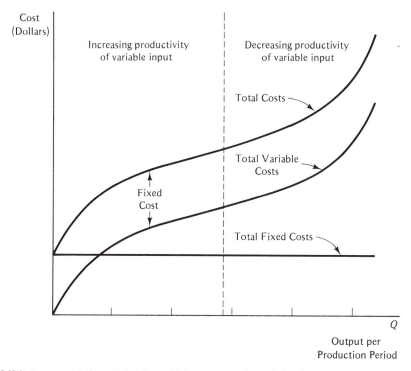

Exhibit 3–1. Total cost, total variable cost, and total fixed cost curves.

stages of production), there are areas exhibiting at first increasing returns to the variable input, then decreasing returns as were shown in Exhibit 2–2. The companion S-shaped TVC curve (as illustrated by Exhibit 3–1) increases less than proportionately with output over the range where the corresponding production function is increasing at an increasing rate. It turns up sharply after decreasing returns set in and is vertical at the level where output is a maximum. Thus, the shape of the TVC curve is determined by the physical nature of the production process. That is why cost theory is sometimes referred to as production theory restated in monetary terms.

Not all TVC curves are S-shaped. Many production response cases exist that exhibit no Stage I of production (no increasing marginal returns). In that case the TVC curve slopes upward and to the right and is concave from above. The hog fattening data in problem 7 of the last chapter can be used to illustrate this case. When total variable costs are plotted (Exhibit 3–2), there is increasing cost or decreasing efficiency throughout

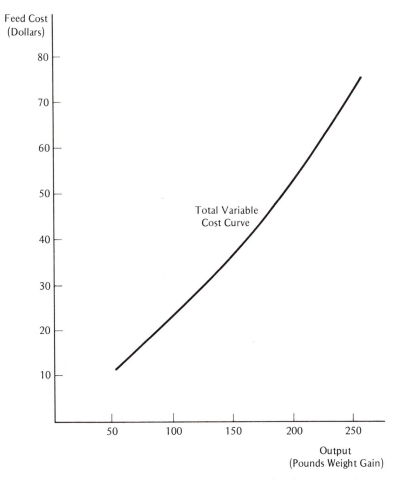

Exhibit 3–2. **Cost function for production response showing decreasing efficiency over entire output range; based on swine fattening study.**

the production range. More feed is required per 50 pounds of gain at each successive weight level. The slope of the cost function becomes progressively steeper. (It may be difficult to see the increasing slope of the curve in Exhibit 3–2, but it becomes obvious when a straight edge is laid alongside the curve.)

Per Unit Cost Curves

The unit costs curves may be more important in decision making than the total cost curves. The livestock or poultry feeder is interested in the cost per pound of gain. The grain producer wants to make sure that costs per bushel of grain are lower than the expected return—plus an extra margin for labor and management and for uncertainty. The feed store operator wants the cost of purchasing, processing, handling, and storing a hundredweight of feedstuffs to be less than the price the feed is expected to sell for. Actually, the unit curves show the same kind of information as the total curves, but in a different form.

The unit cost curves are derived directly from the "total" curves. If Q is the quantity of output produced during the specified period (it is only logical to speak of costs per unit of time, i.e., week, month, crop season, year), then the various unit cost values are computed as:

$$\text{Average fixed cost} \quad = \text{AFC} = \frac{\text{TFC}}{Q}$$

$$\text{Average variable cost} \quad = \text{AVC} = \frac{\text{TVC}}{Q}$$

$$\text{Average total cost} \quad = \text{ATC} = \frac{\text{TC}}{Q}$$

The shapes of the various average cost curves are completely determined by the shapes of the total cost curves. Corresponding unit and total cost curves are shown in Exhibit 3–3. The ATC curve is a summation of AFC and AVC as was the case for the total curves. For example, ATC at point q_0 is an amount C. Cost C is the sum of A (AFC at point q_0) and B (AVC at point q_0). The shape of the ATC curve is totally dependent upon the shapes of the AFC and AVC curves.

Average fixed cost is the fixed cost per unit of output. If output is 1,000 units and total fixed cost is $2,000, then the AFC=$2 per unit. If output is 2,000 units, the AFC changes to $1 per unit since TFC is a fixed amount. Hence, the characteristic of the AFC curve is to be downward sloping over the entire range of output, but to decline at a decreasing rate. For example, a person has certain fixed costs per year on a car (license tag, insurance, depreciation, maybe principal and interest on a loan). The AFC per mile is less if the car is driven 20,000 rather than 10,000 miles.

Average variable cost is directly related to the productivity of the variable input(s). The shape of the AVC curve depends upon the underlying production function. AVC takes on its U-shape because of the increasing and decreasing efficiency of the variable input in the production process.

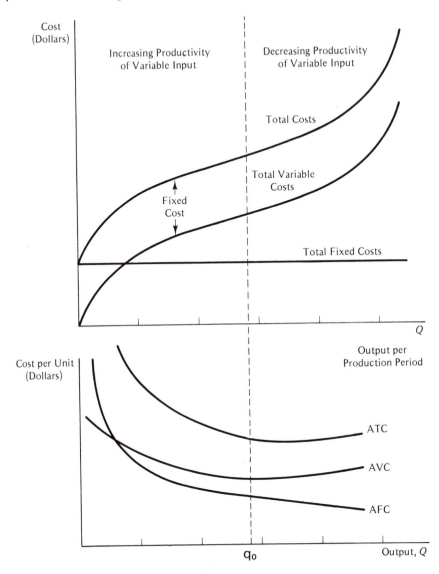

Exhibit 3–3. Short-run total and unit cost curves.

As such, the AVC curve is at its minimum at the point at which average physical product is greatest. It can be shown that when AVC is decreasing, APP is increasing and vice versa. A more detailed explanation can be found in any economic theory text.

It is important to remember that AVC has the characteristic U-shape for the *general* production response case. When there is no Stage I of production, the AVC curve will be upward sloping. This means that variable inputs are being used beyond their level of highest efficiency for the given set of fixed inputs. However, a firm is generally interested in profits, and highest profits are not usually realized at the point of highest input efficiency (lowest unit cost).

The average total cost curve can have a U-shape even when AVC does not. At low levels of output, AFC has the greatest influence on ATC. At higher levels of output when AFC becomes smaller and smaller, AVC has a greater influence and ATC turns upward.

Marginal Cost

A decision maker is generally interested in the additional cost associated with getting an additional unit of output. Simply stated, *marginal cost is the increase in total cost resulting from the production of an additional unit of output.* Marginal cost (MC) is the change in TVC due to a one-unit increase in output. If the TVC curve is increasing at a decreasing rate, the MC curve is decreasing. If TVC is increasing at an increasing rate, then MC is increasing.

To locate the profit maximizing output level, MC must be compared with the marginal revenue (MR) expected from a unit of output. For many agricultural commodities the MR is simply the sales price per unit of the commodity. If selling price is greater than the cost of producing additional units of a product, profits can be increased by increasing output.

Marginal Cost versus Marginal Input Cost

The question of which "marginal" cost concept (MC or MIC) to use in making decisions is a relevant one. The answer depends on (1) the precision with which costs and returns can be estimated and (2) the thought process with which the decision maker is most comfortable.

In the real world of farm decision making, we often cannot accurately specify costs per unit of output until the production process has been completed. Thus per unit costs (MC) are only "known" in theory when short-run decisions are being made. Conversely, a decision maker is generally able to specify marginal input costs fairly accurately, although he or she may have substantial difficulty forecasting production and/or price in order to compute MVP.

Both cost concepts rely on the key issue of estimating the added cost for comparing with some added return. The decision maker who can grasp and successfully apply this general decision criterion should be able to seize profitable opportunities when they present themselves.

APPLICATION OF COST PRINCIPLES: A DAIRY EXAMPLE

A dairy farmer with good quality stock can realize a range of milk production (output) per cow depending upon the ration (i.e., the proportion of grain and roughage) fed. Higher and higher milk levels can be expected as the energy level of the ration is increased.

Several studies have reported the pounds of concentrate needed to produce various levels of milk. The average of the results from three studies are presented (see Exhibit 3–4). Other studies have estimated the annual fixed cost per cow for a 75–100 head dairy herd to be in the $200 to $600 range. These fixed costs include annual charges for land, buildings and equipment, livestock investment, and the fixed costs associated with raising replacements. The wide range of fixed cost estimates results from the differences in the studies. Fixed cost estimates for operating dairies usually fall between $200 and $300 per cow. However, most of

Exhibit 3–4. **Estimated annual quantities of grain fed and milk produced per year from good quality cows**

Output (cwt. milk produced)	Input (pounds of dairy feed)
90	1,250
100	1,770
110	2,350
120	3,050
130	3,900
140	4,830
150	6,000

SOURCES: F. G. Owen and C. R. Hogland, *A Guide for Optimizing Levels of Feeding Dairy Cows*, Nebraska Agriculture Experiment Station, SB-511, 1970. *Hoard's Dairyman*, "A Grain Feeding Program For High Producers," May 1971. Marvin W. Kottke, *Economic Optimum Rates of Feeding in Milk Production*, Storrs Agriculture Experiment Station, Bulletin 349, 1960.

these dairies have been in business many years and their investments were made when things were not as expensive as today. Estimates of per cow fixed costs are $600 to $800 for a new dairy built at today's costs.

It is possible to develop total and unit cost schedules from the data (see Exhibit 3–5). Annual "fixed costs" of $1,170 per cow were assumed. This included per cow fixed costs of $220 on breeding livestock, buildings and equipment, and all nongrain production costs (forage, labor, basic utilities, repairs, supplies, etc.) of $950. "Fixed costs" for this situation were, thus, $1,170 ($950 + $220).

The only variable costs for this example were (1) dairy feed costs and (2) costs that vary with the level of production, e.g., utilities for cooling milk and veterinary expenses, which rise as cows are pushed to higher levels of production. Dairy feed costs of 12¢ per lb. of feed and other variable costs of 2¢ per lb. of feed were used.

Exhibits 3–5 and 3–6 illustrate that (1) it takes more and more dairy feed to get each additional 1,000 lb. of milk per cow; (2) as higher and higher levels of production are divided into TFC, the AFC per unit of milk drops; (3) since it takes more and more feed to achieve higher production, the AVC per unit of milk increases; (4) the ATC curve for this situation is U-shaped; and (5) marginal cost is increasing across the entire range of data provided.

Looking at the unit cost curves, one observes that for this case (no area corresponding to Stage I of production) the AFC and AVC curves are sloping in opposite directions. The ATC curve is flatter than AVC because AFC has a proportionately larger effect at the lower output levels.

It should be pointed out that the TVC and AVC curves are important decision curves for the short run. A dairyman who has already invested in land, cows, and equipment is most concerned about at least

Exhibit 3–5. Cost functions for milk production; fixed costs @ $1,170 per head and variable cost of 14¢ per pound

Output (cwt. milk)	Input (lbs. grain)	TFC	TVC	TC	AFC	AVC	ATC	MC
90	1250	$1,170	$175	$1,345	$13.00	$1.95	$14.95	—
100	1770	1,170	248	1,418	11.70	2.48	14.18	$ 7.30
110	2350	1,170	329	1,499	10.64	2.99	13.63	8.10
120	3050	1,170	427	1,597	9.75	3.56	13.31	9.80
130	3900	1,170	546	1,716	9.00	4.20	13.20	11.90
140	4830	1,170	676	1,846	8.36	4.83	13.19	13.00
150	6000	1,170	840	2,010	7.10	5.60	13.40	16.40

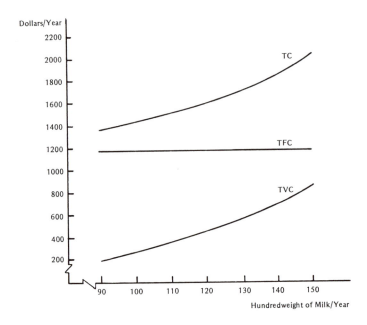

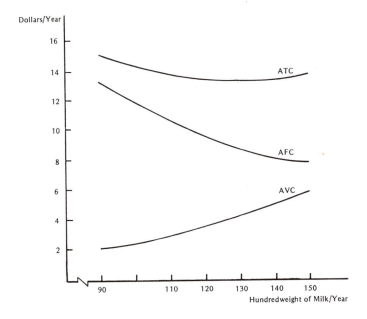

Exhibit 3–6. Short-run cost curves for dairy example: (a) total cost curves; (b) unit cost curves.

covering variable costs. Those are the only costs over which he has much control in the short run.

In this example, TVC have included only feed costs; TFC were constructed to be as inclusive as possible. Such variable costs as utilities, hired labor, vet and medicine costs, any milk-selling costs, and other miscellaneous costs would also have to be covered if a dairyman is to operate in the short run.

The other short-run decision—which milk production level to aim for—would require the dairyman to estimate the milk selling price and compare that with the marginal cost schedule (see last column in Exhibit 3–5).

ECONOMIES OF SIZE

Some managers call long-run cost curves *planning curves*, which is an appropriate description since all costs are variable in the long run. The manager has the option of choosing among a variety of sizes of operations, within certain management and capital limits.

Just as short-run average cost curves are assumed to have a U-shape due to efficiences (and inefficiencies) in resource use, given existing technology, so the long-run curve is assumed to be U-shaped. In fact, the long-run curve is thought of as an envelope curve of the short-run average cost curves for optional plants of various sizes.

The relationship between short-run and long-run cost curves is illustrated in Exhibit 3–7. Four SATC curves represent the short-run unit cost curves for four sizes of firms. There is a most efficient size (S_i) for each plant size; average cost is lowest for that plant size at that level.

The reader will notice that the long-run cost curve does not go through the minimum points of each short-run curve. This is because at that output another larger plant is slightly more efficient; that is, size 2 gives lower average cost than the minimum cost point for size 1. The envelope long-run cost curve is a combination of individual segments of many short-run curves.

A manager is interested in the long-run cost curve because the selection of a profitable operation assumes he will choose an efficient size—one that realizes some of the economies of size. These economies may result from more intensive use of resources, specialization of labor tasks, a higher level of mechanization, or efficiencies in buying and selling. Certainly, large economies of size have been noted for poultry operations and for beef cattle.

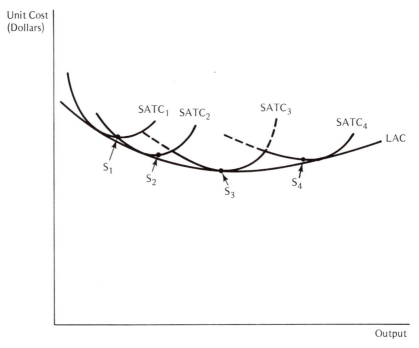

Exhibit 3–7. Short-run cost curves and envelope curve for four farm sizes.

The assumption of a U-shaped long-run average cost curve suggests there are also *diseconomies* of size. At some point the firm becomes so big that cost per unit of output increases. This may result from inability of management to coordinate the many aspects of a business, or it may be due to the spreading of an operation over a wide geographic area.

A study, "Economies of Size in Midwest Hog Operations," illustrated the application of the long-run/planning cost curve concept. The study examined six sizes of confinement farrow-through-finish hog operations with three farrowing intensities, two, four, and six litters per year, for each size. The output range covered was from 110 to 8,300 pigs (see Exhibit 3–8). Variable inputs were feed, storage, bedding, fuel/utilities, sanitation, repairs and maintenance, interest, and labor. Fixed costs included depreciation, taxes, interest on owned capital, and fixed interest charges. Exhibit 3–9 summarizes the unit cost data for the eighteen combinations of size and intensity of use. The short-run average cost curves and an envelope long-run curve for cost per hundredweight of pork produced are presented in Exhibit 3–10.

Exhibit 3–8. Number of sows for six selected capacities and number of pigs weaned for three farrowing intensities

Capacity Level	Number of sows	Intensity levels[1]		
		1	2	3
		Number of pigs weaned[2]		
1	8	110	222	332
2	30	415	830	1245
3	60	830	1660	2490
4	100	1382	2766	4150
5	150	2074	4150	6624
6	200	2766	5530	8300

SOURCE: Finley and Retzlaff, "Economies of Size in Midwest Hog Operations," *Journal of American Society of Farm Managers and Rural Appraisers*, October 1974.

[1]Intensity Level 1:2 farrowings per year (one group of sows farrowed twice per year); Intensity Level 2:4 farrowings per year (two groups of sows farrowed twice per year); Intensity Level 3:6 farrowings per year (three groups of sows farrowed twice per year).

[2]Calculated on 7.0 pigs per litter, adjusted for 1.2% death loss farrowing to weaning.

Exhibit 3–9. Variable cost, fixed cost, total cost per hog, cost per hundredweight, and labor per head for six capacities for three farrowing intensities

	Farrowing intensity		
	1	2	3
Capacity 1			
Variable cost/head	$34.96	$33.68	$33.20
Fixed cost/head	6.67	5.59	5.38
Total cost/head	41.63	39.27	37.58
Cost per cwt.	18.92	17.85	17.08
Labor/head (hours)	1.51	1.26	1.22

Exhibit 3–9. (cont'd.)

	Farrowing intensity		
	1	2	3
Capacity 2			
Variable cost/head	33.09	31.22	30.72
Fixed cost/head	7.21	5.99	5.02
Total cost/head	40.30	37.21	35.74
Cost per cwt.	18.32	16.91	16.25
Labor/head (hours)	1.32	.95	.94
Capacity 3			
Variable cost/head	31.76	30.60	30.50
Fixed cost/head	7.39	6.19	5.19
Total cost/head	39.15	36.79	35.69
Cost per cwt.	17.80	16.72	16.22
Labor/head (hours)	1.00	.94	.94
Capacity 4			
Variable cost/head	$31.79	$31.22	$30.68
Fixed cost/head	7.50	6.23	5.15
Total cost/head	39.30	37.45	35.83
Cost per cwt.	17.86	17.02	16.21
Labor/head (hours)	1.05	1.01	.95
Capacity 5			
Variable cost/head	30.73	30.32	29.87
Fixed cost/head	7.66	6.13	5.29
Total cost/head	38.38	36.46	35.16
Cost per cwt.	17.45	16.57	15.98
Labor/head (hours)	.79	.77	.73
Capacity 6			
Variable cost/head	31.13	30.69	30.08
Fixed cost/head	7.84	6.23	5.19
Total cost/head	38.97	36.92	35.27
Cost per cwt.	17.71	16.78	16.03
Labor/head (hours)	.83	.88	.82

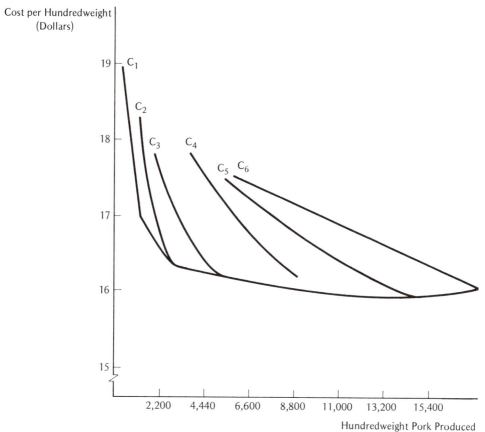

Exhibit 3–10. Derived long-run planning curve showing economies of size: for swine farrow-to-finish facilities, six sizes from 8 to 200 sows.

Several factors associated with economies of size can be pointed out from the study.

1. One efficiency (economy of size) the study shows is in labor. Labor decreases nearly .8 hours per pig from the smallest to the next to largest size (from 1.51 hours to .73 hour).

2. Variable costs, as defined in the study, decrease over $5 per pig (17 percent) from the smallest to the next to largest size.

3. Fixed costs declined 22 percent over the range of output.

4. Most of the economies were realized with the 30-sow unit used at the high level of intensity.

5. The study attempted to look at both (a), the relationship of cost per unit of output to various degrees of facility utilization/intensity levels, and (b), the relationship of cost per unit of output to various sizes of farrow-through-finishing facilities. The former, (a), deals with short-run cost curves while the latter, (b), shows long-run cost to output relationships.

SUMMARY

Much of farm management decision making is concerned with comparing costs and returns of different alternatives. An understanding of the various cost relationships and frequently used terminology is basic to effective decision making. Only a manager who understands the basic relationships can know if he/she is in the ballpark or not. Among the points made in this chapter were:

- Terminology is important in effective communication with other professionals, e.g., bankers, accountants, economists.

- The term *cost* does not necessarily mean a cash transaction, nor is a cash transaction always a cost. A cash outlay may be an investment expense, the cost of which should be prorated over time.

- The planning range is important in the decision of which costs are relevant. In the short run, marginal cost and variable costs are most important. In deciding on the output level to aim for, MC should be used. Variable costs must be covered, even in the short run, if an enterprise/operation is to be continued. Fixed costs also influence the decision regarding continuation of an enterprise; a firm may be "locked in" to certain fixed costs and be forced to continue operation if VC are being covered.

- In the long run a firm must cover all costs, including some difficult-to-allocate overhead costs. The farmer or manager also wants a return on labor.

- Cost functions, particularly the average cost curves, are determined by (a) the physical production response and (b) the price of inputs. The shape of the short-run curves is directly determined by the productivity of variable inputs.

- The long-run cost curve is a valuable planning curve, even though its exact shape is rarely known.

APPLYING THE PRINCIPLES OF CHAPTER 3

1. Which of the following are cash costs? Variable costs?

	Cash	Variable
(a) Depreciation due to use	_____	_____
(b) Utilities to operate a dairy barn	_____	_____
(c) Hired (custom) hay baling and hauling	_____	_____
(d) Real estate taxes	_____	_____
(e) Principal payments on debt	_____	_____
(f) Interest payments on debt	_____	_____
(g) Feed raised on farm and fed to livestock	_____	_____
(h) Marketing costs for fresh vegetables	_____	_____
(i) The expenses of establishing a strand of bermuda grass	_____	_____

2. A farmer has an inventory of 100 tons of alfalfa hay purchased at $30 per ton. Hay prices have now doubled to $60 per ton.

   (a) What is the cash cost?
   (b) What is the opportunity cost?
   (c) What cost should be used in decision making if the hay will either be fed on the farm or carried over until next year?
   (d) What cost should be used in decision making if the farmer would consider selling the hay or feeding it on his farm?

3. A farmer who owns his own combine and normally harvests his own crops is approached by a neighbor who wants 100 acres of his soybeans custom harvested. Which of the following are relevant costs in the farmer's decision?
   (a) Storage costs
   (b) Fuel costs
   (c) Taxes
   (d) Depreciation
   (e) Repair costs
   (f) Opportunity cost of the farmer's time

4. Johnny Quickdollar and Tommy Surething each farm 320 acres. Johnny rents his land for a cash rent of 10 percent of the appraised value. Tommy goes deep into debt and is paying his land off in 15 years with regular principal payments plus 9 percent interest. Both make annual "land payments." Are both payments fixed costs? If so, is there a difference in the degree of fixity?

5. The following table represents the short-run cost curves of one firm. Fill in the blank spaces.

Quantity of output	Total fixed cost	Total variable cost	Total cost	Average fixed cost	Average variable cost	Average cost	Marginal Cost
0	$100	___	$100	___	___	___	___
1	100	$ 30	130	$100	$ 30	$130	$30
2	___	54	___	___	___	77	___
3	___	69	___	33.33	23	___	15
4	100	81	___	___	20.25	45.25	12
5	100	___	200	___	___	___	___
6	100	___	237	16.67	22.83	39.50	37
7	___	176	___	14.29	25.14	39.43	39
8	100	___	320	12.50	27.50	___	___
9	100	280	___	11.11	31.11	42.22	60
10	100	345	___	___	___	44.50	65

(a) What happens to AFC per unit of output as quantity increases? Why?

(b) What happens to AVC per unit of output as quantity increases? Why?

(c) What happens to AC per unit of output as quantity increases? Why?

(d) What happens to MC as quantity increases? Why?

(e) At what level of output would the operator stop production if sales price was $20? $40? $60?

(f) At what level of output would the operator stop production to minimize losses if the expected sale price was $21?

6. A small farmer has 100 forty-pound feeder pigs that will be ready for weaning next week. He has sunk costs of $12 per head. These costs probably include which of the following?

(a) Wages paid his son to care for the pigs and sows

(b) Depreciation of his farrowing houses

(c) Cost of iron shots

(d) Feed costs for the sows and pigs

(e) Utilities to operate heat lamps

Market hog prices recently hit a low of $19 per hundredweight. He expects this price to hold for three to four months. What cost principle should the farmer use in deciding whether to sell the pigs as feeders at approximately $25 per hundredweight or feed them out to 220 pounds?

REFERENCES

Brigham, Eugene and J. Pappas. *Managerial Economics.* Hinsdale, Ill.: Dryden Press, Inc., 1972.

Doll, John P., V. J. Rhodes and J. G. West. *Economies of Agricultural Production, Markets and Policy.* Homewood, Ill.: Richard D. Irwin, Inc., 1968.

Finley, Robert M. and R. E. J. Retzlaff. "Economies of Size in Midwest Hog Operations," *Journal of American Society of Farm Managers and Rural Appraisers,* October 1974, pp. 9–12.

Justus, Fred E., Jr. and C. L. Beer. *A Primer on Costs,* Missouri Extension Publ. C788, Columbia, 1963.

Kay, Ronald D. "An Improved Method for Computing Ownership Costs," *Journal of American Society of Farm Managers and Rural Appraisers,* April 1974, pp. 39–42.

Mantell, L. H. and F. P. Sing. *Economies for Business Decisions.* New York, N.Y.: McGraw-Hill Book Co., 1972.

Spencer, M. H. and L. Siegelman. *Managerial Economics.* Homewood, Ill.: Richard D. Irwin, Inc., 1959.

University of Missouri Agricultural Economics Extension Staff. *Outline of Farm Management,* Miscellaneous Extension Publication. Columbia, Mo., 1964.

Ownership Costs: The DIRTI 5

- Computing depreciation: alternative methods
- Estimating annual interest
- Accounting for fixed repairs
- Recognizing fixed tax obligations
- Shifting risk with insurance

4

The previous chapter illustrated the importance of cost concepts in decision making. Examples showed how cost per unit of product is affected by volume of production. Cost control is basic to a profitable farm business. Fixed, or ownership, costs are incurred regardless of volume of production; thus they deserve special attention.

The objectives of this chapter are to

1. Explain why cost control is important

2. Discuss the items normally included in the ownership cost category

3. Explain and contrast the common depreciation methods

4. Illustrate a method for computing an opportunity cost for "tied up" capital

5. Show how decisions that affect fixed costs also affect farm income

A study in the central United States looked at the differences in costs and returns on 1,700 farms. Exhibit 4–1 reports the gross sales and expenses for the top 400 and bottom 400 farms when rated on the basis of net farm income. The difference in net income per dollar of gross sales is striking. The top group realized net income of 37 cents per dollar of sales while the bottom group received only 4 cents. The researchers could not pinpoint a specific reason for the difference in profitability of the two groups. However, the bottom group was in a different league when it came to cost per unit of production. If the low earning 25 percent had produced their $19,087 gross income for the approximately 63 cents cost per $1 of gross income (as did the high earners), their net incomes would have averaged $7,143 instead of only $766! Ownership costs were an important part of the problem.

Ownership costs have sometimes been termed the DIRTI 5. They are

1. Depreciation
2. Interest
3. Repairs
4. Taxes
5. Insurance

Each of the five factors is discussed below.

DEPRECIATION

It does not make sense to charge the entire cost of newly constructed hog facilities or a silage harvester in the year of purchase or construction. These assets are durable and provide a flow of productive services over time. Since durable assets can contribute to production over several production cycles, their costs should be charged out over the useful life of the asset.

Exhibit 4–1. Income differences among 1,699 farm management association farms

	Top group	Bottom group
Average gross farm income	$49,735	$19,087
Average gross farm expenses	31,122	18,321
Income minus expenses	$18,613	$ 766

Depreciation is a procedure for allocating the used up value of durable assets over the period they are owned by the business or until they are salvaged. By depreciating an asset, an allowance is made for the deterioration in the asset's value as a result of use (wear and tear), age, and obsolescence.

The proportion of the original cost to be depreciated in any one year is largely a matter of judgment and financial management. One aspect of financial management is the influence depreciation will have on income taxes. Another is the desire to have the undepreciated value of an asset reflect the resale value of that asset. That is, the depreciation allowance taken in any year would reflect the actual decline in value of the asset; thus the net worth statement would show the true value of depreciable assets.

Accelerated Cost Recovery System

For tangible property placed in service after 1980, depreciation for tax purposes must be figured under the (1) accelerated cost recovery system (ACRS) or (2) an alternate method that is based upon the straight line depreciation method.

ACRS applies equally to both new and used property placed in service after 1980. Property placed in service prior to 1981, or that does not qualify for ACRS, can be depreciated by straight line, declining balance, or sum of the years-digits methods.

ACRS generally gives much faster writeoff than was allowed under prior law. The ACRS method also removes areas of dispute farmers often had with IRS over (1) useful life of an asset, (2) salvage value, and (3) method of depreciation. However, ACRS depreciation has tax saving as its prime objective. Little consideration is given to actual year-to-year change in value. Thus, for accounting purposes, one of the methods like straight line or declining balance may be more appropriate.

Since life and rate of depreciation are fixed by law, under ACRS the only question to be answered for tax purposes is which recovery period class is appropriate. Property is classified as follows:

1. *3-year property:* Automobiles and light-duty trucks used for business purposes and certain special tools; hogs and some horses; depreciable property with a midpoint life of 4 years or less.

2. *5-year property:* Most farm equipment; grain bins, single-purpose structures and fences; breeding beef and dairy cows; office equipment and office furniture.

3. *10-year property:* Applies to few items used in agriculture.

4. *15-year property:* Includes all depreciable real property (such as buildings) that have an expected life greater than 12.5 years, unless otherwise specified in one of the above classes.

Figuring ACRS Deductions

The deduction under ACRS is figured by referring to a table supplied by IRS in the annual tax booklet. The table is based upon the provisions of the 1981 Economic Recovery Tax Act. The percentage supplied by the table is multiplied by the "unadjusted basis" (original cost) of the property. For example, a light truck purchased for business purposes fits in the 3-year class. The writeoff would be 25 percent in 1984, 38 percent in 1985, and 37 percent in 1986. The entire cost is depreciated; there is no salvage value consideration.

Property acquired in 1986 or later that qualifies as 5-year property would be depreciated as follows: 20 percent in year 1; 32 percent in year 2; 24 percent in year 3; 16 percent in year 4; and 8 percent in year 5. Again, for property acquired in a particular year, a taxpayer should refer to the appropriate tables for that year.

What Can Be Depreciated?

Depreciation can be claimed only on property used in your trade or business or other income-producing activity. Examples are buildings, equipment, breeding stock, patents, and copyrights. Property is depreciable if it

1. Is used in business or to earn rent or royalty income
2. Wears out, decays, gets used up, or becomes obsolete
3. Has a determinable useful life of more than 1 year

Depreciable property can be *tangible* or *intangible*. Tangible property can be seen or touched, e.g., animals and machines. Copyrights and patents are examples of intangible property.

Depreciable property may also be *real* or *personal*. Real property is land and generally anything erected on, growing on, or attached to land. Equipment, tools, animals, and vehicles are examples of personal property. Land itself is never depreciable.

Other Depreciation Methods

Prior to 1981 three other methods were commonly used to estimate depreciation. Those methods may still be appropriate when estimating annual fixed cost of assets. The straight line method may still be used for tax purposes in certain situations. (A taxpayer would want to consult the *Farmer's Tax Guide* published by IRS.)

The three methods discussed below are still appropriate for depreciable assets put into service prior to 1981. The computing formula for each follows.

Straight line:

$$D_s = \frac{OC - SV}{L}$$

$OC =$ original cost or basis
$SV =$ salvage value
$L =$ expected life of the asset in the business

Declining balance:

$$D_d = RV \times R$$

$RV =$ undepreciated value of the asset at the start of the accounting period. In year 1, for example, $RV = OC$. In succeeding years $RV_i = [RV_{i-1} - D_{d,i-1}] \times R$ (salvage value is not deducted from original value before computing depreciation).
$R =$ the depreciation rate. It may be up to twice the rate of decline, $1/L$, allowed under straight line method.

Sum of the years-digits:

$$D_Y = \frac{RY}{S} (OC - SV)$$

$RY =$ estimated years of useful life remaining
$S =$ sum of the numbers representing years of useful life (i.e., for an asset with 5 years useful life, S would be $1 + 2 + 3 + 4 + 5 = 15$).

A comparison of the depreciation that would be taken with each of the three methods for a $1,000 asset with an estimated 10 years' life and projected salvage value of 10 percent of the original cost is given in Exhibit 4–2. The first three years' depreciation for each method would be computed as follows.

Straight line:

$$\text{Year 1:}\quad D_s = \frac{OC - SV}{L} = \frac{\$1000 - \$100}{10} = \$90$$

$$\text{Year 2:}\quad D_s = \frac{\$1000 - \$100}{10} = \$90$$

$$\text{Year 3:}\quad D_s = \frac{\$1000 - \$100}{10} = \$90$$

Declining balance:

$$\text{Year 1:}\quad D_d = RV \times R = \$1000 \times 20\% = \$200$$

$$\text{Year 2:}\quad D_d = (1000 - 200) \times 20\% = \$160$$

$$\text{Year 3:}\quad D_d = (800 - 160) \times 20\% = \$128$$

Sum of the years-digits:

$$\text{Year 1:}\quad D_Y = \frac{RY}{S}(OC - SV) = \frac{10}{55}(1000 - 100)$$

$$= \frac{10}{55}(900) = \$163.64$$

$$\text{Year 2:}\quad D_Y = \frac{9}{55}(900) = \$147.27$$

$$\text{Year 3:}\quad D_Y = \frac{8}{55}(900) = \$130.91$$

There are pluses and minuses for each of the depreciation methods. Straight line, for example, is simple to compute, and it preserves more depreciation for the last half of the life of an asset. This latter factor may be important in the tax considerations of a young farmer who expects taxable income to be rising over time, although with tax loss "carryforward" this is not a particularly big factor.

Declining balance depreciation is also attractive because many assets decline in value most rapidly during the early years of use. Several studies have shown farm machinery values to decline by 50 percent and more within four years of purchase. Certain other equipment, like automated feeding systems, may show even more rapid declines in value.

From Exhibit 4–2 it should be obvious that, for assets held for the duration of their expected life, the total depreciation allowed is the same regardless of the method chosen. For the operator who trades combines

Exhibit 4–2. Comparison of three depreciation techniques

Year	Straight line (10%)	Declining balance (20%)[1]	Sum of years-digits[2]
1	$ 90	$ 200.00	$ 163.64
2	90	160.00	147.27
3	90	128.00	130.91
4	90	102.40	114.54
5	90	81.92	98.18
6	90	65.53	81.82
7	90	52.43	65.46
8	90	41.94	49.09
9	90	33.55	32.73
10	90	26.84	16.36
Total	900	892.61	900.00
Salvage value	100	107.39	100.00
	$1000	$1000.00	$1000.00

Depreciation per year per $1000 of new cost

SOURCE: N. S. Hadley, *et al.*, *Some Economic Considerations in Farm Machinery*, Extension Circular 139, Purdue U.

[1]The depreciation rate is calculated as 20 percent of the value at the beginning of the year. For tax purposes, the rate may not be greater than twice the rate which would be used under the straight line method.

[2]In this system the numerator represents the useful remaining life of the machine and the denominator represents the sum of the number of years of life $(1+2+3+ \ldots +10)$, or $\frac{10}{55}$; second year $\frac{9}{55}$; etc.

or tractors every four or five years, there are some differences in tax considerations for each method, although these are beyond the scope of discussion in this chapter. To pay the legal minimum tax, a manager would use the legal maximum rate of depreciation.

Some special limitations on the depreciation methods are spelled out in the *Farmer's Tax Guide*. Revised each year, the tax guide is made available by the Internal Revenue Service at no cost to farmers. It gives the best simple explanation of depreciation methods.

INTEREST

Money invested in durable assets is tied up and cannot be used for other purposes. This is true whether the money is borrowed or taken out of the firm's bank account. On borrowed money there will be a regular interest payment, a standing obligation which must be met regardless of the use level of the asset purchased with the borrowed money. Likewise, an interest charge should be calculated on equity capital. In this case the charge would be an opportunity cost or opportunity interest. An annual charge should be made because the money invested has alternative productive uses, which may range from earning interest on a savings account to increasing production, e.g., income from acquiring several high quality dairy cows.

Annual fixed interest may be *estimated* by first computing average investment and then multiplying by an appropriate interest rate (r). One computing formula is

$$i = \frac{(OC + SV)}{2} \times r$$

The reader will note that average investment is computed by *adding* original cost to salvage value and dividing by 2. Average investment is a middle value between the acquisition value and the estimated value remaining when the asset is either sold from the business, traded in on new equipment, or discarded because it is economically unproductive. An asset purchased new for $5,000 and scheduled for replacement in five years, when its projected worth will be $1,000, would have an average investment value of $3,000: ($5,000 + $1,000) ÷ 2 = $3,000.

The choice of interest rate, r, will likely depend upon the going interest rate on borrowed money and the rate of return expected from alternative investments in the business. If the best return expected for equity capital is interest on savings, then that should be used for r. If there are several alternate investments with expected yields of 10, 15 and 20 percent, then an r of 15 or 20 percent should be used. An operator with limited financial resources would use the going interest rate on borrowed funds as the *minimum* value for r.

REPAIRS

It is customary to think of repairs as variable costs that depend upon the use level of an asset, that is, wear and tear. Most repair costs are variable costs. Some durable assets, however, deteriorate with time even though they are not used. Fences and buildings are prime examples, although they probably deteriorate even more rapidly with use. The same applies to hoses, belts, and some moving parts on machinery and equipment.

On some farm machinery annual fixed repairs may average as much as 5 percent of new cost. Annual fixed repairs on buildings may be less than ½ of 1 percent. A busy manager should spend time estimating fixed repairs on assets only where the value is expected to be large and should rely on estimates available from planning manuals of management services or public agencies like the extension service for the others.

Some managers prefer to include shelter as another fixed ownership cost. They recognize that if machinery is not housed, depreciation and maintenance costs will be higher. In some areas it is customary to include a fixed cost of 1 or 2 percent of new cost for machinery housing.

Some recent studies have shown housing to have some benefits as well as the annual fixed costs. Trade-in value on five-year-old machinery that had been sheltered from the weather has been 10 to 25 percent greater than similar machinery that was left outside. Of course, this benefit is realized only if you trade in your machinery. However, the higher trade-in value is a reason for not including shelter with the DIRTI 5.

TAXES AND INSURANCE

Personal property taxes are levied on owned machinery in some states. In other states only that machinery that is used for custom work is taxed. Real property taxes are paid on buildings. These taxes come due every year and, again, are unrelated to level of use or productive services provided. Any investment analysis that ignores the annual tax obligation associated with the proposed investment will be incomplete.

Insurance, too, is a fixed cost. Protection against fire, weather, theft, etc., may be required when a financed asset is purchased. That is, the lender may require the asset to be insured as a means of security for the loan. Some operators, particularly those with low equity, will want to insure some of their more valuable assets because of the strain the loss of those assets would place on the financial condition of the business. Other operators will self-insure; that is, they feel they can take risk and choose to do so rather than pay a premium to an insurance company to assume the risks for them. Insurance is discussed further in the chapter on insurance uncertainty (Chapter 20).

Fixed Costs Can Eat into Profits

Ownership costs are important in decision making because of the big investment required in farming and ranching today. Machinery investments over $100,000 per farm are common in many areas. Facilities on a highly mechanized beef, dairy, or hog farm can run into several hundreds of thousands of dollars. As a result, managers have to pay attention to the fixed costs obligations that come with major investments.

For example, consider the ownership costs that go with the purchase of an $80,000 combine. The combine has an expected life of eight years and a projected salvage value of $10,000. Exhibit 4–3 presents the figures summarizing average annual ownership costs. Depreciation and interest are the big factors. That is normal, so a manager will want to spend the most time making sure those estimates are in the ballpark.

It should be pointed out that the depreciation and interest estimates are *average* values. The first few years after purchase, the actual depreciation and opportunity interest will probably be higher than the estimates in the table.

This simple example should illustrate the need to compute and evaluate ownership costs. As a result of such an analysis, a manager might choose to explore some alternatives like (1) purchasing a reconditioned used machine or (2) planning to use custom harvesting. That decision will be influenced by expected level of use. One probably could not afford the machine if it were not going to be used on more than 1,000 acres or the marginal value of a timely harvest resulting from ownership were not particularly high.

In thinking through the ownership costs associated with acquiring a durable asset, a manager should ask.

1. How much is the annual ownership cost?

2. How much will this add to per unit costs of production?

3. What are the alternatives to this particular asset or this way of doing things?

4. Can the same services be obtained at lower cost?

5. Can the business stand this addition to annual fixed costs? Are there other more profitable uses for limited capital resources?

Exhibit 4–3. Figuring ownership costs for an $80,000 combine

1. Annual depreciation (Life = 8 years; SV = $10,000)	$8,750
2. Average interest at 12%	5,400
3. Repairs and housing at 1.5% of new costs	1,200
4. Taxes at 0.3% of new costs	240
5. Insurance at 0.5% of new costs	400
Total Annual Ownership Costs	$15,990

BREAKEVEN

Breakeven analysis is an example of a practical application where the DIRTI 5 get involved. A manager may need to estimate total cost for the business in order to choose a business plan that will yield adequate sales to cover costs. In other cases the manager may want to estimate total costs per acre or per cow in order to compute breakeven income needed. As another example, a grain farmer might want to know how many acres he must harvest in order to own a combine rather than have grain custom harvested.

Among the many reasons a manager needs to know fixed costs are:

1. In the long run you must cover all costs. If you don't, you will use up your assets and have to sell out.

2. In many planning situations, like those mentioned above, it is impossible to make a good decision without knowledge of fixed costs.

3. When developing a marketing plan and deciding on price objectives, a manager must have some estimate of cost per unit (bushel, pound, ton).

As a means of illustrating the use of fixed costs in a breakeven analysis, consider the combine data presented in Exhibit 4–3. Average annual fixed costs were estimated to be $15,990. Those costs are incurred regardless of the level of combine use. But they are only part of the costs of owning and operating a self-propelled combine. There are variable costs for fuel, oil, repairs, and labor. These variable cost items can total $10 per acre. Finally, for a breakeven analysis the farmer must know what custom harvesting would cost.

Assume the appropriate data are as follows:

$$\text{Custom rate} = \$22 \text{ per acre}$$

$$\text{Variable costs of operating own combine} = \$10 \text{ per acre}$$

$$\text{Fixed costs of owning SP combine} = \$15,990$$

The breakeven formula would be:

$$\text{Custom rate per acre} = \frac{\text{annual fixed cost}}{\text{acres}} + \text{VC per acre}$$

For our case, the unknown is A, expressed in acres. The breakeven formula would be solved as follows:

$$22 = \frac{15,990}{A} + 10$$

$$22 - 10 = \frac{15,990}{A}$$

$$12A = 15,990$$

$$A = 1332.5$$

For this situation, not giving any yield or timeliness advantage to ownership, a farmer would need to harvest 1332.5 acres to be indifferent between ownership and custom harvesting. If you only had 1,000 acres it would be less expensive to use custom harvesting ($22,000 vs. $25,990), other things equal.

SUMMARY

The DIRTI 5 are fixed costs that occur after durable assets are purchased whether or not those assets are used. These ownership costs are depreciation, interest, non-use-related repairs, taxes, and insurance.

Ownership costs are greatest during the early life of an asset and decrease as the machine grows older. This fact may have important tax and equity implications.

For planning purposes it is often acceptable to use average values like straight line depreciation and interest on average investment. Such a procedure will underestimate actual fixed costs during those years immediately after an asset's acquisition and overstate the costs in later years. The emphasis in this book is on making sure ownership costs are not overlooked, but are brought into decision making.

Once durable assets are purchased, the operator-manager has obligated himself to a bundle of fixed costs. Further, as pointed out in the previous chapter, although the amount of annual use does not greatly affect total fixed costs, the amount of use has a great effect on the per unit (i.e., per hour, per head, per acre) costs.

APPLYING THE PRINCIPLES OF CHAPTER 4

1. Explain in your own words the reasons for considering the five ownership cost items termed the DIRTI 5.

2. Gene Quicksilver purchased a new tractor for $17,000. He expects it to have an eight-year useful life with a salvage value of $5,000. What depreciation would be taken each year under each of the three different methods?

3. What factors influence the amount of depreciation each year?

4. What are the advantages of each of the depreciation methods?

5. Why should a business make an interest charge on its owned capital?

6. How may interest costs be estimated?

7. How much interest should Gene charge annually on the tractor purchased in question 2 at an interest rate of 12 percent?

8. What is the minimum interest rate a person should charge and why?

9. When are repairs classified as fixed costs?

10. Why are repairs sometimes considered fixed costs and sometimes considered variable costs?

11. Why are taxes and insurance fixed costs?

12. What depreciation strategy would you recommend for a farmer who has one or two good income years followed by a run of bad years? Why?

REFERENCES

Brigham, Eugene and J. Pappas. *Managerial Economics.* Hinsdale, Ill.: Dryden Press, Inc., 1972.

Edwards, Clark. "Depreciation," *Oklahoma Current Farm Economics*, September 1961, pp. 57–64.

Hadley, N. S., S. D. Parsons and D. H. Doster. *Some Economic Considerations in Farm Machinery*, Extension Circular 139, Purdue University, Lafayette, December 1968.

Kay, Ronald D. "An Improved Method for Computing Ownership Costs," *Journal of American Society of Farm Managers and Rural Appraisers*, April 1974, pp. 39–42.

U.S. Internal Revenue Service. *Farmer's Tax Guide*, 1981 edition, Department of Treasury Publication 225, October 1981.

Willett, G. S., O. I. Berge and R. N. Weigle. *Costs of Farm Machinery*, Extension Circular A1766, University of Wisconsin, Madison, August 1972.

Part 3

Monitoring

the Business

Alternative Record Systems and What They Can Provide

5

Effective management calls for sound business practices on the part of the operator to control and manage the use of resources. This means keeping good records of what has happened and having a system that provides the information needed for future planning.

To know where he is going, an operator must know his current position. And to reach a financial goal, he must have a set course and landmarks along the way to guide him. This is the role of records.

There are at least five good reasons for having a record system:

1. To comply with tax reporting requirements and to assist in tax planning and management.
2. To measure financial success and progress of the business over time.
3. To establish a factual basis for comparisons (a) with past years, (b) with goals that have been set, and/or (c) with the performance of other comparable operations.
4. To aid in planning for the future by providing data that will help to estimate the effects of operational changes on economic conditions of the business.
5. To aid in obtaining credit.

In financing agriculture, good farm records are becoming increasingly important. Credit is based in part on the ability of the borrower to repay money, and lenders expect their borrowers to keep adequate records that will show that their businesses are on sound financial footing and that their operations are producing, or will produce, satisfactory income.

In the remainder of this chapter we discuss aspects of the record systems available. Exhibit 5–1 highlights the kinds of records required for farm business analysis.

LEVELS OF RECORDKEEPING SYSTEMS

Tax Purposes

Farm recordkeeping systems can be classified into three levels. The predominant system is one that records cash expenditures, cash receipts, and depreciation on farm machinery and buildings. This level of recordkeeping, in varying degrees of sophistication, meets the requirements for taxpayers who use the cash method of reporting income. The "cancelled check and shoe box method" is the least sophisticated. Many farmers use a simple record book that classifies income and expenses by categories similar to those listed on Schedule F of the 1040 income tax form. Although this kind of record system meets the minimum requirements for reporting, it rarely provides anything more. It meets only one of the five criteria for a good record system.

Exhibit 5–1 Record information needed for various types of farm business analysis

Record information needed	Type of analysis desired					
	Income tax	Profit or loss	Net worth	Cash flow	Enterprise analysis	Family living
Financial Transactions						
Farm income and expense	X	X		X	X	
Nonfarm tax deductions	X					
Nonfarm income and expense	X			X		X
Debt payments				X		
Inventory						
Depreciation schedule	X	X	X		X	
Other farm assets		X	X			
Nonfarm assets			X			X
Record of debts			X			
Production Records						
Feed records					X	
Livestock production					X	
Livestock expenses					X	
Crop yields					X	
Crop expenses					X	

Taxes Plus Some Business Analysis

The second level of recordkeeping, somewhat more complete than the cash expenditure-cash receipts method, is provided in most farm record books sold by commercial companies and universities. Some agribusiness firms give their customers this type of record book. The main difference between this record system and the income tax one is that it provides an organized way of taking a complete inventory. In addition, the farmer can record information on labor used and on crop and livestock production. Many of these systems include a procedure for doing a whole-farm business analysis. Others separate out income and expenses so that the profitability of individual enterprise can be evaluated.

Computerized Business Analysis

The third level of farm recordkeeping is characterized by some of the new, complete, computerized accounting and farm analysis systems. The use of a computer is, however, no indicator of the sophistication and usefulness of the record system. For example, some computer record programs yield only a listing of cash expenses and cash receipts. While the farmer may receive this information monthly and with less work on his part because the information is obtained from bank deposits and checks, it is still nothing more than a glorified income tax system.

The primary advantage of a computerized record system is the capacity to store and classify tremendous volumes of information in a manner that allows quick retrieval. Thus, a complete record system that provides receipt and expense summaries, inventories, depreciation schedules, physical crop and livestock production data, financial data, and enterprise analyses is possible with the computer. Monthly, quarterly, and annual profit and loss or financial summary statements can also be generated with relative ease from a total record system.

Although there are limits to the amount of information these different levels of farm recordkeeping systems can provide, there is no assurance that a particular farmer is utilizing the full potential of the system he employs. The cost and returns associated with a record system, just as with any farm business activity, vary considerably among farmers.

OUTPUT AND USE OF RECORD SYSTEMS

Cash Expenditure–Cash Receipts (Tax Purposes Only)

As indicated earlier, the most common farm record system is the cash expenditure–cash receipts system. If the information is complete and accurate, a manager can observe the income received from cash sales and cash expenditures during the year. Generally available is some type of depreciation schedule that lists the farm machinery, buildings, and perhaps purchased breeding livestock. The possibility of keeping such information should be emphasized. It is surprising how many farm families utilizing this type of recordkeeping system leave the depreciation information with their tax practitioners.

An important limitation of this system is that desired output for decision making is often not provided. For example, without detailed enterprise analysis, one cannot tell what produced the net farm income. Without inventories, one does not know when the output sold during the year was produced. High cash sales during a given year may be the result of selling more than one year's production.

Further, one cannot tell by looking at cash expenses whether they were incurred in producing the crops and livestock that were sold or are prepaid expenses against future production. The farmer may have paid last year's accounts this year or he may have paid for next year's expenses in an attempt to hold his income down for this tax year.

The cash expenditure–cash receipt record system does not provide a systematic way of determining total investment in the business for use in estimating return on capital or other similar measures. It is possible, however, to approximate the capital invested in the business by taking the appropriate data from the financial statement.

"Complete" Farm Business Analysis: The Ideal Farm Record Book

Farmers who completely and accurately fill out the complete farm record book or a computerized record system based upon sound accounting principles have a record of cash transactions, physical quantities (i.e., bushels, pounds, etc., by enterprise), inventory changes, depreciation, and all of the information necessary to compute net farm income. They also have an inventory of total capital used in the business and can compute their return on capital, return on equity, change in net worth, capital turnover, and other financial measures of business performance.

Cash Flow

As managers handle increasing amounts of cash, a cash flow record provides a history of how cash moves in the business. Serving also to project cash flows in the period ahead, the records can monitor actual performance against planned performance. Cash flow is the connecting link between the profitability and the liquidity/solvency of the farm business. These concepts and linkages are discussed in the next chapter.

Past Performance and Forward Planning

The statement that history is useful only if we can profit from it is especially true of farm records. It is a waste of resources to keep records only for tax purposes when, with a little work, much additional management information could be obtained.

It is a fact of life that decisions must be made. A manager without pertinent and reasonably complete data on past performance to indicate progress is at a disadvantage in decision making. For example, an operator deciding between tomatoes and lettuce needs to know the past costs of producing those commodities. A broiler producer who negotiates a contract delivery price for 10,000 birds at a future date had better know what his past costs of production were.

Records provide the manager with information to use with standards of comparisons (size, productivity, efficiency, and organizational consideration) both within and external to the business. The manager can measure actual performance in comparison with planned performance and/or measures of performance of others for the same type of business. In short, records are useful as a monitoring device to correlate actual changes with planned changes and indicate when adjustments are warranted.

Enterprise Accounts

Enterprise accounts are vital in evaluating each of the several enterprises that make up the total farm business. At a minimum they should be broken down between the crop and livestock enterprises. Ideally, each enterprise should have a separate account. Enterprise accounts help farm managers to see which enterprises make the most profit, to determine which production methods within an enterprise perform economically under the individual farm conditions, and to determine what level of output is economically feasible for each enterprise.

Record books are seldom used in the ideal fashion because most farmers stop short of making entries in a manner that facilitates enterprise analysis. Farmers desiring detailed enterprise analyses frequently use computerized systems.

Computerized Enterprise Analysis System

The cadillacs of the farm accounting and analysis systems are some of the more sophisticated computerized farm record programs. It should be quickly noted that there is no magic in the computer for doing recordkeeping. In fact, for most farmers, this method does not reduce the time put into recordkeeping. While requiring about the same amount of time, however, it offers the farmer the potential for obtaining more information. Most of the information that goes into the farm record system is generated on the farm and must be communicated to the computer by the farmer. Despite the various systems for transmitting the data, nobody has found a way to eliminate this task. Some attempts to make it simpler, such as using the information generated when writing a check, create greater problems of incomplete information. Weights, quantities, and the like, for example, often get left out and a follow-up communication to obtain this information is required.

Because computerized record systems require farmers to provide complete information as a condition for participating in the program, they really don't have a choice of participating at less than full capacity. Many of the more sophisticated computerized record programs have the potential for enterprise analysis, but the farmer must take the initiative to assure that the complete information is fed into the system. If he loses interest as he becomes busy during the year, he will receive a printout of incomplete information.

One difficulty of a professional farm management specialist working with different kinds of record systems is that it is hard to find the desired information and to be sure it is in the system output. This is especially true of computer analyses. While they may have a summary page that prints out the answers (for example, net profit, percentage return on capital, cost percentage of output, etc.), they are difficult to accept unquestionably. Any information left out will affect the answer, and many terms, such as profit, are defined differently among the various systems. Therefore, complete knowledge and understanding of statistical computation must precede the use of any record system output.

Some General Observations

Although farm records are a useful management tool, they have several inherent limitations. Most farm decisions are made regarding what will happen in the future. Whether a farm record, which is a collection of historical data about a particular farm, is useful in making decisions for the future depends on how it is used.

Each farm is unique, both from the standpoint of physical resources and the managerial interest and competency of the operator. Over time, farmers tend to overestimate income and underestimate costs. This is a built-in human bias. Farmers, like other people, tend to remember the good experiences and forget the bad. Complete records can help a manager keep estimates realistic.

Based on studies of farmers who participate in computerized record programs and are generally a good cross section of larger, more successful, commercial farms, a number of observations can be made. First, a complete system will help a manager look at all the income and expense information. Because it provides facts, the manager will not have to guess; information will not be biased.

Second, complete records are valuable in providing an accurate picture of the level of performance which a business is achieving. This information is vital when developing a budget for the future to use as a basis for a decision to expand or contract a particular enterprise.

Third, as mentioned earlier, farmers with incomplete record systems tend to underestimate costs. Certain cash costs are easy to identify and usually get charged against the appropriate enterprise. But costs such as tractor fuel, taxes, utilities, etc., must be allocated to several enterprises. These costs of doing business are very difficult to charge against a particular enterprise. One consistently underestimated cost that is not a cost of doing business, but certainly influences ability to pay off a loan, is the cost of family living.

Farmers and ranchers consistently project family living costs lower than what families who are keeping records spend. Not very many people like to admit that they are living high. They will all readily admit that the cost of living is high, but deny that they are living high. Therefore, they may bias their planning by underestimating what their family living costs will be and, as a result, overestimate their ability to repay a loan. At the end of the year, when things did not turn out as expected, they look for reasons and many times miss one of the obvious ones.

In short, records and the resulting benefits from their use are likely to play a more consequential role in the farming/ranching businesses of the future. The cost of wrong decisions is growing. Using records in decision making is just another tool to help minimize wrong decisions and their consequences.

APPLYING THE PRINCIPLES OF CHAPTER 5

1. What basic purpose is served by a recordkeeping system? What information is needed for this purpose? What are the limitations imposed by this information?

2. What are the advantages and disadvantages of a computerized record system?

3. What information should a complete business analysis give the farm manager?

4. What traps can a manager without a complete record system fall into?

REFERENCES

Herbst, J. H. *Farm Management: Principles, Budgets, Plans.* Champaign, Ill.: Stipes Publishing Co., 1980.

James, Sidney C. and Everett Stoneberg. *Farm Accounting and Business Analysis.* Ames, Iowa: Iowa State University Press, 1974.

Business Analysis and Control

- Components of a good record system
- Financial statement lists assets, liabilities, and net worth
- Profit and loss statement as measure of business profitability
- Cash flow analysis
- Financial ratio analysis

6

High among any business's goals are (1) profitability, (2) liquidity, and (3) solvency. Yet some managers who are very capable in the technical and production aspects of their business are completely in the dark when it comes to measures of business status and performance. They leave their record-keeping to a bookkeeper or, worse, use the "shoebox" record system; the only "business analysis" they do is to fill out their tax forms at the end of the year.

Effective managers want to be able to determine the position of a business at any time. They also want a basis for evaluating where the business has been and for projecting where the business is going. This aids their control of the business operation over time.

In this chapter we discuss some of the business analysis forms and ratios a farm/ranch manager can periodically use to evaluate the performance and financial strength of the business.

The many different, excellent recordkeeping systems range from single-entry record books to rather elaborate computer record systems. Most systems have an instruction manual on recordkeeping. How much analysis can be done will vary from one system to another. Most meet the minimum requirements for tax reporting.

ONE RECORD SYSTEM

This is not a chapter on how to keep records. However, for the reader who is unfamiliar with record systems, a set of recordkeeping forms are presented in Exhibits 6–1 through 6–11. This system provides the necessary information for (1) tax reporting, (2) developing an annual profit and loss statement, (3) developing an up-to-date financial statement (balance sheet) at any time, and (4) enterprise accounting so a manager can identify strong and weak segments in the business. Also, a cash flow analysis is an integral part of the system.

A complete record system should include the following components:

- An inventory
- A depreciation schedule
- A financial statement
- A receipts record
- An expense record
- A profit and loss statement
- A cash flow statement
- Production records
- Accounts payable and accounts receivable

Additional records on loans outstanding, payments on social security, and family living accounts may also be kept.

THE INVENTORY AND DEPRECIATION SCHEDULE

Among the first pieces of information the manager needs are an inventory—a complete list of all assets—and a depreciation schedule. The depreciation schedule should summarize original cost; prior depreciation allowances taken; current depreciation; remaining value for each asset; and method of prorating the original cost of capital assets over their useful life. Items like supplies, feed, and grain held for sale are listed on the inventory form but are not depreciated. Machinery, equipment, pur-

Exhibit 6–1.

INVENTORY OF FEED, STORED & GROWING CROPS AND CROP & LIVESTOCK SUPPLIES

LINE		START 19__			END 19__			END 19__			END 19__			END 19__			LINE
		QUANT.	PRICE PER UNIT	TOTAL VALUE	QUANT.	PRICE PER UNIT	TOTAL VALUE	QUANT.	PRICE PER UNIT	TOTAL VALUE	QUANT.	PRICE PER UNIT	TOTAL VALUE	QUANT.	PRICE PER UNIT	TOTAL VALUE	
	PURCHASED FEEDS																
1	Prepared Feeds																1
2																	2
3	Protein Supplements																3
4																	4
5	Vitamins, Minerals																5
6																	6
7	TOTAL PURCHASED FEEDS																7
	STORED CROPS																
8	Corn																8
9	Wheat																9
10	Grain Sorghum																10
11	Soybeans																11
12	Cotton																12
13	Silage																13
14																	14
15	Hay																15
16																	16
17	Straw																17
18	TOTAL STORED CROPS																18
	GROWING CROPS $ invested																
19																	19
20																	20
21	TOTAL GROWING CROPS																21
	CROP SUPPLIES																
22	Seeds																22
23																	23
24	Fertilizer, Lime Applied																24
25	Fertilizer Stored																25
26																	26
27	Herbicides																27
28																	28
29	Insecticides																29
30	Fungicides																30
31	Twine, Etc.																31
32	Fuel																32
33																	33
34	Oil																34
35	Grease																35
36	TOTAL CROP SUPPLIES																36
	LIVESTOCK SUPPLIES																
37	Veterinary Supplies																37
38																	38
39	Bedding																39
40	Other Supplies																40
41																	41
42																	42
43	TOTAL LIVESTOCK SUPPL.																43
44	FORM TOTAL																44

Exhibit 6-2.

INVENTORY OF LIVESTOCK

LINE		START 19__				END 19__				END 19__				END 19__				END 19__			
		NO. HEAD	TOTAL WT.	PRICE PER UNIT	TOTAL VALUE	NO. HEAD	TOTAL WT.	PRICE PER UNIT	TOTAL VALUE	NO. HEAD	TOTAL WT.	PRICE PER UNIT	TOTAL VALUE	NO. HEAD	TOTAL WT.	PRICE PER UNIT	TOTAL VALUE	NO. HEAD	TOTAL WT.	PRICE PER UNIT	TOTAL VALUE
	SWINE																				
1	Purch. Breeding F. 14/15																				
2	Rsd. Breeding - Sows																				
3	- Gilts																				
4	- Boars																				
5	TOTAL BREEDING SWINE																				
6	Hogs																				
7	Pigs																				
8	Gilts																				
9	Boars																				
10	TOT. NON-BREED. SWINE																				
11	TOTAL SWINE																				
	BEEF																				
12	Purch. Breeding F. 14/15																				
13	Rsd. Breeding - Cows																				
14	- Heifers																				
15	- Bulls																				
16	TOTAL BREEDING BEEF																				
17	1-2 years Heifers																				
18	Bulls																				
19	weaned. Heifers																				
20	Bulls																				
21	Steers																				
22	Sucking Calves																				
23	TOTAL NON-BREED. BEEF																				
24	TOTAL BEEF																				
	DAIRY																				
25	Purch. Breeding F. 14/15																				
26	Rsd. Breeding - Cows																				
27	Bred Heifers																				
28	Open Heifers																				
29	Bulls																				
30	TOTAL BREEDING DAIRY																				
31	Heifers																				
32	Bulls																				
33	Steers																				
34	Calves																				
35	TOT. NON-BREED. DAIRY																				
36	TOTAL DAIRY																				
	OTHER																				
37																					
38																					
39	TOT. BREEDING																				
40																					
41																					
42	TOT. NON-BREEDING																				
43	TOTAL																				
44	FORM TOTAL																				
45	TOTAL RAISED BREEDING																				

Exhibit 6-3.   PAGE _____

DEPRECIATION SCHEDULE AND INVESTMENT RECORD: REAL ESTATE

LINE	DATE ACQUIRED	ITEM DESCRIPTION (Kind, size, location) lines 1 to 11: Buildings, Fences, Etc. lines 15 to 21: Land Improvements lines 25 to 27: Land	INVEST-MENT CREDIT	TOTAL COST BASIS	LIFE	METHOD	Annual Rate % or $	Depr. Taken in Prior Years	Rem. Value at Start of Year	END 19__ Depr. This Year	END 19__ Rem. Book Value	END 19__ Depr. This Year	END 19__ Rem. Book Value	END 19__ Depr. This Year	END 19__ Rem. Book Value	END 19__ Depr. This Year	END 19__ Rem. Book Value
1																	
2																	
3																	
4																	
5																	
6																	
7																	
8																	
9																	
10																	
11																	
12		Total Buildings- this page. line 1 to 11															
13		Total Buildings-previous page. line 14															
14		Total Buildings- Lines 12 plus 13															
15																	
16																	
17																	
18																	
19																	
20																	
21																	
22		Total Land Improvements line 15 to 21 this page															
23		Total Land Imp'vmts-prev. page. line 24															
24		Total Land Improvements - line 22 plus 23															
25		Land ____ Acres -original cost															
26		Land ____ Acres -original cost															
27		Land ____ Acres -original cost															
28		Total Land Value-this page. lines 25 to 27															
29		Total Land Value-previous page. line 30															
30		Total Land Value - line 28 plus 29															
31		OWNER'S DWELLING															
32		Total Book Value-this page. ll.12+22+28+31															
33		Total Book Value of Farm ll. 32 plus 33															
34		Total Book Value previous page. line 34															
35		ESTIMATED CURRENT MARKET VALUE															
	1	2	3	4	5	6	7	8A	9A	8B	9B	8C	9C	8D	9D	8E	9E

97

Exhibit 6-4.

DEPRECIATION SCHEDULE: _____ MACHINERY AND EQUIPMENT.

PAGE _____

LINE	DATE ACQUIRED	ITEM DESCRIPTION KIND OF MACHINE, MAKE, MODEL, SIZE	ID. NO.	NEW OR USED	INVEST. CREDIT	COST INFORMATION			ADDITI. FIRST YEAR DEPREC.	SALVAGE VALUE	BALANCE FOR REGULAR DEPREC.	LIFE	METHOD	ANNUAL DEPREC. % or $	DEPREC. TAKEN IN PRIOR YEARS	LINE
						REM'NG BOOK VALUE OF TRADE-IN	CASH. DIFF. PAID	TOTAL COST BASIS								
1																1
2																2
3																3
4																4
5																5
6																6
7																7
8																8
9																9
10																10
11																11
12																12
13																13
14																14
15																15
16																16
17																17
18																18
19																19
20																20
21																21
22																22
23																23
24																24
25																25
	1	2	3	4	5	6	7	8	9	10	11	12	13	14	15A	

Exhibit 6-4. (cont'd.)

DEPRECIATION SCHEDULE:

PAGE

LINE	REM'NG BK. VAL. AT START OF YEAR	END 19__ DEPREC. THIS YEAR	END 19__ REM'NG BOOK VALUE	END 19__ DEPREC. THIS YEAR	END 19__ REM'NG BOOK VALUE	END 19__ DEPREC. THIS YEAR	END 19__ REM'NG BOOK VALUE	END 19__ DEPREC. THIS YEAR	END 19__ REM'NG BOOK VALUE
1									
2									
3									
4									
5									
6									
7									
8									
9									
10									
11									
12									
13									
14									
15									
16									
17									
18									
19									
20									
21									
22									
23									
24									
25									
	16A	15B	16B	15C	16C	15D	16D	15E	16E

MACHINERY AND EQUIPMENT (CONT.)

ESTIMATED CURRENT CASH VALUE

LINE	START 19__	END 19__	END 19__	END 19__	END 19__
1					
2					
3					
4					
5					
6					
7					
8					
9					
10					
11					
12					
13					
14					
15					
16					
17					
18					
19					
20					
21					
22					
23					
24					
25					
	17A	17B	17C	17D	17E

Exhibit 6-5.

DEPRECIATION SCHEDULE: LIVESTOCK FOR BREEDING

PAGE ___

LINE	Date Acq.	I.D. or Lot No.	Item Description	Head in Lot when Acq.	Investment Credit	New or Used	Cost Basis	Salvg. Value	Bal. for Depr.	Life	Method	Annual Depr. %/or $	START OF 19__ Per Head — Depr. in Prior Years	Per Head — Rem. Book Value	head — On Hand	Per Lot — Depr. in Prior Years	Per Lot — Rem. Book Value	END 19__ Per Head — Depr. This Year	Per Head — Rem. Book Value	head — Sold or Died	Head — On Hand	Per Lot — Depr. This Year	Per Lot — Rem. Book Value	LINE
1																								1
2																								2
3																								3
4																								4
5																								5
6																								6
7																								7
8																								8
9																								9
10																								10
11																								11
12																								12
13																								13
14																								14
15																								15
16																								16
17																								17
18																								18
19																								19
20																								20
21																								21
22																								22
23																								23
24																								24
25																								25
	1	2	3	4	5		7	8	9	10	11	12	13A	14B	16A	17A	18A	13B	14B	15B	16B	17B	18B	

PER HEAD DATA

chased breeding livestock, and buildings are included in both the inventory and depreciation schedules. Land improvements like terraces or a deep irrigation well might go on the depreciation schedule, but not necessarily on the inventory (their value might be included in the overall land value). A sample inventory form and depreciation schedule are shown in Exhibits 6–1 through 6–5.

Assets and Their Value

Frequently, the depreciated value of an asset is different from its current market value. In developing a financial statement (presented in the next section), the manager has to decide between "book" value and current value. The asset valuation method(s) selected can greatly influence dollar value of balance sheet items and consequent interpretation of any information reflecting the performance, growth, and status of the business derived therefrom.

Values and methods of valuation of financial statement items should reflect the purpose for which the statement will be used. For tax purposes and for tax and estate planning, one is required to value assets on an adjusted "tax basis," reflecting book value. If, on the other hand, the financial statement will be used to obtain or establish credit, as it often will be, it is advantageous to value all assets at a fair market value. Such valuation is important to decision makers, particularly in evaluating alternatives for investment and resource use.

Regardless of the methods selected to value assets, one should use the same method consistently. Consistency eliminates bias when assessing the financial progress and performance of the farm business and minimizes "paper" profit and losses. The following valuation scheme for assets is suggested when a farmer is interested primarily in the financial performance and progress of the farm business.

Land: Value at cost plus land inflation. Every few years, land values should be updated to conform to an expected market price.

Buildings, depreciable real estate, machinery and equipment: Value at adjusted tax basis (generally purchase price minus depreciation). To do otherwise adds to the "paper" profit and loss problem mentioned.

Working capital such as breeding livestock: Value at conservative market prices. When market prices are relatively high, one may value somewhat lower. As an alternative, some lenders prefer to use the adjusted tax basis to affix value on working capital items.

Livestock purchased for resale, feed, seed, supplies, and other current assets: Value such assets at market value if they are to be used in the next year. Although assets held for sale are likely to appreciate (e.g., stocker steers on pasture and stored grain), the gain is yet to be realized.

FINANCIAL STATEMENT

Assets, once valued, are but one part of the financial picture of a business. A complete picture can be developed in a financial statement. The statement is a valuable document for evaluating business progress or for explaining the financial position of a business to a prospective lender. A financial statement (also referred to as a balance sheet or net worth statement) is a "snapshot" of an individual's or business's financial picture at a given date and is merely the listing of assets, liabilities, and net worth. The accounting equation states that assets minus liabilities equals net worth (assets − liabilities = net worth). One purpose of the financial statement is to illustrate the liquidity and solvency of a business. In addition, information regarding structure of the debt shows the ability of the operation to meet debt servicing requirements.

To represent the business's position accurately, the financial statement should separate personal and business items. However, most farm/ranch businesses are still organized as sole proprietorships or family-owned corporations. Financial statements therefore may reflect both agricultural and nonagricultural assets and liabilities and resulting net worth. A sample financial statement is shown in Exhibit 6–6.

A series of financial statements from consecutive years provides a basis for evaluating the changing financial structure and financial strength of the business. To be most meaningful, these statements should be prepared as of the same date each year. Financial statements are made up of the components discussed below.

Assets

Current assets: These consist of cash or assets that can be converted to cash through the normal operations of the business during the year. Included are accounts receivable (what other persons or firms owe to the business); inventory held for sale; and other near-cash items, such as marketable securities, stocks and bonds, and cash values of life insurance.

Intermediate assets: These assets consist of resources or production items with a useful life of one to ten years. Most of these are used to support production. They do not include assets expected to be sold or converted into cash within the year. Examples of intermediate assets are trucks, equipment, machinery, and breeding livestock.

Generally these assets are also depreciable. Market value may be

EXHIBIT 6-6.
FINANCIAL STATEMENT

As of _____, 19__.

Name _____ Age _____ Address _____
Spouse _____ Age of children at home _____ Phone _____

ASSETS		LIABILITIES AND NET WORTH	
Current Assets		**Current Liabilities**	
Cash (on hand) or in checking	$____	Open or charge acc'ts.:	
Savings accounts & time certificates	____	Feed $____Seed $____ Fertilizer $____	
Cash value of life insurance	____	Fuel & Oil $____ Repairs $____Other farm $____	$____
Marketable bonds and securities	____	Medical & other personal	
Prepaid expenses (for items not yet received)	____	Estimated accrued interest on:	
Notes & accounts receivable (good)	____	Open acc'ts. $____ Notes $____	____
Livestock to be sold Ave. wt: Value/hd.		Intermediate notes	____
____ Steers . . . . ____	____	Long term liabilities	____
____ ____ ____	____	Estimated tax liability (accrued):	
____Heifers . . . . ____	____	R.E. $____; Pers. $____; Income $____	____
____ ____ ____	____	Accrued cash rent	____
____ ____ ____	____	Notes payable within 12 mo. (To whom, maturity,	
____ Hogs . . . . ____	____	purpose)	
____ ____ ____	____	____	____
____ ____ ____	____	____	____
____ Horses . . . . ____	____	____	____
		____	____
Grain, Feed, Seed, & Supplies		____	____
____ Bu. corn ____ bu. gr. sorgh.	____	____	____
____ Bu wheat ____ bu. soybeans	____	That portion of longer term debts due	
____ T. hay (____ alf.____ pr.____other)	____	within next 12 months	
____ T. silage;____T. haylage;____T. straw	____	Intermediate	____
Supplies	____	Long term	____
Cash Investment in Growing Crops		Judgments & mechanic liens	____
____ac. wheat; ____ ac. rye; ____ac. ____		CCC loans: ____ bu. ____, ____ bu.____	____
TOTAL CURRENT ASSETS	$	Other (including relatives)	
		TOTAL CURRENT LIABILITIES	$
Intermediate Assets		**Intermediate Liabilities**	
Machinery, equipment, cars, trucks	$____	(Show only balance due beyond 12 mo.)	
Breeding or work animals not to be sold within 12 mo.			
____ Beef cows;____dairy cows;____bulls		Notes payable	$____
____ 2 yr. old hfrs.;____yrlg. hfrs.		Sales contracts	____
____ Ewes & rams;____horses		Life insurance loans	____
____ Gilts;____sows;____boars		Other intermediate term liabilities	____
Securities not readily marketable			
TOTAL INTERMEDIATE ASSETS	$	**TOTAL INTERMEDIATE LIABILITIES**	$
Fixed Assets		**Long Term Liabilities**	
Farm real estate		(Show only balance due beyond 12 mo.)	
Gross value $____		Mortgages on farm real estate	$____
less: estimated cost of selling $____		Land contracts	____
est. capital gains tax $____		Mortgages on other real estate	____
Net value	$____	Other	____
Non-farm real estate	____		
Household goods	____		
TOTAL FIXED ASSETS	$	**TOTAL LONG TERM LIABILITIES**	$
		TOTAL LIABILITIES	$
		PRESENT NET WORTH	$
TOTAL ASSETS	$	**TOTAL LIABILITIES AND NET WORTH**	$

SOURCE: Bitney, L. L. *et al. A Financial Management Series for Nebraska Farmers and Ranchers.*
University of Nebraska Extension Service and Department of Agricultural Economics.

more or less than book value because of (1) accelerated depreciation taken for tax purposes or (2) inflation which has kept assets from losing value as fast as expected when the asset was initially added to inventory.

Fixed assets: Sometimes referred to as long-term assets, these assets are permanent and consist primarily of real estate and fixed improvements. Although land and improvements are frequently valued as a unit, separate values give a clearer picture of the distribution or structure of capital in the business.

Liabilities

Three groupings—current, intermediate, and long-term—are used to compare liabilities with assets. Such a division permits a realistic appraisal of debt structure.

Current liabilities: These liabilities are due and payable on demand or at stipulated maturities within the operating year, normally a twelve-month period. These include notes and accounts payable, rents, taxes and interest, plus that portion of principal on intermediate and long-term debt due within the next twelve months.

Intermediate-term liabilities: This group of liabilities includes non-real-estate debt and contracts written with the purpose of meeting other seasonal needs. Terms of loans are normally for a period greater than twelve months but less than ten years. Examples include notes for improvements to real estate, equipment purchases, additions to breeding livestock and dairy stock, and other major adjustments in the farm operation. Land debt, if financed over a period of less than ten years, may be included as an intermediate liability.

Long-term liabilities: Debts with repayment periods in excess of ten years. They consist of mortgages and land contracts on real estate less the principal balance due within twelve months.

Net Worth

Net worth is found by subtracting total liabilities from total assets. It reflects the owners' equity in the business and in other personal property. Should the business be sold or liquidated, net worth is an estimate of the amount of money a person would have left over before taxes.

PROFIT AND LOSS STATEMENT

How well has the farm business performed? Did it make a profit or loss? Recent income tax returns are unreliable indicators of how well a business is doing. Rapid depreciation, the selling of crops produced in a prior year, purchase of next year's feed or seed, and other conditions can substantially affect taxable income in any given year. As a result, taxable income may not adequately represent the earning power of a farm business, whereas a profit and loss (income) statement provides information on how well the business actually did over a set time period.

To complete a profit and loss statement, include all expenses and receipts of the business during a specified period (usually one year) and adjust for inventory changes. A good record book or income tax reporting system provides the expenses and receipts information. See Exhibits 6–7 and 6–8 for examples. Inventory changes must account for any change in physical inventory items (number of livestock, number of bushels, etc.) as well as price level movements. In addition, any change in one's financial matters such as cash on hand, accounts receivable and accounts payable (see Exhibit 6–9) must be considered for a true financial picture. Financial statements (beginning and ending), if appropriately completed, provide necessary information for such inventory adjustments.

The profit and loss statement is a useful analytical tool, particularly when statements from a number of years are available for comparative purposes. It reports the return (or loss) to resources used in production. The relationship between income and expenses over time is also shown, indicating whether increased efforts to control costs are warranted.

Monitoring the outlay for capital items over a number of accounting periods gives insight into the capital structure of the business. Capital outlays that are not accompanied by increased income could be lead indicators of cash flow problems and reduced future profit.

The profit and loss statement, with a few adjustments, is useful in determining the business's capacity to undertake and service debts for expansion or investment purposes. Living expenses and income taxes must be subtracted from the annual profit figure to reflect this capacity.[1] In determining actual cash available for investments, one may prefer to add back a portion of the depreciation allowance deducted. In the short run, adjusting for depreciation (i.e. adding back this implicit cost since it is not a direct cash outflow) provides a more realistic measure of dollar amounts actually available for investment and debt servicing purposes. But in the long run, depreciation allowances must be covered to maintain productivity, keep the asset structure intact, and assure peak efficiency and earning capacity of the business.

Exhibit 6–10 shows a sample profit and loss statement. Note that inventory changes are considered when computing farm income. Taxable farm income, if income is reported on a cash basis, could be substantially

---

[1]Under the corporate business organization, adjustment of living expenses is not required since salaries are part of the annual operating expenses.

Exhibit 6–7.

19__ FARM EXPENDITURES

PAGE   **MONTH**

DATE / LINE	TOTAL COST ($ ¢)	check no.	DETAILED DESCRIPTION WHAT WAS BOUGHT, FROM WHOM	FEED (lbs)	FEED ($ ¢) 20	VET. MED. ($ ¢) 21	BREED. FEES, REGIS. ($ ¢) 22	FERT. LIME ($ ¢) 23	CROP CHEM. ($ ¢) 24	SEEDS, CROP SUPPLIES ($ ¢) 25	MACH. REPAIR MAINT. ($ ¢) 26	BLDG., FENCE REPAIR ($ ¢) 27	MACH., TRUCK HIRE ($ ¢) 28	LINE
			subtotals brought from preceding page											
1														1
2														2
3														3
4														4
5														5
6														6
7														7
8														8
9														9
10														10
11														11
12														12
13														13
14														14
15														15
16														16
17														17
18														18
19														19
20														20
21														21
22														22
23														23
			subtotals to next page or totals to summary page F 27											

Exhibit 6-7. (cont'd.)

PAGE ___ MONTH ___ 19__ FARM EXPENDITURES

LINE	CASH RENT	POWER FUEL OIL GREASE	HIRED LABOR	INSUR.	TAXES	UTIL.	TRUCK EXPEN.	AUTO EXPEN.	MISC. FARM EXPEN.	INTER'ST
1										
2										
3										
4										
5										
6										
7										
8										
9										
10										
11										
12										
13										
14										
15										
16										
17										
18										
19										
20										
21										
22										
23										
	29	30	31	32	33	34	35	36	37	38

PAGE ___ MONTH ___ 19__ FARM EXPENDITURES

LINE	NEW INVESTMENTS										
	NON-BREEDING LIVESTOCK		BREEDING STOCK			MACH. & EQUIP.	LAND & BLDG. IMPRV'MT	PRINCIPAL PAID ON BORR'WD FUNDS	NON-FARM EXPEN., INVEST.		
			HEAD	LBS.							
1											
2											
3											
4											
5											
6											
7											
8											
9											
10											
11											
12											
13											
14											
15											
16											
17											
18											
19											
20											
21											
22											
23											
	39	40	41	42	43	44	45	46	47		

Exhibit 6-8.

FARM RECEIPTS

19___

MONTH _____ PAGE _____

LINE	DATE	TOTAL RECEIPTS		DETAILED DESCRIPTION to whom, what, etc.	AMT.: tons lbs. bu.	CROP SALES — KIND: write in below									MISC. FARM RECEIPTS								LINE
															Gov't Paym'ts		Custom Work		Pat. Div., Refunds, Resales		Cash Rent, Other		
		$	¢			$	¢	$	¢	$	¢	$	¢		$	¢	$	¢	$	¢	$	¢	
				subtotals brought from preceding page																			
1																							1
2																							2
3																							3
4																							4
5																							5
6																							6
7																							7
8																							8
9																							9
10																							10
11																							11
12																							12
13																							13
14																							14
15																							15
16																							16
17																							17
18																							18
19																							19
20																							20
21																							21
22																							22
23					subtotals to next page or totals to summary page																			23
						1		2		3		4			5		6		7		8		

108

Exhibit 6-8 (cont'd.)

PAGE   MONTH   19 __   FARM RECEIPTS   PAGE   MONTH   19 __   FARM RECEIPTS

NON-BREEDING LIVESTOCK — KIND: write in below

LINE	HEAD		lbs	$	¢	HEAD		lbs	$	¢
	bot	red				bot	red			
1										
2										
3										
4										
5										
6										
7										
8										
9										
10										
11										
12										
13										
14										
15										
16										
17										
18										
19										
20										
21										
22										
23										

LIVESTOCK PROD'TS — LBS/DOZ/quan — $ — ¢

BREEDING LIVESTOCK — KIND: write in below
HEAD — Quality — Do Not Qualify — bot/red — lbs — $ — ¢

Mach. Equip. Bldg. Sales — $ — ¢
Money Borrowed — $ — ¢
Non-farm Receipts — $ — ¢

LINE
1
2
3
4
5
6
7
8
9
10
11
12
13
14
15
16
17
18
19
20
21
22
23

Exhibit 6–9.

Open Accounts Payable

Includes open accounts at feed, fertilizer, and supply businesses where monthly statement is mailed.

		Date	Added to account	Paid on account		Unpaid balance
				Principal	Interest	$
1	Agency		$	$	$	$
2						
3	Purpose					
4						
5						
6						
7						
8						
9	Terms of payment					
10						
11						
12						

Total interest $

Multipayment Notes and Mortgages Payable

	Description	Date paid	Total payment	Principal	Interest and carrying charges	Unpaid balance
						$
1	Agency		$	$	$	
2						
3						
4	Purpose					
5						
6						
7	Original amount $					
8	Date obtained					
9	Terms of payment					
10						
11						
12						
13						
14						
15						

Exhibit 6–9. (cont'd.)

Single-Payment Notes Payable

Includes all single-payment loans, e.g., $500 for 6 months at 7% interest. Include in the interest column any noninterest loan charges. To allow more room to record loan detail, it may be convenient to use every second or third line.

	Date	Agency	Purpose	Original amount	Terms of payment	Payment		
						Interest	Principal	Date
1								
2								
3								
4								
5								
6								
7								
33								
34								
35	Column Totals			xxx	xxx	$	$	xxx

less because inventory changes are not considered in reporting farm income for tax purposes. That is a reason tax returns are less valuable than profit and loss statements in assessing business performance.

FINANCIAL RATIO ANALYSIS

Financial ratios are obtained from figures provided by the net worth and income statements. The four general groups of financial ratios are (1) liquidity, (2) solvency, (3) profitability, and (4) performance or operational ratios. All ratios except performance ratios can be computed from information provided by the profit and loss statement and the financial statement. Performance (operational) ratios generally require detailed records for each enterprise. Liquidity, solvency, profitability, and performance ratios are helpful in studying the financial trend of a business through the years and/or comparing the operation with similar ones. Ratios may be useful in pointing out problem areas.

Liquidity

Liquidity refers to the ability to meet cash obligations as they come due. The *current ratio* indicates whether current assets are adequate to

Exhibit 6–10.

PROFIT AND LOSS STATEMENT

For 12 Month Period
Ending _____ , 19__

Name _____   Address _____

Cash Farm Income

Grain and hay sales . . . . $ _____

Livestock sales (including breeding animals) . . . . _____

Livestock product sales . . . . _____

Government payments . . . . _____

Custom work . . . . _____

Other cash farm income (including refunds on purchases) . . . . _____

    Gross Cash Farm Income . . . . $ _____

Cash Farm Expenses

Cash operating expenses . . . . $ _____

Breeding livestock purchases . . . . _____

    Gross Cash Farm Expenses . . . . $ _____

Net Cash Farm Income . . . . $ _____

Adjustments

Inventory change . . . . (±) $ _____

Depreciation on machinery and equipment . . . . (−) _____

Depreciation on fixed farm improvements (see income tax depreciation schedule) . . . . (−) _____

Capital gain or loss on machinery & equipment:

    Gross sales of machinery and equipment . . . . (a) $ _____

    Less remaining cost (as per depreciation schedule) . . . . (b) _____

    Capital gain or loss (a-b) . . . . (±) $ _____

Adjustment for real estate sold during the year:

    Gross sales $ _____ , less costs of selling $ _____ . . . . (c) $ _____

    Less net beginning-of-year value from Balance Sheet . . . . (d) _____

    Net adjustment for real estate sold . . . . (±) $ _____

Gross Adjustments to Net Cash Farm Income . . . . (±) $ _____

Net Farm Income (returns to unpaid labor, operators labor, equity and mgt.) . . . . **$ _____**

Non-Farm Income

Operator's wage off farm minus expenses incurred . . . . $ _____

Wife's wage off farm minus expenses incurred . . . . _____

Interest and dividend income . . . . _____

Gifts or inheritances . . . . _____

Gain or Loss on securities . . . . (±) _____

Non-farm inventory change . . . . (±) _____

Net Income — other farms owned . . . . _____

Net Income — non-farm real estate . . . . _____

Net Non-Farm Income . . . . $ _____

Unrealized Income from Change in Real Estate Value

Net end-of-year value of farm real estate (from Balance Sheet) . . . . (e) (+) $ _____

Plus real estate sold this year (Net value from beginning Balance Sheet) . . . . (f) (+) _____

Minus net beginning-of-year value of all farm real estate (from Balance Sheet) . . . . . (g) (−) _____

Minus cost of real estate (land or improvements) purchased this year . . . . (h) (−) _____

Net gain or loss in real estate value . . . . (i) (±) $ _____

Plus depreciation on fixed farm improvements (Same as in "Adjustments" section above) . . . . (j) (+) _____

Net Unrealized Income from Change in Real Estate Value . . . . (±) $ _____

Net Income (Farm + Non-Farm + Unrealized Change in Real Estate Values) . . . . $ _____

        Distribution of Income

        Change in Net Worth . . . . (±) $ _____

        Income and SS Taxes (paid past yr.) . . . . $ _____

        Family Living Expenses . . . . $ _____

            Total (should agree with Net Income above) . . . . $ _____

SOURCE: Bitney, L. L. *et. al. A Financial Management Series for Nebraska Farmers and Ranchers.* University of Nebraska Extension Service and Department of Agricultural Economics.

meet current indebtedness. This ratio is computed by dividing total current assets by total current liabilities. A ratio of 2.5 to 1 indicates that there is $2.50 of current assets to back up each $1.00 of current liabilities. Current commitments are often met by transferring assets such as inventories to cash. Liquidity is influenced in part by profitability of the farm business. In addition, the equity level (extent of leveraging) and debt structure are added factors that influence the ability of businesses to meet current obligations.

Solvency

A business is solvent if total assets exceed total liabilities. The *debt-to-asset* (debt divided by assets) *ratio* is one measure of solvency. A one-to-one ratio would mean a business would just be able to cover all its debts should it be forced to liquidate. A ratio greater than one-to-one would indicate a business could not meet all its obligations and might, therefore, have to declare bankruptcy.

The *debt-equity* (also called debt-to-net worth) *ratio* is another measure of solvency. This ratio shows the ratio of borrowed to owned capital. Lenders are interested in the ratio because they rarely like to provide more than 50 to 60 percent of the capital (i.e., they prefer a debt-equity ratio of 1-to-1, or less) in a farm/ranch business. Such a ratio provides them a measure of investment security. A debt-equity ratio less than one indicates that the owner's net worth exceeds the amount of borrowed funds. Smaller ratios generally mean less of the business's earnings must go toward the payment of principal and interest.

What constitutes a safe ratio will depend upon the profitability of various enterprises in the business and the anticipated economic conditions. A firm showing an increasing debt-equity ratio over time should look for production inefficiencies and/or excessive business (or personal) expenditures.

Profitability

Profitability refers to the difference between costs and returns; it is the amount left over for the resource owners. Because of differences in resources and resource ownership, various measures of profitability are required. A ratio appropriate for a sole proprietor might be inadequate for a farm corporation.

Profitability can be measured by (1) net farm income (returns to labor, management, and equity capital), (2) labor and management returns (net farm income minus return to owner equity), (3) return to total farm capital (net farm income plus interest paid minus return to unpaid family and operator labor and management), (4) return to equity or ownership capital (return to total farm capital minus interest paid), and (5) net profit margin (return to farm capital divided by value of farm production).

Some profitability measures are expressed as a proportion or percentage of a second value or measure (rate of return on investment, equity, etc.). This is necessary for meaningful comparisons over time within the farm business. Ratios also provide standardized statistics for comparative purposes among farms that differ by type, size, resource use, production, and level of technology.

The two most common profitability measures are returns to all resources in the farm business and returns to equity capital. Return on total assets reflects the earnings rate of all assets in the business. Return on equity shows how successful an operation is in using equity capital to attain its key financial goal, as high an income as possible. A high percentage, of course, is preferable.[2]

The reader should recognize the relationship between asset valuation and the key profitability ratios. Undervaluing assets will give (1) an unrealistically high return-total assets ratio and (2) an abnormally high returns-equity ratio.

Businesses considered moderate to highly profitable may find themselves confronted with cash flow problems even if family living expenses are within reasonable limits. Such cases reflect an inappropriate debt structure and repayment schedule. For example, the debt-to-asset ratio may exceed reasonable limits, and/or repayment terms (length of loans) may not coincide with repayment ability. Conversely, some businesses with low or negative profitability can meet cash flow needs through liquidating basic resources or using previously accumulated reserves.

CASH FLOW

A cash flow budget or projection indicates the ability of a business to generate cash inflows (sales, borrowed money, withdrawals from savings, and sale of capital items) to meet its cash demands (cash expenses, principal and interest payments on debt, capital purchases, salaries, or family living expenses) during a specified period of time (see Exhibit 6–11). That the cash flow statement generally projects into the future is useful to

---

[2]The rate of return associated with borrowed money in the farm business must exceed its interest cost or the owners will be losing equity rather than realizing growth.

money managers. It is particularly useful in documenting credit needs and communicating with a lender.

Financial analysis has too often looked only backwards, but today's manager cannot survive on hindsight. With larger and larger sums of money riding on "right" decisions and with profit margins that leave little room for error, the cash flow budget can be used to plan ahead.

Cash flow is the connecting link between the major goals of the farm business: to be liquid, profitable, and solvent. Cash flow is influenced by (1) efficiency of production, as reflected by ratio of operating income to operating expense; (2) debt structure and repayment conditions; (3) purchasing and marketing strategies (timing, inventory, management and control, and sale and replacement of capital items); (4) family living expenditures; (5) tax strategies; and (6) nonfarm income.

A cash flow statement reflects all of the cash transfers that occur in a business. It differs from the financial statement and profit and loss statement in several ways. For example, a new tractor purchase would probably involve a down payment (a cash transaction) that is recorded in the cash flow statement. But only the amount of the down payment and not the full value of the tractor (unless the tractor was purchased outright for cash) is recorded here. The profit and loss statement would reflect only the depreciation (change in beginning and ending inventories) on the tractor. The balance sheet would include the value of the tractor as an asset and the debt against it as a liability.

A cash flow budget is a convenient way to combine all the financial affairs into one report. All farm/ranch business income and expenses, non-business income, loans, debt repayment (and even personal withdrawals and household spending in the case of a family business) can be summarized.

The most effective cash flow statement is an integral part of a total record system. Each month expenses and receipts are summarized; then, as the year progresses, the manager can compare *actual* cash flows to those *projected*. A major benefit of cash flow is the financial control that results from checking actual progress against projected plans.

Preparing a Cash Flow Plan

A cash flow budget is usually prepared for a year and is often used to develop inflows and outflows by month. Cash flow statements can be historical or future-oriented. Developing a historical statement, which records cash transactions for some prior period, is easier and might be a particularly useful experience for the manager preparing his first budget.

A projected cash flow statement is more difficult to prepare because the needed information is not a matter of record, but must be estimated.

Exhibit 6-11.

CASH FLOW   FINANCIAL PLAN OR SUMMARY

	LINE	JAN.	FEB.	MAR.	APR.	MAY	JUNE	JULY	AUG	SEPT.	OCT.	NOV.	DEC.	TOTAL
RECEIPTS														
Crop Sales	1													
	2													
	3													
	4													
Gov't Payments	5													
Custom Work	6													
Dividends,Refunds,Resales	7													
Cash Rent, Other Farm	8													
Non-Brdg Livestock Sales	9													
	10													
	11													
Livestock Products	12													
	13													
OPERATING SALES TOTAL (add lines 1 through 13)	A													
Breeding Livestock Sales	14													
	15													
	16													
Mach.,Equip.,Bldgs. Sold	17													
CAPITAL SALES TOTAL (add lines 14 through 17)	B													
TOTAL FARM RECEIPTS (line A plus B)	C													
MONEY BORROWED summary only	18													
NON-FARM RECEIPTS	19													
TOTAL DOLLARS AVAILABLE	D													
EXPENDITURES														
Feed	20													
Vet.,Med	21													
Breeding Fees, Registr.	22													
Fertilizer, Lime	23													
Crop Chemicals	24													
Seeds, Crop Supplies	25													
Machinery Repair, Maint.	26													
Building, Fence Repair	27													

116

Exhibit 6–11. (cont'd.)

		JAN.	FEB.	MAR.	APR.	MAY	JUNE	JULY	AUG.	SEPT.	OCT.	NOV.	DEC.	TOTAL
Machinery, Truck Hire	28													
Cash Rent	29													
Power Fuel,Oil,Grease	30													
Hired Labor	31													
Insurance	32													
Taxes	33													
Utilities	34													
Truck Expenses	35													
Auto Expenses	36													
Misc. Farm Expenses	37													
Interest (existing obligations)	38													
Non-Breeding Livestock	39													
	40													
	41													
OPERATING EXPEND. TOTAL (add lines 20 through 41)	E													
Breeding Stock Purchases	42													
	43													
Mach.and Equip.Purchases	44													
Land and Bldg. Imprvm'ts	45													
CAPITAL EXPENSES TOTAL (add lines 42 through 45)	F													
TOTAL FARM EXPENSES (line E plus F)	G													
PRINCIPAL PAID existing obligations	46													
NON-FARM EXP. AND INVEST.	47													
FAMILY LIVING	FL													
TOTAL DOLLARS USED (add lines G through FL)	H													
CASH DIFFERENCE FOR MONTH (line D minus H)	I													
CASH BALANCE BEGINNING OF MONTH (line N last month)	J													
CASH AVAILABLE BEFORE BORROWING (line J±I)	K													
SHORT-TERM LOAN PROCEEDS (if line K is negative)	L													
SHORT-TERM LOAN REPAYMENTS (if line K is positive)	M													
CASH BALANCE END OF MO. (line K plus L minus M)	N													
SHORT-TERM CREDIT BALANCE line O last month plus L minus M	O													

However, a historical statement contains valuable data for developing a cash flow statement that applies to the future.

Two things are important to remember about a cash flow statement. First, it includes only cash transactions; purchases with an agreement to pay at a later date are not included until payment is actually made. Second, all cash transactions should be included when they occur. These include borrowing, payments on account, and debt reduction.

Family living considerations: Many farm/ranch businesses are family businesses and the main source of a family's income. Yet expenditures for family living and income taxes are often overlooked in cash flow planning. When family living costs are considered, they are often grossly underestimated. Studies have shown that estimates not based on historical family expenditure records include only about 60 percent of actual expenses. Living expenditures must be accurately estimated if cash flow planning is to be most useful in planning for the future.

Family living expenditures, in addition to being an important expense item, affect the growth of the farm business. Excessive family living expenditures compete with farm/ranch investments that would generate additional earnings. Uncontrolled and unplanned family living expenses can hamper loan repayment schedules. This is why many lenders are interested in family living costs, particularly for young farmers with low equities.

Advantages: Among the most important advantages of cash flow budgeting are that (1) a cash flow projection requires a plan as to enterprise combination and thus encourages production planning and development of marketing strategies; (2) information provided by the cash flow statement permits financial control to be based on comparisons of *actual* performance with *planned* expectations; and (3) cash flow planning facilitates communication between borrower and lender.

PERFORMANCE OR ACTIVITY ANALYSIS (STANDARDS OF COMPARISON)

To analyze performance, one needs to compare what happened with a standard, a measure of what was expected or should have happened. Three types of standards derived from different information sources make comparisons possible. These are (1) historical records (past performance of the business); (2) performance of other firms under similar circumstances (state or association record summaries of the same farm types and sizes); and (3) realistic budgets and projections.

Historical Records

Farm records, properly used, provide a management tool that is not available from any other source. Demonstrating financial progress is easy for a farmer who has kept a complete set of records over the years and prepared financial statements showing the year-to-year changes in assets, liabilities, and net worth. The same records provide a summary of profit and loss over time. Income level and variability from year to year indicate the earning capability of a business under specific resource use and management.

Comparative Performance

Most farm analysis is comparative; in other words, the individual farm business is compared to some standard, generally to similar type farms. A primary reason many states are involved in computerized record programs is to measure the performance of a number of farms as a basis for developing standards or group averages that farmers can use for comparisons. Although this method has the inherent weakness that no two farms are really alike, the performance of a particular farm that does better or worse than the group average should signal the need to pinpoint the cause. Such information facilitates control and enables the application of the "management-by-exception" principle.

Established standards of performance are expressed in both physical and monetary or financial terms. Examples of physical standards are the number of pigs weaned per litter or feed efficiency (i.e., the number of pounds of feed consumed to produce a pound of meat). On the other hand, examples of monetary standards are the dollar costs to produce 100 pounds of meat or milk, and fertilizer costs per acre of grain. These standards of performance may be considered the goals the manager plans to achieve.

Because standards must be feasible, knowing past performance is valuable in establishing them. But accomplishments in a farm business are directly affected by the managerial control. For example, although past records may indicate sales of only 6.5 pigs per litter, the farm manager could set a goal of marketing 8 pigs per litter and achieve this goal if he is willing to do the things necessary. But setting a goal of 10 or 11 pigs per litter may be unrealistic.

Budgeted Comparisons

The main purpose of setting realistic goals and comparing them with actual performance is to help the manager decide where to allocate scarce managerial time. By determining where he/she fell short of his/her goals, a manager can decide where to invest problem-solving and analysis time. By using budgeting or other economic tools, the manager can determine whether striving for the established goals is logical. Evaluating unmet objectives, sometimes called management by objectives, is an economical and efficient management technique.

MEASURES OF PERFORMANCE

Comparative analysis using multiple standards of comparison is often required for an accurate assessment of business performance. No single ratio is adequate; performance indicators are interrelated. Hence, interpretations must be made with caution. For example, a high percentage of purchased feed may be warranted if a dairyman expands the herd without a simultaneous increase in crop acreage. In such a situation, purchased feed costs per hundredweight of milk produced may appear high, but are compensated for by fewer acres (hence, lower investment) and lower crop production expenses. The total feed cost (the value of purchased plus homegrown feed) per cwt. of milk produced is the appropriate measure for comparative analysis.

Investments in buildings, equipment, or machinery provide another example of input substitution. If capital is effectively substituted for labor, increased labor productivity may warrant higher investments in capital items. On the other hand, what appears to be low labor productivity can be balanced by low capital investment expenditures.

Size

Some of the most common ways the size of farm businesses may be measured are listed and discussed below. Over the years, business size has been significantly correlated with profitability. In addition, business size is of interest to managers and farm policy makers because of the economies of scale possible.

1. *Total acres:* An indication of space; says nothing about (a) amount of investment on the land, (b) productivity of the land, or (c) adaptability to various enterprises.

2. *Tillable or crop acres:* Superior to (1) above if concerned with crop farms; still has limitations of (a) and (b). May not be meaningful in comparing livestock farms.

3. *Capital investment per farm:* Because capital investment includes capital in the form of land, this measure is superior to acres. There

is a potential bias in favor of farms that have a high percentage of capital in relation to labor (intensification). An operation that is overinvested in facilities and machinery may show "size," but be a very unprofitable operation.

4. *Value of total annual inputs per farm:* This measure includes cash operating expenditures, plus depreciation on capital investment, plus cost of all labor (including operator's labor), plus interest charge on capital (owned or rented) used in the business.[3]

This is one of the better measures of size if similar rates are charged for similar inputs—particularly land and labor. (One can't charge 8 percent opportunity cost for capital one year and 4 percent the next.) Consideration must be given to (a) capital turnover (capital used to purchase feed for dairy cows may turn two to three times in one year, but investment in a dairy farm is tied up a long time) and (b) changes in price level.

5. *Productive man work units (PMWU):* This is a measure of size in terms of a labor standard—the average amount of work a man can perform in an average ten-hour day using average technology. More popular in some states than others, this measure has these apparent deficiencies: (a) actual labor requirements vary with level of mechanization; (b) work accomplished varies by the man and his efficiency; and (c) the relationship between labor required per unit of enterprise and size is not linear—there are economies in labor use, too.

6. *Cash farm receipts:* Cash farm receipts have become a less reliable measure of size in recent years because of volatile commodity markets and marketing strategies (sales not made in year of production). Therefore, value of farm production appears a more appropriate measure of farm size.

7. *Value of farm production:* Gross sales plus (or minus) the change in inventories of market livestock, crops, equipment, and supplies, minus livestock and feed purchased. This measure is an effort to get at the real production on a farm. One must (a) recognize the potential influence of price level on sales and (b) avoid "paper profits" by valuing assets in inventory differently at beginning of year and at year end.

---

[3]A word of caution is injected regarding the computation of interest charge on all capital. Do not compute an interest charge for "borrowed" capital if it has been expensed with operating expenditures. To do so would be double counting.

Income Performance

1. *Net farm income as a percentage of value of production:* This percentage is a measure of efficiency after adjusting net cash income for changes in inventories, receivables, payables, and depreciation. A desirable goal for most farm types is a net farm income of 30 percent or more of the value of farm production.

For the individual farm, net farm income needs to provide a desirable wage for the family as well as a favorable return on its capital investment in the business.

2. *Net farm income as a percentage of investment:* A figure of 35 to 40 percent for value of production as a percentage of investment along with 30 percent for net farm income (profit) as a percentage of value of production would result in 11 percent as a guide for net farm income (profit) as a percentage of investment. This does not represent a return on capital of 11 percent because profit is a return to both unpaid family labor, management, and capital. Profit does determine the level of wage to the family and the return on the farm capital invested.

3. *Value of production as a percentage of investment:* This ratio, which measures the rate of *capital turnover*, is in terms of the time it takes the farm to produce value equivalent to the investment in the business. It is an indicator of volume and efficiency in the use of capital. A ratio equaling 33 percent means that it takes three years for the farm to "roll over" its capital. The lower the percentage factor, the longer the period of time required for capital turnover.

Capital Investment per Person

This factor depends upon the individual's policy on valuing capital assets. The current and occasionally unrealistic market values used by some farmers are not compatible with the more conservative and/or depreciated values used by others. Also, because the farm investment figures do not include the values of leased land and facilities, a meaningful standard is difficult to define. The best guide is to compare one's farm with the average of a group of farms. Such grouping of farms for comparison purposes entails selecting them to insure the highest degree of homogeneity, i.e., according to scale, capital intensity, type of farm, geographical area, etc.

In a low profit operation, a below average investment in capital per person could indicate that labor is being employed inefficiently.

Efficiency Ratios for the Farm

1. *Investment per tillable acre:* Essentially the same interpretation applies as for capital investment per man. In a low profit operation, an above average investment in capital per tillable acre could indicate that labor and machinery are being employed inefficiently.

2. *Value of production per person:* This figure indicates how productively labor was used. Where only the operator share of production on share rent arrangements is recorded, the value of production per man may be understated. Usually, the landlord's share of crops, but not of livestock, is included. Acceptable ranges of value of production per person will vary by enterprises:

Dairy	$40,000 – $45,000
Hogs	45,000 – 50,000
Beef	45,000 – 50,000
Crops	50,000 – 60,000

3. *Value of production per $100 of production costs:* Production costs include cash operating expenses, depreciation, unpaid family labor, and a charge for equity capital. Earnings immediately below $100 indicate that the production did not cover all of these costs, and that labor and/or equity capital were not fully paid for their contribution. Earnings below $75 to $80 suggest a negative return to unpaid labor and equity and the strong possibility that operating costs and depreciation were not fully covered.

A value above $100 indicates that all costs as figured are covered and that labor and equity earned at least the minimum opportunity cost prescribed. The higher this value, the higher the net earnings (economic profit) of the business.

4. *Fixed costs as a percentage of total production costs:* An acceptable figure here is around 35 percent or less to cover taxes, depreciation, insurance, interest, and repairs. This leaves 65 percent to cover variable cash expenses, unpaid labor, and return on equity capital.

5. *Machinery investment per tillable acre:* The lack of landlord investment data should not affect this value substantially on livestock farms and would probably not affect it at all on grain farms. It is difficult to suggest a standard figure for livestock farms; it varies substantially among enterprises and according to farm and levels of mechanization. Farm record summary reports indicate the following as guides:

Dairy	$90 – $120
Hog	80 – 100
Cattle Feeding	80 – 100
Crop	60 – 170

These figures should be considered along with the value of production per person, and mechanization should be viewed rather closely when above the suggested guides. With high investment in machinery and equipment, the output per person should also be high.

Enterprise Efficiency Ratios (Productivity)

A number of measures reflecting productivity (physical, technical, and monetary) are useful in determining cause and effect relationships for business performance, but they differ according to enterprises. Although some of the most common performance measures are listed below, specific standards are not provided because they differ so greatly by geographical regions.

Crops: While not exclusive, common measures for crops are: (1) value of feed production per feed crop acre, (2) grain yield per acre, (3) hay yield per acre, and so on.

Livestock: Some of the more common measures for livestock enterprises are livestock income per $100 of feed, feed conversion (amount of gain/amount of feed), mortality rate, milk sold per cow, and total value of feed per cow. Feed costs per unit of output depend on many factors, among which are animal health and genetic ability. Often overlooked in analysis of feed costs, however, are the prices *paid* for feed and excessive handling, storage, and transportation costs. Feed wastage is another unmeasured but significant cause of excessive feed costs.

A logical approach to feed costs is to establish whether the problem is price or quantity. Are quantities excessive on a per-animal-day basis or per-unit-of-gain basis? If not, look carefully at price. If cost per unit is not excessive, then quantity must be—if a problem exists. If the problem is quantity, is it quantity per animal-day (indicating waste) or only quantity per pound of production (indicating ration quality, imbalance, or animal health problems resulting in subperformance)? Often, more technical performance measures are required for analysis. As an example, some of the most useful coefficients by selected enterprises are provided in the appendix to this chapter.

SUMMARY

In this chapter we have discussed some of the business analysis forms and ratios that a farm/ranch manager can use periodically to evaluate the performance and financial strength of his business. A complete business analysis requires information provided by:

- An inventory
- A depreciation schedule
- A financial statement
- A receipts record
- An expense record
- A profit and loss statement
- A cash flow statement
- A production performance record
- Accounts payable and accounts receivable

A financial statement is a snapshot of a business financial picture at a specific point in time. It provides a listing of all assets and liabilities and enables an analysis of the liquidity and solvency position.

How well the business performed over a period of time, usually the accounting year, is indicated by the profit and loss statement. It provides information on all expenses, sales, and inventory changes so as to provide data not usually accounted for by income tax returns.

Cash flow analysis is discussed in terms of monitoring the performance of the business and projecting cash needs in accordance with sales, operating expenses, family living expenses, and growth requirements (capital investments).

Finally, the chapter discussed some of the more common comparative performance indicators. Both aggregate business indicators and detailed enterprise productivity measures are provided. These standards of performance are particularly useful for comparing business performance with projected goals for a particular operation as well as comparative performance and growth of different operations engaged in similar production activities.

APPLYING THE PRINCIPLES OF CHAPTER 6

1. What items should be included in an inventory? A depreciation schedule? Both?

2. What are the different methods of valuing assets? Why would one choose a particular method?

3. What purposed does a profit and loss statement serve? Why is it a better indicator of business performance than taxable income?

4. What factors of the farm business influence its cash flow? How does a cash flow statement differ from other statements?

REFERENCES

Baker, Timothy G. and John R. Brake. "Cash Flow Analysis of the Farm Business," Michigan State Bulletin E911, 1975.

Hopkin, John A., Peter J. Barry and C. B. Baker. *Financial Management in Agriculture.* Danville, Illinois: The Interstate Printers and Publishers, 1973.

James, Sidney C. and Everett Stoneberg. *Farm Accounting and Business Analysis.* Ames, Iowa: Iowa State University Press, 1974.

Osburn, Donald D. *et al. Farm Business Analysis Record Book.* Columbia, Mo.: Instructional Materials Laboratory, University of Missouri, 1975.

Schneeberger, Kenneth C. and Donald D. Osburn. *Financial Planning in Agriculture: A Key to Credit and Money Management.* Danville, Illinois: Interstate Publishers, 1977.

Appendix

EGG LAYING PERFORMANCE GUIDES

Egg Production

1. 72 percent of eggs are large, extra large, and jumbo. Egg size has a very marked effect on average price per dozen received.

2. 93 percent grade A eggs.

3. 21 dozen eggs per bird (of average number on hand) over thirteen-month laying period.[1]

4. 63.7 percent average laying percent over thirteen-month lay.

Feed

1. Average 4 pounds feed per dozen eggs produced over thirteen-month lay (open sidewall house).

2. 8,400 pounds feed per 100 birds (of average number on hand) over thirteen-month lay at "standard" laying percent (open sidewall house).

3. Average 3.8 pounds feed per dozen eggs produced over thirteen-month lay (controlled environment house).

4. 7,980 pounds feed per 100 birds (of average number on hand) at standard laying percent over thirteen-month lay (controlled environment house).

---

[1]Average number for month = birds on hand at beginning of month plus birds purchased during the month plus birds on hand at end of month, divided by two.

Average number year-to-date = average number in month 1 plus average number in month 2 plus average number in month 3, etc. . . divided by number of monthly periods.

Mortality

1. Varies by area depending on area disease problems.

2. Generally strive to keep mortality for the total thirteen-month laying period under 14 percent of birds started.[2]

Labor

1. Depends on degree of automation.

2. Guide: 38 hours per 100 birds (of average number on hand) over thirteen-month laying period (open sidewall house).

3. Guide: 1.8 hours per 100 dozen eggs (open sidewall house).

4. Guide: 17 hours per 100 birds (of average number on hand) over thirteen-month laying period (complete automation in controlled environment house).

5. Guide: .8 hours per 100 dozen eggs (complete automation in controlled environment house).

BEEF COW—CALF PERFORMANCE GUIDES

Beef Cow Herd

1. *Calving percentage* (cows calving ÷ cows bred × 100): Calve over 95 percent. Raise over 90 percent to sale weight. Watch how this has been calculated when it is quoted. Many figure it on cows remaining after selling the cows that come back in heat.

2. *Pregnancy-test cows* 75 days after breeding season. This is a *must* for efficient cow-calf management. It takes the profit from 4 or 5 calves to carry an open cow for a year. Sell "open" cows, and if more cows are needed, replace with bred cows.

3. *"Calve out" in a 90-day period.*

4. *Breed to grow calves in cool weather.* Late spring calves growing out in hot weather make slow gains.
   a. Use one yearling bull for 10 to 15 heifers, preferably hand-mated.

---

[2]Birds started, month = birds purchased in month.
Birds started, year-to-date = birds on hand at beginning of enterprise plus birds purchased year-to-date.

b. Use one aged bull for every 20 to 30 cows if bulls are running with the herd. Keep lower number of cows per bull on large rough pastures.

c. Too young and/or too few bulls are a major cause of extended calving periods and low calving percentage.

d. Semen-test bulls prior to breeding season to avoid a short calf crop from too many cows per fertile bull.

6. *Cull cows that can't wean a 500-pound calf every year.*

7. *Death loss*

a. Calf death loss—under 5 percent from birth to sale.

b. Cows—under 2 percent in closely watched herds.

8. *General* guidelines to costs.

a. Feed cost is usually about 50 percent of total cost.

b. Feed cost is usually about 75 percent of variable cost.

c. Variable cost is usually about 75 percent of total cost.

9. *Labor.* 5 to 20 hours per cow per year depending on size of unit with the lower number of hours on operations up around the 400 to 500 cow size.

SWINE PERFORMANCE GUIDES

Farrow and Finish Pigs

1. Feed

a. Good performance: 1 pound pork produced from 4 pounds feed or less.

b. Very efficient operators: 1 pound pork to 3.5 pounds feed or less.

c. Feed cost generally runs 65 to 75 percent of total costs.

2. Labor

a. Under 35 hours per average sow on hand (includes labor for finishing operation).

b. Generally runs 10 to 15 percent of total costs.

3. Pigs farrowed

a. 10 pigs or better from sows.

b. 8 pigs or better from gilts.

c. 85 percent or better of pigs farrowed reach market weight.

4. Gains: 225-pound finished hogs in 5½ months; 1.3 to 1.4 pounds per day average.

Farrow and Sell Pig as Feeder

1. Feed
    a. Average performance: 1 pound pork produced for less than 6 pounds feed.
    b. Efficient operators: 1 pound pork produced for less than 5 pounds feed.
    c. Feed generally runs 50 percent of total costs.
2. Labor
    a. Under 40 hours per sow (average number).
    b. Labor generally runs 15 to 20 percent of total costs.

3. Pigs farrowed same as farrow and finish operation. Wean 90 percent or better.

4. Weaning weights
    a. At eight weeks: from sows, 40 pounds; from gilts, 35 pounds.
    b. At six weeks: from sows, 26 pounds; from gilts, 23 pounds.

Hog Finishing

1. Feed
    a. Good performance: 1 pound pork produced from 4 pounds feed.
    b. Very efficient operator: 1 pound pork produced from less than 4 pounds feed.
    c. Feed generally runs 75 to 80 percent of total costs.
    d. Average feed consumption: 5.6 pounds feed per day with equal mix of 50 to 225 pounds hogs.

2. Strive to average 1.4 pounds salable gain per head per day or better.

3. Death loss: under 3 percent.

4. Feeding margins: see "Cattle Feeding" for example of the effect of buying large feeders at a much higher price than potential selling price.

CATTLE FEEDING PERFORMANCE GUIDES

1. Strive for a cattle feed conversion of 1 pound gain for every 7 to 9 pounds of 14-percent-moisture feed on finishing rations. The better feed conversion will be associated with high concentrate rations.
    a. Rapid gains promote improved feed conversion.
    Finishing Cattle:

(1) At 1.5 pounds per day gain (600 lb. cattle) *maintenance alone* requires 53 percent of feed.

(2) At 2.6 pounds per day gain (600 lb. cattle) *maintenance alone* requires 39 percent of feed.

b. Slow winter gains result in more feed per pound of gain. Slow winter gains usually must be compensated for by cheap spring and summer pasture gains.

Wintering Yearling Cattle:

(1) At .5 pounds per day gain *maintenance alone* requires 77 percent of feed.

(2) At 1.0 pounds per day gain *maintenance alone* requires 62 percent of feed.

2. Feed costs generally run 70 to 80 percent of total production and overhead costs. Operations with high fixed overhead costs may range down below the 70 percent figure.

3. Cattle generally will consume 2.5 to 3 pounds of air-dry feed per 100 pounds of body weight.

4. Strive for 2.75 to 3.00 pounds per day salable gain in finishing period.

5. Death Loss

a. Under 2 percent for long-fed calves.

b. Under 1 percent for long-fed yearlings.

c. Under .6 percent for short-fed yearlings.

6. Feeding margins

a. Operating on a *negative* feeding margin (buying price per pound is higher than selling price per pound):

(1) As the negative margin widens, it becomes increasingly important for the gain added to the feeder animal to make up a higher proportion of the final weight.

(2) Gain must be added at an increasingly lower cost per pound as the negative margin widens.

(3) Gain must be added to the animal at an even lower cost per pound as the amount of gain decreases in relation to the weight purchased.

b. Example:

Purchase 800 pound feeder @30¢   = $240 total cost
Sale   1000 pound finished cattle @28¢ = 280 total sale value
Gain =   200 pounds   = $ 40 increased value
$40 ÷ 200 pounds = 20¢ per pound value of gain produced

Purchase   400 pound feeder @35¢   = $140 total cost
Sale   1000 pound finished steer @28¢ = 280 total sale value
Gain =   600 pounds   = $140 increased value
$140 ÷ 600 pounds = 23.3¢ per pound value of gain produced.

7. Labor Goals:
   a. .8 to 1.0 hour per hundredweight gain.
   b. 2 to 2.5 hours per 100 head days.

DAIRY HERD ENTERPRISE PERFORMANCE GUIDES

Dairy Herds

1. High production per cow is a *MUST*.
   a. Large breeds: 14,000 pounds milk (3.6 percent B.F.) *minimum* per average cow.
   b. Small breeds: 9,000 pounds milk (5.4 percent B.F.) *minimum* per average cow.
   c. Produce a high percent of milk in nonsurplus months.
   d. Keep cows in production 85 to 90 percent of the year.
   e. Keep cows calving every 12.5 months.
2. Replacements and death loss:
   a. Maintain health and quality breeding program to keep annual replacements under 20 percent.
   b. Calves 1 day to 27 months; death loss under 10 percent.
   c. Use only the best sires available on the best cows for replacements.
3. Feed for milking and dry cows:
   a. Ranges from 45 to 60 percent of total cost depending on feeding program and per cow production.
   b. Cow weighing 1,200 pounds requires 16 pounds air-dry feed for daily maintenance plus 8 pounds additional in last two to five months of pregnancy.
   c. 40 pounds of 3.5 percent milk requires about 16 pounds of air-dry feed.
   d. 1,200 pound cow in first six months of pregnancy milking 40 pounds of 3.5 percent milk requires about 32 pounds of air-dry feed daily, 50 percent for maintenance and 50 percent for milk production.
4. Labor:
   a. Annual labor 50 to 75 hours per cow average number depending on type of facilities.

    b. Labor per cwt. milk produced: .5 to .8 hour.

    c. Cost generally runs about 20 percent of total costs.

    d. Sell over 500,000 pounds milk per man annually.

5. General

    a. Gross over $60,000 per man annually.

    b. Gross over $400 per $1,000 invested.

    c. Over $200 gross returns per $100 of total feed cost, including pasture.

Diagnosing Farm Business Problems

HIGHLIGHTS

7

- Systematic troubleshooting
- Checking on earnings sufficiency
- Earnings shortfalls: permanent or temporary?
- Reorganization for improved earnings
- Elimination of operational inefficiencies

The value of problem-solving steps to give organization and direction to decision making was discussed in Chapter 1. One of those steps was problem definition or opportunity recognition.

Systematic steps for efficiently focusing in on the specifics of a problem once the general problem has been identified have also been identified. This step-by-step procedure is referred to as trouble-shooting or problem diagnosis.

The organization and operation of a farm business in agriculture to-day is a complex undertaking that requires numerous skills and abilities. It may be likened to modern medicine, which must not only serve the needs of ill patients but also offer preventive medicine to keep the re-mainder of the population in good health. Just as a good doctor has a procedure for diagnosing a patient's health problem, a competent farm operator or farm management analyst must have a systematic method for evaluating the physical and financial problems of the farm/ranch busi-ness. The purpose of this chapter is to offer such a method, a way of "troubleshooting" the farm business.

When is troubleshooting required? Or, more specifically, what are the symptoms of poor business performance? Farm businesses, like indi-vidual health problems, have different pain levels. A typical and, in part, appropriate response might be to seek remedies when income is low. But an income too low to meet one person's commitments might provide lux-uries for another. In short, one of the first symptoms of a problem is *need*, which, in turn, is reflected by the cash flow requirements of the business. There is no absolute measure; needs among businesses vary because of different requirements and goals.

METHOD OF ANALYSIS

Troubleshooting the farm business, like a doctor's examination and clini-cal diagnosis, employs the process of elimination. One closes in on "where or what it is" by eliminating "where it isn't."

The efficiency of such an approach is obvious. The diagnostician who attempts to guess "where it is" and is unlucky is nearly back at the start, having eliminated only one of perhaps hundreds of possibilities. On the other hand, he may start with a strategic question, to which a yes or a no answer will point in a specific direction. Thus he is much more likely to discover the real problem. One key question quickly eliminates large numbers of unlikely possibilities. Five key questions asked and con-clusively answered in sequence will normally eliminate over 90 percent of all the initial possibilities.

Thus, the suggested analytical approach is to devise a series of ques-tions that ensures that large numbers of possible causes of a farm busi-ness problem will be systematically and logically eliminated. The result is a type of "decision tree," with each question representing a fork in the branching.

The Decision Tree

The five major questions, along with subquestions, can be phrased as follows:

1. Is there a permanent earnings problem?
2. Is the earnings problem due to the size of the business?
3. Is the problem due to enterprise choice or enterprise organization?
4. Is the problem in operations and/or production efficiency?
5. Is the problem one of marketing?

Answers to these basic questions enable one to identify factors influencing below par performance in the farm business.

Exhibit 7–1 represents a decision tree depicting the use of these questions. The starting point or trunk of the tree is determining whether problems or potential problems of business performance exist (the preventive medicine concept). Some of the symptoms might be: (1) the business is unable to meet its financial commitments; (2) the business does not appear to be making financial progress similar to "comparable" farm/ranch businesses; (3) a major change in the business is being considered in hopes of obtaining higher income.

IS THERE AN EARNINGS PROBLEM?

Just as a medical doctor would turn to the function of vital organs, the manager or his adviser may turn to vital performance indicators from the profit and loss and financial statements. These indicators include net farm income, rate of return earned on total assets and equity, value of farm production, cost of production, and various financial ratios.

The preferred information source is the farm business record system. Should the information not be available, the simplified audit approach based upon tax records (see Chapter 8) provides a way to gather and synthesize the bits of information required for a reliable analysis.

Regardless of the availability of information and its source, one must determine whether an earnings problem exists. Two types of earnings problems are possible: (1) the *absolute* earnings problem, which could be reflected by inadequate cash flow to meet financial commitments, low net farm income, and so forth; and (2) an earnings problem in *relative* terms. For example, in the latter case the farm business may be perform-

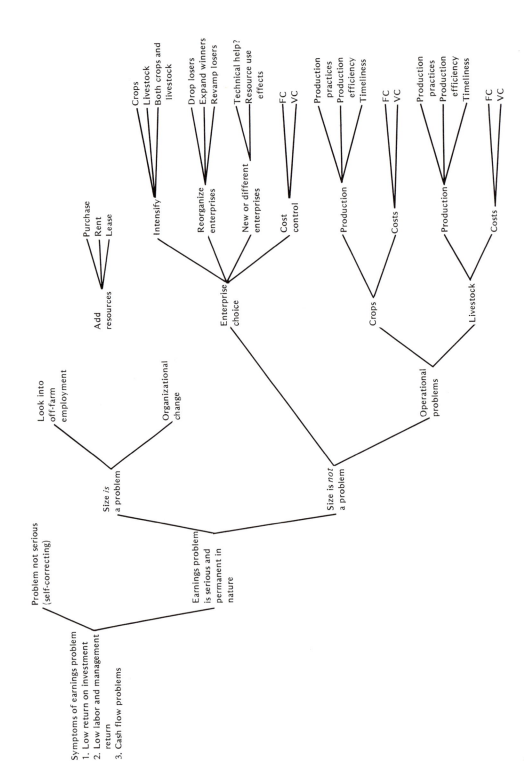

Exhibit 7–1. A decision tree to use in diagnosing a farm's earnings problem.

Symptoms of earnings problem
1. Low return on investment
2. Low labor and management return
3. Cash flow problems

Problem not serious (self-correcting)

Earnings problem is serious and permanent in nature

Size *is* a problem
- Look into off-farm employment
- Organizational change

Add resources
- Purchase
- Rent
- Lease

Enterprise choice
- Intensify
  - Crops
  - Livestock
  - Both crops and livestock
- Reorganize enterprises
  - Drop losers
  - Expand winners
  - Revamp losers
- New or different enterprises
  - Technical help?
  - Resource use effects
- Cost control
  - FC
  - VC

Size is *not* a problem

Operational problems

Crops
- Production
  - Production practices
  - Production efficiency
  - Timeliness
- Costs
  - FC
  - VC

Livestock
- Production
  - Production practices
  - Production efficiency
  - Timeliness
- Costs
  - FC
  - VC

ing so that there are no cash flow problems. Profit measures appear appropriate (10 percent return on investment), but an earnings shortfall is apparent when the business is compared with similar types of farms that have gained 15 percent return on investment. Inadequate earnings, either absolute or relative, warrant proceeding with the analysis.

The Problem: Temporary or Permanent?

The first fork in the decision tree is determining whether the identified earnings problem is of a temporary or permanent nature. If the earnings problem is due to the temporary effects of a particular year, such as drought or flooding, or it is due to a sharp drop in prices or some other event not likely to recur because of shortcomings in the basic management of the farm, the solution may be to select appropriate short-run remedies that will permit the business to weather a bad year.

To ascertain whether an earnings problem is temporary or permanent requires one to normalize for "year" effects. Both production (physical input/output relationships) and price effects must be considered, and deviation from the norm accounted for in this process.

Normalization

The difficulty with normalization lies in determining the norm. Regardless of the obvious limitations associated with establishing a norm, one can approximate the extent of deviations for the year and make quantitative adjustments. For example, if grain yields were 20 bushels lower than normal in the area or community, one can—for appraisal purposes—simply adjust the record (e.g., profit and loss statement) to reflect the effect that a 20-bushel higher yield per acre would have had on sales, feed purchases, or inventory.

Adjustments for price: If the hog-corn price ratio was 25 to 1 and the "average" (or the forecast for the future) has been running only 18 to 1, then it may be crudely estimated that the probable income from hogs for the future is only 72 percent ($18 \div 25$) of what was actually realized in the year in question. Thus, a $40,000 gross sales figure may be "normalized" by multiplying by a factor of .72, thereby resulting in a normalized gross sales figure of $28,000. As another example, if prices were $.30 per bushel higher than believed normal, one could similarly adjust the income measures to reflect the effect of a lower and more nearly normal price.

Production adjustment: what is produced? Perhaps the most difficult normalizing adjustment is where feeder animals are purchased. *The really relevant figure here is the value actually received for the gain put on the animal.*

Gain almost never sells for the price the animal sells for when purchased feeders are involved. If, for example, one farmer-feeder bought 500-pound light yearlings at an average price of $.50 per pound and sold 750-pound feeders at $.40, he really received $.20 per pound for the 250 pounds produced.[1] It is this figure that should be compared or "normalized." Average market prices by grades can be employed in developing suitable standards for assessment of an individual year's deviation from average or normal values.

The normalizing adjustment proposed is, in simplest terms, merely one of quantifying and using one's judgment about how good or bad the year was and how much it biased the record being appraised. It removes the component that created the variation, which cannot be attributed to management.

Adjustment for price–induced inventory effects: When prices change dramatically within a year and when inventories are valued essentially on a market price basis, an accrual basis operating statement is very substantially affected. If a farmer has 300 beef cows on hand each January 1, a $50 per cow drop in valuation from beginning to ending inventory will reduce his accrual basis net income by $15,000 below what it would have been had inventory values been ignored or had the same beginning and ending price been used.

This $15,000 price-induced reduction in inventory is not "*just* a paper loss." It is real enough. Net worth is actually reduced. A similar loss is incurred by other firms with the same inventory affected by the same price change. However, the loss is not normal and does not reflect productivity; it will be offset by a windfall gain whenever prices recover to beginning-of-the-year levels. It is, thus, a "year" effect. Such influences are generally not useful in evaluating management or business performance. Either of these, windfall gains or losses, tends to obscure the effects of management. Thus, normalizing them and other purely "year" effects out of the profit and loss statement is desirable for meaningful analysis.

---

[1]Price actually received for gain can be computed by

$$P_R = \frac{(P_m \cdot W_m) - (P_f \cdot W_f)}{W_m - W_f}$$

where
P_R = price annually received for production or gain
P_m = price received for market animal
P_f = price paid for feeder animal
W_m and W_f = weights of market and feeder animal respectively

Seriousness of Problem

If the earnings problem is temporary, i.e., the problem is self-correcting over time, the manager may not go any farther in his trouble-shooting. However, he may have to implement some short-run measures to cope with the financial or cash flow consequences of the temporary income problem. For example he may have to increase short- or intermediate-term borrowing or dip into savings. This may siphon off resources that had been planned for other purposes.

Suppose it is determined that the income problem is not temporary. Management must then evaluate the seriousness of the problem and determine whether additional analysis and action are called for. Examples of serious earnings problems are:

1. The earnings situation is such that continuing along the same path will erode the financial position of the business and eventually lead to a liquidation or bankruptcy.

2. Cash inflows are insufficient to meet production expenses and asset replacement and, at the same time, provide an adequate return to labor and management.

3. The earnings picture is such that there is little hope for growth of the business.

Such serious problems move a manager to the next branch: deciding whether the problem is due to the size of the business or another related cause.

A PROBLEM OF SIZE?

Many farms and ranches have an earnings problem because they are too small. When the farming bills are paid, there is no money left for making the land payment, for family living, or for business growth.

By size we do not mean just acres of land or head of livestock or poultry. In this context, size refers to volume of production. Is there enough production so that a good manager could normally be expected to make a go of it?

What is "enough" production? That varies by region, type of farming enterprises, family living needs, and level of indebtedness. However, several studies have suggested that farm businesses need to generate

$80–$100,000 in yearly sales if there is to be any hope for a comfortable living for the farm family.

There are knowledgeable agricultural professionals (i.e., extension agents or vocational agriculture instructors) in all areas of the country who have good estimates of the size of unit needed to achieve success in farming. These persons can help a manager who is too small to plan the steps that will be required to (1) develop a viable farming business or (2) develop a part-time farming business that can be supplemented with off-farm income.

The analysis at the size fork in the decision tree may indicate one or more of several possibilities:

1. The business is too small (volume of production).

2. The business is generating adequate volume, but there is insufficient net income.

3. The business has adequate land, machinery, labor, and management, but volume of production is lower than one would expect.

4. One resource is limiting the effective use of other resources.

If one or more of the above seems likely, or is in question, then you need to look at the *organization* of the business and at the manner in which the business is operated.

Organizational Problems

An earnings problem that seems size-related will not necessarily be an organizational (i.e., choice or combination of enterprises) problem. However, as a part of problem diagnosis an analyst may explore one or more of the following possibilities:

1. Will reorganization of present crop and/or livestock enterprises on existing resources increase production/income?

2. Will a reorganization that includes some different enterprises, but existing resources, increase production/income?

3. Can existing resources be used more intensively? Examples are double cropping, drylot feeding of cows, or some other means of growing more crops or animals on the same land.

4. Will the addition of more land, labor, or capital expand production/income more than costs?

5. Are costs of production out of line?

6. Is some combination of the above the answer?

If the analyst has done a good job on the first two troubleshooting questions, she or he should have a good idea which of the above six items are the most likely possibilities. It will probably not be necessary to consider all six. If, for example, the present organization has enterprises that are profitable for other producers, the problem may be either size or costs.

Underutilized resources: It is a rare situation where all farm resources are fully employed. Land is usually the limiting resource. There may be a surplus of labor and/or capital.

A really good manager will often find a way to recombine enterprises and increase production. He/she is able to use the land, labor, and capital resources more effectively than had previously been the case. The budgeting and linear programming techniques explained in subsequent chapters are tools a manager might use to identify enterprise combinations that use resources more effectively.

Too few resources: An expansion will require a new plan from the manager because resources will be used in a different manner. Some new or used machinery, equipment, and/or buildings may be acquired. More (or less) labor may be needed. Purchase, rental, or leasing arrangements can expand the land base. Expanding livestock, machinery capacity, or other capital expenditures can require expansion in the line of credit.

Costs of production: The question of cost of production may be tied up with the organization issue. However, it may also be a separate issue if it appears that the enterprise choice and/or volume of production is appropriate and not a cause of the earnings problem.

We stressed the importance of both fixed and variable costs in decision making in an earlier chapter. The process of diagnosing an earnings problem is a good example where both types of costs may be carefully scrutinized.

Fixed costs such as depreciation, interest, and general farm overhead should be evaluated to see if they are too high for the current farm business size. If they are unusually high, then you will need to (1) see if some costs can be eliminated by selling off underutilized fixed assets or (2) determine if expansion will profitably spread the fixed costs over more production. The desired result is lower fixed costs per unit of production.

If fixed costs don't appear out of line, then you must move to variable costs. Such efficiency measures as (1) machinery variable cost per acre, (2) chemical costs per acre, (3) feed cost per 100 lb. of gain, (4) feed costs per 1000 lb. of milk produced, etc., should be looked at. If any of these items are higher than normal, then the manager should take a close look at production practices or prices being paid for purchased inputs.

Effects of Dropping Losers or Expanding Winners

Based on the organizational analysis, you may want to drop the losers (low earning enterprises) and expand the winners (high earning enterprises) to achieve a greater net income. Most adjustments, however, are not that simple. One must consider how costs and income will change if certain enterprises are expanded or diminished.

Each farm business is unique, partly because of the set of resources included in the business, but also because of the abilities, interests, and desires of the owner and manager. A small enterprise that benefits from some low or zero cost inputs may be very profitable, but if the manager expanded this enterprise beyond the level that could be supported by the low cost inputs, profits might decline or completely vanish. Of a number of examples, one of the most prevalent is the use of beef cattle to glean crop residue and utilize forage from nontillable acreage. The costs of production are low as long as animals are using residues that would otherwise go to waste.

Other enterprises that currently appear to be losers might be converted to gainers by expanding them and increasing the number of units over which fixed costs could be spread. Crop farming, dairying, and poultry are examples where one can frequently improve earnings by expansion.

The Influence of Fixed Costs

Exhibit 7–2 provides an enterprise troubleshooting example. Here, a farmer feeds cattle as one of his major enterprises. As shown, his "normalized" expenses exceed his "normalized" receipts by some $5,000. Assume further that this is the second or third year of such an outcome; hence, the results are reliable.

Exhibit 7–2. Henry Hay's cattle feeding enterprise

Receipts (steer sales)	$40,000	
Cost of feeders	− 15,000	
Gain on purchased steers		$25,000
Minus feed and other costs		− 30,000
Net profit or loss		− $ 5,000

Mr. Hay's "normalized" results over several years suggest that cattle feeding has not been profitable for him. Although the apparent answer is to abandon the enterprise, such a conclusion could be premature.

One must determine the net effect on income of abandoning the project. For the most appropriate decision, one must specify the *behavior* of costs in such a remedial action. Suppose that $8,000 of those costs were sunk, nonsalvageable ownership costs on a feedlot. In effect, abandoning the enterprise would eliminate $25,000 of gain on purchased steers *but only $22,000 of costs.* Gain from abandonment then is a *minus* $3,000! In short, Mr. Hay's gain from what appears to be a logical remedy is to lose $3,000 in income more than that by which he reduces his costs (i.e., to lose $8,000 rather than $5,000).

OPERATIONAL PROBLEMS

If the earnings problem does not appear to be due to size or organization, then one needs to look at operations. Operational considerations refer to the normal day-to-day activities and the manner in which they are carried out. Again, at this fork there are several vital signs that must be checked:

1. Choice of production techniques
2. Production efficiency
3. Timeliness in getting jobs done
4. Some combination of the above

Choice of Production Techniques

There are many ways to obtain production from crop and livestock enterprises. Not all give the same results, however. They may also differ in costs and labor requirements. Tillage in crop production is a good example. There is a wide range of possibilities—from many trips across the field to no tillage. The cost per acre may actually be higher for no till because the added chemicals and fertilizers may cost more than the fuel saved. There will probably be substantial labor savings with no till.

When looking at production practices one should determine if recommended practices are being followed and if production levels are reasonable for the resources. More than that, you should ask if (1) production is acceptable for the inputs used, i.e., production efficiency, and (2) costs of production are reasonable.

Production Efficiency

When we think of production efficiency we normally think of a ratio of output to input. For example, how many pounds of gain did we get per 100 lb. feed fed? Or, how many pounds of milk were produced for each ton of feed fed?

Almost every state has summary record data that show the efficiency levels good producers have been able to obtain in the recent past. One recent study of farrow-to-finish hog units suggested that top operations were getting one pound of pork produced for every 4.1 pounds of feed fed. That included feed to sows, boars, and replacement gilts, in addition to the hogs being fattened.

Some examples of physical efficiency measures are:

1. Average daily gain
2. Feed per pound of gain
3. Calving percentage
4. Pigs weaned per sow
5. Milk produced per cow
6. Eggs per hen
7. Yield per acre

Examples of other efficiency measures are:

1. Machinery cost per acre
2. Chemical costs per acre
3. Variable costs per acre

4. Value of crop production per $100 of crop costs

5. Value of livestock production per $100 of livestock costs

6. Value of farm production per person employed

Timeliness

Some farmers and ranchers use recommended practices, but they cannot seem to get things done in a timely fashion. They are late getting crops planted, or weed control measures are taken too late. Their machinery maintenance program is behind schedule, and they have excessive breakdowns. Maybe they are behind in their sanitation programs, and so they have poor animal performance, or even death losses.

Any of the above mentioned operational problems, and many more you can probably think of, can contribute to an earnings problem. In some cases you will be able to locate these problems by simply visiting with a producer and visiting his or her operation. In other cases you will need to go through the diagnosis steps of looking at size of operation and enterprise choice before you can identify such operational problems as timeliness in getting jobs done.

IS THE PROBLEM ONE OF MARKETING?

There is a large number of farmers and ranchers who are learning that production is only half the job. When soybean prices can fall from $10 per bushel to $7 in a span of a few months or livestock prices can rise by 25%, there is a need for marketing know-how.

Marketing is not some job to be attended to once production is complete. Production and marketing decisions should go hand in hand. The manager must have some price objective in mind. He must also consider the marketing options that may need to be tried in order to achieve that price objective. Should some form of forward contract or hedge be used? Will the commodity be marketed at harvest or will storage be required? What will you do if you cannot get your price objective? How will various marketing options affect taxable income?

In today's volatile economy, a manager cannot leave marketing to chance. A manager who does not keep up with market developments through USDA newsletters and publications and commercially available advisory services is likely to have an earnings problem. Any diagnosis of a farm earnings problem should look at the marketing approach being followed. What prices were received for commodities sold? Were these above or below average prices for the area? The potential benefits of good production management will go unrealized if there is no organized, formal marketing management.

SUMMARY

This chapter provides the reader with a conceptual framework for evaluating the farm business and determining the source of problems when the business is not performing according to expectations.

The first crucial question is to determine whether an earnings problem is truly serious or only temporary. If the earnings problem is permanent and serious, then a manager or analyst will want to look at:

1. The size of the business, measured in volume of production

2. The way the business is organized, i.e., the enterprises and their combination

3. The production practices followed and the resulting production efficiency

4. The marketing plan and effectiveness in realizing above average prices

APPLYING THE PRINCIPLES OF CHAPTER 7

1. List the five questions that make up the troubleshooting procedure.

2. What indicators are used in diagnosing an earnings problem?

3. Why is normalization an important procedure in farm business analysis?

4. What analysis should be followed if a problem is not temporary?

5. What changes are possible if an earnings problem is organizational?

6. Can the expansion of an activity or enterprise that has been documented as a "loser" in terms of profitability ever be considered a wise decision?

7. Why is the understanding and classification of fixed and variable costs important when considering enterprise and farm organization plans (enterprise and scale alternatives)?

REFERENCES

Castle, Emery N., Manning H. Becker and Frederick J. Smith. *Farm Business Management.* New York: The Macmillan Company, 1972.

Jacobs, Victor E. "Trouble-Shooting the Farm Business Record." Paper presented at Champaign, Illinois, September 1973. Available from Department of Agricultural Economics, University of Missouri, Columbia, Missouri.

A Simplified Management Audit with Limited Information

- Estimating net farm income from taxable income
- Measuring value of farm production
- Developing financial measures for business evaluation

What do you do when advice on major financial or organizational decisions must be given but available information on which to base the advice, or decision, is incomplete? Farm advisers and lenders, and sometimes managers themselves, face those situations.

This chapter focuses on a simplified worksheet method that uses the data available on all farms/ranches. It illustrates how the data can be organized so that well-reasoned judgments can be made.

A previous chapter highlighted the use of records for analyzing the financial status of the farm business with respect to profitability, characteristics of the balance sheet, and cash flow from business. Business analysis forms (see Chapter 6 for samples of balance sheet, cash flow form, and profit and loss statement) are highly beneficial in communicating with lenders and planning for the growth and financial requirements of the farm business.

Most of the financial farm management tools available today for evaluating loan requests and determining potential repayment require a considerable amount of data about the individual business. In too many instances, farmers cannot provide the needed data for analyses; or, if they can, it is not in a form to make it readily usable. What are the alternatives available to the business analyst when the farmer is unable to provide the needed data in the form required by the analytical procedure? One alternative is to wait until the farmer adopts a system to collect and thereby provide valid information—not a reasonable alternative.

The purpose of this chapter, then, is to show another alternative: how meaningful business analysis can be performed with limited information that most farmers can provide from their tax returns filed with the Internal Revenue Service and from financial statement(s).

FEDERAL INCOME TAX RETURN: SINGLE PROPRIETORSHIP

Prior to delving into the detailed calculations required for business analysis, familiarity with tax returns and the items that affect taxable income is useful. Such familiarity permits a better understanding of adjustments to taxable income, which are required for a more accurate measure of business performance.

A farmer who operates as a sole proprietor must have sufficient records to complete a set of tax forms. Farm income and expenses are reported on Form 1040F (see Exhibit 8–1). The form summarizes most cash flows for the year, but may not give an accurate picture of business profitability. This is particularly true when the case bases method of reporting is used. The only inventory adjustment that is considered is depreciation. Receipts may be unusually high because production from more than one year was sold. Expenses may be high or low depending on input purchase decisions.

Use of the 1040 Schedule F

Part I: *For cash basis tax filers,* cash farm income and constructive receipts are shown in this section, with the *exception* of income received from the sale of capital assets. This farm income received is also itemized as to the source. The Gross Profit shows on Line 32, Part I. Note that in calculating the Gross Profit the cost of resale items disposed of during the year has been deducted from the gross sale price; therefore, one item of farm expense is actually shown in the income section.

Part II: *For cash basis tax filers,* cash farm expenses and depreciation show in this section. (Depreciation is itemized in Part III.) Total deductions are shown on Line 57. Net Farm Profit is shown on Line 58.

Part III: *For accrual basis tax filers,* Part III reflects farm expenses, either cash or accrued, depending on how the farmer keeps records, *except* that purchases of livestock not entered on the farmer's depreciation schedule will be reflected in Part IV, 1040F.

Part IV: *For accrual basis tax filers only,* farm income, livestock purchases, and beginning and ending inventories are recorded in this section. Note that these inventories will seldom be the same as inventories kept with a record system or those identified on a financial statement because of the various inventory methods permissible for tax filing.

Part V: *For accrual basis tax filers only,* this section is the summary of farm income, expenses and inventory changes, with the net profit reflected on Line 91.

Form 4797 or Schedule D (Gains or Losses on Capital Dispositions)

A sole proprietorship's gains or losses on sales or exchanges of capital assets is shown on Schedule D. This includes capital gains or losses on *breeding livestock* as well as other capital gains or losses which the business may have had. To arrive at farm profitability you must add 1040 Schedule D breeding livestock gains (or losses) to the 1040 Schedule F net profit.

ADJUSTMENTS TO TAXABLE INCOME

Inventory

For an accurate measure of business performance, changes in inventories and open accounts between the beginning and the end of the year must be taken into consideration. Note that cash basis tax filers make no adjustments in net farm profit for such changes. In order to have a true picture of performance, these adjustments must be made. The simplified audit worksheet illustrated by Exhibit 8–2 can provide a means for computing business profitability.

Exhibit 8–1. A sample 1040F Farm Income and Expense Schedule.

(85)

SCHEDULE F (Form 1040)
Department of the Treasury
Internal Revenue Service

Farm Income and Expenses
▶ Attach to Form 1040, Form 1041, or Form 1065.
▶ See Instructions for Schedule F (Form 1040).

1980
17

Name of proprietor(s) *James A. Brown*

Social security number 579 | 28 | 6685

Farm name and address ▶ *James A. Brown RR #1*
Hometown, Your State

Employer identification number

Part I — Farm Income—Cash Method

Do not include sales of livestock held for draft, breeding, sport, or dairy purposes; report these sales on Form 4797.

Sales of Livestock and Other Items You Bought for Resale

a. Description	b. Amount	c. Cost or other basis
1 Livestock ▶ *Heifers bought for resale*	3,450 —	2,000 —
2 Other items ▶		
3 Totals	3,450 —	2,000 —
4 Profit or (loss), subtract line 3, column c, from line 3, column b . . . . ▶	1,450 —	

Sales of Livestock and Produce You Raised and Other Farm Income

Kind	Amount
5 Cattle	
6 Calves	1,658 —
7 Sheep	
8 Swine	
9 Poultry	
10 Dairy products	45,727 —
11 Eggs	
12 Wool	
13 Cotton	
14 Tobacco	
15 Vegetables	
16 Soybeans	
17 Corn	
18 Other grains	
19 Hay	1,133 —
20 Straw	
21 Fruits and nuts	
22 Machine work	504 —
23 a Patronage dividends . . . 272	
b Less: Nonincome items . 22	
c Net patronage dividends	250
24 Per-unit retains	
25 Nonpatronage distributions from exempt cooperatives . .	
26 Agricultural program payments: a Cash . . .	20
b Materials and services	162
27 Commodity credit loans under election (or forfeited) . .	275
28 Federal gasoline tax credit	70
29 State gasoline tax refund	
30 Other (specify) ▶ *Crop Ins. proceeds*	312
Fair Prizes	350
31 Add amounts in column for lines 5 through 30 .	50,461
32 Gross profits* (add lines 4 and 31) . . . ▶	51,911

Part II — Farm Deductions—Cash and Accrual Method

Do not include personal or living expenses (such as taxes, insurance, repairs, etc., on your home), which do not produce farm income. Reduce the amount of your farm deductions by any reimbursement before entering the deduction below.

Items	Amount
33 a Labor hired	2,219
b Jobs credit	
c WIN credit	
d Total credits	
e Balance (subtract line 33d from line 33a) . .	2,219
34 Repairs, maintenance . .	1,618
35 Interest	1,862
36 Rent of farm, pasture . .	600
37 Feed purchased	12,091
38 Seeds, plants purchased . .	1,143
39 Fertilizers, lime, chemicals .	2,249
40 Machine hire	1,100
41 Supplies purchased . . .	1,602
42 Breeding fees	339
43 Veterinary fees, medicine .	1,510
44 Gasoline, fuel, oil	1,025
45 Storage, warehousing . .	
46 Taxes	1,535
47 Insurance	1,053
48 Utilities	1,225
49 Freight, trucking	828
50 Conservation expenses . .	790
51 Land clearing expenses . .	
52 Pension and profit-sharing plans	
53 Employee benefit programs other than line 52	
54 Other (specify) ▶	
Advertising	234
Financial Records	83
Farm Org. Dues	175
Death loss – heifer bought for resale	225 —
55 Add lines 33e through 54 .	33,506
56 Depreciation (from Part III, line 62)	5,010
57 Total deductions (add lines 55 and 56) . . . . . ▶	38,516

58 Net farm profit or (loss) (subtract line 57 from line 32). If a profit, enter on Form 1040, line 19, and on Schedule SE, Part I, line 1a. If a loss, go on to line 59. (Fiduciaries and partnerships, see the Instructions.) | **58** | 13,395 |

59 If you have a loss, do you have amounts for which you are not "at risk" in this farm (see Instructions)? . . . ☐ Yes ☐ No

*Use amount on line 32 for optional method of computing net earnings from self-employment. (See Schedule SE, Part I, line 3.)

Part III   Depreciation (Do not include your home, its furnishings, and other personal items.) If you need more space, use Form 4562.

Description of property (a)	Date acquired (b)	Cost or other basis (c)	Depreciation allowed or allowable in prior years (d)	Method of computing depreciation (e)	Life or rate (f)	Depreciation for this year (g)
60 Total additional first-year depreciation (do not include in items below) (see Instructions for limitation) ➡						1324
61 Other depreciation:						
Barn	1-8-72	6,400	2,048	SL	25	256
Other farm bldgs	Various	9,813	3,259	SL	10-15	784
Car (farm share)	1-7-79	1,900	350	SL	4	350
Truck	1-10-79	2,418	806	DDB	6	537
Farm Mach.	Var.	22,267	7,673	SL	6-10	1,274
Dairy Cows	Var.	3,775	484	SL	5	347
Bulls	Var.	1,200	18	SL	4	138
62 Totals		47,773		Enter here and in Part II, line 56 ➤		5,010

Part IV   Farm Income—Accrual Method (Do not include sales of livestock held for draft, breeding, sport, or dairy purposes; report these sales on Form 4797 and omit them from "Inventory at beginning of year" column.)

a. Kind	b. Inventory at beginning of year	c. Cost of items purchased during year	d. Sales during year	e. Inventory at end of year
63 Cattle				
64 Calves				
65 Sheep				
66 Swine				
67 Poultry				
68 Dairy products				
69 Eggs				
70 Wool				
71 Cotton				
72 Tobacco				
73 Vegetables				
74 Grain				
75 Fruits and nuts				
76 Other (specify) ▶				
77 Totals (enter here and in Part V below)	(Enter on line 86)	(Enter on line 87)	(Enter on line 79)	(Enter on line 78)

Part V   Summary of Income and Deductions—Accrual Method

78 Inventory of livestock, crops, and products at end of year (line 77, column e) . . . .

79 Sales of livestock, crops, and products during year (line 77, column d) . . . .

80 Agricultural program payments: **a** Cash . . . .

                   b Materials and services . . . .

81 Commodity credit loans under election (or forfeited) . . . .

82 Federal gasoline tax credit . . . .

83 State gasoline tax refund . . . .

84 Other farm income (specify) ▶

85 Add lines 78 through 84 . . . .

86 Inventory of livestock, crops, and products at beginning of year (line 77, column b) . . . .

87 Cost of livestock and products purchased during year (line 77, column c) . . . .

88 Total (add lines 86 and 87) . . . .

89 **Gross profits*** (subtract line 88 from line 85) . . . .

90 Total deductions from Part II, line 57 . . . . ▶

91 Net farm profit or (loss) (subtract line 90 from line 89). If a profit, individuals enter on Form 1040, line 19, and on Schedule SE, Part I, line 1a. If a loss, go on to line 92. (Fiduciaries and partnerships, see the Instructions.) . . . . | **91**

92 If you have a loss, do you have amounts for which you are not "at risk" in this farm (see Instructions)? . . . . ☐ Yes   ☐ No

*Use amount on line 89 for optional method of computing net earnings from self-employment. (See Schedule SE, Part I, line 3.)

Exhibit 8–2. Simplified audit worksheet

Name _____   Date _____

Net Farm Income

1. Sale of purchased livestock and other items (Sch. F, line 3, col. b) $_____
2. Sale of market livestock, produce raised, and other farm income (Sch. F, line 31) $_____
3. Gain or loss on sale of breeding livestock and machinery (Sch. D and/or Form 4797) $_____
4. Gain or loss in inventory of grain, feed, and livestock not on depreciation (financial statement or other source) $_____
5. Plus 1040F, line 50 "Conservation" expense from Part II $_____
6. Plus 1040, line 51 "Land Clearing" expense from Part II $_____
7. Total Gross Farm Income (add lines 1–6) $_____
8. Cash operating expenses (Sch. F, line 55) $_____
9. Cost of resale livestock (Sch. F, line 3, col. c) $_____
10. Depreciation (Sch. F, line 56) $_____
11. Total operating costs (add lines 8, 9, and 10) $_____
12. Net farm income (subtract 11 from 7) $_____

Farm Business Earnings

13. Net farm income (line 12 above) $_____
14. Farm accounts payable (beginning of year) $_____
15. Farm accounts payable (end of year) $_____
16. Farm accounts receivable (beginning of year) $_____
17. Farm accounts receivable (end of year) $_____
18. Interest paid (Sch. F, line 35) $_____
19. Value of farm produce consumed at home (est.) $_____
20. Adjusted net farm income (farm business earnings) [line 13 + (lines 14, 17, 18, 19) − (lines 15, 16)] $_____

Return to Factors of Production

21. Adjusted net farm income (line 20) $_____
22. Unpaid labor

		Hours		
operator	a. _____		e. $_____	
family	b. _____		f. $_____	
hired	c. _____			
Total	d. _____(a + b + c)		g. $_____(e + f)	

   h. $\dfrac{\text{Total Hours (d)}}{2400} = $_____ man years

23. Returns to capital (line 21–line 22g) $_____
24. Percentage return to capital $_____

$$\frac{\text{Return to capital (line 23)}}{\text{Avg. total assets (financial statement)}}$$

25. Return to net worth $_____
[returns to capital (line 23) − interest (line 18)]

Exhibit 8–2. (cont'd.)

26. Percentage return to net worth $_____

$$\frac{\text{Return to net worth (line 25)}}{\text{Avg. net worth (financial statement)}}$$

Value of Farm Production

27. Gross farm income (line 7) $_____
28. Subtract purchased livestock (line 9) $_____
29. Subtract purchased feed (Sch. F, line 33) $_____
30. Value of farm production (line 27 minus lines 28 and 29) $_____
31. Value of farm production per man (line 30 ÷ man years of
     labor, line 22) $_____

Financial Ratios (use end-of-year data in computations)

32. Capital Turnover = $\dfrac{\text{Average Total Farm Assets (fin. stmt.)}}{\text{Value of Farm Production (line 31)}}$ $\dfrac{\$\_\_\_\_}{\$\_\_\_\_}$ = _____

33. Liquidity = $\dfrac{\text{Current Assets (fin. stmt.)}}{\text{Current Liabilities (fin. stmt.)}}$ $\dfrac{\$\_\_\_\_}{\$\_\_\_\_}$ = _____

34. Solvency = $\dfrac{\text{Total Assets (fin. stmt.)}}{\text{Total Liabilities (fin. stmt.)}}$ $\dfrac{\$\_\_\_\_}{\$\_\_\_\_}$ = _____

35. Cost Control = $\dfrac{\text{Total Cash Operating Expenses (line 8)}}{\text{Value of Farm Production (line 30)}}$ $\dfrac{\$\_\_\_\_}{\$\_\_\_\_}$ = _____

36. Debt Servicing = $\dfrac{\substack{\text{Interest and Principal Payments} \\ \text{(Sch. F., fin. stmt.)}}}{\text{Farm Business \& Family Earnings (line 20)}}$ $\dfrac{\$\_\_\_\_}{\$\_\_\_\_}$ = _____

One must determine whether farm inventories were essentially the same dollar value at the beginning of the taxable year as at the end. If there has been a buildup in inventory values for the given period, net farm profits as shown on the Schedule F will have to be adjusted upward accordingly. Conversely, if inventory value has decreased over this period, net farm profits will have to be adjusted downward.

Open Accounts

For some farm operations, the above procedure regarding inventory adjustment provides a fairly reliable indication of the unit's profitability. The factors omitted, which could definitely affect profitability, are the changes in *accounts payable* and *receivable*. If this information can be obtained, the profitability figure should be further adjusted. These adjustments are accounted for in Lines 14 through 17 of the worksheet.

Capital Improvements

The practice of "expensing" capital improvements to the farm operation biases measures of business performance. Changing such items as land clearing and conservation "investments" as an annual operating expense lowers operating profits, but the resulting land improvement is usually reflected in the financial statement as an increase in land value. Another example is that of expensing labor used to construct improvements such as buildings. Labor embodied in a capital improvement should not appear as an expense item because it is a component of the investment in a durable asset; an adjustment of net income by the amount of the labor expense is warranted.

The worksheet does not provide an adjustment for labor embodied in a capital improvement, but one can improvise an adjustment from available information. Adjustments for land clearing and conservation expenses are entered on Lines 5 and 6 on the worksheet.

SIMPLIFIED ANALYSIS

The worksheet (Exhibit 8–2) enables one to pull information together systematically from the financial statement(s) and income tax forms to use in computing business and financial indicators for the analysis. The worksheet entries come from entries on the financial statement and tax return forms.

Each section of the worksheet provides a somewhat different, but important, view of the farm business. The first section estimates net farm income; the second, farm business earnings; the third, value of farm production; and the fourth, financial ratios. Because these business analysis statistics have been discussed previously, this section emphasizes sources of information and the mechanics of computation required to generate meaningful business performance indicators. Further in-depth interpretation of the statistics can be found in Chapter 6.

Computing Net Farm Income

The starting point in farm business analysis is to compute as accurately as possible the net farm income produced by the set of resources controlled by the present management. The information requested on Lines 1, 2, 3, 5, and 6 is taken directly from income tax forms. The information requested on Line 4, the gain or loss in inventory during the year, can come from consecutive financial statements or from the inventory in a farm record system.

In many instances, the inventory information must be taken from previously prepared financial statements. Sometimes the financial statement must be adjusted to cover the same time period as the income tax report. Financial statements are frequently taken at the same time of the year, but that time may correspond with the date of the first loan request rather than with the farm's accounting year. Probably most typical is the early spring financial statement. Inventories may be high or low, depending upon the kind of crop year and the farmer's prospective income tax liability.

If the farmer can provide financial statements over a number of years, income and expenses can be estimated with reasonable accuracy because the farm products are eventually sold and payments for inputs made.

Farm Business Earnings and Returns to Production Factors

The farm business earnings section of the analysis form requires information on the value of home-used produce, debts the farm business owes others, and debts others owe the business. These may require some estimating, but the computation can be easily accomplished by following the worksheet instructions. The primary purpose of this section is to compute the earnings on total capital in the farm business and the earnings on the operator's net worth.

Once the earnings capacity of the business has been determined, one also needs to assess the performance and productivity of the major resources. For example, studies have shown that successful farms generally realize $60–$75,000 in business earnings per full-time worker equivalent. Line 22 in the worksheet provides an estimate of total person years employed in the business. That information combined with business earnings (line 20) allows a person to compute earnings per worker.

The computations in lines 23–26, which deal with returns to total capital and equity capital, are also very useful for management. A manager needs to know if the business is earning at a rate as great as the interest rate being paid. If it is not, then net worth (equity) is being used up and the business will soon be in serious financial trouble.

The returns or earnings on total capital may be usefully compared with the performance of other farms to aid the manager in determining whether he is about at par, above, or below. The percentage return on net worth is essential in projecting a farmer's ability to liquidate current debts or implement planned investments.

Value of Farm Production

The third major section of the analysis worksheet is the computation of value of farm production. Many in management feel that this is one of the most important performance indicators in the farm business. The value of farm production can be simply defined as the total farm income, both cash and inventory changes, less purchased feed and purchased feeder livestock. From this definition, one realizes that value of farm production is not the same as net income. Rather, it is a measure of the gross production from the land, plus the value added to livestock above purchased feed and purchased animals. In short, it is the value added that is associated with basic farm production activities.

An example for a cattle feeder is often used to illustrate that value of production is different from total dollar sales. The cattle feeder purchased $100,000 worth of calves and $100,000 worth of feed. He fed the feed to the cattle and then sold the fed cattle for $200,000. What was the value of production for this farm? The answer is zero. The cost of the purchased feeder calves and feed exactly equal the sale price. If, on the other hand, the finished calves were sold for $400,000, value of production would be $200,000. Value of production is not a net income because, out of the $200,000 value of farm production, all other cash costs and fixed costs of labor, investment, etc., would have to be paid.

Financial Ratios

The fourth major section is on financial ratios. Each ratio—capital turnover, liquidity, solvency, cost control, and debt service—looks at a different aspect of the business relative to income and performance.

These ratios have great potential for helping a manager or her/his adviser analyze the business with an eye toward making improvements. They can also help identify weaknesses. Capital turnover, for example, relates the value of farm production to total capital invested in the business. If capital turnover is low, a business will probably have difficulty keeping bills paid. Thus, the manager will need to explore ways to reorganize production in order to increase sales relative to investment. The greater the dollar sales, or better yet, the greater the value of farm production per dollar invested, the greater the potential for making the desired net income—that is, unless the business is very poorly managed. Rapid capital turnover for a losing business will simply force termination more quickly.

The other ratios and their interpretations were presented in Chapter 6. These ratios should be reviewed annually if a manager is to realize the maximum benefit from recordkeeping. The annual summaries should also be kept so that this year's summary ratios can be compared with last year's and the year before that.

By monitoring the information for several years, the analyst, with his knowledge of the ups and downs of agriculture during these years, can develop reasonable judgments about business performance or needed changes. The multi-year period also provides the analyst with information about any trends developing due to internal operational activities and/or external industry trends. Such knowledge may be particularly helpful in planning business adjustments, such as major expansion of existing enterprises or the addition of new ones. Use of the simplified audit will give more realistic and complete information than the tax forms alone. The information is also superior to that available from many simple farm records. A simplified audit can be a valuable aid for a person or family faced with a crucial investment or estate planning decision.

SUMMARY

Business and agencies that work with farmers often require detailed business analysis before they will provide the service, particularly credit, the manager desires. Lack of appropriate information hampers many individuals desiring to perform farm business analyses. Although adequate for tax reporting, many farm record systems are inadequate for providing useful analysis and planning information. This chapter shows how meaningful farm business analyses can be performed with limited information. Basic information is obtained from income tax returns and from financial statements.

The audit approach outlined is a good "second best" to a complete record system. However, the person using the simplified audit approach is cautioned to watch for unusual circumstances that may bias the audit. For example, commodities carried over from a previous year and sold in the current year may cause the business to look unusually profitable. Even though beginning and ending inventory information included in the financial statements should have corrected for this bias, it is possible for estimates to be in error or for oversights in reporting to occur.

As with complete record systems, simplified audits are most useful when they are available for two to three years. By looking at the information for several years, the analyst, with his knowledge of agriculture's ups and downs during these years, can establish reasonable confidence in his conclusions. The multi-year period also provides the analyst with information about any trends that are developing due to internal operational activities and/or external industry trends. This may be particularly helpful as adjustments that are made in the business, for example, major expansion of existing enterprises or the addition of new ones are examined.

APPLYING THE PRINCIPLES OF CHAPTER 8

1. What changes are required for adjusting taxable income to reflect value of farm production?

2. How can business performance be biased by expensing capital improvements?

3. What information is given by the four sections of the worksheet?

4. How does "value of farm production" differ from net income?

REFERENCES

Herbst, J. S. *Farm Management: Principles, Budgets, Plans.* Champaign, Ill.: Stipes Publishing Co., 1972.

Norwood, F. W., P. W. Ljungdahl, S. W. Chisholm and W. R. Chapin. *Accounting for Agricultural Enterprises.* Bryan, Texas: Ryan Printing Inc., 1968.

Part 4

Forward
Planning

Budgeting:
Documented
Decision Making

9

- Budgeting
- Different budget types
- Partial budgeting example
- Partial budgeting plus cash flow analysis

Preparation for effective decision making is a central focus of much of this book. To be able to make logical decisions, a manager must generally complete a logical analysis. Budgeting is one of the most useful and popular analytical tools available to the manager, particularly for short- and intermediate-term planning. When coupled with cash flow analysis, budgeting gives a good indication of profitability *and* cash flow feasibility.

Thorough analysis of alternatives is basic to sound management decision making. A rational manager cannot decide to install an irrigation system on his farm just because a neighbor's system has paid off. He must research its expected impact on the financial position of his business and base decisions on well-documented analysis.

Budgeting is a key analytic and planning tool in all types of businesses. Because of its importance, this chapter endeavors to:

1. Explain what budgeting is and why it is a valuable decision aid

2. Describe the primary types of budgets

3. Discuss the basic data requirements and choice of coefficients for budgeting

4. Explain and illustrate some uses of partial budgeting

A budget is a written plan for future action, including the quantified anticipated results. Budgets indicate what to expect, dollarwise, from a course of action before that action is taken.

The usefulness of a budget depends upon the relative accuracy and degree of realism in portraying the situations under consideration. Production, input, and price coefficients must be consistent with the technical and economic conditions most relevant to the circumstances. Assumptions must conform to the performance reasonably expected of the business and management that will implement decisions based on the budgets.

As a systematic means to planning and to analysis of alternatives, budgeting generally includes some rather specific steps. For farm budgeting the following guidelines should be considered:

1. Specify the overall problem(s) causing the manager or analyst to make the farm budget analysis—his general objectives in the study.

2. Decide whether the analysis should apply to the entire business or to only one segment.

3. Decide whether partial or complete budgeting will be used.

4. Choose the time period to which the budgeting analysis will apply.

5. Decide what data will be needed.

6. Decide how many alternatives will be evaluated/analyzed.

The exact manner in which the different steps are followed will vary with the problem and the business. Further, there may be steps added (or deleted) in particular situations.

As a starting point for conceptualizing the budgeting process, consider the situation of Joe College. As an average student, he is faced with many ways of financing and paying for his schooling and living expenses. There are room and board, books and fees, laundry costs, recreation, car expenses and gasoline, clothing expenses, haircuts, and so on.

Suppose Joe has $360 per month available to meet his various needs. A budget might look like this:

Average budget for one month for Joe College

	Income	
a.	Mom and Dad	$200
b.	Part-time work	160
	Total	$360

	Expenses	
a.	Room and board	$150
b.	Tuition and books (prorated on monthly basis)	110
c.	Club dues and fees	5
d.	Gasoline and car repairs	30
e.	Clothes and laundry	25
f.	Grooming	10
g.	Recreation	30
	Total	$360

Although this is a reasonably complete listing of one way Joe could use the money resources available to him, it is but one of many possible budgets. He could live more frugally, including doing some of his own cooking, to reduce his living expenses. Or he could park his car, dress more casually, or find a job that pays more. Any of these changes would change the budget or require Joe to develop alternative budgets to the one listed above.

Because a budget is written down, it should cause the decision maker or manager (or Joe in the above case) to be thorough in his approach. By putting the data down, he can avoid omitting important variables.

The objective of budgeting is a dollars and cents comparison of possible future actions or ways of organizing a business. The budgeting process should generate a set of plans (outputs, reports) which describe the probable economic and operational consequences of the alternatives considered. For example, the output from comparing several different cropping plans might include (1) expected annual income from each plan, (2) expected cash expenses for each, (3) the differences in labor requirements and their timing, and (4) anticipated differences in machinery investments and ownership costs. A manager comparing cow-calf and dairying alternatives might find the dairy alternative is expected to generate greater income over cash costs (for a given land resource situation). But he might also find the dairy alternative has substantially higher labor and nonland capital requirements.

SOME BUDGET TYPES

Budgets can be used for short-run decision making or longer-run planning. They may encompass the total business or only part of it. The following are frequently used budgeting terms:

1. *Long-term budgets:* These are farm/ranch plans that apply to periods of more than a year. The time period is generally long enough to allow major adjustments or reorganization of a business to occur. The extent to which the future can be reasonably forecast may determine how long is "long." On the other hand, decision makers may decide to settle for the best educated guesses and project beyond the point of reasonably accurate forecasts.

Long-term budgets are frequently used to answer broad "what if"-type questions, such as: "What if I switched from conventional tillage to minimum tillage?" "What if I added an intensive 100-litter feeder pig enterprise?" "What if I developed a custom harvesting and hauling business to supplement my normal farming operation?"

Long-term budgets should be developed with long-term goals firmly in mind, but should have some built-in flexibility. Too much inflexibility may preclude the capacity to adjust to changing conditions.

2. *Short-term budgets:* These budgets are used to evaluate options open to a business during the next few months or the next year. Short-term farm/ranch budgets rarely apply to a period greater than one year.

Short-term budgets may deal with deviations from the long-term plan. Such deviations may make sense because of changed economic conditions, a crop failure due to weather, a change in business goals, or similar factors.

Short-term budgets are useful for answering such questions as "Should I try to double crop this season?" "Should I purchase feeder calves to put on small-grain pasture?" "Should I sell this batch of pigs as feeder pigs or purchase grain and feed them out?" or "Should I apply one more irrigation?"

3. *Complete budgets:* Complete budgets list all costs, both fixed and variable, and returns which affect a business. As a result, the end product is an estimate of a business' profitability. A finished complete budget should give an estimate of the net farm income left to pay the operator for his labor, management, and risk taking.

Complete budgets are used when the decision being made is critical. Some examples are: "Can I make an income I (or my family) will be satisfied with if I go into farming?" or, for a young man going into farming with his dad, "Can this farm, and any additional resources that can be acquired, support two families rather than one?" or, for an established diversified farmer, "What are the consequences of putting in a 1,000-head automated cattle-feeding facility?" For questions like these a decision maker will want as complete an analysis as possible. That means projecting *all* costs—from hired labor to depreciation to telephone and light bills.

4. *Partial budgets:* Determining whether a change in the farm business will be profitable or not does not require preparing a complete budget. A partial budget is a plan that lists only the receipts and expenses that are expected to change with a change in organization. The proposed change may be a small single change (i.e., adding more fertilizer per acre) or a broad, sweeping change in organization. The simple change may compare only a few items and may be accomplished in a few minutes once the analyst is satisfied with the estimates of receipts and expenses. A major business "overhaul" will require a more intensive analysis and may involve several pages of analysis.

The budget for Joe College presented earlier can illustrate the difference between a complete and partial budget. As developed, Joe's budget includes *all* the money he expects to have available to spend during an average month. He also has taken care to include *all* his expected "outgo." He has developed a *complete* budget.

Now, suppose Joe asks the question, "Can I get by on less money per month?" This will require a different budget, an alternative to the one describing his current operating circumstances. He might ask, "What am I willing to change?" If he wants to continue living where he lives now, then room and board would not change. If he wants to stay in school—and he'd better if he wants to keep getting the $200 from home—then the tuition and books expense is fixed. He likes being active on campus so the $5 per month for dues and fees is fixed. Thus, the variable items are his earnings from part-time work and the expenses for car, clothing, grooming, and recreation.

5. *Present-normal plans:* These are "average" plans describing the way the business has normally been organized in the recent past, but not necessarily the last year. They are representative of normal operations; they assume normal livestock numbers and normal acreages of crops under normal conditions. They are sometimes referred to as "benchmark" plans.

6. *Proposed plans:* These are plans developed as an alternative to a present normal plan. Again, reference to Joe College may be useful. Joe has a present-normal plan. He is interested in looking at two alternatives, two proposed plans. They are: present-normal plan—live in dorm as in past; proposed plan A—live in apartment and do some cooking; proposed plan B—join a fraternity.

To evaluate lifestyle alternatives Joe can use either complete or partial budgets. Complete budgets will tell him whether he can cover all expenses with the income provided by his parents and the part-time job. Partial budgets will give the difference between the expenses associated with the three lifestyles.

BUDGET COEFFICIENTS

It is human nature to remember best that which is either most recent or most unusual. But to base the selection of coefficients for use in budgeting on either is to court disaster. The projected outcomes will be biased. A planner needs concrete reasons for choosing these coefficients. Exhibit 9–1 presents the four major budget types and the appropriate technical and economic coefficients to use in each type.

It is generally easier to project costs than returns. For short-run planning, most of the input and expense coefficients can be forecast precisely. For long-run planning, variable input costs often can be estimated by adjusting the average of recent periods for projected trends; "ball-

Exhibit 9–1. Matrix for identifying coefficients for use in budgeting

Budget type	Planning Horizon	
	Short-term	*Long-term*
Partial	Price and production coefficients that are expected in the next year.	Uses average prices and production coefficients adjusted for projected economic and technological trends.
	Includes only costs and returns which are expected to change between present and proposed plans.	Includes only costs and returns which are expected to change between the present and proposed plans.
Complete	Price and production coefficients that are expected in the next year.	Uses average prices and production coefficients adjusted for projected economic and technological trends.
	Includes all costs and returns likely to be incurred in operating the business.	Includes all costs and returns likely to be incurred in operating the business.

park" estimates of average future conditions can be used. Several farm management consulting firms and university agricultural economics departments have developed manuals or newsletters containing estimates of future input cost. The prudent manager will use published sources and make such alterations as are relevant for his planning situation.

For projecting short-run returns, price and production coefficients that are expected to prevail over the next several months can be used. Monthly and quarterly weather forecasts are helpful in projecting crop yields. Reports from the United States Department of Agriculture (USDA) and state crop reporting services are valuable in planting and price forecasting decisions. These agencies issue estimates of planting intentions before the planting season for each major crop; periodic reports on acres planted and crop conditions during the growing season; and, finally, summaries of total acres harvested and estimated yields after harvest. Reports on livestock numbers, marketings, marketing intentions, feed supplies and feedstuffs in storage, fresh and frozen meat in storage, and similar information are also issued periodically. These reports are best obtained directly from the issuing agency or extension service. Although they are usually reproduced in the major farm magazines and newsletters, information may be old by the time it is available through these secondary sources. Most agriculture extension service personnel and USDA agencies like the Soil Conservation Service and Agriculture Stabilization and Conservation Service receive the reports directly and have the latest information.

Experience has shown that managers and professional agriculturalists who work with managers tend to underestimate costs and overestimate income. Because costs occur at many different times, it is easy to forget some of them. Any omission tends to hold the cost figure down. Income, on the other hand, usually comes in at fewer times and is therefore much less frequently overlooked or underreported. It is also common for operators to overestimate production. For example, managers will assume two litters per sow per year, even though actual records have consistently shown hog operations tend to average only 1.8 litters or less per sow. Few operators achieve the production levels magazines advertise or experiment stations achieve under their highly controlled conditions.

PRETESTING A DECISION WITH PARTIAL BUDGETING

Partial budgeting was defined as a planning procedure that lists items of receipts and expenses which change with a change in organization or procedure. The idea of partial budgeting has wide application, particularly for evaluating short-term changes in organization or long-term changes that are likely to involve only one or two enterprises. Partial budgets provide a "test" of changes being considered. For example, a manager may want to assess the effect of replacing one livestock enterprise with another or adding another crop enterprise to an ongoing operating unit.

A simple format for putting down all costs and returns which are likely to change is illustrated in Exhibit 9–2. In addition to computing the estimated change in income, a manager will also want to know the effects on the basic production resources—land, labor, and capital.

Use of the simple partial budgeting format is illustrated with a problem requiring a choice between livestock enterprises (see Exhibit 9–3). The question is, Would it be profitable to reduce the number of beef cows and add a buy-sell stocker steers (backgrounding) enterprise? The manager would like to start by reducing the cow herd by 20 cows. From consulting with a livestock specialist and checking on nutrition requirements, the manager estimates he can run 30 steers year round for a projected 350 pounds of gain each on the same pasture he would use for 20 mother

Exhibit 9–2.

Date _____

PARTIAL BUDGET

Alternative A: (may be Present Plan)
Alternative B:
Business Credits
  A.   Additional Annual Receipts:

      Total Additional Annual Receipts   _____
  B.   Reduced Annual Costs:

      Total Reduced Annual Costs   _____
  Total Annual Credits   _____
Business Debits
  C.   Reduced Annual Receipts:

      Total Reduced Annual Receipts   _____
  D.   Additional Annual Costs:

      Total Additional Annual Costs   _____
  Total Annual Debits   _____
  NET CHANGE IN INCOME
  (Credit minus Debits)   _____

Resource Use Comparisons

	Alt. A	Alt. B
Annual Operating Capital	_____	_____
Ownership Capital	_____	_____
Labor Requirement	_____	_____
Land Use	_____	_____

cows and their calves. Published enterprise budgets plus records the manager has kept on his cow herd provide data for projecting costs and returns.

Budgeting coefficients were chosen to reflect (1) the normal enterprise situation which has existed with beef cows and (2) the expected conditions if the steer backgrounding enterprise is added. Under the present plan, beef cows, a 90 percent weaned calf crop and a 16 percent

Exhibit 9–3.

Date _____

PARTIAL BUDGET

Alternative A: Present Plan Beef Cow-Calf
Alternative B: Backgrounding Steers

Business Credits

A.	Additional Annual Receipts:		
	Value of gain from 30 steers	$6,673.20	
	(30 steers × 750 lb. × $.78/lb.) minus		
	(30 steers × 400 lb. × $.88/lb.) minus		
	3% death loss		
	Total Additional Annual Receipts	$6,673.20	
B.	Reduced Annual Costs:		
	Cash cost of purchased inputs and		
	services for 20 cows (@ $82/hd.)	$1,640.00	
	Total Annual Reduced Costs	$1,640.00	
	Total Annual Credits		$8,313.20

Business Debits

C.	Reduced Annual Receipts		
	9 steer calves × 440 lb. × $.88/lb.	$3,484.80	
	6 heifer calves × 430 lb. × $.82/lb.	$2,115.60	
	3 cull cows × 925 lb. × $.41/lb.	$1,137.75	
	Total Annual Reduced Receipts	$6,738.15	
D.	Additional Annual Costs:		
	Cash cost of purchased inputs and		
	services for 30 steers (@ $74/hd.)	$2,220.00	
	Total Additional Annual Costs	$2,220.00	
	Total Annual Debits		$8,958.15
	NET CHANGE IN INCOME		
	(Credits minus Debits)		− $ 644.95

Resource Use Comparisons

	Alt. A	Alt. B
Annual Operating Capital	$ 1,640	$ 2,220
Ownership Capital	$11,640	$12,780
Labor Requirements	150 hr.	105 hr.
Land Use	Same for both	

replacement rate of young females for old cows was used. Records on the cow-calf enterprise indicate that the average selling weight for steers and heifers has been 435 pounds. For purchased stocker steers, the proposed plan, an average daily gain of 0.96 pounds, is assumed. An average ten cent negative margin (78 cents versus 88 cents) is anticipated between purchase at 400 pounds and sale at 750 pounds. The negative margin was based upon price records at a nearby market. (Of course, in periods of increasing livestock prices the prices for 400-pound calves purchased one year and sold as 750-pound feeders the next would likely show a positive change.) Because this partial budget is considered long-term—getting in and out of cow-calf production is not done easily—normal prices adjusted for trend are used.

Assuming the figures are reliable, the budgeting analysis (see Exhibit 9–3) suggests that a change to backgrounding would not be profitable. Compared to beef cows, steers would require greater annual operating capital requirements but lower labor requirements. Land use would be the same for both alternatives.

It is often desirable to include non-cash input costs in the budget. In this example, hours of operator labor multiplied by an hourly wage could be included as a reduced cost associated with the cow-calf enterprise. Likewise, a labor charge would be included under added cost of the backgrounding enterprise. Pasture could be treated the same way although in this case the pasture charges exactly offset each other and do not change because of the change in enterprise.

This simple example illustrates several things about partial budgets:

1. The end product shows which of two or more ways of doing things is likely to be the *more* profitable. It does not give the single *most* profitable, or optimum, way. There are many other ways of using the pasture made available by a 20-cow reduction in the cow-calf enterprise. Among the alternatives are (a) dairying, (b) running two batches of steers for a shorter time each, (c) grazing heifers rather than steers, and many more.

2. Costs like depreciation, property taxes, insurance, and business overhead, which are the same to the business regardless of the choice between steers and cows, are not included in the analysis.

3. The accuracy of the planning process will be only as good as the input data.

4. The resource use summary highlights the difference in labor and capital resources requirements. The differences between alternatives may be sufficiently large that the manager will choose to include interest and labor charges among the costs and returns that change.

BUDGETING A MAJOR INVESTMENT DECISION

Suppose the decision maker/manager in the above problem farms in an area where weather is a major uncertainty. It just never seems to rain at the right time or in the right amounts. Thus, the manager would like to consider the economic feasibility of irrigating one quarter section of crop-land, but the stakes in this kind of decision are high and mistakes are costly. If the proposal is economically feasible, the manager can finance the investment with a local lending agency. Partial budgeting can provide an analytic framework.

First, the manager must consider the problem setting and the data needed for analysis. The following guideline questions must be answered:

Question 1: What is the overall problem? Because weather is variable, yields fluctuate widely from year to year. This means that income fluctuates too, but irrigation is a means of stabilizing yields. Will irrigation pay for itself over time and give an additional labor and management income?

Question 2: Does the analysis apply to a whole business? Suppose the manager had additional land and capital resources. In that case the irrigation analysis would affect only one segment of the business.

Question 3: Will complete or partial budgeting be used? Partial budgeting is adequate because the proposed change is not expected to alter other segments of the business. The manager should be open, how-ever, to discovering opportunities for adjustments in other parts of the business that are suggested by the analysis.

Question 4: What is the time period? An irrigation decision is gener-ally thought of as an intermediate-term or long-term decision.

Question 5: What data are needed? The investment costs of land forming, if any, water source development, and irrigation system instal-lation are needed. Because this is a long-term analysis, the annual own-ership costs associated with the investments must be estimated. Annual input requirements and costs must also be estimated. Future yields must be forecast, as must future *normal* prices.

Question 6: How many alternatives will be evaluated? For this ex-ample only a present-normal and a proposed plan are compared.

Present plan:	80 acres dryland milo
	80 acres dryland wheat
Proposed plan:	132 acres irrigated corn
	28 acres dryland corn

After the events of the last several years, our manager was a little reluctant to make predictions 8 or 10 years into the future. He used the assistance of an irrigation engineer, agronomist, farm management con-sultant, and his lender to arrive at the budgeting coefficients. By correlating the information they provided, he was able to make an intelligent decision.

Corn was the most profitable irrigated crop among those considered, which included irrigated wheat, forages, and soybeans. Vegetable crops were not considered because of their unusually high labor requirements.

Center pivot irrigation was chosen even though the investment per acre is higher than for alternative systems. Center pivot was justified by the low labor requirement, the availability of good service from a local dealer, and the capability of controlling water application rates. Exhibit 9–4 summarizes the expected investment for the irrigation system and the estimated annual ownership costs (the DIRTI 5 minus repairs). These cost values are $526 and $66 per acre, respectively.

The development of a corn enterprise budget was a key step in the analysis. Particular care was taken in developing the irrigation-related cost coefficients. Specified costs are given in Exhibit 9–5 and are based on the assumptions of (1) water from a well, (2) diesel fuel for power, and (3) 7 to 8 inches of water applied per acre per season. Since no new machinery purchases are anticipated as a result of the irrigation investment, the only change in ownership capital is the irrigation system. An interest charge on operating capital tied up by the enterprise is included among

Exhibit 9–4. Initial investment and annual ownership costs for irrigation system to irrigate 132 acres

			Annual fixed costs as a percent of initial cost				
	Initial cost	Estimated useful life	Depreciation	Interest	Insurance and taxes	Total	Annual fixed cost
Well	$10,500	25	4	6	1	11%	$1,155
Pump and gearhead	9,500	20	5	6	1	12	1,140
Power unit and access.	8,200	14	7	6	1	14	1,148
Pivot unit	1,350	20	5	6	1	12	162
Pipe	3,830	20	5	6	1	12	460
Center pivot system	32,000	15	6⅔	6	1	13⅔	4,374
Land shaping	4,000	—	—	6	1	7	280
	$69,380						$8,719
	$ 526						$ 66

SOURCE: Various irrigation industry companies.

Exhibit 9–5.   Per acre irrigated corn enterprise
budget, projected yield of 150
bushels per acre

Budget item	Value per acre
Production	
Yield (bushels)	150
Gross receipts (@ $3.50/bu.)	$525.50
Variable costs	
Seed	$ 18.50
Fertilizer & lime	75.50
Herbicide & insecticide	26.00
Tillage and planting	25.00
Harvesting and hauling	24.20
Drying	14.00
Irrigation fuel, misc.	23.60
Interest on operating capital	8.70
Total variable costs	215.50
Ownership costs	
Irrigation system fixed costs	66.00
Total specified costs	281.50
Income above specified costs	$243.50

specified costs. Charges for labor, management, and land have not been included because these are inputs the operator will provide and are common to both the present and proposed plans.

The enterprise budgets for milo and wheat are not presented, but the summary values are included in the partial budget. The budgets were based on past records, but updated in line with future expectations that influenced the selection of coefficients for the corn budget.

The final version of the partial budget is shown in Exhibit 9–6. The change is expected to add over $21,000 per year to net income, although the shift to irrigation entails greater labor, capital, and management demands. The larger operating and ownership capital requirements were accounted for in the budgeting process.

Sensitivity Analysis

Although there are many uncertainties in making projections, it is possible to look at a series of different "futures" by making several as-

Exhibit 9–6.

Date _____

PARTIAL BUDGET

Present Plan: 80 acres milo and 80 acres wheat
Proposed Plan: Irrigated corn with central pivot system
Business Credits

A.	Additional Annual Receipts:	
	Value of irrigated corn production	
	(150 bu. × 132 acres × $3.50/bu.)	$ 69,300
	Value of dryland corn production	
	(80 bu. × 28 acres × $3.50/bu.)	$ 7,840
	Total Additional Annual Receipts	$ 77,140
B.	Reduced Annual Costs:	
	Cash production costs for 80 acres milo (@ $172/acre)	$ 13,760
	Cash production costs for 80 acres wheat (@ $129/acre)	$ 10,320
	Total Annual Reduced Costs	$ 24,080
	Total Annual Credits	$101,220

Business Debits

C.	Reduced Annual Receipts:	
	Value of milo	
	(90 bu. × 80 acres × $3.00/bu.)	$ 21,600
	Value of wheat	
	(45 bu. × 80 acres × $4.25/bu.)	$ 15,300
	Total Annual Reduced Receipts	$ 36,900
D.	Additional Annual Costs:	
	Cash production costs for 132 acres irrigated corn	
	(@ $281.50/acre)	$ 37,150
	Cash production costs for 28 acres dryland corn	
	(@ $188.00/acre)	$ 5,264
	Total Additional Annual Costs	$ 42,422
	Total Annual Debits	$ 79,322

NET CHANGE IN INCOME	
(irrigation fixed costs included)	$ 21,898

Resource Use Comparisons

	Present Plan: Wheat and Milo	Proposed Plan: Irrigated Corn
Annual Operating Capital	$24,080	$33,644
Ownership Capital	—	$69,380
Labor Requirement	600	900
Land Use	(Using same acres)	

sumptions. The object is to determine how sensitive the budgeting solution (the net change in income) is to differences in price and production. For example, what if irrigated corn yield is too optimistic by 10 percent? The corn yield coefficient could be reduced from 150 bushels per acre to 135 bushels. The "credits" section of the budget would be reduced by $6930. This would eliminate one-third of the positive expected difference in favor of the irrigated corn alternative, assuming other coefficients are reasonable. Other factors, like expected prices, could similarly be changed and their impact on the income change value assessed. The sensitivity of a budgeting solution to changes in coefficients is a useful indication of the riskiness of proposed alternatives.

Cash Flow Comparison

The irrigation investment discussed above looked profitable on the average. It was suggested, however, that the manager planned to finance the investment with a lending agency. Thus, the manager must also be concerned with the ability to meet interest and principal payments.

Cash flow analysis is a means for projecting the flow of cash in and out of the business for specific time periods, either by months or quarters within a year or by years for the term of a loan.

In the irrigation example, suppose the manager could finance 80 percent of the investment ($55,500) at 12 percent interest. Interest will be paid on the outstanding loan balance. Seven equal principal payments of $7,930 will be made. Interest in year 1 will be $6,660, but it will decrease to $950 in year 7.

In looking at cash inflows, the manager would be interested in the additional net cash inflows from the irrigated corn alternative as compared to the milo-wheat alternative. The irrigated corn alternative is projected to generate an additional $137 or a total of $21,900 for the 160 acres.

The projected irrigation-related cash flow would be as follows:

	Years						
	1	2	3	4	5	6	7
Cash inflow	$21,900	$21,900	$21,900	$21,900	$21,900	$21,900	$21,900
Cash outflow	14,590	13,638	12,687	11,735	10,783	9,839	8,880
Net	$ 7,310	$ 8,262	$ 9,213	$10,165	$11,116	$12,068	$13,020

If the assumptions on price and production are reasonable, the irrigation system should pay for itself and leave $71,154 over the seven years as return on the $13,880 equity capital invested and as a return to labor, management, and risk taking.

SUMMARY

This chapter has explained the essentials of budgeting, with particular emphasis on partial budgets. Among important points made were:

- A budget is a written plan for future action, plus the quantified expected results. Budgets are dollars and cents approximations of an alternative under consideration.

- Budgets can be used to look at the total business (complete) or only part of it (partial). A complete budget is sufficiently detailed to provide an estimate of net farm income; i.e., all projected costs and returns from the largest to the smallest are included. Partial budgeting compares alternatives by looking at only the costs and returns that change with alternative projected plans.

- Either complete or partial budgets can be used in short-term or longer-term planning. Partial budgets are simpler to use and can provide the necessary degree of completeness for most decisions.

- Budgets are future-oriented; hence, most of the numbers used are estimates. Careful attention should be given to the development of these estimates. It is human nature to underestimate costs and overestimate income.

- It is wise to test the results of a budgeting analysis by computing the effect of different levels of key variables on the projected income values. This is known as testing the sensitivity of a solution. Such testing can allow a manager to examine the potential consequences of errors in projecting production or prices before irrevocable commitments are made.

This chapter assumed an informed, knowledgeable management. That is not always the case. Some managers only partially understand the resources available to them. Others have given little thought to enterprise alternatives or alternative means of managing existing enterprises. The basics of resource inventory and enterprise budgeting are the focus of the next two chapters.

APPLYING THE PRINCIPLES OF CHAPTER 9

1. A milo producer has read that he can get approximately 90 days grazing per acre of milo stubble for 450-pound steers. An average daily gain (ADG) of 1.4 pounds per steer can be expected by feeding 4 pounds of protein-concentrate supplement per day. Comparable

steers would normally realize .3 pounds ADG on the milo stubble alone.

The farmer can purchase 450-pound calves now for $40 per hundredweight and expects he can sell them in 90 days at the heavier weight for $38 per hundredweight. He can purchase the protein-concentrate supplement for 7 cents per pound. He expects buying and selling cost and death losses to total $3 per head.

    a. How much can the farmer expect to make (lose) by stocking a 120-acre field with steers for 90 days?

    b. Suppose the farmer stocked half as many calves for 170 days and expected them to sell for $37 per hundredweight. How much can he expect to make (lose)?

2. Joe Bails has been having his 200 tons of hay custom baled for $23 per ton. But he has surplus labor and can get the money to purchase a good used baler. In fact, he can purchase a baler for $4,000 and operate it for an estimated $10 per ton. Joe estimates the annual fixed costs at $1,200 per year. Joe also can bale another 100 tons at $23 per ton for his neighbor, Tom Partimer. Prepare a partial budget showing the profitability analysis for the baler, using the following outline.

Added Receipts

Reduced Costs

               Total Credits

Reduced Receipts

Added Costs

               Total Debits

               Difference (+ or −)

3. A certain swine gestation supplement fed to sows at .3 pounds per day for the 30 days prior to farrowing claims a 150 pound per litter difference (market weight) over a control group not fed the supplement. If the claims are true (litter market weight of 1,431 pounds with supplement, 1,281 pounds without) and you have 50 sows, what can you afford to pay for the supplement if pigs sell for $40/hundredweight.

    a. $ 6.67 per pound

    b.   60.00 per pound

    c.   30.00 per pound

    d. 3,000.00 per pound

REFERENCES

Bitney, Larry L. "Can You Afford to Irrigate?" *Crops and Soils Magazine,* October 1974, pp. 7–9.

Castle, Emery N., *et al. Farm Business Management,* 2nd ed. New York: The Macmillan Co., 1972.

Goodwin, John W. *Agricultural Economics.* Reston, Va: Reston Publishing Co., Inc., 1977.

Hedges, Trimble R. *Farm Management Decisions.* Englewood Cliffs, N.J.: Prentice-Hall, Inc., 1963.

Luening, R. A. "Partial Budgeting," *Journal of the American Society of Farm Managers and Rural Appraisers,* April 1974, pp. 33–38.

Schneeberger, K. "Irrigation in the Midwest—Can It Pay in the 1980s?," *Big Farmer/Entrepreneur,* March 1981, pp 10–14.

Farm Resource Inventory

- Resources are basic to production
- A resource inventory considers the attributes of all resources, including services
- Quantity of resources is important, but so are quality and flexibility
- Readily accessible services can facilitate efficient production
- Future resource use and potential should be considered

10

At any given time a manager has control over a set of resources—land, capital, labor, and management. The business may own all or part of the resources. In most cases additional resources could be controlled if the manager decided the business could profitably employ additional borrowed capital, hired labor, or rented land.

In this chapter we discuss:

1. The need for resource inventory

2. Some resource attributes a manager should consider as he/she inventories

3. A classification of resources that is broader than land, labor, and capital

Deciding what resources to use and how to use them is one major responsibility of management. Such decisions are not made once and forgotten; they must be made again and again as technical and economic conditions change. The beginning operator or one who is very limited in one or more of the basic resources may find decisions about resource use relatively frequent and very difficult. An established operator with a profitable farming operation, on the other hand, may only make resource decisions about reallocation when there are major shifts in commodity prices or when land is added. Nevertheless, all managers are faced with resource allocation decisions as they strive to attain their respective goals.

RESOURCE INVENTORY

Some managers are too narrow in their thinking when they evaluate the nature and potential of resources they manage. Stop and look at Exhibit 10–1. This is one way of representing the variety of things a manager might consider. There are many attributes, or factors, that affect the productivity and profitability of resources.

The individual cells in Exhibit 10–1 are empty on purpose. We want you to visualize the items that you think should go in each cell. Some items that apply to the cells are discussed on the following pages. The discussion is not meant to be all-inclusive, but should give a framework for inventorying resources and should stimulate consideration of other items that might be peculiar to a particular region.

LAND

Land is probably the first resource to receive attention in any farm business—logically so, since land is basic to most agriculture production and

Exhibit 10–1. Resource inventory matrix

Attributes	Resources			
	Land	Labor/ mgmt.	Capital	Services
Quantity				
Quality				
Availability				
Flexibility				
Future				

in most cases represents the major capital asset managed, even though it may be rented. Numerous attributes of land influence the value of that resource in production. Among these are:

1. The total amount available and the division between cropland, pasture, timber, and wasteland
2. The fertility of productive land
3. Location—accessibility
4. Topography
5. Size and shape of fields
6. Rigidity and/or flexibility of use

Quantity

The amount of land controlled is closely related to business volume for many farm businesses, such as cattle ranches and grain farms. Net earnings are heavily dependent upon volume and efficiency of production. The income equation can be stated as:

$$\text{Net Business Earnings} = \text{Volume of Production} \times \text{Earnings per Unit Produced}$$

Experience through the years has shown that profits left over at the end of the year are closely related to the gross sales during the year, as illustrated by Exhibit 10–2. One avenue to greater sales volume is a larger land base.

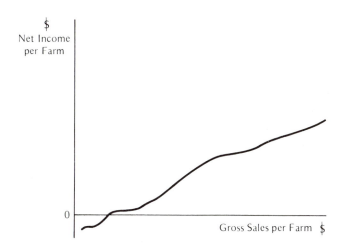

Exhibit 10–2. The generalized gross sales–net income realization.

Quality

Size itself is not a guarantee of high income. Net earnings are determined by both quantity and quality of land. The grain farmer with only 200 acres of land will have limited sales volume. If that 200 acres is also poor quality, the production and income potential will be further constrained.

A number of quality, or productivity, factors have been identified by soil scientists. Among these are texture, depth of topsoil, internal drainage, subsoil permeability, slope, natural fertility, pH (acidity or alkalinity), and water-holding capacity.

The quality factors can be determined with the help of (1) soils tests, (2) soils maps, and (3) the assistance of soils specialists. Soils tests on each field and/or pasture will indicate the general fertility level. Soils maps are available for each farm at many county Soil Conservation Service (SCS) offices. Exhibit 10–3, a reduced SCS photo of a farm, shows the location of major soil series. The soil series description includes information on slope, soil texture, depth, and water-holding capacity. Both private and public services are available for providing current soils tests or farm soils maps. Check with SCS or local extension personnel for more information if soils data are inadequate.

Developing quality indexes: A manager must weigh the various quality factors as he struggles with a means for classifying land for economic purposes. Although the technical advice of SCS and extension specialists should not be overlooked, the manager must interpret it in view of his own business situation and objectives. For example, erosion control measures like terraces and rotation cropping patterns may get low priority in the short run when managers are faced with cash flow problems and limited capital.

The economic principles studied in Chapter 2 suggest a method of classifying land. That is, allocate the land to its most profitable use consistent with the manager's business objectives. This is not necessarily the use that maximizes production.

A simple classification that has proved useful for many managers is one that divides the land into five capability classes. (This classification differs somewhat from SCS classes.)

Capability class 1: Land suited for intensive cropping. This includes level to nearly level upland or bottomland and terraced upland that can be cropped year after year. It is not subject to more than slight erosion regardless of treatment. The land may be irrigated or nonirrigated. Double or triple cropping may be practiced in some regions.

Capability class 2: Land suited for limited cropping. In humid areas

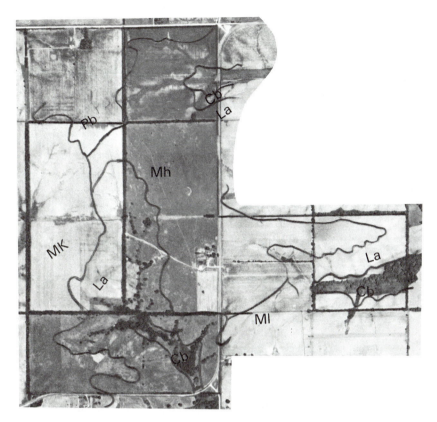

Exhibit 10–3.   A Soil Conservation Service photo of a farm.

this class includes land with sufficient slope that continuous row-cropping results in substantial erosion, even if terracing is done. Such land might be in a rotation that includes row crops, small grain crops, and/or pasture. In arid regions Class 2 land may be row-cropped every other year.

Capability class 3: Land sufficiently steep that it must be used for either small grains or small grains and hay or pasture in rotation.

Capability class 4: May include fairly good land, but has severe limitations and restrictions in use. As a rule it is best used for pasture or hay.

Capability class 5: Wasteland and timberland that has minimal value for pasture.

Once soils are grouped into capability classes, the manager is in a position to use economic or other criteria to determine land use within capability classes. A sample classification sheet is shown in Exhibit 10–4.

Exhibit 10–4.

LAND USE CLASSIFICATION

	Field letter	Acres in field	PRESENT (OR PROPOSED) LAND USE					
			CLASS 1 Intensive row cropping	CLASS 2 Limited row cropping	CLASS 3 Small grain continuous if terraced or rotation of sm. grain and hay	CLASS 4 Permanent pasture	CLASS 5 Timber or woods pasture	CLASS 6 Farmstead roads, etc.
	(1)	(2)	(3)	(4)	(5)	(6)	(7)	(8)
1								
2								
3								
4								
5								
6								
7								
8								
9								
10								
11								
12								
13								
14								
15								
16								
17								
18								
19								
20								
21								
22	Total acres							
23	Class 1 acres							
24	Class 2 acres							
25	Class 3 acres							
26	Class 4 acres							
27	Class 5 acres							
28	Class 6 acres							

Availability and Flexibility

Location and topography are two important land attributes. Location affects

1. Distance to trade centers

2. The ease with which those trade centers can be reached

3. The variety and number of alternative input suppliers and marketing outlets from which to choose

4. Climatic factors like amount and distribution of rainfall, temperature range, length of growing season

5. Pest problems from insects, noxious grasses and weeds, and harmful soil microorganisms

6. Constraints or regulations due to zoning, pollution controls, proximity of neighbors, opportunities for expansion

7. Access to public services

8. Price of land and/or rental rates

Because distance can be translated into fuel and travel-time costs, land remote from trade centers may increase costs, reduce profits, or reduce the number or kind of services that can be obtained from dealers, veterinarians, bankers, and public agencies. In a few cases, location may increase buying and selling options. Being halfway between two trade centers and in the normal trade area of both may provide opportunities to take advantage of the competition between several sellers (buyers).

Topography is difficult to separate from land quality factors, but includes some other variables. Topography influences

1. Flexibility of land use among crops or between crops and pasture

2. Erosion hazards and the need for terraces, strip cropping or minimum-tillage farming

3. Field shape and size—if, for example, there are steep slopes, rivers or streams, sloughs or swamps, rock outcroppings

4. Because of the above factors, choice of machinery

Future Adaptations

As the perceptive manager looks at the land resource, he will see beyond what is and try to visualize what can be. Perhaps the land can be used more efficiently (and profitably) by

1. Filling in ditches and gullies

2. Terracing

3. Removing fences or trees

4. Installing underground tile

5. Shaping or leveling the land to eliminate wet spots or improve drainage

6. Installing irrigation

7. Constructing levees to reduce flooding

The reader can probably think of other opportunities.

LABOR

The people who live and work there are one of the most important resources on any farm. Their aptitudes, desires, training, and capability for accomplishing their tasks have an important influence upon how well other resources are utilized.

The labor resource is peculiar to each farm situation. Some large units have many hired laborers, whereas in some family operations the one major laborer is the operator, and supplemental labor is available from family members during weekends and vacations. And, of course, there are farm operations with labor resources between these extremes.

Besides the number of workers, a farm's labor supply and labor product is determined by the hours worked per day and the number of days per year each worker is available. Worker output is also influenced by the machines and equipment used, the degree of mechanization.

On quality, a manager must recognize that no two persons are alike: they differ in their capabilities, work habits, attitudes, personality traits, ambitions, and willingness to accept responsibilities. Some workers, like some managers, are capable of only simple, repetitive tasks. Others can handle a wide variety of tasks and responsibilities. Although trite, the old saying "you get what you pay for" is often true, especially when applied to hired labor.

Good quality labor is also productive labor. Thus, a manager should regularly look at such productivity factors as (1) value of production per full-time worker, (2) labor per tillable acre, (3) labor per animal unit, e.g., dairy cow or sow, and (4) labor cost per $100 of gross production. Although these values can be influenced by the degree and level of mechanization on a farm, there are standards (available from the Extension

Service in most states) that should be consulted for comparative purposes. A manager may find that labor is not performing up to standard. He may need to implement policies and/or procedures for improving labor productivity. Alternatively, a new job assignment may be in order for one or more employees. In certain cases, an employee may have to be terminated.

Labor productivity can sometimes be improved by increasing the capital investment and technology per laborer. In such cases the manager will want to look at the "bottom line." What is the added cost of the mechanization/technology and what does it add to profits? Substituting machinery for labor is sometimes costly.

Availability and Flexibility

The time at which labor is available may be more important than the quantity. Family labor available in the summer may be worth very little if the peak labor period is in the spring. In some areas it is also difficult to hire seasonal or part-time help on a daily or weekly basis.

A labor worksheet (see Exhibit 10–5) is one means of estimating labor supply by period (e.g., month, quarter, planting time, lambing season, vegetable harvest). This budget can then be matched with projected labor demands.

Labor can be either fixed or variable. Labor that has no alternative employment is fixed, as is labor hired on a full-year basis. It cannot be stored. You use it or lose it.

Flexibility of labor depends upon the capability and attitude of labor, the level of mechanization, and the age and health of workers. Employees or family members who are well paid and happy with their work are more likely to be flexible.

Future Outlook

Labor is a dynamic resource. Children come and go. The manager ages. Hired labor becomes more or less available with changing economic conditions within a community. These factors should be kept in mind as a manager "sizes up" the labor resource.

CAPITAL

Capital resources include investments in (1) livestock; (2) buildings and equipment to care for livestock; (3) farm machinery to use in growing crops; (4) buildings, tools, shop, etc., to house and maintain machinery; and (5) money used to operate the business.

Exhibit 10–5.

LABOR ESTIMATE WORKSHEET

	(1)			Total hours for year (2)	Distribution of hours			
					Dec. thru March (3)	April May June (4)	July Aug. (5)	Sept. Oct. Nov. (6)
1	Suggested for full-time worker			2400	600	675	450	675
2	My estimate for full-time worker							
3	LABOR AVAILABLE							
4	Operator (or Partner No. 1)							
5	Partner No. 2							
6	Family labor							
7	Hired labor							
8	Custom machine operators							
9	TOTAL LABOR AVAILABLE							
10	DIRECT LABOR NEEDED BY CROP AND ANIMAL ENTERPRISES							
11	Crop enterprises	Acres	Hr./Ac.					
12								
13								
14								
15								
16								
17								
18								
19								
20	TOTAL CROP HOURS NEEDED							
21	Animal enterprises	No.Units	Hr./Un.					
22								
23								
24								
25								
26	TOTAL ANIMAL HOURS NEEDED							
27	TOTAL CROP AND ANIMAL HOURS							
28	Estimated indirect hours							
29	TOTAL HOURS LABOR NEEDED							
30	TOTAL HOURS AVAILABLE							
31	Overload (L. 29 minus L. 30)							
32	Underload (L. 30 minus L. 29)							

Quantity and Quality

It is easy to tie up a large number of dollars in capital items. In fact, farmers are often accused of having too much equipment or equipment that is too large. However, in developing the inventory of capital, a manager determines what is at his disposal; there is no requirement that all capital be used. As a result of the inventory, a manager may decide to dispose of (or acquire) some assets.

In these days of high interest costs, there can be a substantial opportunity cost of being overinvested in machinery, equipment, or buildings. There are, however, some very good reasons for having capital resources that are adequate, reliable, and in good condition. Good quality capital items can contribute to:

1. Increased production through improved timeliness

2. Increased price through improved quality

3. Increased price through storage

4. Reduced labor cost

5. Improved labor productivity because (a) jobs are made easier, (b) more jobs can be done in the same amount of time, or (c) some of the drudgery is eliminated.

Quantity of capital also relates to the availability of borrowed funds. What is the owner's equity? How much borrowing power does that equity have and at what interest rate?

Quality is also important when reviewing nonland capital. What is the state of repair of machinery and buildings? If a given capital item is in disrepair, is it needed and what will it cost to make it a useful, dependable, and productive asset?

Availability and Flexibility

Availability relates to how operationally useful the capital items are and whether they lend themselves to an efficient operation. Capital items vary in their availability and flexibility. A hog-finishing floor that is directly across the road and upwind from a neighbor's house is inflexible and may be unavailable. Storage bins scattered around over a farm are neither as available nor as flexible as a well-planned, integrated grain handling system. Field and power equipment that is too small for the job is available but uneconomical to use. A tractor cannot be simultaneously used for plowing and powering a grinder-mixer although with planning it may be available for multiple uses. Money tied up in crop production is not available for livestock investments. An inventory of capital items considers more than the accounting required to prepare a balance sheet.

Flexibility is the quality of having alternative uses. For example, a stantion-type milking parlor is not very flexible. A large, open loafing barn is much more so. A tractor with picker attachment is more flexible than a self-propelled cotton picker.

Degrees of flexibility apply also to the use of money. An operator with a heavy debt load in land, equipment, and facilities has little flexibility in deciding how to use a year's net earnings. It will be required to meet principal and interest obligations and family living expenses. As a consequence, management may have to pass up unusually profitable opportunities.

Future Values

When inventorying capital assets, a manager must recognize that most items depreciate with time. The inventory taken a year from now will differ from the one taken today. Some thought and energy should be invested in assessing the quality and usefulness of capital resources at some future time, say five years ahead, in addition to the current assessment. Where there are capital inadequacies, a manager must evaluate the feasibility of (1) borrowing money; (2) leasing machinery, equipment, or facilities; (3) hiring someone else to provide the item; or (4) building up a cash reserve for a down payment on a needed item. Budgeting and cash flow planning will help the manager select from among the options.

SERVICES

Some businesses are large enough to be self-sufficient in terms of needed services. A large 50,000-head cattle feeding operation likely has its own grinding-mixing-storage complex, a machine shop and mechanic, a full-time veterinarian, a machinery dealership or franchise, and so on, so that inputs and equipment can be purchased at the lowest cost. Many family operations are self-sufficient in some areas. Managers should be fully aware of the variety of services needed for them to operate most efficiently. The farmer who is the only irrigator in his area or the dairy farmer with some exotic automated feeding system can lose valuable time, and probably money, while awaiting service from a dealer 200 miles away.

As mentioned above, there is a strong correlation between location and the services that are available. An operator in the sparsely populated ranching areas of the Southwest has a narrower range of services to depend upon than do cash grain farmers in the more diversified farming areas. A crop producer in a predominately livestock area may be similarly disadvantaged.

A number of services are available from public agencies like the Forest Service, Farmers Home Administration, Soil Conservation Service, Cooperative Extension Service, or from private firms. The latter may include financial institutions; machinery and equipment dealers; repair and maintenance service firms of all kinds; livestock input suppliers and providers of health services; suppliers of fertilizer, seed, fuel, or chemicals; and custom operators.

Quality factors include dependability, experience and knowledge, promptness in responding to requests, and an attitude of standing behind sales or services. Here, too, a manager usually pays for what he gets, although business firms have different objectives in providing their services. Some offer capable, dependable service as a means of attracting or holding business, especially in areas such as providing feed ingredients or agricultural chemicals where there is substantial sales competition. Others give superior service because they are known as reputable firms and are interested in maintaining that reputation. In any case, a manager should not expect service to be free. Service is a valuable asset for timely and efficient production.

Again, a manager should attempt to project the future availability of services. An area experiencing substantial out-migration from agriculture is likely to have fewer suppliers in the future, although the firms that remain may be able to give higher quality service. On the other hand, an area which is just developing in a particular agricultural activity (irrigation or vegetable production, for example) should expand in support services with the passage of time.

MANAGEMENT

The discussion of the management resource in Chapter 1 made the point that managers have different capabilities. Those capabilities should be reflected in the profitability of the farm business.

It should also be obvious that the manager may not be the most qualified person to assess the management resource. It is difficult to be objective about one's own capabilities and limitations. Most managers, however, recognize some of their strong and weak points, and other people provide feedback which should aid them in self-evaluation. For example, labor management capability may be indicated by the output from hired laborers and the turnover in workers. Managers also get feedback when a lender refuses (or agrees) to loan money at the prime rate being extended other managers.

The quality of the management resource should not remain static. Good managers are open to opportunities to learn and improve on their ability, and they seek out capable advice on problems or questions about which they are inexperienced or incapable.

FROM INVENTORY TO PLANNING

The preceding discussion has pointed out that resources are the foundation of any business, although firms differ in the quantity and quality of resources controlled. Once the resources are inventoried and the strengths and limitations identified, a manager is nearly ready to (1) develop a plan for operating a farm/ranch, (2) reorganize an existing operation, or (3) expand a business. However, there is generally an intermediate step of accumulating and organizing pertinent facts on specific enterprises which might be included in a farm plan. The next chapter focuses on enterprise budgets and the process of estimating costs and returns. Other sections of this book focus on economic and management techniques (linear programming, whole farm budgeting, records) and criteria for choosing among plans.

APPLYING THE PRINCIPLES OF CHAPTER 10

True-False Questions

_____ 1. A manager's goal should be to make clever resource use decisions that can remain in effect for the rest of his career.

_____ 2. The level of gross sales influences the net income of a farm.

_____ 3. An important part of a resource inventory is the manager's judgment of various attributes of each resource.

_____ 4. The major capital asset managed on most farms is buildings and equipment.

Labor Estimate Worksheet

1. Complete a Labor Estimate Worksheet, using Exhibit 10–5 as an example, for a hypothetical farm as described below. What is the labor overload or underload for the year and for each season? If the children leave the farm, reducing family labor to zero, what will happen to the over- or underload?

Labor available:

Operator: 250 hours per month, each month

Family: 80 hours per month, September–April; 200 hours per month, May–August

Labor needs by enterprise:

Soybeans: 90 acres, 5.2 hrs./ac./yr. distributed as follows:

December–March:	0.10 hr./ac./month
April and May:	0.90 hr./ac./month
June and July:	0.65 hr./ac./month
August and September:	0.15 hr./ac./month
October and November:	0.70 hr./ac./month

Wheat: 15 acres, 3.8 hrs./ac./yr. distributed as follows:

June and July:	0.80 hr./ac./month
August and September:	0.70 hr./ac./month
October and November:	0.40 hr./ac./month

Corn: 80 acres, 7.6 hr./ac./yr. distributed as follows:

December–March:	0.22 hr./ac./month
April and May:	1.50 hr./ac./month
June and July:	0.50 hr./ac./month
August and September:	0.40 hr./ac./month
October and November:	0.85 hr./ac./month

Barley: 10 acres, 3.8 hr./ac./yr. distributed as follows:

June and July:	0.80 hr./ac./month
August and September:	0.70 hr./ac./month
October and November:	0.40 hr./ac./month

Perennial Pasture: 50 acres, 0.07 hr./ac./yr. distributed as follows:

April and May:	0.005 hr./ac./month
June and July:	0.010 hr./ac./month
August and September:	0.015 hr./ac./month
October and November:	0.005 hr./ac./month

Timber Pasture: 120 acres, 0.07 hr./ac./yr. distributed as follows:

April and May:	0.005 hr./ac./month
June and July:	0.010 hr./ac./month
August and September:	0.015 hr./ac./month
October and November:	0.005 hr./ac./month

Hay: 46 acres, 5.4 hr./ac./yr. distributed as follows:

April and May:	0.20 hr./ac./month
June and July:	2.50 hr./ac./month

Litters: finished hogs, 40 units, 20 hr./unit/yr. distributed as follows:

December–May, August and September:	2 hr./unit/month
June, July, October and November:	1 hr./unit/month

Beef Cows: 35 units, 7/hr./unit/yr. distributed as follows:

December–March:	0.70 hr./unit/month
April, May:	0.20 hr./unit/month
October and November:	0.55 hr./unit/month
June–September:	0.50 hr./unit/month

(Estimate indirect labor needs as 20 percent of Total Crop and Animal needs. Distribute the indirect hours to months of low direct labor needs.)

2. Complete a similar Labor Estimate Worksheet for your family's farm or for some other operation with which you are familiar. How is this useful to the manager for long-range planning?

REFERENCES

Castle, Emery N., *et al. Farm Business Management*, 2nd ed. New York: The Macmillan Co., 1972.

Fenton, T. E., *et al. Productivity Levels of Some Iowa Soils*, Iowa State Agricultural Experiment Station Special Report 66, April 1971.

Hedges, Trimble R. *Farm Management Decisions*. Englewood Cliffs, N.J.: Prentice-Hall, Inc., 1963.

Justus, Fred E., Jr. "Farm Managers: It's Time to Take an Inventory," *Journal of American Society of Farm Managers and Rural Appraisers*, October 1967, pp. 19–23.

Kay, Ronald D. *Farm Management*. New York, N.Y.: McGraw-Hill Book Co., 1981.

Using Enterprise Budgets

- Format for enterprise budgets
- Production practices define enterprise budget content
- Relating data needs to budget content
- Data sources
- Adjusting for variance in gross receipts
- Some nonmonetary differences can be included in analysis

11

A manager-planner cannot chart the course of resource use in a business without goals and objectives and sound data on alternatives. Once goals are defined, resources are inventoried, and data on alternative means for using resources are developed, the decision maker is in a position to perform the analytical and decision-making steps of management.

Partial budgeting as an analytical tool was discussed in Chapter 9. Simple enterprise budgets were introduced at that time to illustrate their use as a source of data for budgeting. This chapter contains the details of enterprise budget development and further illustrates their use.

Enterprises are the building blocks of farm plans. *An enterprise has defined or recognizable inputs and measurable outputs or services.* Enterprises are most frequently distinguished by their end products; wheat, alfalfa hay, and beef cow-calf are examples. However, other segments of an operation, such as custom harvesting, grain storage, or pasture production, may be treated as enterprises.

The purpose of enterprise budgets is to provide economic data to assist the farm/ranch manager in evaluating options. Depending upon the objective, the budgets may be used in short-term planning (this month or this season, for example) or longer-term planning and evaluation.

This chapter focuses on the economic aspects of enterprise evaluation once the basic production techniques (i.e., varieties, choice of chemicals, ration, feed conversion) are established. After reading this chapter the reader should understand:

1. The basic format used in enterprise budget construction

2. What differentiates one enterprise budget from another

3. The difference between budgets developed for short-term and long-term planning

4. Special characteristics of enterprises which may not be specifically included in an enterprise budget, but which can influence enterprise choice

SAMPLE ENTERPRISE BUDGETS

Sample budgets for corn and wheat are presented in Exhibit 11–1. These budgets represent single points on production functions. A different fertilizer combination or no-till farming rather than conventional tillage would require developing new budgets (or altering the ones shown) and would represent another point on a production function.

An enterprise budget has several parts. One part gives expected production per unit (acre, head) and the associated gross sales (see Part A, Exhibit 11–1). This defines the production level of the enterprise: 150 bushels of grain, 450 pounds of gain, 18 tons of silage.

The next part of a budget (see Part B, Exhibit 11–1) summarizes variable production inputs and their costs. The set of inputs is defined by the production practices and/or ingredients to be used; for example, minimum tillage versus conventional tillage or a high roughage ration versus a high concentrate ration.

The variable costs, sometimes called direct costs, can differ with the size of the enterprise (one would expect economies of size) and the meth-

Exhibit 11–1. Per acre enterprise budgets for corn and wheat
An example assuming medium productivity soils, above average
management

		Corn	Wheat
Budget item	Units	Value per acre	
A. Production			
Yield	bushels	120	50
Gross Receipts[1]	$	420	212.50
B. Variable Inputs			
Seed	$	13.50	8.50
Fertilizer and lime	$	49.00	25.50
Herbicides and insecticide	$	18.00	.50
Machine operation	$	24.50	14.00
Drying	$	14.40	—
Interest on operating capital and miscellaneous costs	$	19.50	8.00
Total Variable Costs	$	138.90	56.50
Income above Variable Costs	$	281.10	156.00
C. Ownership Costs			
Machinery, equipment, and storage	$	32.00	19.00
Taxes and land maintenance	$	9.00	8.25
Farm overhead	$	4.50	4.50
Interest on land[2] @ 11%	$	143.00	143.00
Total Ownership Costs		188.50	174.75
Return to Labor, Management, and Risk	$	92.60	−18.75
Labor @ $5/hour	$	22.50	10.00
Return to Management and Risk	$	70.10	−28.75

[1]Corn @ $3.50/bu., wheat @ $4.25/bu.

[2]Land @ $1300/acre.

ods or technology used. Both size and methods will influence the cost estimates used.

Gross sales less the cost of variable inputs gives expected income above variable costs. Also known as the *gross margin*, this figure is an estimate of the return to land, labor, capital, management, overhead, and risk.

The fixed, or ownership, costs section of the budget (Part C) summarizes items for which there may not be a direct cash outlay. Some of these costs, like the DIRTI 5 machinery ownership costs, are somewhat difficult to allocate to individual enterprises. However, an attempt to develop realistic cost values is necessary to get at the real profitability of an enterprise. Ignoring significant fixed costs may result in erroneous decisions. The major consideration in allocating fixed costs is to be consistent from one enterprise to the next. Items like machinery ownership costs, building and facilities ownership costs, a return to land, and a portion of annual farm overhead costs are normally included in fixed costs. Fixed labor, either family or hired, may also be charged here.

Subtracting labor, capital, and land costs from income over variable costs gives an estimate of income over all costs on a per unit basis. The return estimate is sometimes referred to as the *return to management and risk*.

MORE THAN ONE BUDGET PER ENTERPRISE

There are a number of ways (sometimes called processes) of managing any enterprise to get the desired end product or output. An example is the beef cow-calf enterprise, wherein the desired output is a marketable stocker calf. However, the calf may be calved in the fall or spring. It may receive creep feed or it may not. The cow may be wintered on high quality roughage or dry grass and protein supplement. Thus, the set of production practices followed—the process—defines the specific characteristics of the cow-calf enterprise.

An enterprise budget is constructed to summarize the costs and returns expected for a particular set of production practices. Consequently, there can be as many budgets for an enterprise as there are logical combinations of production practices. Each enterprise budget would be analogous to a point on a production function (or production surface, depending upon the number of practices varied). This can be illustrated with creep feeding (see Exhibit 11–2). The graph assumes all production practices are identical, with the exception of creep feeding. Suppose the two points on the production function considered are points A and B. Point A is equivalent to no creep feeding. Point B is one of many possible creep feeding levels. The corresponding enterprise budgets are shown in Exhibit 11–3. The differences in the two budgets are (1) level of output, i.e., pounds of live calf marketed per cow; (2) amount and cost of creep feed; (3) slight differences in operating and ownership capital requirements per cow; and (4) slight differences in labor requirements (it takes only a short time to set up a creep feeder and keep it replenished with feed).

PURPOSE OF BUDGET INFLUENCES CONTENT

The use to which an enterprise budget is put will influence its construction. Some managers are interested in annual cash flow so they want to know how much the direct (out-of-pocket) cost will be to get a certain

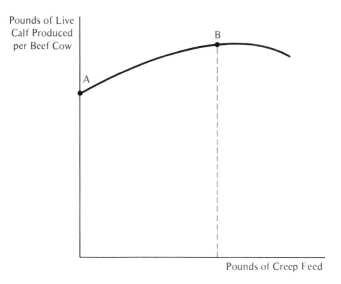

Exhibit 11–2. Two points on a production function used as a basis for enterprise budget construction.

level of output. The variable costs are the most important, with fixed costs of lesser significance, at least in the short run.

A crop producer may separate preharvest and harvest-related costs because of a need to decide between the use of a crop for grain or forage. Separating out costs by use period also assists in planning operating capital needs.

Other planners want enterprise budgets to reflect all costs. Such a budget would be particularly relevant for a manager trying to assess the long-term profitability of a particular farm plan or a new investment like an irrigation system or livestock feeding facility.

The trends in costs must be carefully considered so that cost estimates reflect the appropriate future conditions, such as the consequences of inflation and changing input supply-demand conditions.

Earlier discussion has stressed the importance of realistic estimates for prices and production. The chapter on partial budgeting discussed the value of using different coefficients depending on the planning horizon. The same considerations apply in the development of enterprise budgets.

Prices and output (yield, gain) are probably more difficult to predict than costs. As a result, when developing enterprise budgets for use in *planning that extends beyond the current year*, it is common to use long-term average prices and yields and adjust them for any prevalent trends. For example, if livestock prices have just been through the down phase of a price cycle but appear to be "turning around," a manager-planner may

Exhibit 11–3. Beef cow-calf; fall calving; 90% calf crop; replacements saved; calf sold in August; creep feeding vs. no creep feeding

Budget item	Creep-fed	Not creep-fed
Production		
Calves sold	$354.50	$345.25
(.75 calves per cow)		
Cows sold	53.00	53.00
(.15 cows per year)		
Gross receipts	$407.50	$398.25
Variable Inputs		
Grain	31.00	21.00
Protein	21.00	20.00
Hay	64.00	64.00
Pasture	76.50	76.50
Machinery and equipment	15.00	15.00
Vet and medicine	6.00	6.00
Breeding charge	5.00	5.00
Marketing and transportation	14.00	14.00
Interest on operating costs	18.40	18.00
Miscellaneous costs	12.00	12.00
Total variable costs	$261.90	$250.50
Income above variable costs	$145.60	$147.75
Labor	8.0 hours	7.5 hours

use higher prices than the average of recent years. Similarly, if average crop yields have been unduly affected by unusual weather or pests, the yield value used in the enterprise budget can be adjusted to reflect more normal conditions.

Managers preparing enterprise budgets for *short-run planning* (this year) should use prices and yields that are expected to prevail—after getting the best outlook information available. If current prices are consistent with supply-demand and cost relationships, or if government programs are setting a floor under prices, the manager should be able to develop reasonably accurate short-term price projections.

Of course, at times it will be very difficult to project either short- or long-run values. Then it is wise to develop several sets of budgets based upon the manager's judgment of the set of events most likely to prevail. The manager can compare the different budgets and choose the one most consistent with his perception of the future and the productive capacity of the farm/ranch business.

TIPS ON OBTAINING DATA FOR ENTERPRISE BUDGETS

A manager-planner would like to have enterprise budgets that closely represent the average situation he expects to encounter. However, to develop a large number of enterprise budgets is a time-consuming and costly process. In fact, to develop specific budgets for a particular farm based upon actual experience would require several years data on the crop and livestock enterprises of interest. Even then, the data would be limited to enterprises that had been included on the farm in the past.

Fortunately, there are alternatives to developing everything from scratch. Data are available to managers from a number of sources. For example, formal *input-output research studies* have been and are being done by researchers in government, at universities, and in industry. Reported in special bulletins, government reports, and the popular media, these studies frequently collect their enterprise data from nearby experiment farms or from experiments run on operating farms. The farm manager may need to adjust the research data for differences in soil type, climate, or special production techniques used in the experiments.

Summaries of *surveys* of operating farmers are another useful data source. Although these data give a benchmark of current practices and associated production, they frequently do not reflect what is possible using the latest technology and management practices. Such surveys are regularly reported in extension service publications, trade publications, and the popular media.

Farm *record data*, summarized annually in many states and areas within states, are extremely valuable in obtaining representative coefficients to use in enterprise budgets. These records permit a manager to check research results against what good farmers are really doing. For example, based upon feeding trials, the production scientists may determine feed requirements for various classes of livestock. However, because the requirements were developed under controlled conditions, they may underestimate the actual requirements of an operating feeder. Record data from area farms with top management may be the most useful information a manager can get.

Prepared budgets are another possibility. Extension and vocational agricultural farm management specialists, as well as commercial farm management services, have sets of representative budgets for the common enterprises in an area. These budgets are often available for the asking and are frequently updated annually. Generally developed by professional specialists, these enterprise budgets represent their "best educated guess" based on knowledge of research results, experience and observation, and sound judgment. The operating manager can modify these budgets, often with the advice of a competent professional, to closely represent his expected situation.

The Firm Enterprise Data Systems (FEDS) Budgets

The Economic Research Service of USDA has initiated a systematic approach to the development and maintenance of farm enterprise budgets. Known as FEDS (Firm Enterprise Data Systems) budgets, this system got its impetus from the Agricultural and Consumer Protection Act of 1973, which requires USDA to keep up-to-date estimates on the cost of producing certain commodities.

The FEDS budgets represent the average current technology being used in crop and livestock enterprises by sub-areas within every state. There are some 1,000 individual crop budgets and nearly 500 livestock budgets. Prices and yields are updated annually.

Copies of the FEDS budgets are available from each state university, generally an agricultural economics department, and certain USDA agencies in each state. Sample FEDS budgets are included in Exhibits 11–4 through 11–6.

The FEDS budgets are comprehensive. They not only summarize estimated costs and returns but, in the case of livestock, also estimate the investment. Exhibit 11–4 is a FEDS budget for a 200-cow ranching operation in the northern Great Plains. The 1980 nonland investment was projected to be $286,536, or $1,345 per cow unit. Weaned calf percentage was 72 percent. Prices would be considered on the high end of the scale.

The budget shows income above variable costs to be a plus $197.48 per cow. However, the fixed capital and land costs total $402.77. The net result is a minus $205.29 return above all costs. These data would suggest that the rancher who has most land paid for would have a positive cash flow (although the return to land would be less than 1 percent), but the highly leveraged young rancher is likely to be in for bad times—if this budget is representative of his situation.

Exhibits 11–5 and 11–6 illustrate the type of information available in FEDS crop budgets. Note that operating costs are separated into preharvest and harvest costs.

MORE THAN DOLLARS AND CENTS

Enterprises, like resources, have peculiar characteristics and management demands. Average costs and returns are only part of the data needed for evaluating them. Some enterprises have high labor demands; others have high capital demands. Some enterprises require large amounts of purchased inputs; others do not. Some enterprises give rapid capital turn-

Exhibit 11–4. A sample FEDS livestock budget.

TITLE: REGION 2: COW - YEARLING BUDGET -- HERDS 200-499 HEAD (GP-2)   1979

```
--------------------------------------------------------------------------------
1. INVESTMENT SUMMARY                        CURRENT REPLACEMENT    AVERAGE ACQUISITION
                                              TOTAL      PER UNIT    TOTAL      PER UNIT
        LIVESTOCK                          155423.94      729.69  155423.94      729.69
        EQUIPMENT                           52719.19      247.51   20188.61       94.78
       *TRACTORS AND TRUCKS                 31200.00      146.48   21028.80       98.73
       *OTHER MACHINERY                     52435.00      246.17   35341.19      165.92
     TOTAL                                 286536.37     1345.24  226740.75     1064.51
     (*FULL INVESTMENT COST - ITEMS MAY SERVE MULTIPLE ENTERPRISES)
--------------------------------------------------------------------------------
```

2. PRODUCTION	UNITS	QUANTITY	WEIGHT	PRICE	VALUE/UNIT	VALUE	VALUE/ PRODUCTION UNIT
STEER CALVES	HD.	47.00	4.63	96.44	446.52	20986.30	
HEIFER CALVES	HD.	13.00	4.49	85.75	385.02	5005.23	
FEEDER STEERS	HD.	35.00	6.92	83.30	576.44	20175.26	
FEEDER HEIFERS	HD.	17.00	6.27	75.73	474.83	8072.06	
CULL COWS	HD.	36.00	9.80	48.35	473.83	17057.88	
TOTAL RECEIPTS						71296.69	334.73

3. VARIABLE COSTS	UNITS	NUMBER OF UNITS	PRICE	VALUE	COST/ PRODUCTION UNIT
PRIVATE RANGE	ACRE	3177.0	0.0	C.0	0.0
PAST. RENT/LEASE	ACRE	1637.0	0.97	1587.89	7.45
CROP RESIDUE	ACRE	239.0	0.0	0.0	0.0
PUB GRAZ-BLM	AM	315.0	1.89	595.35	2.80
PUB GRAZ/FOREST	AM	71.0	2.03	144.13	0.68
PUB GRAZ-STATE	AM	58.0	1.55	89.90	0.42
GRAZING ASSOC.	AM	321.0	6.45	2070.45	9.72
HAY (PROD.)	TN.	277.0	26.34	7296.18	34.25
HAY (PURCH.)	TN.	31.0	54.50	1689.50	7.93
PROTEIN SUPP.	CWT.	14.5	10.43	151.24	0.71
GRAIN (PROD.)	TN.	4.3	102.07	438.90	2.06
GRAIN (PURCH.)	TN.	5.8	101.28	587.42	2.76
SALT & MINERALS	CWT.	77.0	7.61	585.97	2.75
VET & MED	DOL.	850.7	1.00	850.70	3.99
TRUCKING	DOL.	408.4	1.00	408.40	1.92
MARKETING	DOL.	6.4	1.00	6.37	0.03
HIRED LABOR	HR.	871.1	3.29	2865.92	13.46
FAMILY LABOR	HR.	1108.3	3.29	3646.31	17.12
MACH FUEL & LUBE				2342.12	11.00
MACHINERY REPAIR				2078.55	9.75
EQUP FUEL & LUBE				246.84	1.16
EQUIP REPAIR				803.93	3.77
INTEREST ON OPER CAPITAL	DOL.	7121.51	0.10	747.76	3.51
TOTAL VARIABLE COSTS				29233.80	137.25

```
--------------------------------------------------------------------------------
4. INCOME ABOVE VARIABLE COSTS                             42062.89      197.48
--------------------------------------------------------------------------------
5. OWNERSHIP COSTS (REPLACEMENT, TAXES,
      INTEREST, AND INSURANCE)
        MACHINERY                                           6137.66       28.82
        EQUIPMENT                                           3849.43       18.07
        LIVESTOCK                                          19522.48       91.65
        LAND TAXES                                          2959.23       13.89
     TOTAL OWNERSHIP COSTS                                 32468.80      152.44
--------------------------------------------------------------------------------
6. OTHER COSTS
        LAND CHARGE (LAND PRICE)                           47779.30      224.32
        GEN FARM OVERHEAD                                   1336.00        6.27
        MANAGEMENT CHARGE ( 7.00% OF TC-LAND-PURCH. LVSK)   4205.55       19.74
     TOTAL OTHER COSTS                                     53320.86      250.33
--------------------------------------------------------------------------------
7. TOTAL OF ABOVE COSTS                                   115023.37      540.02
--------------------------------------------------------------------------------
8. RETURN TO RISK                                         -43726.69     -205.29
--------------------------------------------------------------------------------
```

FOOTNOTE: WEANING RATE 72%, REPLACEMENT RATE 19%,   04/01/77
           YEARLINGS AS % OF FEEDER SALES 46%,   KERRY GEE
           COWS/BULL 18, SUPP FEEDS AS % OF TOTAL 32%,   10/15/80
           PRIVATE RANGE AS % OF TOTAL FEED 44%,
           CATTLE PRICES AS REPORTED AT OMAHA,
           GRAIN PRICE IS SEASONAL AVG FOR OATS IN S.D.

```
        ENTERPRISE CODE: 119000004        MACHINERY COMPLEMENT NO.  8
        AREA CODE  _2/30/_0/_0            EQUIPMENT COMPLEMENT NO.  8
        FILE NO.  56                      PARAMETER SET 30
        HEAD REPRESENTED  319.5 (000)     EDITION NO.  0
        PRODUCTION UNIT DIVISOR   213.    NAME SET 2
        LAND CHARGE METHOD  2             INTEREST CHARGE METHOD 21000
        LAG-PERMANENT STRUCT 20           LAG-OTHER EQUIPMENT  4
DATE PRINTED:
```

211

Exhibit 11-5. A sample FEDS crop budget.

PREPARED BY FIRM ENTERPRISE DATA SYSTEM, NATIONAL ECONOMICS DIVISION, ESS IN COOPERATION WITH OKLAHOMA STATE UNIVERSITY, STILLWATER, OKLA. FEDS BUDGETS ARE PREPARED FOR RESEARCH PURPOSES AND ARE NOT OFFICIAL USDA ESTIMATES OF PRODUCTION COSTS.

TITLE: SOYBEANS - OHIO - AREA 100   1979

	UNIT	PRICE OR COST/UNIT	QUANTITY	VALUE OR COST PER ACRE	COST PER UNIT OF PRODUCTION
1. GROSS RECEIPTS FROM PRODUCTION:					
SOYBEANS	BU.	6.250	36.800	230.00	
TOTAL RECEIPTS				230.00	
2. VARIABLE COSTS:					
PREHARVEST:					
HERBICIDE	ACRE	13.570	1.000	13.57	0.37
HERBICIDE APPL.	ACRE	3.000	0.050	0.15	0.00
SEED	LBS.	0.165	64.900	10.71	0.29
NITROGEN	LBS.	0.163	5.500	0.90	0.02
PHOSPHATE	LBS.	0.189	26.300	4.97	0.14
POTASH	LBS.	0.093	30.800	2.86	0.08
LIME	TN.	8.390	0.080	0.67	0.02
FERTILIZER APPL.	ACRE	1.950	0.110	0.21	0.01
TRACTOR FUEL & LUBE	ACRE			4.99	0.14
TRACTOR REPAIRS	ACRE			2.12	0.06
MACH FUEL & LUBE	ACRE			1.51	0.04
MACH REPAIRS	ACRE			2.24	0.06
MACHINERY LABOR	HRS	3.730	2.260	8.43	0.23
OTHER LABOR	HRS	3.730	0.600	2.24	0.06
INTEREST ON OP. CAP.	DOLS	0.106	23.816	2.52	0.07
TOTAL PREHARVEST				58.10	1.58
HARVEST:					
CUST COMB & HAUL	ACRE	15.100	0.180	2.72	0.07
MACH FUEL & LUBE	ACRE			2.05	0.06
MACH REPAIRS	ACRE			1.84	0.05
MACHINERY LABOR	HRS	3.730	0.657	2.45	0.07
INTEREST ON OP. CAP.	DOLS	0.106	0.0	0.0	0.0
TOTAL HARVEST				9.06	0.25
TOTAL VARIABLE COSTS				67.16	1.82
3. INCOME ABOVE VARIABLE COSTS				162.84	4.43
4. OWNERSHIP COSTS (REPLACEMENT, TAXES, INTEREST, INS.)					
TRACTORS				6.86	0.19
MACHINERY				23.08	0.63
TOTAL OWNERSHIP COSTS				29.94	0.81
5. OTHER COSTS					
LAND CHARGE (SHARE RENT)				96.62	2.63
GEN FARM OVERHEAD				7.94	0.22
MANAGEMENT CHARGE (10.0% OF TC-LAND)				10.50	0.29
TOTAL OTHER COSTS				115.06	3.13
6. TOTAL OF ABOVE COSTS				212.16	5.77
7. RETURN TO RISK				17.84	0.48

Exhibit 11–6. A sample FEDS specialty crop budget.

PREPARED BY FIRM ENTERPRISE DATA SYSTEM, NATIONAL ECONOMICS DIVISION, ESS IN COOPERATION
WITH OKLAHOMA STATE UNIVERSITY, STILLWATER, OKLA. FEDS BUDGETS ARE PREPARED FOR RESEARCH
PURPOSES AND ARE NOT OFFICIAL USDA ESTIMATES OF PRODUCTION COSTS.

TITLE: ALFALFA HAY MICHIGAN - ENTIRE STATE   1979
   HARVESTED FOR HAY ONLY

	UNIT	PRICE OR COST/UNIT	QUANTITY	VALUE OR COST PER ACRE	COST PER UNIT OF PRODUCTION
1. GROSS RECEIPTS FROM PRODUCTION:					
ALFALFA	TN.	42.380	3.100	131.38	
TOTAL RECEIPTS				131.38	
2. VARIABLE COSTS:					
PREHARVEST:					
SEED	LBS.	2.160	4.080	8.81	2.84
NITROGEN	LBS.	0.201	12.000	2.41	0.78
PHOSPHATE	LBS.	0.190	32.000	6.08	1.96
POTASH	LBS.	0.093	75.000	6.97	2.25
BORON	LBS.	0.230	1.000	0.23	0.07
LIME	TN.	8.390	0.022	0.18	0.06
CHEMICALS	ACRE	0.760	1.000	0.76	0.25
TRACTOR FUEL & LUBE	ACRE			1.10	0.35
TRACTOR REPAIRS	ACRE			0.44	0.14
MACH FUEL & LUBE	ACRE			1.24	0.40
MACH REPAIRS	ACRE			0.91	0.29
MACHINERY LABOR	HRS	3.700	1.051	3.89	1.25
INTEREST ON OP. CAP.	DOLS	0.106	9.360	0.99	0.32
TOTAL PREHARVEST				34.03	10.98
HARVEST:					
BALER TWINE-WIRE	BL.	14.100	0.270	3.81	1.23
TRACTOR FUEL & LUBE	ACRE			7.04	2.27
TRACTOR REPAIRS	ACRE			2.06	0.67
MACH FUEL & LUBE	ACRE			0.30	0.10
MACH REPAIRS	ACRE			3.66	1.18
MACHINERY LABOR	HRS	3.700	2.724	10.08	3.25
INTEREST ON OP. CAP.	DOLS	0.106	5.197	0.55	0.18
TOTAL HARVEST				27.50	8.87
TOTAL VARIABLE COSTS				61.53	19.85
3. INCOME ABOVE VARIABLE COSTS				69.85	22.53
4. OWNERSHIP COSTS (REPLACEMENT, TAXES, INTEREST, INS.)					
TRACTORS				8.09	2.61
MACHINERY				16.84	5.43
TOTAL OWNERSHIP COSTS				24.92	8.04
5. OTHER COSTS					
LAND CHARGE (CASH RENT)				21.77	7.02
GEN FARM OVERHEAD				6.93	2.24
MANAGEMENT CHARGE (10.0% OF TC-LAND)				9.34	3.01
TOTAL OTHER COSTS				38.04	12.27
6. TOTAL OF ABOVE COSTS				124.49	40.16
7. RETURN TO RISK				6.89	2.22

213

over; others take several years. Exhibit 11–7 summarizes some of the peculiar characteristics of a few popular enterprises. The relationships are somewhat arbitrary, and some enterprises fare better in certain geographical areas than others.

When trying to decide for which enterprises budgets should be constructed, a manager should develop comparisons like the ones presented in Exhibit 11–7. The process of accumulating the basic data and the analysis which goes into developing the comparisons contributes to logical decision making. While developing a comparison like Exhibit 11–7, for example, a decision maker might uncover data like that presented in Exhibit 11–8. The fluctuation in income above variable costs over time is not likely to be reflected in an enterprise budget developed for "average" conditions, but it is a very important factor to most managers. Sensitivity analysis was discussed in Chapter 9. It is one means to evaluate the potential impacts of income fluctuations upon a business.

COMMENTS ON ENTERPRISE BUDGETS

Obviously, a manager must use time economically in developing enterprise budgets. Sets of feasible budgets will vary from farm to farm and from region to region, but a manager should be careful to include all relevant budgets. Ignoring an enterprise because no one else in the community has it may be a serious management error. Recognizing oppor-

Exhibit 11–7. Some comparative factors for selected enterprises

	Hogs	Beef feeding	Beef cows	Dairy	Crops
Management					
Buying and selling	Avg.	Most difficult	Easy	Avg.	Avg. to Difficult
Feeding and handling	Difficult	Difficult	Easy	Difficult	—
Disease control	Difficult	Avg.	Easy	Avg.	Easy
Pest control	Avg.	Easy	Easy	Avg.	Difficult
Labor	High	Avg.	Low	High	Avg.
Investment	Avg.	High	High	Low	Avg.
Cash Flow	Good	Avg.	Poor	Excellent	Avg.
Income Variability	Avg.	High	Avg.	Low	Avg.
Return to Capital and Management	High	Avg.	Poor	Avg.	Avg. to High
Land Area/Return	Low	Low	Highest	High	Medium

Exhibit 11–8. Relative profitability of livestock enterprises
Midwest, recent ten-year period

Profit odds	Farrow-to-finish hogs	Fed cattle	Dairy	Beef cows
High Return	30%	20%	20%	20%
Average Return	30%	10%	40%	30%
Breakeven	10%	20%	20%	10%
Loss	10%	20%	10%	30%
Serious Loss	20%	30%	10%	10%

SOURCE: Farm Records Summaries from Illinois, Iowa and Missouri.

tunities is still an important management function. Conversely, relying only on budgets as a basis for decisions may be unwise. As was illustrated in Exhibit 11-7, there are enterprise factors other than average costs and returns which managers should consider.

Finally, a word of caution. It is common to think one can do better than average. Every manager should try; some succeed. However, a manager should not assume that he/she can always do a better job than others.

Here are some examples of "myths" in management planning and budget construction to watch out for: (1) 100 percent calf crop—only the superior managers consistently wean as high as 95 percent; (2) all animals weaned are sold—this, too, is unusual, as replacements must be kept or the breeding herd will be depleted in a few years; (3) all acres planted are harvested—harvested acreage is frequently 5 to 15 percent less than planted acreage; (4) 200 bushel corn or 60 bushel wheat—some farmers do much better in a given year, but are not likely to keep it up year in and year out; (5) a cow carried year-round on two acres; and (6) one pig finished on 8 bushels of grain.

SUMMARY

Farm management is more than deciding whether to be a crop farmer or livestock farmer/rancher, or some combination thereof. A decision maker should have good data upon which to base the decisions. Basic to selecting a farm plan or choosing between farming systems is (1) thorough knowledge of the available resources and their capability and (2) accurate data on feasible enterprises that might be combined to use the resources profitably. This chapter has suggested:

• Profitable decisions about resource use presuppose good data on alternative enterprises that might use the resources.

• Enterprise budgets are the building blocks for economic planning and analysis on farms. These budgets contain basic cost and returns data and are built upon realistic estimates of feasible input-output relationships.

• There are other enterprise characteristics like income variability, labor requirements, and capital demands which influence (a) the decision of which enterprise to budget and (b) choice between enterprises.

Succeeding chapters discuss tools and techniques for (1) developing whole farm organization comparisons, (2) selecting optimal farm/ranch plans, and (3) developing investment strategies using enterprise budgets as the data base.

APPLYING THE PRINCIPLES OF CHAPTER 11

Multiple Choice

_____ 1. An enterprise budget contains:
(a) the amount of resources available for use by the manager
(b) variable production inputs, and their costs, for an activity
(c) predicted total annual profits for the farm or ranch
(d) a plan for reorganizing a farm

_____ 2. An enterprise has more than one budget because:
(a) managers differ in their knowledge of alternative practices
(b) different managers prefer different practices
(c) a number of production processes produce similar results
(d) no manager uses the same production practices year after year

Sample Enterprise Budgets

Using the following information, prepare a simplified enterprise budget. (Not all of the items in Exhibit 11–1 will appear in this budget.)

Corn Silage, 70 percent moisture, yielding 13 tons per acre.

Price per ton = $15.00.

Seed: 20,000 per acre required @ $0.50 per 1,000

Fertilizer:
anhydrous N: 120 lb/acre @ $0.15/lb.
dry N: 20 lb/acre @ $0.20/lb.

P_2O_5:   50 lb/acre @ \$0.20/lb.
K_2O: 110 lb/acre @ \$0.10/lb.
lime application @ \$2.50/acre

Crop chemicals and supplies	\$14.00/acre
Custom machine hire	2.00/acre
Machinery: fuel, oil, and repairs	19.00/acre
Miscellaneous	5.00/acre
Effective operating capital	
interest rate = 9%	24.44/acre
Ownership costs	25.00
Land charges (rent or interest)	45.00/acre
Wage rate	4.00/hour
labor required = 8.5 hours/acre	
Return to management from	
gross receipts	7 percent

REFERENCES

Allison, John R. *Beef Production in Georgia: Resource Used and Operator Characteristics,* Georgia Agricultural Experiement Station Research Bulletin 134, February 1974.

Castle, Emery N., *et al. Farm Business Management,* 2nd ed. New York: The Macmillan Co., 1972.

Forster, D. L. and B. L. Ervin. *Foundations for Managing the Farm Business.* Columbus, Ohio: Grid Publishing, Inc., 1981.

Hedges, Trimble. *Farm Management Decisions.* Englewood Cliffs, N.J.: Prentice-Hall, Inc., 1963.

Justus, Fred E., Jr. and A. I. Overall. "Studying Financial Performance of Dairy Enterprises." *Journal of American Society of Farm Managers and Rural Appraisers,* April 1975, pp. 26–30.

Lanpher, Buel F. "Management and Policy Implications of Cost and Returns Budgets: Extensions Role in Formulation and Use," *Southern Journal of Agricultural Economics,* July 1975, pp. 27–32.

Mueller, A. G. and R. A. Hinton. "Farmer Production Costs for Corn and Soybeans by Unit Size," *American Journal of Agricultural Economics,* December 1975, pp. 934–39.

Purdue University Extension Staff. *Farm Planning and Financial Management,* Purdue University Cooperative Extension Manual ID-68, 1975.

Williams, Ed and D. E. Farris. *Budgeted Costs and Returns of Fifteen Cattle Feeding Systems,* Texas A & M Agricultural Experiment Station Bulletin MP-1022, February 1972.

Whole-Farm/Ranch Planning

- Purpose of whole-farm planning—to identify high-profit plans
- Select cropping system before selecting livestock
- Necessity of modifying crop plans to ensure usage of fixed livestock facilities
- Farm plan must be feasible as well as profitable
- Feasible farm plan provides sufficient earnings to meet debt-servicing requirements
- Basic planning rule for identifying profitable plans

12

Whole-farm planning is concerned with total resource use within the farm business, in contrast to analyses of only part of a business or simple investment decisions. The purpose of whole-farm planning is to identify high-profit plans that are consistent with farm business goals and also to determine possible constraints that confront the manager.

Farm planning is simply charting a course from where one is to where one wants to go. The procedures and techniques involve the logical formulation of a blueprint or guide to achieve selected goals that have been set for the business. The purpose of whole-farm planning, given specific goals and resource limitations (real or self-imposed), is to select a combination of enterprises that maximizes utility (usually income) from the resources over a given planning horizon.

A couple of points about whole-farm planning are emphasized:

1. Farm planning is "forward planning." It involves the formulation of expectations about the future—particularly input-output relationships, product prices, and costs of production.

2. Farm planning serves only as a guide to decision making. Its value lies in providing a comparison among alternative courses of action and in developing a logical and systematic procedure to carry out the chosen course.

Block budgeting, a systematic approach to farm plan evaluation, is used. Planning worksheets are provided to help a manager or business analyst systematically identify and consider resource requirements and returns associated with alternative plans.

The discussion in Chapter 9 pointed out that there will likely be occasions when the consequences and complexity of some problem will dictate a complete analysis of a business. That is, there are some decisions that are so crucial, they affect the entire course of the business. For example, a young person who has been working regularly off-farm and farming part-time must at some point ask the question: Am I satisfied with my current situation or should I go into full-time farming/ranching? Answering that question requires a thorough analysis.

In this chapter the emphasis is on the whole-farm budgeting method, which uses the systematic approach sometimes referred to as "block budgeting." In Chapter 9 we discussed the partial budgeting technique for analyzing changes in only a portion of the farm/ranch business. Computerized methods of farm planning are also available. One computer method, linear programming, is discussed in the next chapter.

BLOCK BUDGETING

Block budgeting is a means of analyzing a total business and comparing the economic consequences of alternative plans. An important strength of the method is its simplicity. Combining enterprise "blocks" or units that contain requirements for land, labor, and capital (basic and often limiting resources) enables one to build alternative plans which are then compared. A unique feature of this process is that it enables a separate evaluation of returns from crop and livestock enterprises.

PLANNING THE CROPPING SYSTEM: GENERAL CONSIDERATIONS

The procedure for inventorying land resources was discussed in Chapter 10. Land is the basic resource and primary source of income on most farms. While livestock may account for a large part of the receipts on many farms, feed is the most important livestock input; and it is the land that produces feed.

To combine enterprises in an optimum manner, use the *planning rule: Select enterprises that yield the highest return to scarce resources* (the equimarginal principle). Land, for most farmers/ranchers in the short run, is the limiting factor of production.

Application of the planning rule suggests that returns per acre of land should be maximized in most operations. A common planning mistake, resulting in less than maximum returns, is to select livestock enterprises and then fit land use to the livestock enterprises.

Generally, decisions regarding kinds and acreages of crops or improved pasture to be grown should be made before selection of livestock. Even if it is not practical to change the present livestock operations because of a large fixed investment (dairying for example), one should first determine the most profitable cropping system. Having determined this, one tests the adaptability of the crop plan to present livestock facilities and scale of operation. However, if existing livestock facilities have multiple uses, the kinds of livestock best suited to the cropping system can be selected after the cropping system is established.

If a farm has a large fixed investment in livestock facilities, it may be necessary to tailor crop production to accommodate use of the facilities.

The goal is to maximize returns to all resources, and "value in use" for some fixed resources may exceed any salvage value. This means that returns to numerous variable inputs associated with use of fixed resources exceed that of any alternative use.

If cropland is available, highest net farm income is most likely when a farmer devotes the greatest amount of land possible to high-profit crops, consistent with reasonable soil conservation. An index of this use is often referred to as the intensity of land usage (a ratio of land in high profit crops/forages to total land).

PLANNING THE SELECTION OF LIVESTOCK ENTERPRISES: GENERAL CONSIDERATIONS

A number of factors influence the selection of livestock enterprises for farms. In many parts of the country, livestock is the sole means of utilizing land resources; in some geographical areas grazing may be the only profitable means of harvesting produce of the land. In other areas a combination of livestock and crops may provide the greatest net farm income, although livestock enterprises provide the major portion of farm income.

Resources required for livestock production vary widely, in terms of both fixed and variable inputs. Factors that should be considered in selecting livestock enterprises are:

1. Amounts of grain and forage crops produced in the cropping system or available in the area
2. Regularity and stability of net income
3. Amount and distribution of available labor
4. Distribution of labor requirements for livestock during the year as compared to labor requirements for crops
5. Skill and personal preferences of the manager
6. Available markets (especially for poultry, milk, and eggs)
7. Capital requirements and rapidity of capital turnover

The main purpose of a livestock enterprise, where land resources are suited to a number of crop and livestock enterprise uses, is to increase farm income. Over the long run, livestock enterprises would be expected to increase incomes, when they:

1. Provide a market or use of pastures and other forages (particularly crop residue) that otherwise would not be marketed;
2. Provide year-round employment to the farmer and his family members; and

3. Provide higher returns to grain and forage production by marketing the crops through livestock.

PUTTING THE PLAN TOGETHER

The following planning procedure—step by step—is suggested:

Step 1: Establish general goals.

Step 2: Inventory resources.

Step 3: Establish more specific goals.

Step 4: Identify and itemize major problems.

Step 5: Summarize investment capital.

Step 6: Summarize the selected cropping system.

Step 7: Summarize the livestock system, if any.

Step 8: Summarize and evaluate the income and profitability of the plan.

Step 9: Evaluate the economic feasibility of the plan from the standpoint of cash flow and resource availability.

Step 10: Compare the results of the alternative plans and choose one for long-term development.

Steps 1 through 4 provide background information and a basis for evaluating and comparing all plans developed. They need not be repeated for each alternative farm plan except as they influence the capital investments required, as summarized in Exhibit 12–1.

Steps 1 through 3 were discussed in previous chapters. At that time, work forms were provided for evaluating and itemizing land and labor resource availability in a systematic fashion.

Steps 5 through 9 should be completed for each alternative to be compared. Usually, the present plan of operation is evaluated first using the budgets and technology level selected for evaluating all alternative plans.

Step 10 is one of decision making, comparing the various alternatives and selecting the one to be implemented.

THE PRESENT-NORMAL SITUATION

Once goals have been established and resources inventoried, a manager needs to determine the normal profitability of the current operation. This can be done with a present-normal plan which summarizes the "average," or normal, results expected from enterprise combinations that the

Exhibit 12–1.

FARM INVESTMENT CAPITAL

Present Plan ✓
Alternative No. _____

	Item & description	Year to invest	New cost	Average value[1]	Total value
	(1)		(2)	(3)	(4)
1	Breeding livestock (present or alternative):				
2	Cows _____ (units) x $ _____ /unit =			$	
3	Sows _____ (units) x $ _____ /unit =				
4	Other _____ (units) x $ _____ /unit =				
5	TOTAL BREEDING LIVESTOCK CAPITAL (sum Lines 2, 3, 4)				$
6	Machinery & equipment (present)			$ 40,000	
7	Added machinery & equipment:[2]				
8			$	$	
9					
10					
11					
12					
13	TOTAL MACHINERY & EQUIPMENT CAPITAL (sum Lines 6, 8, 9, 10, 11, 12)				$ 40,000
14	Buildings & facilities (present)			$ 16,000	
15	Added buildings & facilities:[2]				
16			$		
17					
18					
19					
20	TOTAL BUILDING & FACILITIES CAPITAL (sum Lines 14, 16, 17, 18, 19)				$ 16,000
21	Land & land improvements (present)[3] _320_ ac. x $ _1200_ /acre =			$ 384,000	
22	Added land & land improvements:[2]				
23			$		
24					
25	TOTAL LAND & LAND IMPROVEMENTS CAPITAL (sum Lines 21, 23, 24)				$ 384,000
26	TOTAL FARM INVESTMENT CAPITAL (sum Lines 5, 13, 20, 25)				$ 440,000

[1] Present system values for Lines 6 and 14 are depreciated values (such as those on depreciation schedule). For new machinery and equipment added in alternative system, average value equals approximately 1/2 of new cost. For new buildings, fences, and facilities added, average value equals approximately 3/4 of new cost. For non-depreciable items (such as land), average value equals new cost.

[2] Disinvestment may also be considered in alternative plan. Values of machinery, equipment, facilities, land, etc., not needed in alternative plan are entered as negative figures in Column 3.

[3] Does not include value of dwelling, farm buildings, fences, and facilities.

manager has previously operated. The present-normal plan is not meant to represent the plan of any single year, but is an average plan over the most recent three to five years. Such a plan would provide a "benchmark" for comparison with alternative (new) plans.

The Jones Farm

As a means of illustrating the whole-farm planning procedure—and use of the planning worksheets—a hypothetical Jones farm will be used. The present-normal Jones farming operation consists of 320 acres. Three hundred acres of Class I land can be used for intensive row cropping. Jones has been growing corn. The remaining 20 acres is wasteland and farmstead.

Farm improvements consist of a 20,000-bushel shelled corn facility, a machine shed, and a farm dwelling. All tillage and harvesting equipment, valued at $40,000, is owned by the Jones family. Note the entries on Exhibit 12–1 (present plan) for each of these capital items.

Investment Capital Worksheet

Use the Farm Capital form (Exhibit 12–1) to estimate the farm investment capital for the present plan (and for each alternative plan considered). *Farm investment capital* is defined as the average value of intermediate and long-term owned farm assets. Current farm assets (inventories of market livestock, feed, crops, etc.) *are not* included as farm investment capital.

Average value of breeding livestock units includes investment in the breeding animal (sow, cow, etc.) plus the share of sire and replacement animal per unit. Average value for machinery, equipment, buildings, land, and the like, is explained in footnote 1 of the table. The total values (line 26, column 4) are transferred to the farm plan evaluation form (Exhibit 12–2).

The Cropping System

Exhibit 12–3 is a systematic means for summarizing the expected outcome associated with the normal cropping plan. It is used to calculate total income over variable costs, labor hours, and farm feed production for the cropping system. In conjunction with development of Exhibit 12–3, the following procedure is suggested:

1. Complete a farm map (an aerial photo map with acreage calculations would also suffice). Developing a cropping system and a field layout plan go hand in hand. A good place to start in developing a long-run cropping system is to evaluate the productivity of the present system.

Exhibit 12–2.

SUMMARY: CAPITAL, LABOR, INCOME, & RETURNS

Present Plan ✓
Alternative No. _____

	Item (1)	Details (2)	Totals (3)
	FARM INVESTMENT CAPITAL:		
1	Breeding Livestock (Form 12-1, Line 5)	$	
2	Machinery & equipment (Form 12-1, Line 13)	40,000	
3	Buildings & facilities (Form 12-1, Line 20)	16,000	
4	Land & improvements (Form 12-1, Line 25)	384,000	
5	AVERAGE FARM INVESTMENT CAPITAL (Form 12-1, Line 26)		$ 440,000
	DIRECT LABOR REQUIRED:		
6	Crop labor hours (Form 12-3, Line 20, Col. 8)	900 hrs.	
7	Livestock labor hours (Form 12-4, Line 11)	hrs.	
8	TOTAL HOURS DIRECT LABOR (sum Lines 6, 7)		900 hrs.
	INCOME OVER VARIABLE costs:		
9	Crop income over variable costs (Form 12-3, L. 20, Col. 7)	$ 32,400	
10	Livestock income over variable costs (Form 12-4, L. 14)		
11	TOTAL INCOME OVER VARIABLE COSTS (sum Lines 9 and 10)		$ 32,400
	OTHER CASH COSTS & NET CASH INCOME:[1]		
12	Hired labor: _____ no. men x $_____ /year =	$ 0	
13	Cash rent paid: _____ acres rented x $_____ /acre =	0	
14	Real estate & property taxes (es. 1% of Line 5)	4,400	
15	Building insurance & repairs (est. 3% of Line 3)	480	
16	Miscellaneous expense (est. 2% of Line 11)	648	
17	TOTAL OTHER CASH COSTS (sum Lines 12, 13, 14, 15, 16)		$ 5,528
18	NET CASH FARM INCOME (Line 11 minus Line 17)		$ 26,872
	DEPRECIATION:[1]		
19	Machinery & equipment (est. 20% of Line 2)	$ 8,000	
20	Buildings & facilities (est. 10% of Line 3)	1,600	
21	TOTAL DEPRECIATION (Line 19 + Line 20)		$ 9,600
	RETURNS:		
22	Farm profit[2] (Line 18 minus Line 21)		$ 17,272
23	Family labor & mgt. charge (est.) _____ hrs. x $_____ /hr.=	$ 6,000	
24	Return to farm investment capital (Line 22 minus Line 23)		$ 11,272
25	Rate earned on farm investment capital (L. 24 ÷ L. 5)		3.0%
26	Interest on farm investment capital (6 % of Line 5)	$ 26,400	
27	Return to family labor & management (Line 22 minus L. 26)		$ -9,128

[1] Percentage estimates are only guidelines.

[2] Estimated return to family labor, farm investment capital and management.

Exhibit 12-3.

SUMMARY: CROPPING SYSTEM

Crop & land use	Total acres[1]	PER ACRE BUDGETS Avg. yield	Income over variable costs	Hours direct labor	BUDGET TOTALS Produc- tion	Income over variable costs	Hours direct labor	FARM FEED PRODUCTION Corn equiva- lent[2]	Silage tons	Hay tons	Pasture AUM's[3]
(1)	(2)	(3)	(4)	(5)	(6) 2x3	(7) 2x4	(8) 2x5	(9)	(10)	(11)	(12)
CORN	300	100	108	3.0	30,000	32,400	900	30,000			
TOTAL CROP ACRES											
Farmstead											
Idle land											
TOTALS						32,400		30,000			

1 When land is double cropped, list first and second crops separately. Circle acreage of second crop and do not add circled figures in Col. 2.

2 To calculate corn equivalent bushels, multiply feed grain yield in Column 6 by C.E. factor (corn = 1.0, grain sorghum = .95, barley = .77, and oats = .50).

3 AUM= animal unit month.

226

2. On each field, write in the crop(s) presently on the land.

3. On Exhibit 12–3, check "Present Plan" (√) and enter in column 1 all the crops and uses of land for the current year, showing all second crops resulting from double cropping on a separate line and circle the acreage in column 2. This is a computational aid to avoid duplications in the Totals row at the bottom of the worksheet. Double-cropped acres must not be added to total acres.

4. Refer to the farm map, and total the acreage of each crop and land use and enter in column 2.

5. Select yield level appropriate for long-range planning. This could come from budgets like those presented in Chapter 11 or some other appropriate budget source.

6. Transfer per acre data directly from the selected budgets to columns 3,4, and 5 of Exhibit 12–3.

7. Complete computations on Exhibit 12–3 according to instructions.

Crops and their required land use are accounted for in columns 1 and 2. Per acre crop budget information (columns 3, 4, and 5) is used to calculate the totals (columns 6, 7, and 8). Note that interest paid on crop operating capital is part of the variable costs per acre. Per acre budgets for crops on rented land should be adjusted for yields and income over variable costs as needed. Transfer budget totals in column 6 to the appropriate farm feed totals (columns 9, 10, 11, or 12).

Compute a farm total (line 20) by adding columns 2, 7, 8, 9, 10, 11, and 12. These totals are required for additional planning and analysis. Transfer totals of columns 7 and 9 to Exhibit 12–2, lines 9 and 6, respectively. Transfer totals of columns 9, 10, 11, and 12 to livestock summary, line 8, if appropriate.

Income (gross receipts minus variable costs) derived from growing 300 acres of corn amounts to $32,400.

The cropping system of the Jones farm is relatively simple because it is being used for illustrative purposes. A normal grain farm might have 2 to 4 crops and/or forage enterprises.

Evaluating Income Levels

The test of profit power for farm organization alternatives is accomplished by the use of Exhibit 12–2. The earning power of the current system generally requires no additional investment (an exception, of course, would occur if a capital item has been completely depreciated and continued production requires investment above normal upkeep).

Farm investment capital figures are transferred from Exhibit 12–1 to Exhibit 12–2, making sure that any *added* investments—for breeding livestock, machinery, buildings, etc.—needed for a particular alternative are included in the totals before transferring to Exhibit 12–2. Labor requirements and income over variable costs for crop and livestock enterprises included in each alternative may be transferred directly from the cropping and livestock system summaries.

Space is provided in lines 12 through 18 of Exhibit 12–2 for computing indirect cash costs not allocated to specific crop and livestock enterprises and for computing depreciation deductions on lines 19 to 21. Farm profits and returns to labor, capital, and management can then be computed for each alternative.

The "Present" Jones Operation Summary

The highlights of Exhibit 12–2 show that farm profits were about $17,000. Subtracting a family labor and management return of $6,000 leaves a residual of $11,000 as a return to total investment capital. Imposing a required rate of return at 6 percent interest for farm investment capital, thereby letting the residual reflect labor and management return, results in a negative return.

ALTERNATIVE PLAN(S)

The present-normal plan is only one of many alternative organizational possibilities for a set of farm/ranch resources. A manager may be interested in the profit potential from other plans. In fact, the possibility of increased income is often the impetus for the planning and budgeting process.

The development of alternative plans competes with other demands on a manager's time. He is not likely, therefore, to develop more than two or three alternatives. Answers to one or more of the following questions may help him choose which alternatives to budget:

1. Are available resources used in their most profitable way? For example, are all row-crop acres planted to row crops?

2. Is volume of production adequate or is expansion needed?

3. Will expansion contribute to greater efficiency or will it require major new investments?

4. Are present livestock enterprises well suited to resources?

Developing tentative answers to these and related questions provides the basis for detecting weaknesses in the present-normal plan. It also provides insights for logical new enterprise combinations.

To be consistent, the development of alternative plans should be based upon the same general price, production, and technology assumptions as the present-normal plan. Some adjustments may be made in cases where alternative plans will allow greater efficiency or timeliness. The same set of worksheets should also be used in budgeting alternative plans.

The Jones Alternative

Harry Jones wants to determine the feasibility of adding a swine enterprise (farrowing to finish) to his farming operation. Since no livestock facilities are available, he must start from scratch in constructing farrowing, nursing, and finishing facilities.

Jones decides to consider individual farrowing houses, confinement nursery and growing, and confined finishing facilities. Estimated investment capital in the amount of $61,900 is required for these facilities. Detailed cost estimates for each facility are shown in Exhibit 12–4 (alternative farm plan). Note how (following instructions in Exhibit 12–4) averages were computed to provide a "constant" or level annual estimate for investments.

The Alternative Crop Plan

Before formulating alternative cropping plans, particular attention should be devoted to the intensity with which land is utilized, ignoring land requirements of livestock. Continuous row-cropping is the highest intensity of land use. Land capability Class I enables such row-cropping intensity because of its inherent characteristics of soil and topography that result in minimal erosion.

Many farms have acreage which has potential for higher land use classifications, hence an opportunity for more acreage devoted to higher income crops. Poorly drained bottom land, whose current highest and best use might be pasture, might easily be moved to tillable acreage (continuous) by tilling and/or land-forming activities. Rolling land subject to erosion might be terraced and brought into continuous crops with minimum soil loss.

The choice of cropping alternatives is also influenced by the expected use and disposal of crop production. If livestock enterprises are to be included in long-run plans, the kind of feed required may affect the choice of crops and pastures. As a general rule, the operation should be as nearly self-sufficient for all forage needs of livestock enterprises as possible, including pasture, hay, and silage because in many areas a reliable market for forages is not available. If hay must be transported considerable distances to meet shortages, costs increase. Whether self-sufficiency is economically feasible will depend on the alternatives and the opportunity cost involved.

After alternative cropping systems have been formulated, new sum-

Exhibit 12–4.

FARM INVESTMENT CAPITAL

Present Plan _____
Alternative No. ✓

	Item & description	Year to invest	New cost	Average value[1]	Total value
	(1)		(2)	(3)	(4)
1	Breeding livestock (present or alternative):				
2	Cows _____ (units) x $ _____ /unit =			$	
3	Sows _60_ (units) x $ _70_ /unit =			4,200	
4	Other _____ (units) x $ _____ /unit =				
5	TOTAL BREEDING LIVESTOCK CAPITAL (sum Lines 2, 3, 4)				$ 4,200
6	Machinery & equipment (present)			$ 40,000	
7	Added machinery & equipment:[2]				
8	Grinder mixer		$ 4,000	$ 2,000	
9					
10					
11					
12					
13	TOTAL MACHINERY & EQUIPMENT CAPITAL (sum Lines 6, 8, 9, 10, 11, 12)				$ 42,000
14	Buildings & facilities (present)			$ 16,000	
15	Added buildings & facilities:[2]				
16	60 Individual farrowing houses		$ 15,000	7,500	
17	Hog nursery		16,500	8,200	
18	Finishing floor + equipment		26,400	13,200	
19					
20	TOTAL BUILDING & FACILITIES CAPITAL (sum Lines 14, 16, 17, 18, 19)				$ 44,900
21	Land & land improvements (present)[3] _320_ ac. x $ _1200_ /acre =			$ 384,000	
22	Added land & land improvements:[2]				
23			$		
24					
25	TOTAL LAND & LAND IMPROVEMENTS CAPITAL (sum Lines 21, 23, 24)				$ 384,000
26	TOTAL FARM INVESTMENT CAPITAL (sum Lines 5, 13, 20, 25)				$ 475,100

[1]Present system values for Lines 6 and 14 are depreciated values (such as those on depreciation schedule). For new machinery and equipment added in alternative system, average value equals approximately 1/2 of new cost. For new buildings, fences, and facilities added, average value equals approximately 3/4 of new cost. For non-depreciable items (such as land), average value equals new cost.

[2]Disinvestment may also be considered in alternative plan. Values of machinery, equipment, facilities, land, etc., not needed in alternative plan are entered as negative figures in Column 3.

[3]Does not include value of dwelling, farm buildings, fences, and facilities.

maries should be prepared for each, with proper identification for future comparisons: Alternative A, B, C, etc. The crops, uses of land in each system, and the summary of each alternative should then be completed on Exhibit 12–5 as was done for the "present" system. For each alternative, the budget totals in columns 7 and 8 should be transferred to Exhibit 12–6 for whole farm analysis.

The revised cropping system for the alternative Jones farm plan is almost identical to the present plan. All tillable acreage is devoted to corn, with the exception of five acres required for the swine enterprise. Income from corn grown under the alternative farm plan (295 acres) is estimated at $31,860.

Livestock Worksheet

Exhibit 12–7 provides space for summarizing and evaluating each livestock system. Labor requirements, feed requirements, income, and a comparison of feed requirements to feed production from the cropping system are summarized.

The choice of enterprises to be included in *alternate livestock* systems should depend, primarily, upon the most productive and profitable cropping system if cropland is available, rather than vice versa. Livestock enterprises can often be supplementary to cropping activities. That is, livestock can be expanded with little or no reduction in output of crop enterprises.

Total farm feed required for livestock enterprises is found on line 7. Total farm feed produced (line 8) is entered from Exhibit 12–5. The difference in production and requirements (feed balance) is entered on line 9. The feed balance is a vital statistic for planning purposes.

After enterprises have been selected for alternative plans, the size of forage consuming enterprises (the number of total units in column 2 of Exhibit 12–7) can be adjusted according to the evaluation on line 9. The guideline should be to utilize fully the forage produced in the cropping system. Pasture carrying capacity in low-production periods determines the size of the enterprise. Management that increases carrying capacity in periods of low pasture yields can pay large economic dividends. Neither a surplus nor a deficit of feed grains is a problem since a market for buying and selling grains is readily available in most places.

The alternative farm plan considers adding 60 sows. The annual feed requirements expressed in corn equivalents amount to 12,000 bushels. Since almost 30,000 bushels are produced annually, over one-half of the crop will continue to be marketed as cash crop. Projected income over variable costs as the result of adding the swine enterprise amounts to $16,500 (see Exhibit 12–7).

Exhibit 12-5.

Present Plan ✓
Alternative No. _____

SUMMARY: CROPPING SYSTEM

(1) Crop & land use	(2) Total acres[1]	PER ACRE BUDGETS			BUDGET TOTALS			FARM FEED PRODUCTION			
		(3) Avg. yield	(4) Income over variable costs	(5) Hours direct labor	(6) Production	(7) Income over variable costs	(8) Hours direct labor	(9) Corn equivalent[2]	(10) Silage tons	(11) Hay tons	(12) Pasture AUM's[3]
					2x3	2x4	2x5				
CORN	245	100	108	3.0	29,500	31,860	885	29,500			
TOTAL CROP ACRES											
Farmstead											
Idle land											
TOTALS					29,500	31,860	885	29,500			

When land is double cropped, list first and second crops separately. Circle acreage of second crop and do not add circled figures in Col. 2.

To calculate corn equivalent bushels, multiply feed grain yield in Column 6 by C.E. factor (corn = 1.0, grain sorghum = .95, barley = .77, and oats = .50).

[3] AUM = animal unit month.

Exhibit 12–6.

SUMMARY: CAPITAL, LABOR, INCOME, & RETURNS

Present Plan_____
Alternative No. ✓

	Item	Details	Totals
	(1)	(2)	(3)
	FARM INVESTMENT CAPITAL:		
1	Breeding Livestock (Form 12-1, Line 5)	$ 4,200	
2	Machinery & equipment (Form 12-1, Line 13)	42,000	
3	Buildings & facilities (Form 12-1, Line 20)	44,900	
4	Land & improvements (Form 12-1, Line 25)	384,000	
5	AVERAGE FARM INVESTMENT CAPITAL (Form 12-1, Line 26)		$475,100
	DIRECT LABOR REQUIRED:		
6	Crop labor hours (Form 12-3, Line 20, Col. 8)	885 hrs.	
7	Livestock labor hours (Form 12-4, Line 11)	1680 hrs.	
8	TOTAL HOURS DIRECT LABOR (sum Lines 6, 7)		2565 hrs.
	INCOME OVER VARIABLE costs:		
9	Crop income over variable costs (Form 12-3, L. 20, Col. 7)	$31,860	
10	Livestock income over variable costs (Form 12-4, L. 14)	16,500	
11	TOTAL INCOME OVER VARIABLE COSTS (sum Lines 9 and 10)		$48,360
	OTHER CASH COSTS & NET CASH INCOME:[1]		
12	Hired labor: _____ no. men x $_____ /year =	$ 0	
13	Cash rent paid: _____ acres rented x $_____ /acre =	0	
14	Real estate & property taxes (es. 1% of Line 5)	4,751	
15	Building insurance & repairs (est. 3% of Line 3)	898	
16	Miscellaneous expense (est. 2% of Line 11)	967	
17	TOTAL OTHER CASH COSTS (sum Lines 12, 13, 14, 15, 16)		$ 6,616
18	NET CASH FARM INCOME (Line 11 minus Line 17)		$41,744
	DEPRECIATION:[1]		
19	Machinery & equipment (est. 20% of Line 2)	$ 8,400	
20	Buildings & facilities (est. 10% of Line 3)	4,490	
21	TOTAL DEPRECIATION (Line 19 + Line 20)		$12,890
	RETURNS:		
22	Farm profit[2] (Line 18 minus Line 21)		$28,854
23	Family labor & mgt. charge (est.) _____ hrs. x $_____ /hr.=	$ 7,000	
24	Return to farm investment capital (Line 22 minus Line 23)		$ 21,854
25	Rate earned on farm investment capital (L. 24 ÷ L. 5)		5
26	Interest on farm investment capital (6 % of Line 5)	$ 28,506	
27	Return to family labor & management (Line 22 minus L. 26)		$ 346

[1] Percentage estimates are only guidelines.

[2] Estimated return to family labor, farm investment capital and management.

233

Exhibit 12-7.

SUMMARY: LIVESTOCK SYSTEM

Livestock unit	Total Units	PER UNIT BUDGETS Income Over var. costs	Hours direct labor	PER UNIT FARM FEED REQUIREMENTS Corn equivalent	Silage tons	Hay tons	Pasture AUM's	BUDGET TOTALS Income over variable costs	Hours direct labor	TOTAL FARM FEED REQUIREMENTS Corn equivalent	Silage tons	Hay tons	Pasture AUM's
(1)	(2)	(3)	(4)	(5)	(6)	(7)	(8)	(9)	(10)	(11)	(12)	(13)	(14)
								2x3	2x4	2x5	2x6	2x7	2x8
60 sows	60	275	28	200				16,500	1,680	12,000			

7   Total farm feed requirements (add Cols. 11, 12, 13, and 14)   12,000

8   **Total farm feed available** (Crop-summary, Cols. 9, 10, 11, and 12)   29,500

9   Farm feed surplus (+) or shortage (−)
    (difference of Lines 7 and 8)   +17,500

10   Total Income Over Variable Costs (add Col. 9)   16,500

11   TOTAL HOURS DIRECT LABOR (add Col. 10)   1,680

12   Adjustment of Income Over Variable costs
    for Value of Surplus Pasture: −

13   If surplus pasture, multiply surplus _____ $\times$ $ \frac{(Line\ 9,\ Col.\ 14)}{\$_____/AUM} =$

    ADJUSTED TOTAL INCOME OVER VARIABLE COSTS
    (subtract Line 13 from Line 10)   16,500

The "Alternative" Jones Plan Summary

Adding the swine enterprise to the farrowing operation inreased cash farm income dramatically—$14,872 to be exact (see Exhibit 12–6 of alternative plan). The swine addition to the plan, given labor availability and feed requirements, meshes well with the grain system. Labor for the total operation, although slightly exceeding that of a one-man operation, can be handled by an operator and his family.

EVALUATION OF CASH-FLOW FEASIBILITY

After comparing the long-run profitability of various alternative farm plans, one or two may seem quite promising from the standpoint of long-run profits. In the Jones example only one alternative was considered, but many possibilities exist.

Farm reorganization, in addition to being profitable, must also be feasible. *Feasibility* requires a farm plan to generate income sufficient to meet additional debt-servicing requirements associated with added capital outlays (investment) for new enterprise combinations. Often the returns from farm organizational changes lag behind capital outlays required for those changes. This lag results in cash flow problems during the transition from the present-normal plan to the alternative plan.

For example, erection or expansion of new livestock facilities are often accompanied by undercapacity utilization because of the start-up time required. Hence, income often falls short of the expected budgets. While this could be due to mechanical and technological problems, it also may result from management limitations. The producer may still be learning the business.

Financing also significantly influences cash flow. The loan repayment schedule is often not designed to coincide with loan repayment ability. A common mistake is that of financing intermediate and long-term capital items with short-term finance schedules. Although profitable, the investments do not generate the cash flow required by debt servicing because the economic life exceeds the finance period.

Exhibit 12–8 provides a method for calculating the feasibility of a proposed plan from the standpoint of cash flow. This calculation is only an approximation because it represents only one typical year in the long-run plan. But it is a crucial first step to help identify a plan which is completely unworkable from the cash flow standpoint—of utmost importance *before* capital investments are made.

The Jones Plan Cash Flow

Exhibit 12–8 (debt repayment and available cash) shows that under any reasonable repayment plan, the swine investment of $62,000 appears feasible. Additional interest payments, when combined with servicing

Exhibit 12–8.

SUMMARY: DEBT REPAYMENT & AVAILABLE CASH
(optional)

Present Plan_____
Alternative No. ✓_____

	Item	Details	Totals
	(1)	(2)	(3)
1	Net cash farm income (Exhibit 12-6, Line 18)	$41,744	
2	Non-farm income	5,000	
3	Total net cash income (Line 1 + Line 2)		$46,744
4	Interest paid on I.T. & L.T. debts	$ 9,000	
5	Est. income tax & Social Security	5,000	
6	Family living expenses (estimate)	12,000	
7	Subtotal (sum Lines 4, 5, 6)		$26,000
8	Cash available before payments (Line 3 minus Line 7)		20,744
9	Total annual principal payments (from other records)		16,000
10	Net cash available or balance (Line 8 minus Line 9)[1]		$ 4,744

[1]May be used for replacement of capital items, new investments, and cash reserve.

debts outstanding (interest payments on principal), amount to an estimated $9,000. This leaves $20,744 available annually for principal paydown. In this example, only $16,000 was needed for principal payments.

SUMMARY

Whole-farm planning, as opposed to partial analysis, is concerned with total resource use within the farm business. The purpose of whole-farm planning is to identify high profit plans consistent with farm business goals and possible constraints that confront the manager.

1. Farm planning is "forward planning." It involves the formulation of expectations about the future—particularly input-output relationships, product prices, and costs of production.

2. Farm planning serves only as a guide in decision making. The primary value lies in providing comparisons among alternative courses of action and in developing a logical and systematic procedure to carry out a chosen course of action.

The basic planning rule for identifying profitable plans is to select enterprises and investments that yield the highest return to scarce resources. Land, for most farmer/ranches in the short run, is the limiting factor of production.

Generally, decisions regarding kinds and acreage of crops or improved pasture to be grown should be made before selection of livestock. Even if it is impractical to change the present livestock operations because of a large fixed investment (dairying for example), one should determine the most profitable cropping system. After this is determined, test the adaptability of the crop plan to present livestock facilities and scale of operation. However, if livestock facilities have multiple uses, the kinds of livestock best suited to the cropping system can be selected after the cropping system is established.

Should a farm have a large fixed investment in livestock facilities, it may be necessary to tailor crop production to accommodate usage of the facilities. The goal is to maximize returns to all resources.

Step-by-step procedures (including work forms) are provided to test profitability and feasibility of alternative farm plans (different enterprise combinations). Feasibility analysis relates to cash flow management and is of vital importance in evaluating alternative farm plans that differ with regard to capital outlays. A given farm plan, in addition to being profitable, must generate sufficient earnings to provide for any additional debt service (repayment) requirements associated with investments made.

APPLYING THE PRINCIPLES OF CHAPTER 12

1. Why is land an important resource in farm planning?

2. Can the intensity of land use classification on a given farm be changed?

3. Why is it suggested that the cropping system be developed before the livestock system?

4. How do the concepts profitability and feasibility as used in farm planning differ?

5. When a major investment(s) is required for a given farm plan, indicate methods one can use to minimize the financial burden associated with changes.

REFERENCES

Herbst, J. H. *Farm Management: Principles, Budgets, Plans.* Champaign, Illinois: Stipes Publishing Co., 1976.

Missouri Farm Management Staff. *Missouri Farm Planning Handbook, Manual 75.* Columbia, Mo.: University of Missouri-Columbia, 1981.

Linear Programming

- Linear programming is a superior alternative to budgeting when solving complex allocation problems
- Linear programming solutions are only as good as the input data
- Linear programming solutions are optimal for the data set used
- Applications in production agriculture are for selecting high-profit farm plans and least-cost rations

Managers are confronted with decisions about how to organize and/or allocate resources. The methods for making the decisions, some of which have been explained in earlier chapters, are varied. Sometimes a decision can be made by applying a simple economic principle; at other times a detailed process like whole-farm planning is in order. Some cases have so many alternatives and interrelationships that a computer is much more efficient than trying to solve the problem manually.

This chapter explains the basics of the linear programming (LP) analysis technique. The topics covered include:

1. Definition and areas of application

2. A comparison of budgeting and linear programming

3. A graphic example

4. A computer plus a manager

LINEAR PROGRAMMING DEFINED

Linear programming is a computational method for determining the best plan or course of action from among all the possible plans when there are many alternatives, a specific objective, and limited means or resources. Thus, linear programming methods are primarily applied to the general class of problems known as allocation problems.

The problem of formulating a least-cost livestock ration is an example of a complex allocation problem. Many different feed ingredients can go into the ration; each has a different price. But what combination of corn, oats, wheat, milo, cottonseed meal, soybean meal, fish meal, linseed meal, bone meal, dehydrated alfalfa, corn silage, bran, hulls, etc., should be used to give the desired gain at the least cost? Linear programming is the most efficient means of answering an economic question like "What is the least cost ration?"

Linear programming is also efficient for planning the use of scarce resources so that returns can be maximized. In farm planning, the manager must choose among livestock and crop enterprises (alternate ends) given the limitations of land, labor, and capital (alternate means). Linear programming can be used to determine the maximum income potential of the resources available to an operator-manager. It is also useful in projecting whether a desired level of income is attainable from a certain farm situation.

Agri-business managers have used LP to (1) determine the types and quantities of products to manufacture; (2) decide the blend or mix of petroleum and fertilizer products; (3) select production schedules and inventory plans for products with seasonal demands; and (4) choose optimal shipping and transportation schedules for materials and products.

LINEAR PROGRAMMING AND BUDGETING

A logical question might be: Aren't the goals of programming and budgeting the same? In fact, determining the profitability of different farm plans is the goal of both budgeting and linear programming, but they are complementary rather than competitive methods. Linear programming is a more exact and more inclusive technique than budgeting. Furthermore, linear programming can be applied to complex least-cost and transportation problems that do not lend themselves to budgeting.

Budgeting is not used to find the unique combination of enterprises that gives maximum profits; it is usually used to compare only two or three alternative farm organizational plans. Budgeting would be too time consuming and costly for determining which of 50 to 100 different organizational plans would be most profitable. Linear programming has the advantage for large scale problems. When the problem is small scale—a limited number of comparisons are being made—budgeting is probably more appropriate.

Linear programming and budgeting, as applied to farm planning problems, require identical information. Both require (1) a complete and accurate inventory of the limiting resources and special conditions; (2) enumeration of alternative crop and livestock enterprises that use the resources and their projected production per unit; (3) estimates of product prices; and (4) estimates of production costs for the various enterprises. Each of the four data requirements is discussed in more detail below.

Constraints

A process for inventorying farm resources was detailed in Chapter 10. It was pointed out that the existence of resource restrictions forces a manager to select among alternatives. In linear programming, constraints refer to the quantity and, in some cases, the quality of land, labor, and capital available, or which may be made available, for production purposes. A constraint may also refer to a special condition set by a manager, such as no more than 50 acres of hay or 30 dairy cows, or a government regulation like an allotment or a zoning or environmental requirement.

In the process of establishing farm planning constraints, a manager must answer such questions as: How many acres of cropland/pasture are available? How many acres can be row-cropped? How many acres can be irrigated? How much labor is available during each work period or each month? How many head can the farrowing facilities (or feedlot, or dairy barn) handle in a year? How many farrowings per year am I willing to oversee?

Alternative Means

The concepts of enterprises and processes were discussed in Chapter 11. An enterprise was defined as a segment of the business that can be readily separated out, like irrigated corn, wheat, or steer fattening. A process can be an enterprise, but is generally more precisely defined. It refers to a particular set of production practices associated with an enterprise—for example, minimum tillage wheat fertilized with 60–40–40 (N–P–K) fertilizer. An example of a cattle feeding *process* might be 600-

pound yearling steers purchased in December and placed on a 60–40 ration of milo and corn silage for a period of 200 days. It is not unusual in linear programming to consider a dozen or more different enterprises with one to five different processes per enterprise. For example, there might be beef cow-calf processes for fall, winter, and spring calving, and creep feeding and no-creep feeding options for each of the different calving alternatives.

The basic resource requirements of each process must be determined: this means feed, seed, fertilizer, labor, and machinery requirements must be quantified. Basic enterprise (technical unit) budgets will be valuable in ascertaining these various coefficients.

Production, Prices, Costs

Answers from linear programming, as with any planning and analysis technique, are no better than the input data used. Thus, estimates of yields, average daily gain, or pounds of milk produced for various processes must be made carefully. Obviously, equal care should be given to choosing prices and costs as a basis for the analysis. Mistakes in input-output coefficients give incorrect answers. However, a major advantage of linear programming is the ease with which a coefficient can be changed, a new computer run made, and the effects of the change on projected profits or farm organization examined.

THE LOGIC OF LINEAR PROGRAMMING: A GRAPHIC EXAMPLE

A farm manager may ask, "How can I use my cropland, labor, and operating capital most profitably in the production of grain and forage?" He has specified his constraints and some alternative means to use the resources. Since no mention is made of machinery or management, these are not assumed to be restrictions on the planning process.

To simplify the analysis, only two processes, grain and forage, are used. To determine the most profitable combination, the following must be known:

1. The amounts of land, labor, and operating capital available

2. The amounts of land, labor, and operating capital required by the grain and forage process/enterprises

3. The costs of producing grain and forage

4. The expected production per acre of grain and forage

5. The expected selling price per unit of grain and forage

The last three items allow income above costs to be estimated.

Exhibit 13–1 presents the basic input data needed for a simple linear programming analysis. Resource constraints include 160 acres of cropland, 300 hours each of spring and summer labor, and $20,000 operating capital. The two alternative crop processes use different combinations of the resources to produce an acre of the process. It is the difference in resource requirements that provides the basis for asking the question: Should only grain, only forage, or a combination be produced? Assuming the objective is maximum income, a simple budgeting exercise is not likely to give the optimal answer, even for a problem as simple as this one.

Step One: Specifying Constraints and Processes

To determine the most profitable resources allocation between grain and forage, one must first know how many units of each process (enterprise) can be produced with each resource. This is accomplished by dividing the coefficient opposite each resource and under each process into the number of units of the resource available. For example, if cropland alone were limiting, either 160 acres of grain or forage could be grown. However, all constraints must be considered simultaneously. Exhibit 13–2 summarizes the acres of forage alone or grain alone that can be produced with each of the constraints.

Note that the *most limiting resource* is *not* the same for each enterprise. Spring labor would limit grain production to 100 acres, but summer

Exhibit 13–1. Data needed for linear programming example

Constraints		Processes	
Resource	*Units available*	*Grain*	*Forage*
Cropland	160 acres	1.0	1.0
Spring labor	300 hours	3.0	1.5
Summer labor	300 hours	.5	2.0
Operating capital	$20,000	100.0	60.0
Net Returns per Acre		$90	$55

Exhibit 13-2. Production possible by resource for linear programming example

	Acres possible by constraint	
Resource available	Grain	Forage
160 acres cropland	160	160
300 hours spring labor	100	200
300 hours summer labor	600	150
$20,000 operating capital	200	333

labor is most limiting on forage. If the same resource were scarce and limited both enterprises, determining the most profitable solution would be simple. The enterprise giving the greatest net returns based upon the maximum acres allowed by the limiting resource would be chosen. This assumes that none of the other resources could be substituted for the limiting resource.

However, the solution to our problem is not simple. Producing only grain uses up spring labor and would give $9,000 net returns, but leaves surplus cropland, summer labor, and operating capital. Producing only forage would use all summer labor, use 150 of 160 cropland acres, and generate an estimated $8,250 in income, but would leave surplus spring labor and operating capital. It would appear that a combination of grain and forage would be more profitable. But what combination?

Step Two: Defining the Region of Feasible Solutions

A graphic approach will illustrate the process of determining the optimum solution to the grain-forage problem. As a beginning, a graph is constructed by plotting grain acreage on the horizontal axis and forage acreage on the vertical axis. The maximum number of each process can be represented for each limiting resource by points on the respective axes corresponding to the units computed and included in Exhibit 13-2. For example, points A and B in Exhibit 13-3 represent the maximum acres of grain and forage that would be possible if cropland alone were the limiting resource. The straight line connecting points A and B shows all the combinations of grain and forage (160 and 0, 150 and 10, 140 and 20, etc.) that would use up the fixed cropland resources.

Exhibit 13-4 includes the line showing the cropland constraint and the lines for each of the other resources. Each line defines the production possibilities for a particular resource, ignoring the other resources.

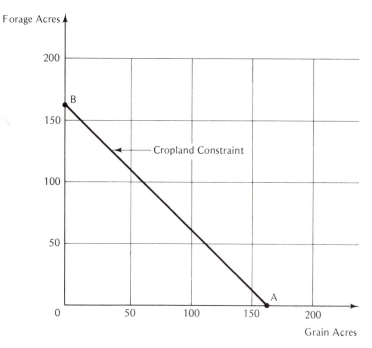

Exhibit 13–3. All possible combinations of grain and forage, given a 160-acre cropland restriction.

One advantage of the graphic method is that the effects of restrictions or constraints on a decision can be represented visually. Consider the line for the operating capital resource (line GH). The line is at a level such that some other resource is always more limiting; that is, it lies to the left or below line GH. Thus, although operating capital is a resource, in this case it is not a limiting resource. Operating capital will not influence the decision about the optimum combination of grain and forage.

The shaded area in Exhibit 13–4 indicates the region of feasible solutions. Any combination of grain and forage that lies in the shaded area, including all points along the perimeter line FIJC, is possible. Combinations above or to the right of FIJC are not possible because at least one resource is limiting.

Step Three: Locating the Optimum Feasible Solution

Points on FIJC might be viewed as the frontier of production possibilities for grain and forage. Some point on the frontier will satisfy the

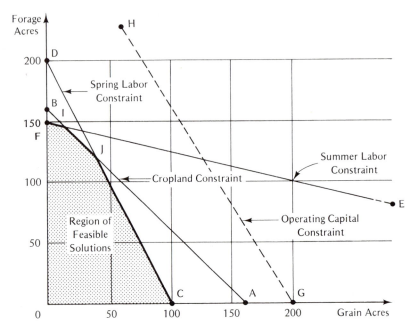

Exhibit 13–4. All resource restrictions plotted and region of feasible solutions identified for hypothetical 160-acre cropland farm.

objective of maximum possible income from the set of resources that has been specified. Once the alternatives are defined by the points on this frontier (production possibilities), the points are measured against the profit-maximizing objective.

One method of determining the optimal solution is by trial and error. By computing the income from all combinations of grain and forage represented by points F, I, J, and C on the production possibilities frontier, the best possible solution can eventually be discovered. This computation is not difficult for the simple two-product example. The resulting income from each organization is as follows:

Point C: (100 acres grain × $90) + (0 acres forage × $55) = $9,000

Point J: (40 acres grain × $90) + (120 acres forage × $55) = $10,200

Point I: (13.3 acres grain × $90) + (146.7 acres forage × $55) = $9,266

Point F: (0 acres grain × $90) + (150 acres forage × $55) = $8,250

Thus, for returns of $90 and $55 per acre respectively for grain and forage, point J indicates the most profitable combination from the resources available. The return figure should be considered a net return to land, labor, and capital because charges for these resources were not included in computing the $90 and $55 values.

An alternative method for locating the most profitable solution relies on the "relative profit" of the grain and forage processes. The ratio between net returns from grain (G) and forage (F) is $G = 1.636 \, F$. The relationship, based upon the net return values of $90 and $55, can be transformed into an *equal-profit line* that has the slope $-1.6/1.0$. Total net return realized would depend upon the product quantity combination chosen. Exhibit 13–5 shows the region of feasible solutions (from Exhibit 13–4) and a "family" of equal-profit lines superimposed on it. All lines have some portion within the feasible region. Line O is the greatest distance from the origin, yet still touches the feasible region. It identifies the optimum solution as point J, the same point chosen by the trial and error approach. Students of economic theory should relate this approach to the basic product-product model.

The optimal solution uses all land and spring labor, but still there is surplus summer labor and operating capital. Nevertheless, no solution for the specified resources will give greater profits unless (1) some operating capital can be used to acquire additional cropland or spring labor, or (2) some summer labor can be substituted for spring labor. In such cases the problem would have to be structured again (new lines drawn) consistent with the altered conditions assumed.

This simple graphic example illustrates the principle of linear programming. The graphic approach is, however, capable of handling problems of only limited complexity and is a special, rather than a general, method. The chief limitation is the restriction to two independent variables. A more complex case would have a large number of possible combinations like those represented by points F, I, J, and C in Exhibit 13–5. The search for the optimal points in what mathematicians call an N-dimensional space is mathematically possible and can be greatly simplified by using a computer.

COMPUTER-ASSISTED DECISION MAKING

Computerized linear programming has paid off well for many farmers. One cattle feeder reduced his cost of gain by 1.6 cents per pound without reducing average daily gain. At 400 pounds gain per steer, that cost re-

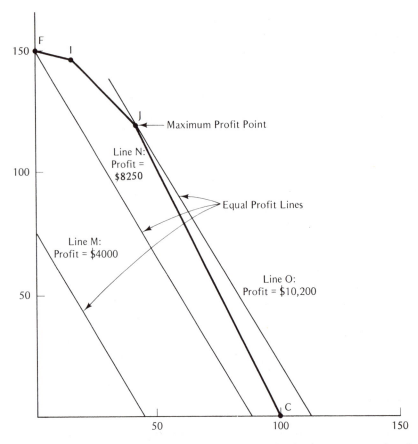

Exhibit 13–5. Maximum profit point determined by linear programming for hypothetical 160-acre farm.

duction meant a $6.40 per head savings. And that savings translated into $6,400 added income per year for the farmer's 1,000-head system.

But the computer is only a tool. Large scale planning problems require *both a manager and a computer*. Although the computer is necessary for the computations that would take a manager days or even weeks to complete, the manager is essential (1) to define the problem, (2) to choose the set of enterprises/processes and provide the coefficients, and (3) to interpret the solution and determine whether solutions for some alternative situations should be generated.

Once the basic data are developed, a manager can use a computer linear programming model to provide answers to a multitude of "what if?" type questions. Some examples of these questions are:

1. What if a full-time worker could be hired for $10,000 per year?
2. What if an additional 320 acres pasture could be rented?
3. What if reduced-tillage were added as a production practice and double cropping could be accomplished in at least half the years?
4. What if farrow-to-finish confinement facilities were added?
5. What if cotton prices increased by 15 cents per pound?
6. What if I went into partnership with my son or daughter?

Many resources and enterprises are likely to be considered and resource constraints and production coefficients may change. Thus, a manager could probably benefit from a linear programming analysis of the above questions.

Although the results from linear programming least-cost rations are generally put to use immediately, the time frame for implementing most profit maximization analyses is up to five years. It takes time to switch from dairying to hogs or from a cropping system using four-row, forty-inch per row equipment to eight-row, thirty-inch per row equipment.

The profit-maximization linear programming approach to planning is generally most useful to a manager at a major decision point. The profit potential can be estimated for optimal use of the available resources. Then the income consequences of changes in resources, enterprises, or prices can be programmed.

Exhibit 13–6 presents the results of a linear programming computer analysis applied to a 350-acre farm suited to crops and livestock. The resource situation was as follows:

Resource	Amount available
Class 1 capability cropland	175 acres
Class 2 capability cropland	75 acres
Pasture land	100 acres
Hog facilities to accommodate	50 sows
January–March labor	600 hours
April–June labor	700 hours
July–September labor	750 hours
October–December labor	600 hours
Operating Capital	$40,000

Exhibit 13–6. Computer output for profit maximization linear programming problem.

EXECUTOR. MPS/360 V2-M6

SECTION 1 - ROWS

NUMBER	...ROW..	AT	...ACTIVITY...	SLACK ACTIVITY	..UPPER LIMIT.
1	VALUE	BS	50511.76	50511.76498-	NONE
2	LANDA	UL	175.00	.	175.00
3	LANDB	UL	75.00	.	75.00
4	PASTLA	UL	.	.	.
5	PAST	UL	.	.	.
6	JANMAR	UL	600.00	.	600.00
7	APRJUN	BS	557.27	142.72150	700.00
8	JULSEP	BS	711.66	38.33517	750.00
9	OCTDEC	UL	600.00	.	600.00
10	OPCAP	UL	40000.00	.	40000.00
11	IRRIGA	UL	120.00	.	120.00
12	CORNTR	UL	.	.	.
13	INVCAP	EQ	.	.	.
14	STEERT	UL	.	.	.
15	HAYGL	BS	.	.	.
16	HAYG	UL	.	.	.
17	CORNBYUP	BS	.	20000.00000	20000.00
18	FARFINUP	BS	40.44	9.55709	50.00

SECTION 2 - COLUMNS

NUMBER	.COLUMN.	AT	...ACTIVITY...	..INPUT COST..
19	IRCORN	BS	120.00	137.00
20	SHEEP	BS	117.13	40.00
21	FPIG1	LL	.	168.50
22	FPIG2	BS	40.44	219.50
23	FPIGA	BS	628.03	33.00
24	FARFIN	LL	.	603.00
25	INVES	BS	120.00	32.10
26	CORNBY	LL	.	2.85
27	CORNSL	BS	10473.38	2.60
28	BECOMA	LL	.	96.00
29	RECOJF	LL	.	118.25
30	BECOSO	LL	.	134.50
31	WHMIA	BS	19.06	165.50
32	WHMIB	BS	75.00	146.25
33	SCBUYL	BS	.	136.00
34	SCWG	LL	.	64.00
35	BSFF	LL	.	293.00
36	BSDEFER	LL	.	339.00
37	SYSSGR	LL	.	172.00
38	SWFSG	LL	.	165.50
39	PASTIM	BS	.	22.00
40	PASTUI	LL	.	14.50
41	SOYBEAN	LL	.	92.00
42	GLHAYBUY	LL	.	40.00
43	GHAYBUY	BS	38.65	35.00
44	GLHAYPAS	LL	.	53.00
45	GNHAYPAS	LL	.	66.50
46	NICORN	BS	35.93	97.00

The manager had 24 different processes he wanted to consider.

In less than 40 seconds and at a computer time cost of less than one dollar, the computer determined the optimum organization of:

120 acres irrigated corn
36 acres dryland corn
94 acres wheat-milo double-cropped

117 ewes producing spring lambs
 40 sows
628 feeder pigs purchased and finished out
 39 tons of hay purchased

The projected income over costs (all investment in irrigation was required to be paid in seven years) was $50,511. The return figure is a return to land and other fixed capital, interest on operating capital, and a return to labor and management. Two "what if?" questions were also developed. They were:

1. What if hogs and sheep were removed from the list of enterprises to be considered?

2. What if irrigation, hogs, and sheep were all eliminated from consideration in the optimum plan?

The computer results for question (1) suggest income would drop, on the average, from $50,511 to $44,884. But 980 fewer hours and $24,000 less operating capital would be required. Buy-sell steers (100 head) was the livestock enterprise that came in. Crop acres changed very little.

Eliminating irrigation from consideration [question (2)], dropped projected income to $38,911. Double-cropped milo and wheat was the major crop process, and buy-sell steers was the primary livestock enterprise.

If the resource restrictions and enterprises/processes are representative of the existing and/or potential situation, then the manager for whom the programming analysis was developed can decide what direction his farm business should take. He obviously will consider the goals for the business and the different requirements in labor, capital, and management for the three farm plans developed by the computer. After studying the results, he may decide on additional linear programming computer runs.

One word of caution: The primary contribution of any quantitative method like computer programming is to narrow the judgment portion of decision making, not to eliminate it. While most of the technical and economic phases of a problem can be expressed explicitly and directly in linear programming, many qualitative and intangible human factors cannot. It is important to recognize that the optimal LP solution is not necessarily the optimal overall solution to a problem. Managerial judgment must interpret the mathematical solution in the total context of the farm/ranch firm and its goals.

SUMMARY

Linear programming will never replace budgeting or record analysis as a planning aid for managers making decisions. However, linear programming is particularly applicable to a broad range of farm planning problems that involve optimization. This chapter has:

- Explained the close relationship between budgeting and linear programming. Both require sound, accurate data on production processes, prices and costs, and resource constraints. Both have the objective of determining the profitability of alternatives.
- Demonstrated the logic of linear programming through a simplified crop decision problem using graphic analysis.
- Presented one sample of an application of computer linear programming, a farm planning problem in profit maximization.

The reader should be aware that many agriculture problems have the common characteristics of (1) limited resources, (2) competing ways by which those resources can be utilized, and (3) an objective, that is, maximizing profit or minimizing costs. If these three characteristics can be satisfactorily quantified, then applying the linear programming technique may pay off substantially. There are farm management and other professionals in most areas across the country who are ready to help, usually for a minimal fee.

APPLYING THE PRINCIPLES OF CHAPTER 13

1. What is linear programming?
2. To what kind of problems is LP best applied?
3. How does LP differ from budgeting?
4. What assumptions or conditions are required for a problem to be solved by LP?
5. What is a constraint, and how does it affect the solution to an LP problem?

REFERENCES

Beneke, R. R. and R. D. Winterboer. *Linear Programming Applications to Agriculture*. Ames, Iowa: Iowa State University Press, 1973.

Finley, R. M. and Dean Brown. *Linear Programming, A New Farm Management Tool.* Nebraska Extension Service Bulletin EC 60-815, 1961.

Heady, Earl O. "Simplified Presentation and Logical Aspects of Linear Programming Technique," *Journal of Farm Economics*, December 1954, pp. 1035–1048.

Stockton, R. S. *Introduction to Linear Programming.* Homewood, Ill.: Richard D. Irwin, Inc., 1971.

Part 5

Business Organization and Resource Management

Types of Farm Business Ownership

14

The family farm is an American institution. Some are saying that this institution is slowly but surely falling prey to those inescapables, death and taxes. The farm where father and mother, sons and daughters served as the management, labor, sales and marketing staff, accountant, and credit manager is coming under many pressures. Among these pressures are limited periods of peak management efficiency, legal problems during the transfer of ownership from one generation to the next, too few tax dollars, too little equity capital, and too much drain on what equity capital there is.

More and more farm operations are reviewing their current legal business organization and investigating the advantages and disadvantages of the three major organizational forms highlighted above.

The choice of organizational structure is a very important decision for farmers, one that should be made only after carefully weighing both short-run and long-run effects and discussing the various factors with an attorney or other qualified adviser. This chapter points out some of the major considerations associated with choosing the legal business organization.

THE SOLE PROPRIETORSHIP

The terms *sole proprietorship* and *individual proprietorship* are often used interchangeably. They usually refer to *an individual who owns, manages, assumes all the risk, and derives all the profit from a business.* Most farm businesses in the United States are the sole proprietorship type. A sole proprietor holds all rights in the business except those reserved for society, like eminent domain and police power. There may also be restrictions like pollution regulations or rights to use water from a stream or ground water for irrigation.

How Is the Sole Proprietorship Created?

The sole proprietorship is the easiest structure to begin or end. It can have the most flexible purpose for its operations and usually needs no government approval—although some licences or certificates for certain activities like applying pesticides may be necessary. There are fewer government regulations and restrictions on the individual proprietorship than on any other form of business.

Ownership of a sole proprietorship business should not be confused with ownership of assets like land, livestock, and supplies. A sole proprietor may rent land and operate machinery and grow crops or livestock purchased with borrowed money. That one person is solely responsible for the business is the factor that makes the business a sole proprietorship.

The sole proprietorship is the oldest and most widespread legal structure. As a result, little doubt remains as to laws regulating its legal rights and obligations. Likewise, the relationships are clear between a sole owner and his or her agents, creditors, and others with whom he/she has business dealings.

The Major Attractions

In the individual proprietorship, the business owner is the boss. Decision making and operations, policy and goals rest in one individual. Concentration of management avoids the problems of disagreements among owners. The sole proprietor receives the rewards of good management and labor directly. He can, and often does, employ assistants to whom he assigns various details of the operation. The sole owner can hire the services of a professional manager, accountant, lawyer, or agriculture production specialist; and he reaps the rewards or penalties of those he hires.

The sole proprietorship has flexibility. The owner can quickly and easily expand or contract the size of the business, add or eliminate enterprises, and increase or decrease his inventory as he sees fit. As the decision maker and the only person who must be satisfied, the sole owner theoretically can act more quickly than when several individuals are involved in the decision. This does not alway work in practice because the individual proprietor may put off a difficult decision rather than make it.

Other Considerations

The sole proprietorship is taxed at individual rates which range from 16 to 50 percent of taxable income. A private citizen working in Ohio can have a sole proprietorship farm business in Kansas, providing he has the management ability, without being taxed differently on his federal tax return from a sole proprietor Kansas farmer.

Although sole proprietorships have no legal time limit on them, they are not fundamentally perpetual. The owner's illness may derange the business; death ends it.

In single proprietorships, capital for operations and/or investment may be obtained by borrowing, by purchasing on credit, or by investing from profits. Thus, the sole owner is responsible for acquiring the capital needs and is liable for all the debts of the farm business. In a sole proprietorship, the farmer's personal assets and farm assets are lumped together. As a result, a creditor with a claim against the farm business can force payment from personal assets if farm assets are inadequate to meet the claim. Conversely, assets of the farm business may be required to pay off personal debts the proprietor may incur.

This lumping together of all assets is especially significant when an accident occurs in the farming operation. All the assets of the farmer are on the line if he is legally responsible for the accident; property that is completely unrelated to the farm could be taken to pay the damages. By the same token, all of the farm-related assets can be reached by someone to whom the farmer is liable for a completely non-farm–related accident.

Members of the family may be hired by the sole proprietor in some kind of employer-employee relationship so that the younger member is paid a wage for the services rendered the business. More than likely, however, the owner will be planning to bring the younger members of the family into an owner and manager role if they wish to remain on the farm. A family with these intentions should look to the partnership or corporate structure to better meet their needs.

THE PARTNERSHIP

A *partnership* is *a voluntary association of two or more persons to carry on, as co-owners, a business for profit.* This does not mean that the property used in the business must be co-owned, but that the business as a business enterprise must be owned by all partners. The partnership may own all, some, or none of the property used in the business. Partnerships are governed by a code of rules called the Uniform Partnership Act, and additional rules may be adopted in the partnership agreement.

There are two basic types of partnership structure: the ordinary, or *general*, partnership and the *limited* partnership. The important distinction between the ordinary and limited partnership is that limited partners cannot have management control in the business, but they do have priority over general partners in the recovery of capital investments. The limited partnership has achieved its primary agricultural application in large-scale livestock operations, particularly feedlots.

Most of the following discussion of partnerships relates to ordinary partnerships.

The Major Attractions

The opportunity to pool capital and/or know-how is a major attraction of the partnership. A partnership is the simplest business for two or more persons to start and terminate. It has the same flexibility of purpose and operation as a sole proprietorship and needs no governmental approval. A partnership may look attractive to a father and son who wish to farm together. The legal and recordkeeping requirements are far fewer than for a corporation. Many young farmers may be unable to compete in farming unless they get into a partnership arrangement.

How Is the Partnership Created?

A partnership is created by an oral or written agreement. In some cases a partnership may be implied without an agreement if the business is being carried on as a partnership. The only legal requirement is that two or more persons combine for the purpose of conducting business. Many times a partnership will be orally created and simply involve an agreement to divide profits in a specified manner. While this may at first seem acceptable, many problems can arise under such an agreement.

Even a written agreement is likely to miss some potential problem areas, but it also eliminates many areas of disagreement. Some examples of the sticky problems which need to be spelled out at the start of a partnership are:

1. Suppose one partner furnishes all the land. What return on land investment will he be paid?

2. Suppose one partner contributes his cattle to the partnership. How are offspring divided?

3. Suppose one partner uses his combine to harvest the crops of the partnership. Should he be paid the going custom rate for harvesting, or is this part of his contribution to the partnership business?

Partnerships do not succeed long unless the partners trust each other and have faith in each other's ability to make sound, objective business decisions.

General Legal Characteristics

Some of the characteristics that point to a partnership are as follows:

1. Whether or not each person involved participates in management decisions

2. Whether assets are owned individually or jointly

3. Whether or not profits are shared

4. Whether or not losses are shared

5. Whether or not the parties have operated under a firm name

6. Whether or not the parties have a joint bank account for use in business transactions

7. Whether they keep a single set of business records

An agreement might provide for one or more of the above characteristics and not necessarily be a partnership. No one factor is controlling. All are applied to the particular arrangement to determine whether in sum it is a partnership.

The above characteristics are used to determine if an agreement is, in fact, a partnership. The following are some other legal factors that partners, or potential partners, should consider.

1. Unless specified otherwise in the agreement, legally each partner has an equal voice in management control and a majority of the partners control business decisions.

2. Both real and personal property may be owned in the partnership name. Unless the agreement expressly states otherwise, each partner has an equal partnership interest and has an equal right to possession and control of partnership property for purposes of carrying on the business of the partnership. Often individual partners agree to contribute the use of their personally owned property to the partnership business. In such cases, title to such property remains in the person contributing it. Also, the partnership may lease needed real and personal property as an alternative to the partnership assuming ownership of the assets.

3. Profits and losses are divided in accordance with the specific agreement; partners do not normally draw compensation for their services and any withdrawals or "wages" should usually be treated as advances on their share of profits. Profits do *not* have to be distributed on the basis of the relative amount of capital contributed by the respective partners.

4. A partnership must have its own records, especially for income tax purposes. Although it pays no income taxes, a return showing partnership income tax information must be filed. The partners then pay individual taxes on their share of the partnership income, as specified in the partnership agreement.

Liability Considerations

Legally it is possible to create either an ordinary or a limited partnership. Each member of an ordinary partnership is, individually, fully responsible for all debts owed by the partnership. A limited partner in a limited partnership risks only the capital he has invested in the business; his status is more like that of a stockholder of a corporation.

If an ordinary partnership does not have sufficient assets to pay its debts, each partner can be held personally liable for the partnership's debts and obligations. This rule holds true whether the partnership debt arises out of a contract entered into by the partnership or from an accident for which the partnership is liable. The partnership itself is liable for loss or injury caused to any person by the wrongful act or omission of a partner if he is acting in the course of business or with the consent of the other partners. Carried to its conclusion, this means each partner is liable for the wrongful acts of a co-partner if the co-partner is doing partnership business.

Contrary to popular belief, the liability of a partner does not extend to personal debts and obligations of the other partner(s). The personal debts of a partner are collected from that individual's assets to the extent possible. If the partner's assets are not sufficient to meet these debts, the creditor may take legal action to require the partnership to pay the debtor-partner's share of partnership income to his creditor until the debt is discharged. This procedure is quite important because it permits the partnership to continue to operate without being hindered by the personal financial problems of an individual partner.

Occasionally a partner may be held liable for partnership debts *after* he has withdrawn from the partnership. A creditor who advances credit to the partnership may be depending on the personal credit of a particular partner in doing so. For this reason, a withdrawing partner remains liable for debts contracted prior to his withdrawal. As a practical matter, this means that a partner cannot escape liability when times get hard by simply withdrawing from the partnership.

A withdrawing partner can take steps to avoid liability for partnership debts. If he gives notice to creditors who had previously done business with the partnership, he will not be liable when credit is subsequently extended. He may avoid liability to all others—that is, to creditors who have not previously done business with the partnership—by publishing notice in local newspapers that he has withdrawn.

For other legal considerations, the reader is referred to one of the excellent publications listed at the end of the chapter or to a qualified attorney.

The Family Partnership

The family partnership has been important in the past and will probably be more important in the future because of the vast financial requirements of farming today. The combination of the wisdom and experience of parents or relatives and the energy or labor of a son, daughter or nephew makes a potentially good team. A partnership is a convenient mechanism by which a younger family member can gradually assume managerial responsibilities. Although this has obvious advantages over thrusting one into a decision-making position with no experience, the decision to form a family (e.g., parent-child, brother-brother) partnership should be based on careful consideration of family circumstances and goals, as well as on factors discussed in the sections above.

In family partnerships, the senior member (usually a parent) may be making a considerable sacrifice. For example, the parent may have accumulated sufficient resources to rent out land, take life more easily, and still have a satisfactory income. Forming a partnership with a child/children or other relations often necessitates expanding the business, borrowing more money, taking on additional risk, and the parent's working as hard as ever for an additional number of years. In other cases, the son farms with his father and finds at age 40, "Dad is still the boss and I am still the kid."

A family partnership seems to work best when only one child is involved. As more children become involved, particularly if some have jobs in another town or state, the opportunities for family disagreements increase. A family partnership should be adopted only if it does a better job in meeting personal and family objectives than the alternatives (sole proprietorship and corporation).

Terminating a Partnership

A partnership may be terminated by agreement between the partners or by operation of law. Dissolution under a partnership agreement generally occurs when the term or business in the agreement is finished. If no duration is fixed by the agreement, then either partner may terminate the partnership at will. Dissolution by operation of law occurs in the event of death, bankruptcy, or incapacity of any partner, or by an event which makes the continuation of the business unlawful. If a court is shown that the partnership cannot continue without loss, the court may dissolve the partnership.

Although a partnership is easy to terminate, careful thought should be given this area at the time the partnership begins. Looking ahead will allow a fairly high degree of continuity of management and ownership at the death of a partner if continuation is an objective. Or it will minimize hard feelings between the partners should one party wish to leave the business.

The above outline of only a few of the possible considerations in a partnership points to the need for legal advice when working out the partnership arrangement.

THE CORPORATE STRUCTURE

A third business organization, the *corporation*, is defined as *a legal entity separate and distinct from the shareholders who own it, from the individuals who manage it, or from its employees.* It is created by state law and organized for the purpose of carrying on a business for profit. The corporation, as a separate "legal person" apart from the shareholders, has most of the legal rights and duties of an individual. It can make contracts, transact business, hold property, sue, and be sued. The concept of legal separate-

ness sets the corporation apart from the partnership and sole proprietorship.

The Internal Revenue Service recognizes two types of corporate
structures, the regular corporation and the Subchapter S corporation. The
regular corporation is also referred to as a Subchapter C corporation. The
Subchapter S corporation is frequently known as a pseudo- or tax-option
corporation. The major difference between the two corporate structures
is in the method by and the rate at which they are taxed by the federal
government. The regular corporation is taxed at the rate of 15 percent on
the first $25,000 of taxable income; 18 percent on taxable income between
$25,000 and $50,000; 30 percent on the third $25,000; 40 percent on the
fourth $25,000; and 46 percent on all taxable income above $100,000.[1] The
Subchapter S corporation is not taxed directly, but is used as a conduit to
transfer income to the individual shareholders. The shareholders are then
taxed at their individual rates, much like the partner of a partnership. Income is transferred to the shareholders in the same form that it was received by the corporation. Thus, long-term capital gains for the corporation are proportionally allocated to the shareholders and are treated as
long-term gains on their individual income tax returns.

The basic requirements of a Subchapter S corporation are: (1) it can
have only one class of stock; (2) it can have no more than 25 shareholders; (3) it cannot have a nonresident alien as a shareholder; (4) it cannot
receive more than 80 percent of its gross receipts from foreign sources;
(5) all shareholders must elect to be taxed as a Subchapter S corporation;
and (6) not more than 20 percent of the gross receipts can be derived
from rents, royalties, dividends, and interest. Again, careful thought
should be given to the choice between the two corporate structures.

How Is the Corporation Created?

The steps of incorporation may vary slightly from state to state but
generally include the following:

1. Certain responsible people are needed to organize and become
officials in the new corporation. In most farm corporations, the interested persons are family members or close friends. They will
likely become the officials of the corporation.

---

[1]Tax rates have varied somewhat in recent years due to federal tax legislation. An attorney or tax accountant can provide the current tax rates.

2. A special document called the "articles of incorporation" is filed with the designated state official. These articles, along with the by-laws, make up the charter governing the relations between the corporation, its owners/shareholders, the officers, and the board of directors.

3. An initial tax and certain filing fees will probably be required.

4. In order to do business for which the corporation was formed, certain official meetings must be conducted to deal with specific details of organization and operation.

The following are the steps followed by one family that created a farm corporation:

1. Listed goals

2. Retained the services of an experienced attorney

3. Engaged a certified public accountant to set up record accounts

4. Obtained state charter

5. Divided stock as prescribed when setting goals

6. Issued stock certificates

7. Held first stockholders meeting; elected board of directors; adopted the bylaws of the corporation

8. Elected officers

9. Set wages and salaries and settled on remuneration for assets leased to the corporation

10. Established fiscal year

Generally speaking, if the organization of a corporation is properly planned, the transfer of property or money to the corporation and the receipt of stock by the shareholders is not a taxable event. The basic requirement is that the incorporators receive 80 percent of the stock of the corporation. The income tax basis the corporation takes in assets transferred to it is the same as the shareholder had in the assets, and the shareholder's basis in his stock is the same basis as he had in the assets. This arrangement defers taxes until such time as the shareholder sells his stock.

Unlike the organization of a partnership, the termination of a corporation is generally a taxable event. With careful tax planning, it is possible to plan the termination so that the gain is taxed at the favorable long-term capital gain rate.[2] This type of planning is very technical and will require competent tax counsel; however, any expense for this advice will likely be more than repaid in tax savings from careful planning.

Some states are very specific in their requirements on farming corporations. In Oklahoma, for example, the conditions are:

1. There shall be no shareholders other than natural persons, estates, banks, or personal trustees of trusts for the benefit of natural persons or corporations;

2. Not more than 20 percent of the corporation's annual gross receipts shall be from any source other than farming or ranching or allowing others to extract minerals from the land;

3. There shall be not more than ten shareholders unless the shareholders in excess of ten are related as lineal descendants or by marriage.

Any parties considering incorporation should obtain a qualified person familiar with the requirements in their state. A corporation is the most complex, formal, and expensive method of organization to form. Organizational costs for a farm corporation may be as low as $300, but can range to $1,000 or more.

Timing may be important in incorporation, as is the case with any business venture. Selection of the "right" time depends on both the particular circumstances and the major purpose of incorporating. A person with substantial personal assets besides a farm operation might want to incorporate as soon as possible if he is interested in separating the farming venture from other businesses and limiting personal liability in the farming venture. There likewise may be practical reasons for delaying incorporation, such as using up old tax losses, letting inventories reach a low level, or waiting until the end of a production year.

The Major Attractions

The corporation offers advantages that are unparalleled by the other legal structures. These benefits include continuity of management, limited personal liability, income tax minimization, estate planning, and specialization of management decision making.

---

[2]This tax treatment has been debated in Congress and may be eliminated in future tax legislation.

Most farm corporations are family corporations with no equity capital contributed from outside agriculture. However, more and more unrelated farmers are pooling their capital, labor, and management to form corporations. The corporate form of business has a strong attraction because of this pooling opportunity.

There are also special employee benefit and medical plans in which corporations can participate, but in which sole proprietorships and partnerships cannot. In some cases the benefits are attractive enough to swing the interested parties toward incorporation.

Limited Liability

An important characteristic of the corporation is the limited liability of the shareholders for the acts and obligations of the corporation. If the business fails or if, for some reason, the business is sued for negligent acts of its officers or employees, the shareholder is only risking the amount she/he has invested. Personal assets not included in the corporation are not at risk. It should be noted that this limited liability is of benefit only to the extent the shareholder has assets that are not included in the corporation. In other words, if the family farmer is going to transfer all assets to the corporation, limited liability is nearly meaningless. Conversely, a shareholder's corporation is not directly liable for that shareholder's personal obligations. Suppose an individual shareholder's creditor seeks satisfaction from the shareholder's property. The creditor may be awarded the shareholder's stock, but the corporation, as a separate legal entity, will continue.The creditor may be able to get the shareholder's stock to satisfy the debt, but he will not be able to reach the corporate assets. This means the corporation—that is, the farm itself—will remain intact and in operation.

Continuity of Operation

A corporation exists as long as the shareholders desire, if it continues to fulfill the requirements of the law. Simply stated, this means the corporation's life may be perpetual or be shortened as the shareholders see fit. The shareholders of a corporation come and go, die and leave the shares to heirs, with no effect on the operational continuity of the corporation. As a practical matter, the death of an important member may have serious consequences for the actual decision-making processes and operation, but the separate legal entity continues to exist. Proper planning will facilitate solution of practical problems which arise upon the death of a key shareholder.

The perpetual life of a corporation may be a hazard, particularly to minority shareholders. Many farm corporations pay out most of their earnings in the form of salaries and bonuses to minimize the double-tax aspect (see below). While this is acceptable to shareholders who are also employees, a son or daughter not employed by the corporation and not receiving dividends may not realize a return on his assets comparable to what assets of equal value would earn elsewhere. Furthermore, the minority shareholder may find it difficult to withdraw from the business because there is no ready market for his or her shares in the farm business. Without a ready market for the stock, a person may be "locked in" to the corporation, subject to the rule of the majority.

Arrangements for requiring or permitting the purchase of stock by the corporation or the remaining shareholders may be included in the articles of incorporation, bylaws, or by separate side agreements. As noted above, a corporation must fulfill requirements of law to be allowed by the state to continue. If the corporation fails to meet these requirements, the corporation will be terminated by the state and the articles of incorporation are forfeited.

Tax Aspects

Certain corporations are in a rather unusual position under the federal income tax laws. The "small corporation," a category in which most family farm corporations fit, may be taxed as a regular corporation or choose to be taxed under provisions very similar to those for a partnership.

As mentioned earlier, the regular corporation is taxed at a rate of 15 percent on the first $25,000 of corporate profit and at a rate of 46 percent on all corporate profit above $100,000. In reality, however, that may not be the end of the tax question for a family farm using the regular tax rules. After the money has been reported as profit and taxed, it will ordinarily be distributed to the shareholders. Upon distribution to the shareholders, it will be taxed to them as a dividend, which is ordinary income.

It should be noted that this problem is not as significant as it first appears because any salary paid to a shareholder employee is a business expense, a deduction to the corporation, and income to the employee. Thus, to the extent that corporate earnings can be paid to the shareholder employees as salary, the double tax problem is avoided. One warning should be mentioned at this point. The salary arrangement for avoiding the double tax will be successful only to the extent that the salaries are paid for services actually rendered and only then to the extent that the compensation is reasonable for those services. This principle will almost surely defeat any attempt to pay an off-farm shareholder who has little or no contact with the farm operation. As a practical matter, however, in most family farm operations all potential profits can be paid out as salaries.

The election to be taxed as a small corporation requires that *all* shareholders consent. If a new shareholder buys into the corporation during a tax year, he is given a chance to consent. Just as the shareholders and the corporation may elect into this method of taxation, they may also elect out. If they fail to meet any of the requirements during a tax year, their status as a small corporation for tax purposes is automatically terminated retroactively as of the first day of their current tax year. In either case, the corporation can not reelect the small corporation tax method for a period of five years following termination.

Estate Planning

Estate planning has been a major factor in the development of family farm corporations. This is particularly true when the net assets of a husband and wife approach or exceed the level at which federal estate taxes become effective. The corporate structure, if executed properly, tends to allow a shareholder to minimize estate taxes at his or her death and, thus, conserve more of the estate for heirs.

Less red tape is involved in transferring shares of stock, either by gift or sale, than bulky assets like land, machinery, and livestock. Thus, the corporate business form may facilitate the transfer of a farm business from parents to children, although the process is complicated when there are several children and only one or two who wish to farm. A parent who wants to keep the farm intact for heirs who wish to farm may need to use nonfarm assets to equalize or make fair the distribution of assets among heirs.

COMPARING THE THREE STRUCTURES

Preceding sections have pointed out special characteristics of the three primary farm/ranch business structures. Choosing a business structure on only one special characteristic, estate planning for example, can lead to faulty decisions. Although one factor may have more weight (estate planning in the case of parents who desire to pass the family business on to the next generation efficiently), all characteristics of each structure should be considered. One means for comparing the business structures is on the basis of:

1. Resource acquisition
2. Continuity of existence
3. Liability of the owners
4. Participation in management
5. Compensation of management
6. Transferability of ownership
7. Tax planning[3]

Resource Acquisition

All farm businesses are concerned with having adequate resources to allow the business to attain certain objectives. The three business types vary particularly in ability to acquire capital. It is in the area of capital acquisition that the sole proprietorship may be most limited. The only source of capital in a sole proprietorship is from either prior earnings or debt from lending institutions. However, the amount a creditor will loan a farmer depends on earnings potential and personal wealth. Consequently, the funds obtainable will always be limited by the farmer's own circumstances.

Because of the need to realize economies of large size, capital requirements have outstripped the earnings potential of many agricultural firms in the recent past. Thus, new sources of capital or additional methods of moving funds into agriculture have been examined. One of these is to use the multiowner business organization. Partnerships often can raise funds more easily because the resources of several individuals are combined in one undertaking. Because several individuals are liable for a partnership debt, the partnership may be able to borrow on better terms than some sole proprietorships and corporations. Some of the larger feedlots are good examples of the use of the partnership structure to obtain new sources of capital.

The corporate structure may also facilitate the acquisition of capital. Like the partnership, a corporation allows and facilitates the pooling of capital by two or more individuals. In addition, during the estate transfer process, the corporation structure may encourage nonfarm heirs to maintain their ownership in agriculture and keep their inherited capital in the farm firm. However, the nonfarm heir will expect to be paid a return on inherited capital if the equity is left in the farm business.

---

[3]For further information see Thomas and Boehlje, *Farm Business Arrangements: Which One for You?* University of Minnesota, Extension Bulletin 401, 1976.

The corporate form of business organization also provides more longevity or a longer planning horizon for the farm firm. When a sole proprietor dies, the farm firm is frequently dissolved and divided among the heirs. However, a properly organized corporation will allow the farm firm to continue doing business as a single unit even after the death of the major shareholder. Thus, the corporate structure may help a farm firm attain and maintain an efficient and profitable size because lending institutions are aware that the business will continue operating when a parent (or other major shareholder) dies and the farm will not be dissolved. This awareness may encourage the lending institution to provide larger amounts of money for financial needs.

However, there may be disadvantages of the corporate structure with respect to borrowing funds from certain lenders. For example, to borrow funds from Federal Land Bank Associations and Production Credit Associations, the personal signature of a major stockholder may be required. Farmers Home Administration regulations are somewhat restrictive on farm corporations except for soil and water conservation loans. Thus, if a farmer hopes to borrow from one of these sources he/she must make sure that the firm, organized as a corporation, will qualify for their loans.[4]

The opportunity for labor and management specialization in multiowner firms is a plus for these structures over the sole proprietorship. Some partnerships and corporations are large enough to hire the best management at very high salaries, but that situation is limited primarily to the large farms in Florida, California, and the Southwest. The axiom of two heads being better than one still seems generally applicable, even for family farm corporations. It may be very difficult for a sole proprietor to be competent in all the areas of production, marketing, finance, and labor management required on commercial farms today.

Continuity of Existence

As indicated earlier, continuity of existence may increase the ability to acquire capital. Although sole proprietorships are under no legal time limit, they are not perpetual and are limited by the lifetime of the proprietor. Again, multiowner structures have significant advantages with respect to business continuity. The death of an individual in the farm operation does not mean the death of the farm as an entity. To maintain

---

[4]The major agricultural lenders seem to be getting less restrictive on farm corporation loans each year.

continuity in the case of death may be more costly for a partnership than for a corporation because it may be necessary to purchase the deceased partner's interest.

Continuity of existence is particularly important to consider in estate planning and in arranging for the transfer of a farm business from one generation to another. Multiowner organizations facilitate the transfer of property between generations without destroying the firm as a "going concern." The corporation seems superior to partnerships or sole proprietorships in terms of continuity.

Liability of the Owners

The degree to which owners of the farm business risk legal liability for the debts of the firm is a cardinal consideration. A single proprietor is personally liable for all business debts, to the extent of owned property. Likewise, each member of an ordinary partnership is, himself, fully responsible for all debts owed by the partnership, irrespective of the amount of his/her own investment in the business, unless otherwise specified. In a limited partnership, a limited partner is liable only for his/her contribution. Corporations seem to have a real advantage, as far as risk goes, over other legal structures. Creditors can force payment on their claims only to the limit of the farm corporation's assets, except in circumstances where a shareholder is also a director or a manager, who may be personally liable as well. Personal liability of corporation directors and officers most frequently occurs where their personal signatures are required in addition to corporate signatures. Cosigning of notes is frequently required with small farm corporations, and the advantage of limited liability is lost by the individual(s) who cosigns.

Participation in Management

To what extent the owners will participate in management decision making should also be considered in deciding on a business organization. There are positive and negative sides to this issue. When more than one person is involved in management (and each has the opportunity to specialize), the quality of the management input usually improves. At the same time, the potential for conflict between managers increases, and disagreements may be serious enough to result in the organization being dissolved. The sole proprietorship has no such problems with conflicts, but also offers fewer opportunities to specialize. The corporate structure may lead to conflicts; but unlike the partnership, if one manager decides to leave, the corporation does not have to be dissolved.

Compensation of Management

The sole proprietor is the sole recipient of the profits of the farm business. He gets everything that is left once bills have been paid and such fixed obligations as taxes and principal payments on debt are met. There is a strong incentive to work hard to make that profit figure as large as possible. Unfortunately, profits are highly variable from year to year in most farm businesses.

Ordinary partnerships are much like sole proprietorships with regard to compensation, but the importance of deciding on the distribution of profits ahead of time cannot be stressed too strongly. The potential of higher profits resulting from specialized management may be a factor favoring a partnership over a sole proprietorship.

Profit sharing and fringe benefit programs can be used to compensate corporate employees, even in the family farm corporation. Furthermore, a constant salary for management and employees can be established and bonuses paid in exceptionally profitable years. Most fringe benefit programs can be treated as ordinary expenses in the corporate structure, whereas similar outlays cannot be used for tax advantages in sole proprietorships or partnerships.

Transferability of Ownership

The transferability of ownership is another important consideration. It includes not only the transfer of property, but also the transfer of the management responsibility associated with that property. In many cases parents tend to think only about how to transfer their assets to the children or heirs. However, to make sure that those assets have the highest economic productivity for the heirs, parents should also be sure that the children have the opportunity to learn how to manage the assets.

Because the sole proprietorship is dissolved when a person dies, this business structure provides little assistance in transferring managerial responsibility to the next generation. In contrast, the corporation and the partnership facilitate the transfer of the firm as an entity. The multi-owner structures facilitate not only the transfer of assets, but also the transfer of management and financial responsibility from owners to heirs.

Recordkeeping

To be sure, all businesses should keep complete and concise records, but the requirements vary. The sole proprietor must have records adequate to prepare a defensible tax return. The partnership, too, must file an annual tax form. However, it should have a complete set of books so any individual partner can know how the business stands at any given time. Complete records will minimize the opportunities for disagreement among partners.

Doing business as a corporation requires a more comprehensive set of records than either a sole proprietorship or a partnership. In addition to regular accounting records, it must keep minutes of (at least) annual meetings of shareholders and the board of directors. Some state agencies may also require annual reports.

Tax Planning

The income, estate, and gift tax regulations on the different business structures will be a major concern. The counsel of a competent, experienced attorney or accountant should be obtained. Each situation is sufficiently different that it is difficult to generalize and say one structure is superior for a given group of businesses while another structure is best for a different group. Selection of a business organizational form will be based upon what the parties involved want to achieve.

In the case of income taxes, the sole proprietorship is taxed at rates ranging from 16 to 50 percent of taxable income. In a partnership, taxable income is transferred through to the individual owner-partners and they pay taxes on their share at the rate determined by their total taxable income. The upper limit tax rate for a regular corporation is 46 percent. Like the partnership, income in a Subchapter S corporation is transferred to the shareholders and taxed at individual rates.

A family corporation may provide the liquidity and flexibility that will result in substantial savings of federal gift and estate taxes when an estate is transferred from one generation to the next. Moreover, the corporate organization facilitates changing the ownership structure of the farm firm without affecting the asset structure by transferring shares of stock as gifts to the heirs.

SUMMARY

Every farm operator or potential operator should give careful consideration to the legal structure under which the farm/ranch will operate. The stakes may be high. The decision should involve a careful examination of the financial structure, the decision-making process, the goals of the parties, the physical make-up of the operation, and the various tax brackets of those involved, to name just a few. These factors are different in every situation. What is right for one may not be right for another. The advice of an attorney will be beneficial in analyzing business needs and in discussing in more detail the points raised in this chapter. The important choice of a legal structure should be an informed management decision.

APPLYING THE PRINCIPLES OF CHAPTER 14

1. Must the property used in a partnership be co-owned?

2. Is it true that a partnership can own only real property in the partnership's name?

3. There are some differences in the liability of partners to a partnership and parties to a corporation. What are they?

4. What are some disadvantages of partnerships? Corporations?

5. How might a corporation fit into a family's estate planning?

6. Which of the three business structures is likely to require the most recordkeeping? Is that bad?

7. How does a Subchapter S corporation differ from a Subchapter C corporation? Why would you consider a Subchapter S corporation?

8. Do partnership profits have to be shared 50–50?

9. How does the method by and the rate at which a regular (or Subchapter C) corporation is taxed differ from that of the Subchapter S corporation?

10. What is a way to minimize the effect of double taxation in farm corporations?

REFERENCES

Boehlje, Michael. "Economic Considerations in the Choice of a Business Organization," *Oklahoma Current Farm Economics*, March 1972, pp. 13–26.

_____. "Limited Partnerships and Investment Trusts for Real Estate Ventures," *Journal of American Society of Farm Managers and Rural Appraisers*, April 1974, pp. 73–80.

Harl, Neil E. *Farm Estate and Business Planning*. Skokie, Illinois: Agri-Business Publications, 1980.

Harl, Neil E. and J. C. O'Byrne. *The Farm Corporation*. Iowa State Univ., NCR Extension Publ. No. 11, 1981.

Levi, D. R. "Incorporating and Perpetual Indebtedness as a Financial Tool," Department of Agricultural Economics, University of Missouri, July 1969.

_____. *Incorporating the Washington Family Farm Business*, Washington Extension Service Bulletin 650, January 1974.

_____. *Organizing the Washington Family Farm Business as a Partnership*, Washington Extension Service Bulletin 651, January 1974.

Matthews, S. F. and D. R. Levi. *Missouri Agricultural Law*. Columbia, Mo.: Lucas Brothers Publishers, 1976.

Small Business Administration. *Choosing the Legal Structure For Your Firm*, Management Aids Series No. 80, Washington, 1966.

Thomas, Kenneth H. and M. D. Boehlje. *Farm Business Arrangements: Which One for You?* University of Minnesota Extension Bulletin 401, 1976.

Tucker, James. "The Legal Structures for Organizing Your Farm Business," University of Missouri Agricultural Economics Paper 1973–51, Columbia, 1973.

Credit Sources and Credit Factors

A large part of financial management revolves around choosing those alternatives which give the highest payback at an acceptable level of financial risk. Another important aspect is being businesslike in the acquisition and use of credit. A manager who does not attempt to anticipate the questions a lender will have is not likely to get the best loan terms the lender is capable of extending. Further, a good financial manager will probably find that one lender is best for some types of credit while some other creditor may be best in other situations.

Several credit sources are available to the qualified, credit-worthy borrower. Some lenders specialize in operating loans; others, in long-term credit. Still others make both long- and short-term loans. The following discussion of credit sources gives a general sketch of the primary agriculture creditors, the services they provide, and how they obtain money for their lending operations.

PRODUCTION CREDIT ASSOCIATIONS

Production Credit Associations are legally owned cooperative organizations, each operating within its federally chartered territory under adopted bylaws. Farmers, ranchers, and others who borrow for eligible purposes make up the membership of the associations. PCAs exist for the express purpose of *providing short- and intermediate-term credit* to agriculture.

As specialists in short- and intermediate-term credit, PCAs provide (1) dependable credit to qualified borrowers and (2) knowledgeable agricultural-finance consultants. Money is nearly always available regardless of market conditions, whereas commercial banks and insurance companies find it more difficult to maintain their supply of loanable funds to agriculture during periods of tight money. The experience of PCAs in agricultural lending enables them to service the demand for larger, more specialized loans that are characteristic of agriculture today.

PCAs have also begun to offer ancillary services like computer recordkeeping and analysis, equipment leasing, and specialized savings options. Because of their primary interest in agriculture, many PCAs have special loan programs for members of 4-H and Future Farmers of America.

When a farmer borrows from a PCA, he purchases capital stock (Class B stock) in the association. This member-owned stock plus accumulated surplus provides the capital base for the association. Farmers who continue as active borrowers retain their stock in the PCA. A farmer who becomes an inactive member may have the stock either refunded or converted to nonvoting stock (Class A stock).

By becoming a stockholder of the PCA, the borrower has a voice in the affairs of the association and is entitled to one vote at the annual meeting (each member has one vote regardless of the amount of stock owned). Policy of the PCA is set by a board of directors elected from the general membership. Each member has a vote in electing directors and is also eligible to serve on the board (barring any conflict of interest).

Although PCAs are local institutions, they do not depend upon local funds for lending purposes. PCAs obtain their loan funds primarily from the sale of members' notes and mortgages to a Federal Intermediate Credit Bank (FICB), which also supervises the lending activities and operations of the PCAs. The FICBs obtain funds through the sale of securities to the investing public. The PCAs may also obtain part of their lending funds through direct loans from the FICB and from the association's own income.

Interest rate to borrowers is determined by the cost of FICB securities sold on the nation's money markets. PCAs operate on an interest spread designed to cover their basic cost of operation. Any profits of PCAs, above necessary expenses and legal reserves, are returned to members. Currently, PCAs are multi-billion dollar lenders and rank as a major source of short- and intermediate-term credit.

PCA loans have maturity dates up to seven years and are usually tailored to fit the farm operation and the time income is available for repayment. Money is advanced as needed and interest is paid on the outstanding balance. The only limitation on loan size is the condition that the loan must be a sound credit need of the borrower and a financially safe commitment for the PCA. There is no fixed rule as to security. Security requirements vary by type of loan and the financial and management capacity of the borrower.

COMMERCIAL BANKS

Commercial banks continue to be a major source of agricultural credit. Although their share of the farm credit market has declined slightly over the past decade, they continue to account for over 35 percent of the total production agriculture loan volume.

Commercial banks offer several advantages to their agricultural borrowers. Two attractive features are competitive interest rates and "one-stop service" for short- and intermediate-term capital loans and long-term real estate loans.

Because banks offer a full range of banking services (i.e., checking and savings accounts, legal counseling, safe deposit boxes, financial counseling), they are able to get to know their customers. Through regular contact, trust and confidence is established. It is normal, then, for the customers to turn to the bank when they need credit.

Commercial banks will probably make three to four times more short-term than long-term agriculture loans. The rates of interest and other terms and conditions of such loans vary with the bank. To a bank, "long-term" is often ten years. Consequently, banks are not likely to be interested in a thirty-year agriculture real estate loan.

When banks do make true long-term agriculture loans it is probably as a service to a bank's farmer, rancher, or grower customer. The loan becomes a part of the general banking relationship between the farmer and the banker. Frequently the bank does not hold these long-term loans but places them with an insurance company or savings and loan association. Or the country bank may call upon a larger neighboring bank or city correspondent bank to participate in larger long-term loans.

Many banks in agricultural areas have agriculture departments with loan officers who specialize in agricultural lending. Loan plans and terms are geared for the needs and repayment capacity of farm and ranch borrowers.

The money loaned by commercial banks is obtained largely from depositors. Because the capital structure of country banks is often limited, many banks must limit the size of any individual loan they can make. Because quite often this limit is lower than the credit needs of many of their agricultural borrowers, commercial banks use other sources to supplement their own funds.

These sources include rediscounting of notes with Federal Reserve Banks and with larger metropolitan commercial banks. Most large city banks maintain a correspondent banking department that specializes in providing agricultural credit through affiliated country banks.

A relatively new way of supplementing local bank credit is through participation loans with PCAs and guaranteed loans with the Farmers Home Administration. Under the PCA joint participation loan, a commercial bank may, for example, advance funds to a farm or ranch borrower up to its lending limit. The balance of the funds needed to serve the borrower are then provided by a local PCA. Although two lenders are involved, from the borrower's standpoint the financing is handled as a single loan.

MERCHANTS AND DEALERS

It is a common practice for a farmer to purchase goods or services "on time" from general stores, feed dealers, machinery and implement companies, appliance stores, and automobile dealers. He usually agrees to pay for these goods at the end of the month or at a time when he expects to sell livestock, grain, or other products. Tractors and other farm equipment may be bought on a sales contract that provides for a reasonable down payment or trade-in and payment of the balance within a specified time.

Most merchant credit is short term. The interest rate may vary widely from one merchant to another. A usual practice is to charge no interest if a bill is repaid within a specified time, normally a month or less, and then charge a certain percentage per month on any outstanding balance. There is frequently no written agreement. The merchant agrees to allow the buyer to purchase on credit up to some maximum at his usual interest rate. Sales contracts involving the purchase of machinery or equipment usually include a specified interest and/or carrying charge.

Some dealers make a practice of selling strictly for cash. This usually results in lower prices for their goods since their cost of operation is lower. If a farmer doesn't have the cash to do business with the store that doesn't extend credit, the farmer can borrow from a regular lender in order to make his cash purchases. This is justified when the interest cost of borrowed money is less than the difference between buying from the "cash" store and buying at a "credit" store.

Since credit from merchant or dealer sources sometimes contains "hidden costs," farmers and ranchers usually obtain credit at lower costs when borrowing from a regular lender and paying cash for the goods they purchase.

LIFE INSURANCE COMPANIES

Life insurance companies tend to specialize in large, long-term loans on land. Insurance companies are interested in profits. Thus, they may be big holders of farm loans when they don't have better lending options for their money. A change in economic conditions may find their funds moving from farm loans to other investment options. Over the recent past, insurance companies have held about 10 percent of the long-term rural real estate credit.

Life insurance companies that make a number of farm loans will have well-organized loan departments staffed with professionals in credit and rural real estate appraisal. Loans are usually made through an agent of the company. Loans may also be made indirectly through correspondents such as mortgage brokers, mortgage companies, or commercial banks.

FEDERAL LAND BANKS

For more than half a century, the nationwide system of twelve federal land banks, one in each farm credit district, has been providing farmers and ranchers with long-term farm real estate loans. These loans are secured by first mortgages on real estate in rural areas and made through more than 500 local federal land bank associations. Loans are made to farmers, growers, ranchers, certain corporations engaged in agricultural production, rural residents, and selected farm-related businesses.

The federal land bank system is the leading institutional supplier of farm real estate financing and is a multi-billion dollar lender. It obtains loan funds through the sale of securities to investors on the nation's money markets. These securities are backed by the mortgages held by the banks and the net worth of the banks. They are not directly insured or guaranteed by the government.

Land banks have variable interest rate plans in effect, providing that interest rates may be lowered or raised depending on the cost of money to the banks. This allows the banks to adjust quickly to changes in the money markets and makes funds available at competitive rates to all borrowers.

Since the federal land banks are cooperatively structured, a borrower becomes a voting member of his local federal land bank association. Through this arrangement the associations are completely owned by their member-borrowers. In like manner, the associations completely own the banks. Thus, the system is cooperatively owned and controlled by the farmers it serves.

Federal land bank associations may loan up to 85 percent of the appraised value of rural real estate. However, most of the loans are for less than 75 percent of the appraised value. The term of the loan depends upon the borrower's desires and financial ability, but normally ranges from five to forty years.

Although they are primarily agricultural lenders, land banks make rural residence and farm-related business loans. Rural residence loans may be made for the purposes of building, buying, remodeling, improving, refinancing, or repairing a home. A farm-related business is one that furnishes custom services directly related to on-farm operating needs. Examples of such businesses are custom combiners, chemical applicators, or custom haulers.

FARMERS HOME ADMINISTRATION

The Farmers Home Administration (FmHA) is an agency of the U.S. Department of Agriculture. FmHA has over thirty different loan authorizations from water and sewer district loans to farm operating loans. The primary authorizations for agricultural production are for (1) farm ownership loans, (2) farm operating loans, (3) soil and water conservation loans, and (4) farm emergency loans.

Farmers Home Administration is a decentralized agency with 42 state offices and over 1,700 county offices. Most loan applications are made at the county offices and many can be approved at the local level. Larger and specialized loans are reviewed by district and state committees.

A borrower of FmHA agricultural credit must be a family size operator and be at least a part-time farmer. The borrower may receive part of his income from nonfarm employment, but farm income must be a substantial portion of the total family income. Labor must be furnished primarily by the farmer-borrower and his family, and he must be unable to obtain sufficient credit elsewhere at reasonable rates and terms.

The amount of money FmHA has available for the various farm loan authorizations varies from year to year. Funds are authorized by Congress through special legislation each year. Because of the nature of the agency, FmHA normally charges lower interest rates than other agricultural lenders.

Farm management counsel is given to FmHA borrowers to help them improve their management ability and improve their financial position. When one has gained the financial strength to become eligible for a loan from a commercial lender, the borrower is obligated to repay the FmHA loan and borrow from another source.

Long-term credit from the Farmers Home Administration is obtained principally for the development, purchase, and improvement of family-type farms by farmers who are unable to secure credit from other institutional sources. The financing program is worked out by the local FmHA representative to fit the needs and earning capacity of the individual farmer. During the course of the program the farmer receives counsel and supervision from the FmHA representatives. Long-term FmHA loans are attractive because of lower interest rates and loan maturity up to 40 years. Each borrower is expected to refinance a long-term loan when it is financially feasible to rely solely on normal commercial credit sources.

For further information and specific details concerning Farmers Home Administration, the reader should check with a county or state Farmers Home Administration office. At the time of this writing, Congress is discussing several changes in the FmHA.

INDIVIDUALS

Personal credit is the oldest source of credit. Debt to individuals is still the largest single source of long-term debt. Debt to individuals is often attractive because the money may be borrowed at lower interest rates than from commercial financial institutions. Further, in the case of long-term credit, individuals frequently require a lower down payment than is necessary when borrowing from institutional agriculture lenders.

Frequently a farmer who sells his farm and retires accepts part of the selling price in the form of a mortgage loan (commonly called a contract) on the farm. The interest on the loan provides the seller income on which to live, and such an arrangement usually results in a saving on personal income tax. Rather than the full gain from the sale being taxed in one year, it is spread over several tax years.

Whether a loan from an individual is satisfactory depends entirely upon the parties involved and the terms of the contract. Before borrowing from an individual, the farmer should thoroughly acquaint himself with the individual's reputation as a lender and be sure the terms fit his requirements. Furthermore, the death of an individual lender is likely to affect the status of the loan, whereas no such risk is present when borrowing from an institutional lender.

The proportion of total agriculture credit held by the various sources has been approximately as follows:

Banks	28%
Life Insurance Companies	8%
Cooperative Farm Credit System	29%
Farmers Home Administration	5%
Dealers and Individuals	30%

IS THE BORROWER CREDIT WORTHY? THE LENDER'S VIEWPOINT

The variety of sources of loanable funds discussed above suggests credit is available—at a price. There are several factors which practically all lenders consider (although they weigh the factors differently) and of which the borrower should be aware. Broadly, lenders look at:

1. Management
2. Repayment capacity or business volume and efficiency
3. Loan purpose
4. Loan security
5. Financial position and progress
6. The economic climate

Management: The primary focus here is on the individual, the borrower. What sort of person is he or she? Very likely, the character of the borrower comes first. Does she/he have a history of paying on time, of being honest and truthful in her/his dealings?

When a net worth statement is developed, is it complete? Are all liabilities, as well as assets, listed? Second, does the borrower demonstrate prior planning? For instance, has the borrower carefully thought through the potential loan (the amount needed and for how long), and does he/she have a plan for repayment? Finally, has he or she demonstrated the ability to manage? This does not necessarily mean ability to manage a farm. A young person starting a business will have to rely on a reputation of managing whatever resources he or she has had.

Repayment capacity: The ability to use the desired funds profitably is difficult for a lender to assess. The lender will probably place some emphasis on the past business record: past earnings are the business's report card. But what will the income and cost situation be after the new investment or application of funds?

In attempting to assess repayment capacity, the lender and borrower must determine the amount of income the business will generate, the expected annual expenses, the payment on prior debt obligations, and family living needs. No surplus means no debt repayment capacity—unless something gives.

The borrower can furnish some evidence of capacity by developing a budget to show the expected effect of the additional funds on the profitability of the business. Additionally, repayability can be illustrated with net income statements or cash flow statements adjusted to show the expected change in receipts and expenses if the firm had the benefit of the proposed borrowed funds. Such projections should be based upon careful and realistic analysis, as explained in earlier chapters.

Other factors that might influence a lender's assessment of repayment capacity are (1) the size of the farm business (in terms of gross sales generated); (2) the past production record (bushels per acre, pounds of milk per cow); and (3) other cash demands (family living needs, other debt). Potential income risk due to price and/or production variability would also be considered (remember the earlier discussion of variability of income from different enterprises).

Regarding repayment capacity, it might be useful to digress and discuss why lenders sometimes appear "too conservative," particularly to the borrower. There are two important factors, at least to lenders: (1) loans are becoming larger and (2) expansion of agriculture businesses may involve greater uncertainty.

As to the first, when the number of loans becomes smaller and the balance of each is larger, each loan becomes a higher percentage of the lender's total investments. The loss due to an error in only one loan can have a significant impact and put the lender in a shaky financial position.

The problem is further complicated by the increasingly specialized nature of some larger agriculture units. In many instances the process of expanding the size of the business is not a gradual one, but of necessity requires rather large changes in size. In dairying or confinement hog operations, for example, modernizing frequently requires substantial infusion of capital as the manager shifts toward a lower point on the long-run cost curve and takes advantage of economies of size. Shifting from a 30-cow dairy to a 300-cow dairy may be more efficient, from an investment standpoint, than making several jumps of 30 cows each. Yet making such large single changes poses serious problems not only for the dairyman, but for the lender as well. He finds himself in the uncomfortable position of needing to project management and repayment capacity for a totally untested scale dimension. The managerial skills of one who is quite successful with 30 or 60 cows may be inadequate to handle 300 cows.

Loan purpose: What is the borrower to do with the money? This question is obviously related to repayment capacity. The biggest questions here are: (1) Is the credit to be used for an income-generating purpose, i.e., will the loan be self-liquidating and not be a drain on other productive enterprises? and (2) Is the projected use the optimal use given the set of alternatives, the resources already available in the farm business, and the operator's ability? The creditor will likely place differential weight on operating versus investment (or ownership) debt. In the former case, the primary effects are on current year income. Debt for a longer term has more severe cash flow implications because it does not have the rapid turnover expected from annual operating credit.

The smart borrower is profit-oriented. He or she chooses to borrow on projects that will turn a profit without unnecessary risk to equity capital. He/she will use credit for new machinery, exotic breeds of livestock, or heavy fertilizer applications—if they are profitable. He is not adverse to feeding Holstein steers rather than choice whiteface. He will settle for a 14,000-pound herd average for his dairy rather than 16,000 pounds if the profit is not there to pay for the feed required to get the extra production. He will agree to a horizontal silo when he prefers an upright.

Loan security: The creditor's first obligation is to the success of his business or to the people whose money he is lending. He is interested in a safe loan or accounts payable. For some short-term loans the creditor will require no security. The borrower's character, as discussed above, is adequate.

Most loans require some security. To provide the security, the borrower pledges clearly described assets such as land, machinery, livestock, or stocks and bonds to the creditor. This pledged security is called collateral—that is, identifiable property that has a market value.

Financial position and progress: A creditor wants his or her accounts receivable (notes receivable) to be with farm businesses that are solvent, profitable, and growing. The two principal documents he or she is likely to use to determine these conditions are the financial statement (balance sheet) and net income statement (profit and loss sheet). The former is the major yardstick of solvency, and the latter of profits. A continuous series of these two statements over time is the principal device for measuring financial stability and growth potential. Other measures, like the debt/equity ratio or rate earned on investment, may be used as well.

It is particularly likely that a lender providing substantial intermediate or long-term credit will consider past net income performance. Although income varies widely from year to year, the history of several years will tell the lender if the prospective borrower is average or above. Has the applicant been going forward or backward in recent years?

Out of interest in security, the lender may try to assess the borrower's capacity to withstand a "lean" year, or perhaps two. The financial statements also show other debts and their potential debt-servicing demands.

It seems logical that younger farmers will have more debt in relation to their net worth than older farmers. Their limited financial position means younger farmers must choose enterprises that make greatest use of limited capital. To do so requires sound economic analysis, careful planning, and a willingness to use physical energy and a high level of educational training.

WHAT TO EXPECT FROM A LENDER

Some farmers and stockmen have the opinion that a borrower is at the mercy of lenders. That need not be the case. In fact, it should rarely be the case. Just as a cattle feedlot operator has to keep resources (labor, facilities, land) in use and cattle moving through the lots to make a profit, so a lender must keep resources busy.

Lenders make profits by lending their money. Dealers use credit as a means of attracting clients, being competitive with other sellers of merchandise, and building customer loyalty. However dealers usually recognize that their primary function is to merchandise products, not to finance them.

In addition to (1) a competitive interest rate and (2) loan maturity that is consistent with the repayment capacity of a proposed loan, a borrower should expect some or all of the following qualities from a lender or creditor:

1. Financial reliability
2. Agriculture knowledge
3. Competent and confidential consultation

Financial reliability/responsibility: A good lender should know his or her business. He/she should understand, and be able to explain, the various financing arrangements, contracts, financial statements, and credit documents. He/she should be able to explain the implications of alternative financing strategies for a business. When a farmer has financial or legal questions the lender cannot personally handle, he/she should have access to competent professionals who can answer them.

For sound requests, a lender should be ready to provide, or help secure, all necessary credit. If a request does not measure up to good credit practices, the lender should say "No" and be able to explain why.

A reliable lender will be around to finance one's credit needs next year and the year after that. He should have adequate reserve to meet a borrower's expanding credit needs and must have loanable funds even in times of tight money or financial "droughts."

A lender's policy during "hard times" is also important. A lender who is concerned about a borrower's welfare will not cut a borrower off during temporary periods of low income. Neither will he carry a borrower too long.

Agriculture knowledge: A lender should understand agriculture and its peculiar problems and be informed of new developments in agriculture and in financing agriculture. A trained, experienced agricultural lender who has had an opportunity to observe successful farmers will be in a position to pass along information about profitable operations or techniques. The benefits of such insight may provide constructive alterations in production or financial plans.

A dependable consultant: A lender should be interested in the borrower's success and be willing to confer periodically about the business. Of course, the discussions, particularly those on financial matters, should be held in strict confidence.

The lender should be open to questions about financing procedures—that is, the lender's commitments, the borrower's commitments, actual APR, and other relevant items. He/she should also be willing to appraise the borrower's financial position and financial statements frankly.

Able to advise on matters beyond the farm gate, a good lender should be informed on the state of the economy and the directions that economic forces such as interest rates and demand for agricultural products are likely to take. A lender who is knowledgeable about major economic issues can simplify the decision-making process for a manager.

SUMMARY

The decisions on where to establish credit and for what terms can mean the difference between success and failure in farming and ranching. Wise use of credit is more than simply getting the lowest interest rate or the biggest loan. This chapter has pointed out that:

• There are a variety of potential sources of agriculture credit. Some, like PCAs and merchants, specialize in short- and intermediate-term credit. Others, like Federal Land Banks and insurance companies, deal in long-term credit.

• There are several factors about a borrower and the proposed loan that a lender is likely to try to "size up." These include the manager, repayment capacity of the business, loan purpose, loan security or collateral, and financial position and/or progress of the business.

• A wise borrower will shop around. While cost of the loan is important, there are other valuable services that competent lenders can provide. These services might include (1) tax or estate planning, (2) cash flow and financial planning and (3) consultation on nonfarm economic variables that are likely to have an impact on agriculture.

APPLYING THE PRINCIPLES OF CHAPTER 15

1. Natural Farms, Inc., has two different projects in which they would like to invest. They currently have a debt-equity ratio of 40,000: 80,000. Project A will require debt of $10,000 and Project B will require $30,000. Lender X will loan the full $40,000 at 12% interest and Lender Y will loan the first $10,000 at 9% and the next $30,000 at 13%. Does this relate to principles discussed in this chapter?

2. Why are individuals a continuing major source of long-term credit?

3. Why are commercial banks a popular source of short-term credit?

4. Is the Farmers Home Administration a part of the Cooperative Farm Credit System? Who can borrow from FmHA?

5. Suppose you were a well-established, successful rancher who wanted to borrow $20,000 for three years. What lenders might you visit?

6. A young, part-time farmer holds down a job paying $700 per month. He is just getting started in farming and is having difficulty meeting his farming bills. What lenders might he logically visit?

7. A lender is a source of credit. Is money the only service you should expect from a qualified agricultural lender?

REFERENCES

American Bankers Association. *Agricultural Credit Analysis Handbook.* Washington, D.C.: American Bankers Association, 1975.

Evans, Carson D., *et al. Balance Sheet of the Farming Sector, 1974,* Agriculture Information Bulletin No. 376, Economic Research Service, USDA, Washington, D.C., 1974.

Farm Credit Administration. *The Farm Credit Act of 1971.* Washington, D.C., 1972.

_____. *The Cooperative Farm Credit System,* Circular 36, Washington, D.C., March 1974.

Farm Credit Banks of Louisville. *Credit in Agriculture.* Louisville, Ky: Farm Credit Banks, 1974.

Hopkin, John A., Peter J. Barry and C. B. Baker. *Financial Management in Agriculture.* Danville, Ill: The Interstate Printers and Publishers, Inc., 1973.

Lee, W. F., M. D. Boehlje, A. G. Nelson and W. G. Murry. *Agricultural Finance,* 7th ed. Ames, Iowa: Iowa State University Press, 1980.

Schneeberger, K. C. and D. D. Osburn. *Financial Planning in Agriculture.* Danville, Ill: The Interstate Printers and Publishers, Inc., 1977.

Swackhammer, G. L. and R. H. Erickson. "Agriculture's Future Credit Needs and the Farm Credit System," *Agriculture Finance Review,* July 1971, pp. 6–14.

Capital Use and Credit Planning

- Categories of capital items
- Use of borrowed or leased capital to improve earnings
- Definition of leverage
- Effect of ratio of borrowed to owned capital on risk
- Influence of type of loan and lender on interest charges
- Influence of interest rate, repayment period, and type of loan on amounts required for loan liquidation

16

Capital is a collective term applied to *the assortment of productive inputs that have been produced.* The broad category of capital is often broken down into (1) operating, or working, capital and (2) ownership, or investment, capital. Operating capital refers to inputs or resources like feed, seed, and fuel that are normally used up within a production year. Investment capital refers to durable resources like machines and buildings in which money invested is tied up for several years. The quanity of capital is generally measured in terms of monetary value. Although land is sometimes included in a broad definition of capital, it is treated separately in farm management.

Several factors that influence decisions about use of capital, particularly borrowed capital, are discussed in this chapter. The topics included are:

1. What is capital?
2. The alternative uses of capital
3. Use of capital by farmers
4. The principle of increasing risk
5. Time and interest rate
6. Types of loans
7. The true interest rate

To the average person on the street, capital probably means money, stocks, or savings. That definition is too narrow. An important feature of capital is that someone had to be willing to forego immediate consumption so monies could be "invested" in productive inputs or capital assets. These capital items (1) may be used up during the next year in the production process or (2) may be durable assets such as livestock, equipment, or buildings which contribute to, or facilitate production processes.

The large volume of capital used in agriculture today requires that farm and ranch operators be able to manage both owned (equity) and borrowed capital effectively. As the ratio of borrowed to total capital increases, the risk of losing equity capital increases.

ALTERNATIVE USES OF CAPITAL

The income potential from a bundle of resources will be influenced by the choice of enterprises, the scale of enterprises, and the manager's choices in the purchase and use of productive capital.

Dealing with alternatives is what management is all about. Some of the tools for evaluating alternatives (e.g., partial budgets, cash flow budgets, financial statements) are discussed elsewhere. It is assumed that careful analysis will be given to major capital use decisions, although what is major will vary with the size of the business. A $5,000 expenditure may be major to a beginning farmer and of little significance to a large firm with abundant resources. Several questions on economic feasibility are appropriate regardless of business size:

1. Will it work on this firm/farm?

2. Have all the costs been considered? Are there hidden costs?

3. Will this use of capital necessitate others? Expansion of a hog enterprise likely means greater building and equipment needs and greater annual operating capital for feed, veterinary expenses, and so on.

4. How does this outlay affect flexibility? Is the firm being committed to a long-term fixed expenditure that will affect capital use decisions in the future?

5. How urgent is the capital outlay under consideration?

6. Will the decision to invest in one capital use alternative shut out some other alternative? There is a limit to funds, both owned and borrowed, which can be made available for capital outlays. The decision to spend money on a nice barn and elaborate fences may prevent the acquisition of a more productive resource or asset.

CAPITAL USE BY FARMERS AND RANCHERS

Almost everyone is familiar with the substantial capital demands in all forms of business, including farming and ranching. The total value of agriculture capital (including land) in the United States has climbed to approximately $1 trillion from $50 billion in 1940. Yet, the number of farms has been decreasing. It is common for viable farming operations to involve more than $600,000 in capital. Some representative, highly efficient, *one-man* farm situations developed by USDA suggested an optimal size, in terms of capital managed, of more than one-half million dollars. (See Exhibit 16–1.) Obviously, this does not all have to be *owned* capital. The capital requirements have more than doubled since 1973.

Debt per farm has also been increasing rapidly, especially among younger, aggressive operators. Evaluation of successful commercial farms in a number of states has found many where one-half or more of capital managed is rented or borrowed. The pressure to grow is likely to continue, and farm businesses are likely to grow faster than will be permitted by reinvesting annual savings from net income. Because it thus seems reasonable that demand for credit will continue to expand, much of this chapter is devoted to decisions about credit use.

CREDIT

Credit has been defined as the capacity to borrow. It is the right to incur debt for goods and/or services and repay the debt over some specified future time period. The business has use of a productive good while it is being paid for.

There are good reasons for using credit beyond the fact that funds generated within the business are inadequate. Using borrowed funds can (1) increase the returns on equity capital, (2) allow more efficient labor utilization and (3) increase income. Consider the case of an above average farmer who earns a 15 percent return on total capital managed, but who only has 40 percent equity. Exhibit 16–2 shows he could pay 8 percent interest (or rent) on the 60 percent of total capital managed he does not own and still realize 25.5 percent on his own capital. (See the last column, first row of Exhibit 16–2.) The table also reports the return to equity capital for several other levels of return to total managed capital and levels of borrowed capital. It is also obvious that the operator should earn greater than 8 percent, the interest rate he is paying, on total capital or his own position will suffer.

The process of using borrowed, leased, or "joint venture" resources from someone else is called *leverage*. Using the leverage provided by

Exhibit 16–1. Seven technically optimum one-person farms (adjusted to 1980 price conditions)

Region	Acres	Land capital		Other capital	
		1973	1980	1973	1980
Montana					
Wheat-barley	1,960	$245,000	$ 710,000	$ 57,000	$171,000
Kansas					
Wheat-grain sorghum	1,950	200,000	516,000	55,000	165,000
Indiana					
Corn-soybeans	800	480,000	1,747,000	130,000	390,000
Louisiana					
Rice-soybeans	360	108,000	270,000	50,000	150,000
Delta					
Cotton-soybeans	600	255,000	637,500	80,000	240,000
California					
Irrigated cotton	400	320,000	896,000	64,000	192,000
Irrigated vegetables	200	400,000	1,080,000	85,000	255,000

Exhibit 16–2. Percentage return to equity capital for alternative levels of return to all capital and equity positions; 8 percent assumed paid on borrowed capital

Percent return on total capital	Percent total capital borrowed		
	20	40	60
15	16.8[1]	19.7	25.5
10	10.5	11.3	13.0
5	4.3	3.0	.5
3	1.8	−.5	−3.0

[1]A 15% return of total capital managed becomes a 16.8% return on owned capital for an 80% equity position.

someone else's capital, the operator makes his/her own go farther than it otherwise would. For instance, a person who puts up $1,000 and borrows an additional $4,000 is using 80 percent leverage. The objective is to increase total net income and the return on one's own equity capital.

PRINCIPLE OF INCREASING RISK

The example above illustrated how an operator could improve the earnings on his own capital by using someone else's. But in the situation sometimes referred to as the increasing risk case, he could stand to lose. The principle of increasing risk may be stated thus: As the debt-to-equity ratio increases, the risk of losing one's own equity also increases (see Exhibit 16–3). Stated another way, the safety of a person's own net worth decreases as the equity percentage of total capital managed decreases. This is illustrated for a situation of $10,000 equity capital and varying levels of debt (Exhibit 16–4). Cases of +15 percent and −15 percent return on all capital for varied equity levels are examined. Interest on borrowed capital is assumed at 8 percent. Compare the earnings on equity rows for the +15 percent and −15 percent return cases. The "bite" taken from equity by a loss escalates faster (15, 38, and 84 percent) than the "gain" on equity (15, 22, and 36 percent) realized from the positive return case.

The principle of increasing risk explains why many managers do not go into debt to the full extent possible. They do not borrow money on capital items to the point that expected added returns equal the cost of borrowed funds and expected profits are maximized. Instead they under-

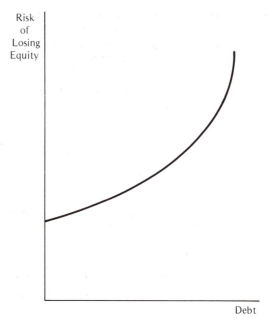

Exhibit 16–3. The principle of increasing risk.

estimate the profitability to allow for uncertainty associated with short-run and long-run decisions.

TIME AND INTEREST RATE

Any good book on money management suggests that the borrower/debtor "shop around" for credit. Among the comparisons to be made are (1) time allowed for repayment (loan maturity), (2) interest rate, and (3) service charges, or points, that may be added to the loan. These three factors determine the cost of the loan.

Since interest is a "rent" for the use of borrowed funds, it is logical that total interest increases with the length of the repayment period. Exhibit 16–5 presents the different amounts of interest repaid on a $10,000, 8 percent loan, when the repayment periods are varied from 5 to 30 years (assuming annual interest payments on unpaid loan balance and equal annual principal payments). In this example it costs $4,000 to spread the $10,000 repayment out over ten additional years. The manager must decide if the additional length of the repayment period (the loan maturity period) is worth the cost. The manager must of course also assess the ef-

Exhibit 16–4. Illustration of principle of increasing risk

	Percent equity		
	100%	50%	25%
Own capital	$10,000	$10,000	$10,000
Borrowed capital	0	10,000	30,000
Total capital	$10,000	$20,000	$40,000
Return of Plus 15%			
Income above costs	1,500	3,000	6,000
Cost of borrowed funds	0	−800	−2,400
Return above capital costs	1,500	2,200	3,600
Earnings on equity	15%	22%	36%
Return of Minus 15%			
Loss above costs	−1,500	−3,000	−6,000
Cost of borrowed funds	0	−800	−2,400
"Real" loss	−1,500	−3,800	−8,400
Earnings on equity	−15%	−38%	−84%

fects of various length repayment periods on cash flows. This example assumes the annual payment to include both principal and interest. Exhibit 16–6 shows the *average annual* payment for each loan maturity period, assuming the same conditions as above. By stretching out the repayment time, the payment due each year is reduced. This, of course, increases the total cost of the loan. The extra time can be worth the extra cost if it (1) permits staying in business rather than foreclosure or (2) allows greater flexibility in management's response to other profitable ventures and, consequently, greater profit over time.

Exhibit 16–5. Total interest repaid on a $10,000 loan; annual installments; interest rate at 8 percent on unpaid balance

Years of loan			
5	10	20	30
$2,400	$4,400	$8,400	$12,400

Exhibit 16–6. Annual average principal plus interest: $10,000 loan at 8 percent equal annual principal payments

	Years of loan			
	5	10	20	30
Annual P+i=	$2,480	$1,440	$920	$747

TYPES OF LOANS

There are a number of ways to classify loans: (1) installment versus single payment, (2) short-term versus long-term, (3) secured versus unsecured, (4) simple interest versus add-on, versus discount, and versus balloon. Each is briefly described to illustrate the variety of options and the possibility of getting a loan that suits one's needs by shopping around for credit.

Short-term: This is credit that is usually paid back in one year or less. In agriculture this type of credit is used to finance seed and fertilizer for crop production, feed and feeder livestock, wages for hired labor, machinery and equipment purchases, or family living expenses. Usually lenders expect short-term loans to be repaid after their purposes have been served—for example, after the crop is harvested or feeder animals are sold.

Loans for operating inputs like feed and fertilizer are assumed to be self-liquidating. That is, although the inputs are used up in the production, the added returns from their use will repay the money borrowed to purchase the input, plus interest. (It may also be assumed that the astute manager has figured in a risk premium and a return to labor and management.) Loans for investment capital items like machinery are not likely to be self-liquidating in the short term. Loans for family living expenses are not at all self-liquidating and must come out of net cash income after all cash obligations are paid.

Intermediate-term (IT): This is credit extended for several years, generally one to five years. This type of credit is normally used for purchases of buildings, equipment, and breeding stock. IT loans are used to purchase inputs that require longer than one year to generate sufficient returns to repay the loan.

Long-term: Loans for which repayment exceeds five to seven years and may extend to 40 years are classified as long-term. This credit is extended on assets (such as land) which have a long productive life in the business. Some types of land improvements, such as land leveling, orchard development, reforestation, land clearing, and drainageway construction may be financed with long-term credit.

Unsecured loan: Many lenders will hand out money on no other basis than a promise to repay. The borrower does not have to put up collateral; the lender relies on credit reputation. Unsecured loans sometimes carry a higher interest rate than secured loans and may be difficult or impossible to arrange for the business with a poor credit record.

Secured loan: This loan involves a pledge of some or all of a business's assets. The lender requires security as protection for its depositors against the risks involved in the use planned for the borrowed funds. The borrower may be able to bargain for better terms by putting up collateral, which is a way of backing one's promise to repay.

Installment loan: With this loan the borrower or credit customer repays a set amount each period (week, month, year) until the loan is cleared. Installment credit is similar to charge account credit, but usually involves a formal legal contract for a predetermined period with specific payments. With this plan the borrower usually knows precisely how much will be paid and when.

Single payment: With this type of loan the borrower pays no principal until the note comes due. Because he/she must eventually pay the debt in full, it is important to have the self-discipline to set aside money to be able to do so. This type of loan, sometimes called the "lump sum" loan, is generally repaid in less than a year.

Simple interest: Sometimes called a loan for which interest is paid on the unpaid loan balance, this loan requires the borrower to pay interest only on the actual amount of money outstanding. Interest is paid only for the actual time (e.g., 30 days, 90 days, 4 months and 2 days, 12 years and one month) the money is used.

A loan at simple interest at 12 percent a year means you pay 12 cents a year for each $1 you borrow. If you borrow $100 at 12 percent for a full year and make no principal payment until the end of the year, you would have full use of the money for a year. At the end of the year you would repay $112. If you repaid the loan in 6 months the interest would be half, or $6.

Add-on interest: Under this method, the borrower pays interest on the full amount of the loan for the entire loan period. Interest is charged on the face amount of the loan at the time it is made and then "added on." The sum of the principal plus interest is then divided equally by the number of payments to be made. The borrower is paying interest on the face value of the note although he/she has use of only a part of the initial balance once principal payments begin. This type of loan is sometimes called the "flat rate" loan.

On an add-on loan, the interest charge is added to the loan or purchase. On a 12 percent per $100 loan for a year, you would repay $112. If you make monthly repayments you do not have full use of the money for the entire year. Month by month you are retiring the debt, but are still paying on the full $100 at 12 percent. If you repay $100 plus 12 percent in 12 monthly installments of $9.33 each for a total of $112, your true annual interest is 21.4 percent. That is nearly double what you may have thought you were paying. That is because you only have an average debt, considering the monthly repayment, of approximately $50.

Discount or front-end loan. In this loan the interest is taken out first; that is, the interest is calculated and then subtracted from the principal. A $5,000 discount loan at 10 percent for one year would result in the borrower only receiving $4,500 to start with, and the $5,000 debt would be paid back, as specified, by the end of a year.

On a discount loan, the lender discounts or deducts the interest in advance. On a $100 discounted loan at 12 percent, you are handed $88 rather than $100. But, you repay the full $100. The true annual interest rate for a 1-year loan of $100 with equal monthly installments of $8.33 for a 12 percent discount loan ($88 actually received) would be 24.2 percent.

Balloon: Sometimes referred to as the "last payment due," the balloon loan normally requires only interest payments each period until the final payment, when all principal is due at once. The concept is the same as the single payment loan, but the due date for repaying principal may be five years or more in the future, rather than the customary ninety days or six months for the single payment loan.

In some cases a principal payment is made each time interest is paid, but because the principal payments do not amortize (pay off) the loan, a large sum is due at the loan maturity date.

Amortized loan: The amortized plan is a partial payment plan where part of the loan principal and interest on the unpaid principal are repaid each year. The standard plan of amortization, used in many intermediate and long-term loans, calls for equal payments each period, with a larger proportion of each succeeding payment representing principal and a small amount representing interest. The repayment schedule for a ten-year standard amortized loan of $10,000 at 7 percent is presented in Exhibit 16–7.

The constant annual payment feature of the amortized loan is simi-

Exhibit 16–7. Amortization of $10,000 loan in 10 years by equal annual installments; interest at 7 percent

Year	Unpaid principal at beginning of year	Payment at end of year		
		Interest	*Principal*	*Total*
1	$10,000.00	$ 700.00	$ 724.00	$ 1424.00
2	9,276.00	649.30	774.70	1424.00
3	8,501.30	595.10	828.90	1424.00
4	7,672.40	537.10	886.90	1424.00
5	6,785.50	475.00	949.00	1424.00
6	5,836.50	408.60	1015.40	1424.00
7	4,821.10	337.50	1086.50	1424.00
8	3,734.60	261.40	1162.60	1424.00
9	2,572.00	180.00	1244.00	1424.00
10	1,328.00	93.00	1331.00	1424.00
Total	—	4240.00[1]	10000.00	14240.00

[1]Figures in this column are rounded and do not total exactly as shown.

lar to the "add-on" loan described above, but involves less interest because it is paid only on the outstanding loan balance, as with simple interest. The annual payment for the ten-year, $10,000, 7 percent loan is separated into principal and interest in Exhibit 16–7. Amortization tables, which can be used to determine the regular payment for an amortized loan, can be found in almost any finance book or Appendix Table 3 of this book. The $1,424 annual payment for the ten-year loan was determined by using the amortization factor (AF) of 0.1424 and multiplying that by $10,000, the face value of the loan.

As another example, suppose new equipment was being financed with an 18-year, $25,000 note at a 9 percent interest rate. Using Appendix Table 3, find the AF (0.1142) and multiply by $25,000. The annual payment is $2,855. A total of $51,390 would be repaid in the eighteen years. This amplifies the comments made earlier about the effect of time and interest rate on amount paid back over time—in this case, $25,000 borrowed and $51,390 repaid.

THE TRUE (APR) INTEREST RATE

The discussions of time and interest rate and different types of loans should make the reader aware of the opportunity for confusion when it comes to borrowing money or purchasing items on credit. The opportunity for confusion exists even though Truth-in-Lending legislation was passed that states a borrower must be told *both* the finance charges and the annual percentage rate (APR)—also called the *effective interest rate*—before a loan is granted.

Consider the car buyer who contacted four lenders about an automobile loan for $2,470 to be repaid in 36 equal monthly payments. The lenders quoted interest rates from "one percent per month" to "five and one-half percent add-on" and monthly payments from $82.04 to $86.00. Obviously, some lenders did not quote the true APR. Thus, it was necessary to turn to a reliable finance book for a formula to compute APR (see formula below). Exhibit 16–8 summarizes the quoted finance charges, monthly payments and interest rates, plus the true APR for each lender. All lenders gave the true finance charges for the stated monthly payments, but the variance in quoted and actual interest rates was surprising.

Estimating APR

$$\text{Rate} = \frac{6 \times m \times C}{3P(n+1) + C(n-1)}$$

m = Number of payments per year
C = Total finance charges
P = Original loan balance (principal)
n = Total number of payments made over the term of the loan

The above discussion is not mean to discredit lenders; however, it does point out that financial decision making requires a manager's careful attention. The facts must be both collected and analyzed.

Three similar IT loans are presented in Exhibit 16–9 to illustrate the

Exhibit 16–8. Comparative schedule of monthly payments and quoted interest rates for a $2,470 loan for 36 months

Lender	Total finance charges	Monthly payment	Interest rate quoted	Effective annual percentage rate
Bank A	$499.28	$82.48	5.5% add-on	12.3%
Bank B	518.00	83.00	7.0% add-on	12.8%
Bank C	626.00	86.00	10.3%, plus service chg.	15.2%
Credit Union M	483.44	82.04	1% per mo.	12.0%

Exhibit 16–9. Repayment schedule for three different "10 percent" loans: semiannual payments

	Plan I simple interest	Plan II add-on	Plan III discount
Original loan balance	$6,000	$6,000	$5,400
Payment 1	1,300	1,300	1,000
Payment 2	1,250	1,300	1,000
Payment 3	1,200	1,300	1,200
Payment 4	1,150	1,300	1,100
Payment 5	1,100	1,300	1,100
Payment 6	1,050	1,300	1,050
Annual Percentage Rate (APR)	10%	16.0%	11.1%
Quoted Rate	10%	10%	10%

potential difference in finance charges and APR for the three loan types discussed earlier. The basic loan in the illustration is a three-year, $6,000 loan with $1,000 semiannual principal payments plus interest at "10 percent." The loan repayment plans are:

Plan I: Simple interest on unpaid loan balance

Plan II: Add-on interest on the original loan balance

Plan III: Discount loan: the first year's interest is discounted from the loan balance and only $5,400 is received. Interest in years 2 and 3 is the same as would be charged on a simple interest loan.

Although the nominal rate for the three loans is 10 percent, the annual percentage rate varies from 10 to 16 percent.

YOUR CREDIT RATING

To get credit, some lender must consider you a good risk. Thus, your credit standing is a major asset to protect. You build up your standing over time. You will take it with you if you move. Credit bureaus and other credit-related institutions share information from coast to coast. In today's high technology world it is easy for the lending community to share information about your ability and reliability in meeting your obligations.

If your credit application is turned down, do not consider the case closed. It is your right to know why you have been denied credit. The company or lending institution denying you credit must inform you of their reasons. The reason may be the result of inaccurate information shared about you by some credit bureau or other agency. Inaccurate credit information can be corrected, and the revised information furnished to a prospective lender.

See to it that information you provide a prospective lender or creditor will stand investigation. If you fail to give full or truthful information, you will damage your credit record. That is a serious error in financial management.

SUMMARY

This chapter has provided a framework for viewing capital use decisions and has discussed some factors and sources to consider in using credit. Among the points made were:

- The term *capital* applies to many assets, not just money.

- What is economically feasible for one farm business may not be at all feasible for another. Managers must consider their particular financial circumstances, as well as the capacity of existing resources (and/or proposed additions), in determining the soundness of proposed financial commitments.

- Use of borrowed capital has been increasing rapidly. Because the increased use of debt makes decisions more risky, planning and analysis become increasingly important.

- Interest rate and loan maturity (repayment period) affect the cost of a loan, hence, cash flows. A twenty-year, 8 percent loan will result in interest paid equal to the original face value (balance) of the loan.

- There are many different types of loans and financing arrangements. In spite of Truth-in-Lending legislation, a borrower should know how to figure the "true" annual percentage rate on a loan.

Once a manager determines credit needs and understands the factors that influence the cost of a loan, he/she is ready to choose a lender and arrange financing.

APPLYING THE PRINCIPLES OF CHAPTER 16

1. List some operating capital items regularly used in farm or ranch businesses in your area.

2. A tractor is a durable asset; so is a feed grinder-mixer. Is a cow a capital item? Why?

3. What are some potential "hidden costs" associated with the decision to expand a confinement cattle feeding enterprise?

4. Estimate total capital managed, both operating and ownership capital, for a farm or ranch in your area. What proportion is operating capital? What portion is nonland ownership capital? What portion is land capital?

5. What is leverage? What are its hazards?

6. What is the leverage position of a person with $120,000 in assets and $80,000 in debts?

7. What is the true interest rate on a $500 loan paid back in 11 equal monthly payments of $55.

8. Check the computation of APR in Exhibit 16–9. What is n in each case? What is C? How much is P?

REFERENCES

Bailey, Warren R. *The One-Man Farm.* ERS-519, Economic Research Service, USDA, Washington, D.C., August 1973.

Brown, Thomas G. "Meeting the Challenge of Credit Demands with Farm Financial Planning." Paper presented to the Arkansas PCA Directors Conference, Little Rock, Arkansas, December 1972.

Carson, E. E. and P. R. Robbins. "Debt—How Much?" Department Paper 73–26, Department of Agricultural Economics, Purdue University, 1973.

Evans, Carson D., *et al. Balance Sheet of the Farming Sector, 1974.* Agriculture Information Bulletin No. 376, Economic Research Service, USDA, Washington, D.C., 1974.

Hopkins, John A. and T. L. Frey. "Financing Agriculture in the Great Plains," in *Proceedings of Seminar on Agricultural Finance in the Great Plains.* G.P. No 51, Kansas Agricultural Experiment Station, 1970.

Hopkin, John A., Peter J. Barry and C. B. Baker. *Financial Management in Agriculture.* Danville, Ill.: The Interstate Printers and Publishers, Inc., 1973.

Schneeberger, K. C. and T. G. Brown. *Before You Borrow.* Missouri Extension Science and Technology Guide 410, January 1970.

Schneeberger, K. C. and D. D. Osburn. *Financial Planning in Agriculture.* Danville, Ill.: The Interstate Printers and Publishers, Inc., 1977.

Small Business Administration. *The ABC's of Borrowing.* Management Aids Series No. 170, Washington, D.C., 1969.

Swackhammer, G. L. and R. H. Erickson. "Agriculture's Future Credit Needs and The Farm Credit System," *Agriculture Finance Review.* July 1971, pp. 6–11.

Land Acquisition and Use Strategies

HIGHLIGHTS

- Land: the basic income-producing resource
- Leasing as an alternative to land ownership
- Influence of goals and financial position on choice of land control method
- Use of income capitalization approach to determine land value
- Leasing options: cash, flexible cash, and share leases
- Sharing of returns under equitable lease

17

Although it is commonly recognized that inputs/technologies such as machinery, fertilizer, and confinement livestock facilities can substitute for land, within limits, the amount of land controlled by an operator continues to be one of the most common measures of a firm's size.

For the individual manager, land acquisition questions generally revolve around issues like "How much land do I need to attain a desired level of income?" or "Should I own or rent land?" or "If I rent land, what leasing arrangement should I choose?"

After reading this chapter the reader should be familiar with (1) the major issues associated with the buy versus rent decision and (2) analytical approaches for evaluating leasing and purchase options. Some topics covered are:

1. The incentives to control land
2. An approach to land valuation
3. Advantages and disadvantages of ownership
4. Leasing options
5. Leasing equity considerations
6. Some advantages and disadvantages of leasing
7. A framework for comparing leasing with purchasing

Land is a basic, if not *the* basic, ingredient for agricultural production. It is the distinguishing characteristic that sets farming and ranching apart from other businesses.

The total amount of land is essentially fixed. The amount available for agricultural production has decreased slightly due to expansion of cities, new highways, and other public uses. On the other hand, the land base has been expanded through the reclamation of some arid and forest areas. The amount of land in specific use categories expands and contracts according to the relative price of various inputs and products. As product prices go up relative to input prices, there is an incentive to use land more intensively, and vice versa.

INCENTIVES TO CONTROL LAND

There are two major reasons to gain control of land. *Land has the ability to produce (1) income and/or (2) satisfaction.* From an agricultural perspective, both factors are important; but for the operating farmer or rancher, the income-generating aspect is primary. Although some farmers are in a position to speculate on land, most want to control land (frequently more land than they now control) because their livelihood depends upon the resources they operate. Land is a basic and major resource.

While this chapter emphasizes agricultural aspects of land value and use, it is well to mention some of the competing demands for agricultural land: (1) urban expansion for residential, industrial, or roadway uses; (2) public and private recreational uses, such as national parks and forests, amusement parks, golf courses, and weekend homesites; (3) public service facilities, such as interstate highways or lakes for flood prevention, irrigation, and/or power generation; and (4) land speculation.

LAND OWNERSHIP

For both part-time and full-time farm/ranch operators, land ownership may seem essential to a secure base of operations. Although the owned unit may only be a few acres, the operator who sees the need for an investment in specialized buildings or facilities can construct them on the owned land over which the operator has control.

Land purchase to expand an existing unit is another reason for ownership. Such an expansion may be justified by spreading costs or permitting the adoption of new technologies. However, leasing added land may offer the same opportunities. A manager-operator should be careful to consider the alternatives and ask, "Am I purchasing land because it is economically feasible or for some other reason?"

Land ownership is a major goal of many farmers and ranchers. They receive great satisfaction from owning the land they operate. Ownership may also result in capital accumulation through appreciation. Though less liquid than assets like stocks and bonds, land values do change over time; during recent decades those changes have generally been appreciations in values. Although the values varied by localities, agricultural land appreciated at a rate greater than 5 percent per year over the last two decades. Exhibit 17–1 shows the very favorable appreciation some land owners realized during the 1965–1976 period and compares that with the Dow-Jones stock index. Such a situation, however, has not generally been the case. During the twenty years after World War II, the Dow-Jones index increased about twice as fast as farmland.

Without a doubt, land appreciation has been a big factor in the ability of owners to increase their holdings of land. Increased land values make it easier for those purchasing on long-term mortgages to acquire even more land as a result of equity appreciation.

AN APPROACH TO LAND VALUATION

During the past two decades, a majority of the land purchased has been to enlarge existing farms or ranches. For persons considering land purchase, three questions stand out:

1. What is the land worth to me? That is, what returns, including cost savings and potential capital gains, are expected as a result of a certain land purchase?

2. What am I able to pay for land in terms of cash flow repayment? What is the sum of the down payment plus the maximum debt I can pay off?

3. What are the opportunity costs of tying money up in land as compared to other investment options open to me?

Several methods can be used in evaluating the question of land worth. One popular method is the *adjusted income capitalization approach.* This approach is particularly relevant for the person buying land to use in farming or ranching. The income capitalization method involves determining the estimated net income that can be earned each year by the property in question and then, by using an appropriate interest rate, estimating the maximum price the property will support.

The usual approach for estimating annual returns is budgeting. A budget for the determination of net income from a 1,200 acre cattle ranch

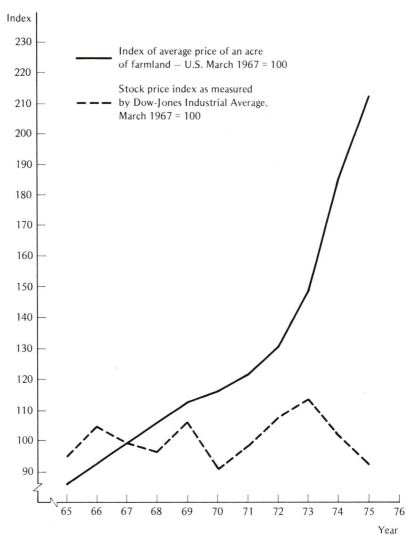

Exhibit 17–1. Trends in land and stock prices, 1965–76.

is illustrated in Exhibit 17–2. A stocking rate of 12 acres per cow is assumed, so the budget is for a 100 head beef-cow herd. Interest at 9 percent is charged on money tied up in cattle; labor is charged at $3 per hour. Feed and other input prices are based upon the average of recent years and adjusted for projected inflation or other trends. Gross receipts are based upon normal production and estimates of future price conditions.

Exhibit 17–2. Production requirements and projected income for 100 head beef cow herd on a 1,200 acre cattle ranch; spring calves sold in the fall as stockers or feeders

Nonland Capital items	No.	Estimated value each	Total value
Eqpt., hay storage, corrals, etc.			$ 28,000
Brood cows	100	550	55,000
Bulls	4	1,500	6,000
Replacement heifers	16	400	6,400
Machinery, trucks			79,000
Total			$174,400

Item	Description	Value
Gross receipts		
Cull cows	14 cows × 970 lb. × 48¢ per lb.	$ 6,518
Calves	72 calves × 450 lb. × 85¢ per lb. (avg.)	27,540
Total		$ 34,058
Variable Inputs		
Winter feed and minerals		$ 5,147
Vet. and medical		467
Bull depreciation		500
Hauling and marketing		345
Miscellaneous costs		3,906
Interest on operating capital @ 11%		494
Total Variable Costs		$ 10,859
Nonland Costs		
Interest on livestock capital		$ 7,640
Interest on machinery and equipment capital		4,247
Taxes		1,250
Family labor @ $4.00/hour		2,800
		$ 15,937
Return to Land, Risk and Management		$ 7,262

An estimate of return to land, management, and risk taking is computed by subtracting all costs, including a charge for labor, from gross receipts. The net return value is $7,262. This is the net income value that is capitalized in estimating the value of the 1,200 acre ranch.

Capitalization?

The $7,262 is an estimate of the average income that will be realized each year in the future if the 1,200 acre ranch is purchased. However, as

Chapter 18 shows, it makes good economic sense to strongly prefer a dollar today over a dollar some time in the future. For this reason, it is helpful to express future income in terms of current (or present value) dollars when there is decision to make. This is done by discounting future income by a reasonable rate of interest—called the discount rate (r).

The present value of a future income amount is computed by multiplying income by $1/(1 + r)^n$ where n equals the year in which the income will be realized. This is the standard present value (PV) formula:

$$PV = \frac{A_1}{1+r} + \frac{A_2}{(1+r)^2} + \frac{A_3}{(1+r)^3} + \ldots + \frac{A_n}{(1+r)^n}$$

If the net income to land ($7,262) can be expected to be constant in amount from year to year and to continue indefinitely, the present value formula gives the same result as the capitalization formula: $V = A/r$. The discount rate, r, should be the rate of return that the operator can earn on other investments of equal risk and uncertainty as land purchase, i.e, the opportunity cost of capital. A minimum figure would be the interest rate that could be earned on a savings account. Another way to choose a discount rate is to use the interest rate paid when borrowing money.

The discount rate does make a difference. For example, the value of $7,262 capitalized at 5 percent (7,262 ÷ .05) is $145,240. Capitalized at 8 percent, the estimated land value would be $90,775. Stated another way, if a person paid $145,240 for the ranch, he/she could expect a 5 percent on the investment.

What Is Wrong?

It is highly unlikely that a 1,200 acre ranch could be purchased for $145,240 ($121 per acre). You may ask, "What is wrong?" The answer is, "Nothing—if our figures are correct." If the production, prices, and costs are reasonable and the discount rate chosen makes sense, this particular ranch cannot support an investment greater than $145,240—or less if a discount rate above 5 percent is used—on strictly an income basis.

There may be adjustments to the estimated value that should be considered. Some of these are:

1. Adjustments for appreciation. Land prices have been increasing so a buyer may pay more than the income capitalization approach would suggest because the property is expected to be worth more in the future.

2. Adjustments for size. Larger tracts usually sell for less per acre than smaller tracts of comparable quality.

3. Adjustments for location: location with regard to roads, markets, and centers of economic activity affect land prices.

4. Adjustments for minerals. The proportion of mineral rights that go with a tract will influence the property value.

5. Adjustments for buildings. Houses, barns, and quality of fences are factors that enter into the value of a property.

Advantages of Ownership

Land has generally been a sound investment in the past. The average price today is 3.5 times the price of two decades ago. Land has been good security even though some purchases have not realized a particularly good annual *cash* return. (Some stocks don't pay very well either.) It has become a cliché to say that farmers live poor and die rich, but there is a lot of truth in the statement.

However, some farmers have taken real advantages of the windfall gains they realized from land appreciation. As their equity position has been improved by increases in land value, these farmers have turned around and borrowed more money on the "new equity." That is, they have used the leverage principle. In some cases the use of high levels of leverage has caused operators to have to sell out because they couldn't make their payments after successive poor income years (recall the principle of increasing risk?).

It is almost universally understood that farmers and stockmen would prefer land ownership to leasing. However, ownership can have real disadvantages, particularly for farmers trying to get started.

The Primary Disadvantages

Land is an expensive resource. It is often difficult for an operator-manager to purchase land because the down payment or finance charges are too high to meet the payments with the cash income received. As a consequence, the farmer doesn't have enough money to buy the feed, seed, and other necessary productive inputs and still have enough money to live on. The operator is in a cash-flow bind. That is the problem a purchaser of the land in the ranch example above would probably have.

If principal and interest payments are too high relative to annual net income, the farmer will be unable to invest in other high return alternatives in a way that allows him to develop his potential management ability.

An operating farmer considering a land purchase should not lose sight of the questions presented earlier:

1. What is the land worth to me?
2. What am I able to pay for land in terms of cash flow repayment?
3. What other uses do I have for my money?

FARMLAND LEASING OPTIONS

Leases are contracts in which the landlord (lessor) gives the tenant (lessee) possession and use of certain assets, such as land, for a specified time period and for specified consideration (i.e., money, a share of the production, or both). A lease is a business agreement, either written or oral, between two or more parties. Having the provisions written down reduces the chances of misunderstanding

The three main types of land leases used are cash rent, crop-share, and livestock-share. The labor-share and flexible rent leases are popular in some areas. A description of each type of lease and its advantages and disadvantages follows.

Cash Lease

Rent is a payment for the use of capital assets owned by someone else. Rent compensates the owner for the assets and for keeping them in serviceable condition. An owner should be compensated because he/she will have costs such as (1) interest on investment, (2) taxes, (3) repair on buildings and facilities, (4) insurance, and (5) depreciation or obsolescence of some assets.

Cash leases are generally relatively simple. The tenant pays the landowner either a fixed amount per acre or a lump sum for the use of the farm resources. In return the tenant gets all the income. Provisions in the lease generally include the terms of the agreement; any restrictions of the landowner on the use of land, such as the specification of certain crops or fertility treatments; and requirements about the maintenance of fences, terraces, drainage ditches, or other special features associated with the land. The amount and method of paying rent are also specified. Beyond this, the tenant may have a free rein in planning crop and livestock production on the tract leased. This type of lease is attractive to a landowner who (1) prefers a certain income each year, (2) knows very little about farming or doesn't want the bother of management and/or (3) does not live in the area.

Among the advantages of cash leases are the following:

1. The cash lease is simple. There is little chance for misunderstanding.

2. The landowner is assured of a definite, steady income. He/she, therefore, has little risk involved. Because of the certainty of some income, a landlord may cash rent at a lower rate than he would ask for a crop- or livestock-share lease.

3. The owner is generally relieved of responsibility for making any operating decisions. This is particularly relevant in the case of an absentee landowner or for retired persons who own land.

4. The tenant has complete management control other than the provisions agreed to by the tenant and landlord at the time the contract is made. This generally gives the tenant great flexibility in fitting the leased property into his total farming operation.

The cash lease also has disadvantages. The lease payment is a fixed cost to the tenant regardless of the level of production or profits; thus, a cash lease is more risky for the tenant. On the other hand, the landlord does not share in the unusually profitable years, although he/she also takes fewer income risks.

A landlord may get a tenant who will exploit the land: one, for example who is not concerned with conservation or will overgraze pastures. These practices will lower the normal productivity of the land. Conversely, a tenant may find a landlord slow or reluctant to maintain buildings and facilities adequately. Problems such as these can be avoided by specific lease provisions.

Another difficulty is that of establishing a lease amount both parties feel is fair. The landlord will probably be in the driver's seat if the tract is more productive or larger than average for the area. Small, "cut-up," or poorly located tracts command a lower rent.

Crop-Share Lease

Share renting of cropland is a system for sharing the income and is not based upon a specific amount of money. The landowner receives a share of the crop as a return on the land and other resources used in the business. The share of income going to each party varies geographically but is typically influenced by (1) customary leasing arrangements in the area, (2) the contribution of each party, (3) the degree to which variable input costs are shared, and (4) profitability, which varies from year to year.

Cash rent for buildings or pasture may be appropriate where a tenant leases a whole farm but has a crop-share arrangement on only the cropland.

In developing a crop-share lease agreement, a landowner and tenant should keep the following in mind:

1. The risks involved with regard to weather and other natural hazards are shared by both parties.

2. Both parties share in increased production, which may result from the adoption of improved technologies.

3. In leases that have a provision for the landowner to share in the costs of variable inputs, the capital requirements of the tenant will probably be lower than if he had cash rented. This would lower the tenant's risk. Or, said another way, the landlord is sharing more of the production risks.

4. A landowner is likely to share more decision making in a crop-share lease than a cash lease. Although many landlords are very knowledgeable and can make a significant management contribution, this limits the decision-making freedom of the tenant.

5. Landowners are rarely involved in the day-to-day decisions.

The following are some major difficulties that can arise with a crop-share lease:

1. Determining a fair and equitable method of sharing production based upon each party's contribution.

2. Adjusting the lease to fit the cost of new technology, such as irrigation or drying equipment.

3. Deciding who makes the final decision on an annual cropping plan.

4. Determining the crop share or payment for forage crop production.

5. Determining an acceptable charge for the farm residence or livestock buildings used by the tenant or the employees. Who should maintain these buildings and/or residences?

Livestock-Share Lease

The problems—and the opportunities—with livestock-share leases are much like those of crop-share. Some people have land that they are unable to use directly. Others have time, management ability, and livestock (or access to money to purchase livestock). Both parties see an opportunity to improve their income, or achieve some other goal, by joining resources and capabilities in a livestock-share lease. There are many variations in livestock-share lease terms because of the differences in resources furnished and the production program on the individual farm or ranch.

The most common terms in a livestock-share lease are that the land-owner furnishes the land and buildings, the tenant furnishes the labor and most equipment, and they share in the investment in the animals. Expenses may or may not be shared depending upon the provisions of the lease agreement. The importance of a well thought-out, written agreement cannot be overstressed.

Among advantages and disadvantages of the livestock-share lease are:

1. It may provide an opportunity for a farmer or stockman with limited capital to gain control of a business large enough to provide a satisfactory income. This is particularly relevant for the young or low-equity operator.

2. It may provide an opportunity for an older farmer or rancher to retire, yet keep the business unit intact. This allows a continued use of past capital investment and may allow the landowner to share in the labor and management.

3. It may give the tenant a direct outlet for grain or forage produced elsewhere in his operation.

4. Risks are shared. Tenant does not face a fixed rent payment regardless of production and prices. Landlord has more variable income from year to year but is in a position to share in returns of very good years.

5. A livestock-share lease arrangement is complex; it lends itself to many differences in opinion. This may lead to problems in deciding how income should be shared.

6. Decisions on growth and expansion, types of animals, and production methods must be made, but by whom?

Flexible Rent Lease

The big fluctuation in grain and some livestock prices in the 1970s caused more landowners to be interested in crop- and livestock-share leases. Landlords who had their land contracted for cash rent did not share in the favorable returns. On the other hand, tenants who had cash leases were generally very happy because they got all the windfall gains of the high prices. One attempt at equalizing such gains or serious losses is the flexible rent lease. The goal is to keep some aspects of a cash rent contract, but allow the landlord to share in the windfall gains in periods of unusually high profits and in losses during periods of adversity (low production and prices).

The flexible rent clause comes into play if the actual gross income per acre exceeds some predetermined value or some expected yield multiplied by an agreed-on normal price. The agreement might have the landlord receive a certain percentage of any gross income above the predetermined amount. The specific percentage is determined through negotiation between the two parties.

A Leasing Checklist

Any time two or more parties join together in a business arrangement, dissatisfaction or disagreement is possible. Some problems can be avoided by planning ahead. Key points to consider in leasing arrangements are:

1. Make sure there is an economic gain for both the landowner and the tenant. Without a profit, somebody will be unhappy and the arrangement is likely to fall apart after a year or so.

2. Make sure all parties have agreed on the contribution each is to make to the leasing arrangement.

3. Keep accurate and complete records and have all parties agree on who should keep them.

4. Discuss and decide how differences in opinion will be resolved.

5. Decide which party has responsibility for what jobs or enterprises.

6. Agree on a means for sharing expenses and production. Try to share the production/income equitably; misunderstandings will be reduced.

7. Decide when a settlement of business earnings or rent will be made.

8. Agree on the responsibility for maintaining buildings, facilities, and land fertility.

9. Make sure the lease provides for legal protection of both parties. A landlord/tenant doesn't want the agreement construed as a partnership.

10. Put the lease in writing! A written lease protects the heirs if one of the original parties dies. In case of a dispute, a written lease prevents many legal problems by forcing all parties to consider explicitly the terms they are agreeing to.

11. Decide how the lessee is to be compensated for improvements but not used up before the lease between landlord and tenant is terminated.

Leasing Equity Considerations

The previous sections have illustrated that landowners and tenants can have competing objectives. The resulting lease is generally a compromise. But how can an equitable compromise be developed? What is a fair lease?

Although there is no pat answer, the concept of "returns according to contributions" has gained widespread support. The idea is to look at all the contributions of each party, not just cash expenses or land. A 50–50 sharing of seed, fertilizer, and chemicals does not necessarily mean the landlord and tenant should split the income 50–50. Some value should be attached to labor, management, and risk taking, as well as to machinery and land—factors which vary from one situation to another. The weights placed on these factors will depend upon the personal characteristics and preferences of the parties to the lease.

Exhibit 17–3 illustrates the process one landlord and tenant went through to determine the contribution of each in the production of a grain crop. The machinery cost values were based upon local custom rates for tillage, planting, and harvesting. Fertilizer, seed, and chemical costs were shared 50–50. A labor wage of $3 per hour was used as an

Exhibit 17–3. Estimating landlord and tenant contributions in a crop-share lease, an example

Item	Total cost	Tenant cost	Landlord cost
		Per Acre	
Fertilizer, chemicals, and seed	$ 60	$30	$ 30
Tillage and planting	15	15	—
Lime	5	—	5
Harvesting and hauling	15	15	—
Labor at $3/hr.	12	12	—
Real estate taxes	4	—	4
Land charge ($1,000 × 7%)	70	—	70
Management (5% of gross)	9	9	—
Total Contributions	$190	$81	$109
Percent of Contributions		42.6%	57.4%

opportunity cost on labor. The land charge was based upon the opportunity cost of the landlord's money. The landlord could have put the $1,000 invested per acre of land into certificates of deposits at a local financial institution and earned at least 7 percent on the money. The landlord also paid the real estate taxes and the cost of lime to maintain soil fertility.

The "contributions" approach is a useful technique for helping each party see the other party's side. The final terms to the lease can then be reached by bargaining between the landowner and the prospective tenant.

LEASE OR PURCHASE?

There is no concrete answer to the lease versus buy question. The farmer or rancher interested in the agricultural value of the land and in providing a livelihood from the land has to ask some special questions. For most operators/managers the first question is, "What is the expected cash flow for lease compared to purchase?" This can be estimated by budgeting through the expected annual costs and returns and then subtracting the annual payment, be it principal and interest or rent. The tax angles of each method of control should get special attention. The "after tax" comparison may be just the opposite of the "before-tax" result.

Without a doubt, leasing adds the control of land to a farm firm with a minimum of financial disturbance. In the short and intermediate term, leasing will likely require lower liquidity than purchase. No cash outflow requirements beyond the lease payment are created.

The second question will probably relate to the benefits derived from ownership. A purchase, or contract to purchase, allows a buyer to realize the windfall gains associated with land appreciation, but there is also the possibility that local land values could decline, in which case the buyer would be worse off. Some above average managers have been able to combine land appreciation with the wise use of leverage and to build very profitable farm businesses from a meager start.

A third major question is the effect of purchase on the borrowing capacity of the farm business. Creditors are going to allow just so much debt relative to equity and then they will call a halt. They want to be sure that (1) the borrower can service his debts and (2) the debts are secured by assets which will allow the loan to be paid if the borrower defaults on the obligation. More important, at least for the farmer-borrower, is the wise use of borrowing capacity. Use of credit for land purchase will preclude the use of that credit for some alternative purpose. The opportunity cost concept is an important aspect of the lease versus buy decision, particularly for the young or growing operator-manager.

SUMMARY

In this chapter we have discussed some of the options that exist for gaining control of land. The desirable method of control will vary with individuals or firms, their goals, and their financial positions. Among the major points of the chapter are:

• The land control decision is influenced by the individual's or firm's objectives. Are the objectives those of a producer or investor? The way that question is answered definitely colors the approach taken in the lease versus buy question.

• The main reasons people want to own land are (a) for income, (b) for the satisfaction they get from ownership, and (c) for reducing uncertainty regarding the future control of that asset.

• For farmers and ranchers (whether leasing or buying) three questions must stand out.
   (a) What is the land worth to me?
   (b) What am I able to pay for land in terms of cash flow repayment?
   (c) What other uses do I have for my money?

• The income capitalization approach is a useful technique for estimating the agricultural value of land.

• Factors, in addition to agricultural income, which contribute to land value include (a) value of undeveloped mineral rights; (b) speculative, or appreciation, value; (c) site or location value; (d) value for add-on purposes; and (e) intangible value associated with ownership. The importance given each of these factors will vary from person to person.

• Parties to a lease are likely to have competing objectives. These objectives will influence the choice between a cash rent or share arrangement. They will also influence the negotiation of the lease terms once the type of lease is chosen.

• A means to arrive at an equitable lease where returns are shared is based upon the contributions of each party to the lease.

• A written lease is desirable from both a legal and economic standpoint.

APPLYING THE PRINCIPLES OF CHAPTER 17

1. Why do people want to own land?

2. Who do farmers and ranchers compete with for land?

3. Suppose you wanted to purchase a property that is expected to generate $8,000 income per year over the next 25 years. How might you estimate the amount you could pay for the property?

4. Using discount rates of 5 percent and 7 percent, estimate the amount you could pay for the property described in question 3.

5. What are the differences between a cash rent and a crop-share lease. What are some advantages and disadvantages of each to the tenant? Landowner?

6. What is the basic idea behind developing a lease arrangement where returns are shared according to contributions? What contribution is the landowner likely to make? What contribution is the tenant likely to make?

REFERENCES

Hopkins, John A., P. J. Barry and C. B. Baker. *Financial Management in Agriculture.* Danville, Ill.: Interstate Printers and Publishers, Inc., 1980.

Jeffrey, D. B., C. D. Maynard and L. A. Parcher. *Suggestions for Buying or Selling A Farm.* Stillwater, Ok.: Oklahoma Cooperative Extension Service Circular E-786, Oklahoma State University, 1966.

Luckham, W. R. "How Much Can You Pay for Agricultural Land?" *Virginia Agricultural Economics.* No. 271. Blacksburg, Va.: Virginia Polytechnic Institute and State University, July–August 1975.

Matthews, Robert C. *Do It Right the First Time.* St. Louis, Mo.: Doane Agricultural Service, Inc., 1973.

Scott, J. T. and F. J. Reiss. *Farm Lease Theory and Changing Technology.* AE 4196. Urbana-Champaign, Ill.: Department of Agricultural Economics, University of Illinois, October 1968.

Stoneberg, E. G. *Improving Your Farm Lease Contract.* FM 1564. Ames, Iowa: Cooperative Extension Service, Iowa State University, November 1970.

Part 6
Investment
Analysis

Investment Analysis and Decision Making

- Time value of money
- Process of discounting
- Process of compounding
- Influence of interest charge on size of discounted cash flows
- Cash inflows and outflows in investment opportunities

18

When should scarce capital resources be allocated to investments rather than annual operating inputs? How can time be incorporated into the decision-making process when comparing investments with different periods of productive use? Economic feasibility has been explained in terms of profitability and cash flow analysis. However, capital expenditures are often large permanent commitments that influence the earning power of the business for a number of years. There is a need to go beyond feasibility. The amount and timing of cash flows differ by alternative. To insure a wise investment decision, a manager will probably evaluate the profit potential of several alternatives. Such an analysis requires that one determine the amount of capital required for each investment, forecast the added earnings and benefits likely to occur, and use a realistic method to evaluate and select among investment alternatives.

Paying for labor to irrigate a growing crop or applying nitrogen to the crop are examples of activities that have both costs and benefits for a single production period. On the other hand, alternatives such as sealed storage for ensiling forage or high moisture feed grain, orchards, and confinement livestock buildings are examples of investments that have costs and returns over a number of production periods.

The investment criterion available to aid decision makers, termed the *index of profitability,* has two major aspects: (1) other things being equal, larger benefits are preferred to smaller ones; (2) other things being equal, early benefits are preferred to later benefits. As discussed later in the chapter, these "other things" are such characteristics of the investment as length of life, size of investment, and other unique characteristics. Here, however, the discussion concerns the importance and influence of early investment benefits relative to those occurring later.

TIME VALUE OF MONEY

Understanding that the value of money is influenced by time is important in evaluating the profitability of investment opportunities. Money values change with time because of the many alternative uses of money.

The Effect of Interest

Suppose one dollar were loaned today for one year at 8 percent simple interest payable at maturity. One year hence, creditors would receive one dollar principal plus interest of 8 cents for a total of $1.08. The generalized formula for this transaction is $A = p + (p \times r \times t)$, where p is equal to principal, r is equal to the interest rate expressed as a decimal, and t is equal to the number of years the annual growth factor is at 8 percent. Two conclusions can be reached: (1) the value one year hence of $1.00 loaned today at 8 percent simple interest will be $1.08; (2) $1.08 payment received in one year has a current or *present* value of $1.00, given an 8 percent simple interest rate. Dividing $1.00 to be received in one year by $1.08 (a dollar plus the interest at 8 percent rate), we can say that $1.00 to be received one year hence has a value *today* or present value of .9259 dollars.

In this example, there was only one interest payment and that took place at maturity. An individual with a two-year loan of $1.00 at 8 percent, with interest received at maturity, would receive $1.16. This is an accurate simple interest calculation if all the interest were payable at maturity; but in real life the first $.08 of interest will probably be paid at the end of the first year, and the second $.08 of interest will be payable at the end of the second year. When the interest on such a loan is payable makes a great deal of difference. If interest payments are made before maturity (for example, monthly, quarterly, semiannually or annually), the creditor has the alternative of reinvesting them or spending interest payments when received.

The fact that interest is often paid before maturity leads to compound interest calculations, which assume one or a series of interest payments before maturity. For example, suppose the same dollar were loaned for two years at 8 percent per annum. Compound interest payable at the end of the first and second years with the first interest payment reinvested at 8 percent results in the following calculations: (1) interest earned during the first year amounts of $.08; (2) reinvestment of the first year interest payment of $.08 at 8 percent interest is equal to $.0064. In other words, total interest earned during the second year amounts to $.0864 ($.08 on the original $1.00 plus interest on interest). Adding the total interest earned during the two-year period (.08 + .0864) to the original $1.00 principal yields a total payment of $1.1664 at the end of the second year.

The growth of money over time by reinvesting accrued interest may be expressed in a mathematical formula: $p(1+r)^t$. This procedure of finding the value of a given sum of money at some future time period is known as *compounding*.

To find the value (current or present) of an amount of money to be acquired in the future or a distant time period, one may use a discounting formula: $p(1+r)^{-t}$ or $p\ 1/(1+r)^t$. *Discounting* is a process of finding the present value of a given amount of money to be received in some future time period.

Use of Mathematical Tables in Compounding and Discounting

Computations associated with discounting and compounding are greatly simplified by the use of mathematical tables. Appendix Table 1 provides the future values of $1.00 compounded at different interest and various time periods. To use a math table, one must find the intersection of the interest rate desired and the appropriate time period. For example, to find that the future value of $1.00 invested today at 5 percent becomes $1.05 in one year, one locates the intersection of 5 percent and one year. What is the value of $250 placed at a savings account at 10 percent interest for a period of ten years? The compound table shows us that $1.00 amounts to $2.5937 (tabular value) in ten years at 10 percent. Therefore, $250 times 2.5937 amounts to a total of $648.43.

The present value factor for $1.00, ten years from now at 10 percent interest, is .3855 (intersection of 10 percent with ten years in Appendix

Table 2). Multiplying the future value of $648.43 times the discount factor (.3855) yields $249.97. (The reason the sum does not exactly equal $250 is due to rounding error.) Discounting and compounding are the opposite sides of the same concept.

Use of Annuity Tables

What is the present value of an investment return that provides $100 *each year* for five years, assuming a discount factor of 8 percent? The solution to this problem is found by multiplying $100 by the present value factors for the 8 percent interest rate (from Appendix Table 2) for years one through five—that is, $100 times .9259 + $100 times .8573 + $100 times .7938 + $100 times .7350 + $100 times .6805. Adding these individual multiplications would result in a present value sum of $399.25. The same answer can be obtained by the annuity table in Appendix Table 4 entitled "The Present Value of Annuity of 1." A tabular value 3.9927 is found at the intersection of 8 percent and five years, which, when multiplied by $100, gives the present value of the flow of money. The five individual multiplications required to compute the present value of the $100 annual flow of funds for the five year period is simplified to only one multiplication.

An annuity, by definition, is an event occurring annually. In this case, $100 is received each year for five years; therefore, an annuity table is used. On the other hand, if one received $100 the first, second, third, and fourth years, but $400 the fifth year, an annuity table could not be used.[1]

COST OF CAPITAL AND SELECTING THE DISCOUNT RATE

The cost of capital is crucial to the investment analysis. Before discussing the different techniques of investment analysis for determining present worth, suggested procedures for selecting a discount rate are discussed.

The present value measures of an investment's economic worth depend on the use of an appropriate discount rate (or rate of return). *The appropriate rate is the firm's cost of capital.* This rate, when determined, provides a yardstick for testing the acceptability of any investment; those that have a high probability of achieving a rate of return in excess of the firm's cost of capital are acceptable.

How can one estimate a farm firm's cost of capital? Some possibilities are: (1) to use the interest rate attainable by "investing" in lending institutions (deposits or securities) *before taxes* as an estimate of opportu-

---

[1]One could use the annuity table in conjunction with Appendix Table 2.

nity cost of capital; and (2) to determine the *weighted average after-tax cost of capital,* which reflects the costs of all forms of capital the firm uses. The two basic sources of capital are *borrowed capital from lending institutions* and *ownership or internal capital representing profits reinvested in the business.*

To estimate the weighted average cost of capital, one needs to determine: (1) the present cost of borrowed or leased funds from each source; (2) an average cost of internal capital as reflected by the percentage of equity in business and risks being taken; and (3) an adjustment for income tax effect. Suggested procedures for determining these rates are presented below.

Cost of Borrowed Capital

Methods of determining reliable rates for borrowed capital vary among individuals. The difficulty arises because of the different proportions of long-term and short-term debt among farmers.

Lenders' interest rates vary by type of lender. The Farm Credit System's (Federal Land Banks and Production Credit Associations) variable rate lending is keyed to money market conditions; hence, predicting capital costs through time is imprecise. Less difficulty exists, however, when borrowers have considerable long-term borrowings at fixed rates.

For simplicity, assume an individual real estate debt of $100,000 outstanding with an insurance company at 8.25 percent interest rate. In addition, short-term borrowings over the past few years have averaged $10,000 per year at average rates of interest of 6.75 percent.

The average interest rate (weighted average) on borrowed capital is:

Amount (1)	Interest rate (2)	Interest charge (1 × 2)
$50,000	8.25	$4,125
$10,000	6.75	$ 675
		$4,800 Total interest

Dividing total interest paid ($4,800) by capital borrowed ($60,000) provides an average rate of 8 percent.

Cost of Ownership (Equity) Capital

Cost of ownership capital is the difficult one to nail down. Theoretically, one knows that the cost of ownership capital is the *opportunity cost* of placing the owner's funds elsewhere in comparable risk situations. Opportunity costs are likely to vary among farm firms because they differ (1) in abilities to find alternative uses of equity, (2) in management abilities, and (3) in riskiness of the operations.

As a guide for selecting an appropriate ownership cost of capital, use the condition *that the cost of equity or owner capital should be equal to or greater than the cost of borrowed capital.*[2] As a result, one can develop a scale that reflects to some degree the individual's management abilities, age, degree of risk, etc. The scale could begin with the cost of borrowed capital as a *minimum*, then increase according to different situations.

Low risk average ability	Moderate risk moderate ability	High risk high ability
8%	10%	12%

Average Cost of Capital

Using a balance sheet or other information, one can estimate the percentage of the sources of capital in the business. Assume that the farmer has a 50 percent equity (or will average about half borrowed and half owned over the investment period). The average cost of capital is estimated in Exhibit 18–1.

The After-Tax Average Cost of Capital

If the owner is in the 20 percent (marginal) tax bracket, each $1.00 of interest paid on borrowed money will reduce taxes $.20 since interest paid is a business expense. If the owner could get a 10 percent return elsewhere, the after-tax return of this alternative would be 8 percent. An-

Exhibit 18–1. Cost of capital estimates

	(1) Percent of capital	(2) Interest cost	Weighted cost (1×2)
Equity capital borrowed	50	.10	5.00
Bank	40	.09	3.60
Insurance company	10	.08	.80
			9.40

---

[2]This assumption is based on the premise that there is a *higher risk* cost of the owner's money sunk in the business. However, the owner may view the opportunity cost at *less* than the actual interest cost of money in some cases—land used for low return enterprises, for example.

other aspect of this computation is that the 8 percent after tax is 80 percent of 10 percent (ignoring capital gains effects). Thus, adjustment of the average cost of capital to an after-tax cost is needed:

$$10.0 \times (1. - .20) = 8.0 \text{ percent}$$

Selecting an appropriate cost of capital can be simplified by developing tables reflecting different owner equity conditions and cost of borrowed capital. Exhibit 18–2 shows the results when the cost of borrowed capital is 7 percent.

DEVELOPING THE CASH FLOW BUDGET

A wide variety of capital budgeting decisions are confronted. For example, a person living in town who has a good job has an important capital investment decision when determining whether to return to a rural area and engage in farming. His decision is quite different from that of someone already engaged in farming. The latter has viable, ongoing farming operation capital. Budgeting decisions that confront the person already in business might be whether to add an additional enterprise and drop a present one; to erect a durable machine shed or one not so durable; or to buy a new or a used combine. Although the alternatives are quite different in their makeup, all of these decisions have something in common: they all have cash outflows and cash inflows. Cash inflows in the farm business may result from increasing farm business output or, conversely, reducing costs associated with a constant farm output. Regardless of what kind of investment opportunity is considered, a sound evaluation must be preceded by fully identifying all dollar outflows (investments) as well as all dollar inflows that are a result of the investments.

Exhibit 18–2. **Average cost of capital when borrowed capital is 7 percent under different equity positions**

	Owned capital cost scale					
Percent equity	7.0%	8.0%	9.0%	10.0%	11.0%	12.0%
0%	7.0	7.0	7.0	7.0	7.0	7.0
25%	7.0	7.25	7.5	7.75	8.0	8.25
50%	7.0	7.5	8.0	8.5	9.0	9.5
75%	7.0	7.75	8.5	9.25	10.0	10.75
100%	7.0	8.0	9.0	10.0	11.0	12.0

Partial Budgeting to Estimate Net Benefits

Previous discussion of the partial budgeting process provides a background and indicates the kind of information that must be identified and, in fact, quantified. The importance of each component in a partial budget cannot be overemphasized. Because there are few cases in which benefits and costs are known precisely beforehand, estimation involves prediction; and because the future is uncertain, such predictions may vary widely. The important point is that some analysis of possible alternative outcomes is essential. Both the estimate of benefits, as reflected by the added returns or reduced cost, and the opportunity cost, as reflected by the added costs or reduced returns portion of the partial budget, must consider an evaluation of these alternative outcomes.

One way to consider the uncertainties associated with investments that have benefits and costs occurring over a considerable time in the future is to estimate different levels of expected benefits and costs. These costs and benefits predictions can be the basis for developing net benefits, such as (1) the best or most reasonable estimate, (2) a pessimistic estimate, (3) an optimistic estimate. Such estimates provide a basis for taking into account the consequences of unexpected or unforeseen situations associated with the investment. To clarify this point, assume an individual is considering the investment opportunity of producing swine under confinement housing, i.e., complete confinement. Such a system requires housing for farrowing, nursing, and finishing activities. Without getting into the technicalities of swine production, the numerous systems available vary in cost as well as in expected benefits. Apart from cost, obvious benefits to such a system would be reduced death loss, reduced labor requirements, and improved feed efficiency, all of which would combine to give the product more profit than would be attained under a different system of production. The problem arises when one begins to quantify the extent of these benefits: How many more pigs are saved? What is the feed efficiency? How much labor is saved? Still another uncertainty is what market value should be attached to the physical production estimate. What is the possibility of $60 hogs, $50 hogs, $30 hogs or even $20 hogs? Production uncertainties, when combined with market uncertainties, are the basis for estimates of different net benefits associated with a given confinement system.

SUMMARY

Outlays for capital expenditures differ from the more traditional production expenses in that returns, and sometimes expenses, occur over a number of years.

Money has time value—a dollar received in some distant period is not worth $1.00 today. *Discounting* is the process of finding the present value of a given amount of money in the future. The procedure of finding the future value of a given sum of money at some distant time period is known as *compounding*.

Uncertainty regarding expected returns exists with every investment. One way to consider the uncertainties associated with investments is to estimate different levels of expected benefits and costs. These estimates may be considered (1) the best or most reasonable estimate, (2) a pessimistic estimate, (3) an optimistic estimate.

APPLYING THE PRINCIPLES OF CHAPTER 18

1. Why is capital budgeting and investment analysis important?

2. Why does money have a time value?

3. What is compounding?

4. What is discounting?

5. How is a discount rate determined?

6. How does depreciation influence the size of discounted cash flow?

7. By what methods can investment uncertainty be considered in an analysis?

REFERENCES

Aplin, R. D., G. L. Cosler and C. P. Francis. *Capital Investment Analysis Using Discounted Cash Flow,* 2nd ed. Columbus, Ohio: Grid Inc., 1977.

Bierman, H., Jr. and S. Smidt. *The Capital Budgeting Decision.* New York, N.Y.: Macmillan Co., 1960.

Johnson, R. L. *Financial Decision Making.* Pacific Palisades, Calif.: Goodyear Publishing Co., 1973.

Quirin, C. D. *The Capital Expenditure Decision.* Homewood, Ill.: Richard D. Irwin Inc., 1967.

Weston, J. F. and E. F. Brighan. *Managerial Finance,* 5th ed. Hinsdale, Ill.: The Dryden Press, 1975.

Choosing Between Alternative Investment Opportunities

19

- Techniques for determining profitability of investment opportunities
  Payback
  Accounting rate of return
  Present worth techniques
- Influence of taxes on profitability
- Effect of cash flow available for taxes and loan servicing on investment
- Investment risk
- Feasibility and profitability of investment

When managers make investment decisions they are making decisions that will affect the financial affairs of the business for several years into the future. An unwise investment decision can cause the financial position to be eroded and can lead to business failure. Well-reasoned investment decisions, on the other hand, can move a farm/ranch business along the path to growth and greater success.

Regardless of the kind of investment, some systems must be developed to determine the profitability of the investment opportunities, and some method must be used in ranking the alternatives that confront a manager. Managers used to understand the different capital budgeting techniques for comparing investments. This chapter discusses some of the useful evaluation techniques and measures and points out advantages and limitations of each.

TECHNIQUES OF ANALYSIS

Investments in such capital items as land, fixed livestock facilities, and equipment have far-reaching implications for the farm's earning power, its growth, and even in some instances its survival. A number of techniques are available for determining acceptability of investment opportunities. The first three sections of this chapter describe them and discuss their relative merits.

Payback

The index of profitability or decision rule associated with the payback investment analysis technique is simply a measure of the time required for the cash income for a given investment to return the initial investment outlay. In absolute terms, four years might be the recoupment time period selected by the manager.[1] That is to say, any investment that requires a time period greater than four years to return the initial outlay would not be considered acceptable. Those investments having quicker paybacks (paying off or liquidating the present value of investment costs) are preferred to those requiring a longer payback period.

Understanding and applying the payback technique, in addition to others, to investment decisions can best be shown by a simple problem. Assume there are two investment opportunities, A and B, that have investment costs of $1,000 each. Investment A has a life of 5 years, investment B, 6 years. Assume further that their profitability index or cutoff period is 4 years. The result of applying the decision rule to each investment is shown in Exhibit 19–1. Note that investment A returns $900 of the initial cost of $1,000 at the end of the second year. The third year has a return of $300, but only $100 of this amount is required to cover the complete initial cost ($1,000). Dividing the required return of $100 (the additional cost that needs to be recouped) by the return of $300, results in .3 years; therefore, investment A has the payback period of 2.3 years. On the other hand, investment B returns the $1,000 by the end of the fourth year. Since 4 years was the index of profitability, one can conclude that both investments A and B are acceptable. However, if only one of them can be made, one would select investment A because it returns the original cost in 2.3 years instead of the 4 years for investment B.

---

[1]In general, managers arbitrarily select the payback period (index of profitability). For example, some farm managers state that they want investments to pay out in a period not to exceed 10 years. To increase objectivity in selecting cutoff or payback periods, some managers select payback periods by computing the reciprocal of the cost of capital. For a 10 percent rate, this would be a 10-year payback period $(1 \div .10 = 10)$. A 20 percent rate would result in a 5-year time period.

Exhibit 19–1. Cash flow and profitability analysis of investments A and B by payback method when costs of A and B are $1,000 each

Year	A Cash flow*	B Cash flow*
1	500	100
2	400	200
3	300**	300
4	200	400**
5	100	500
6		600

*Cash flow is gross income minus variable costs.

**Indicates year in which initial investment outlay is repaid.

Although the above technique is widely used in the business world, it has some major disadvantages which conflict with previously stated criteria regarding desirability of investments. Its major disadvantage is that it ignores benefits that occur in any period of time after the cutoff period associated with the index of profitability. Supposedly, the $500 and $600 returns associated with years five and six for investment B are completely ignored in the analysis process. Another disadvantage of this technique is that no consideration is given to the time value of money. A dollar received during the first year is given the same weight as a dollar received in the fourth year.

The Average or Accounting Rate of Return

The average rate of return technique measures the profitability of an investment as an annual percentage of the capital employed. Average earnings after depreciation are divided by average investment. Exhibit 19–2 shows a calculation of the rate of return when the straight line depreciation technique is used. No salvage value is assessed for the $1,000 investments. Note that average costs (investment outlay) for A and B were computed by averaging the average book value at the beginning and at the end of the investment period. An advantage of this technique over the payback method is that all returns associated with all years of the investment were considered. Nevertheless, although all benefits were considered in the investment analysis, the time value of money was not considered. As with the payback period, this is a major disadvantage of

Exhibit 19–2. **Analysis of investments A and B by average rate of return method**

				Investment A			
Year	1	2	3	4	5	Average	
Cash flow	500	400	300	200	100	300	
Depreciation	200	200	200	200	200	200	
Net cash flow	300	200	100	0	(100)	100	
Book value							
Jan. 1	1000	800	600	400	200		
Dec. 31	800	600	400	200	0		
Average	900	700	500	300	100	500	

$$\text{Average rate of return} = \frac{100}{500} \times 100 = 20 \text{ percent}$$

				Investment B			
Year	1	2	3	4	5	6	Average
Cash flow	100	200	300	400	500	600	350
Depreciation	167	167	167	167	167	167	167
Net cash flow	(67)	33	133	233	333	433	183
Book value							
Jan. 1	1000	833	666	499	332	165	
Dec. 31	833	666	499	332	165	0	
Average	916	750	582	416	248.5	83	499

$$\text{Average rate of return} = \frac{183}{499} \times 100 = 36.7 \text{ percent}$$

the average rate of return approach. Another disadvantage is that the index of profitability or decision rule is not clearly identified. For example, previous analysis suggests that when the added returns exceed the cost of adding the variable input, one should include the additional input to maximize profits. Applying the same logic to investment analysis, one might conclude that if the average rate of return of an investment is 10 percent, increased profits would result when the cost of capital is less than 10 percent. This logic is in error. The computed rate of return is not directly comparable to the rate of interest charged by lending agencies, nor is the average rate comparable to rates of return quoted by fiduciary instruments such as bonds. In ranking investment alternatives, however, one would obviously prefer those with the largest computed rates of return. Of investments A and B, investment B is preferable with a 37 percent rate of return, which exceeds that of A by approximately 17 percent.

Note, however, that this decision conflicts with the ranking previously based on the payback technique. The payback technique ranked investment A over B because the initial investment cost of A was recovered in a shorter time period.

PRESENT WORTH TECHNIQUES

Four different methods of evaluating investment alternatives are discussed under the category of present worth techniques: (1) benefit/cost ratio, (2) net present value method, (3) the amortization method (annual costs and annual benefits approach), and (4) the internal rate of return. Although each procedure has its own unique advantages and disadvantages, they have one thing in common: each technique considers the time value of money, which previously discussed methods do not. Benefits that vary in amounts as well as time are standardized by the process of discounting and/or compounding to enable fair and comparable evaluations. As observed earlier, the results of adjusting for the time value of money are greatly influenced by the interest factor.

Benefit-Cost Ratio

The benefit-cost ratio is computed by dividing the present value of the cash inflow by the present value of cost flow outlays. In other words, it compares benefits relative to costs. The index of profitability of this technique is indicated by the numeric value of the ratio; an investment would need a ratio value in excess of one to be considered profitable. A ratio of one would indicate that benefits and costs are balanced and the decision maker would be indifferent to the investment. Benefit-cost analysis calculations of A and B are shown in Exhibit 19–3. The discounted cash flows associated with investments A and B presented in the table are shown for discount rates of 10, 19, and 20 percent. Remember that discount factors are found in the Present Value of $1 table (Appendix Table 2). Since the cash flows of A and B are different for each year, one cannot use an annuity table to simplify present value calculations. Therefore, each individual cash flow for a given year must be discounted separately and the results added to get the total present value of the given cash flow. The present value of benefits associated with investment A, when benefits are discounted at a 10 percent rate, is $1,210. Dividing benefits by cost yields a ratio of 1.21. Since the ratio exceeds a numeric value of 1, the investment is considered profitable. A simple interpretation would be that the investment is returning $1.21 for every dollar invested. *Do not*, however, conclude that the rate of return is 21 percent. This point will be clarified at a later time. The benefit-cost ratio for in-

Exhibit 19–3. Discounted cash flows of investments A and B: investment costs of A and B are $1,000 each

Year	Discount factor and amounts at 10% rate			Discount factor and amounts at 19% rate			Discount factor and amounts at 20% rate		
	Factor	A	B	Factor	A	B	Factor	A	B
1	.91	455	91	.84	420	84	.83	415	83
2	.83	332	166	.71	284	142	.69	276	138
3	.75	225	225	.59	177	177	.58	174	174
4	.68	136	272	.50	100	200	.48	96	192
5	.62	62	310	.42	42	210	.40	33	200
6	.56		336	.35		210	.33		198
Sum of present value		1,210	1,400		1,023	1,023		994	985
Benefit-cost ratios		1.21	1.40		1.023	1.023		.994	.985

vestment B is 1.40. Investment B is the preferred investment because its ratio exceeds that of investment A.

Exhibit 19–3 also shows some other interesting results. Note how the total present values of benefits change with different discount rates. As discount rates increase, present values decrease because the cash flows of investments A and B differ with the number of years. For example, at the 10 percent discount rate, the total present value of investment B exceeds that of A by $190. Discounting at the 19 percent rate results in no difference. At the 20 percent rate, the total present value of the cash flow of investment A exceeds that of B. These variations highlight the fact that selection of a discount rate is very important in investment analysis.

Net Present Value Technique

The net present value technique can be considered a "first cousin" to the benefit-cost ratio. Net present value is simply the difference between the present value of benefits and the present value of costs. In other words, one merely subtracts costs from benefits, rather than dividing benefits by costs.

The index of profitability of the net present value technique is to accept all projects that have a positive net present value. That is, discounted benefits must numerically exceed discounted costs.

Using the net present value to determine the profitability of any given investment will give roughly the same results as the ratio of benefits to cost. Different rankings can be obtained when projects are rank-ordered by level of profitability, depending on which evaluation technique is used. The benefit-cost ratio more accurately reflects the relative profitability of various investment opportunities. Because of this advantage, the benefit-cost ratio is generally recommended over the net present value technique.

To illustrate the different results in ranking, assume that investments D and E are under consideration. Assume further that investment D has an initial cost of $5,000. Associated with this investment is a present value of benefits of $6,000 at a given discount rate. Dividing $6,000 by $5,000 yields a benefit-cost ratio of 1.2. On the other hand, investment D has an initial cost of $10,000, but its present value of discounted benefits equals $11,000. Therefore, the benefit-cost ratio is equal to 1.1. These two ratios indicate that both investments are profitable, but if a choice must be made, investment E (which has a ratio of 1.2) would be selected.

In contrast, the net present values of both investments (D and E) are equal. An initial cost $6,000 minus $5,000 provides a net present value of $1,000 for investment D. Investment E, in like manner, yields a net present value of $1,000 ($11,000 minus $10,000); given these results and applying the index of profitability for the net present value technique, one would be indifferent to investments D and E.

Amortization Technique

As with all other present worth techniques, this particular method of analysis likewise considers the time value of money. Amortization places all costs and benefits on an annual basis. This procedure is widely used by engineers in their project evaluations. A possible advantage, particularly to the noneconomist, is that confusion associated with benefits and costs expressed in present value terms are reduced when converted to an annual basis. Any cost estimate or benefit estimate, when converted to a present value, can be converted to an annual basis by using an amortization table (Appendix Table 3).

Assume an investment alternative has an initial cost of $1,000. Assume further that the required rate of return, the opportunity cost of money, is 8 percent and the investment has a life of five years. To convert the $1,000 present cost to an annual cost, one merely consults Appendix Table 3, the amortization table, and multiplies $1,000 by the tabular value of .2504 (value at the intersection of five years at 8 percent). In other words, $250 over a five-year time span is the same as $1,000 today, when the time value of money is considered. Assuming this investment has expected annual benefits of $300 each year for the five years and that there is no salvage or terminal value, the benefit-cost ratio can be found by dividing 300 by 250, which yields a ratio of 1.2.

In the previous example, note that benefits were equal for each of the years the investment had returns. Although this method of analysis may be used when they differ from year to year, additional arithmetic is required. Investments A and B are examples of investments with different annual returns. Discounting the returns of investment A at an 8 percent discount rate results in a total present value of $1,262. The benefit-cost ratio at an 8 percent discount would be 1.26. To convert the present value of benefits to an annual basis, again use the amortization table. Annual benefits amount to $316, determined by multiplying $1,262 × .2504. Combining annual benefits and costs of $316 and $250 respectively yields a benefit cost ratio of 1.26. One obtains the same ratio by dividing total present value of benefits by total present value of costs.

Internal Rate of Return

The internal rate of return technique is often referred to as the marginal efficiency of capital and also "Fisher's rate of return." By definition, *the internal rate of return is the discount rate that equates the present value of benefits with the present value of costs.* Rather than selecting a rate to use in discounting, this process requires one to solve for the discount rate. The discount rate is the unknown.

The index of profitability associated with this technique is to select an investment as long as the internal rate of return exceeds the cost of capital to the firm. If a computation results in an internal rate of return equal to the cost of capital, one would be indifferent as to whether investments were made (breakeven point). This result is equivalent to a benefit-cost ratio of one. A major advantage of the internal rate of return technique over the other present worth methods is that one does not have to select the discount rate. Its major disadvantage, relative to the other present worth techniques, is the difficulty in computations. Without the use of a computer, one must rely upon trial and error procedures to find discount rates that discount all future returns to equate with initial costs or present value of all costs.

The internal rate of return computations for investments A and B require one to find a discount rate that discounts the future returns until they equal $1,000. A look at the total present value of all benefits associated with investment A shows that the internal rate of return is somewhere between 19 and 20 percent (Exhibit 19–3). At a discount rate of 19 percent, the present value of benefits still exceeds the $1,000 cost by $23.00. However, discounting at a 20 percent rate results in a total present value of $994, which is less than $1,000. Therefore, the internal rate is something less than 20 percent but greater than 19 percent.

TAX CONSIDERATIONS

The discussion of investment analysis thus far has been limited to profitability analysis in its simplest form. The influence of taxes on investment decisions has been deliberately omitted to simplify as much as possible the computations necessary for considering the time value of money. Taxes are obviously important in the investment analysis because they influence the amount of money one has left to pay toward investment outlays.

Tax considerations influence investment profitability and feasibility (cash flow) in terms of (1) cost of capital, (2) the cash flow after taxes (depreciation) and (3) investment credit provisions (initial cost).

Depreciation

The objective is to compute the cash flow after taxes. How this task is accomplished may be illustrated by disclosing additional characteristics of the previous investment B and of the decision maker considering it. Assume that the decision maker is in a 20 percent marginal tax bracket and that investment B has a salvage or terminal value of $400. Also, suppose that the straight line depreciation technique has been selected and that the required rate of return is 10 percent. Exhibit 19–4 shows the detailed calculations necessary to derive the cash flow after taxes. With the straight line technique, depreciation amounts to $100 each year over the six-year life of the investment. Therefore, subtracting depreciation from the cash flow before taxes gives the amount of taxable income for each year, shown in column 4 (Exhibit 19–4). After taxable income is computed, one multiplies the expected marginal tax rate by the additional income generated for the business. With a 20 percent tax rate, one multiplies the taxable income by 20 percent to get the amount of income tax payable as a result of the investment. Subtracting the tax from the cash flow before taxes provides the cash flow after taxes, shown in column 6. Note that depreciation was considered only for the purpose of determining income after taxes. A common mistake in investment analysis is to treat depreciation as an annual expense. To do so is in error; treating depreciation as a cost results in double counting of costs because the initial cost of the investment is accounted for by the present value of costs.

Exhibit 19–4. Influence of taxes on cash flow and profitability: investment B*

(1) Year	(2) Cash flow	(3) Depreciation	(4) Taxable income (col 2 − 3)	(5) Tax charge (.20 × col 4)	(6) Cash flow after tax (col 2 − col 5)	(7) Discount factor	(8) Discounted cash flow at 8%
	$	$	$	$	$	8%	$
1	100	100	0	0	100	.93	93.00
2	200	100	100	20	180	.86	154.80
3	300	100	200	40	260	.79	205.40
4	400	100	300	60	340	.74	251.60
5	500	100	400	80	420	.68	285.60
6	600	100	500	100	500	.63	315.00
		600					1,305.40
						Present value of salvage	252.00

*Assumes 20 percent tax rate, straight line depreciation, salvage value of $400, and required rate of return of 10 percent.

Effect of Tax on Discount Rate

The concept of the effective cost of capital was introduced in a previous section. Recall that the effective cost of capital was influenced by tax considerations and that one's marginal tax rate was the primary determinant. The required rate of return of 10 percent in our example results in an effective discount rate of 8 percent, which is computed by multiplying 10 percent by (1 – the marginal tax rate). Therefore, one discounts at an 8 percent rate rather than a 10 percent rate after considering the influence of taxes.

One additional tax consideration pertains to the salvage value of an investment. Recall a previous assumption that investment B had a salvage value of $400. An investment with salvage value or terminal value has an additional benefit associated with it although such benefits cannot be obtained until the end of the investment period. With this specific example, the salvage benefit occurs at the end of year six. The consequence of waiting until the end of the investment period is considered in Exhibit 19–4; the present value of the salvage value ($400) is $252. Adding the total present value of the cash flow to the present value of the salvage value results in investment B having a total present value of benefits of $1,557.40.

Investment Credit

The effect of investment credit is to reduce the initial (effective) cost of the investment. Generally, computational consideration of investment credit can be accomplished by subtracting investment credit allowances from the present value of costs (that is, amounts qualifying for investment credit times rate of investment credit—now quoted at 10 percent). If an investment is considered at the beginning of a calendar year and income tax payments are not due one year or more in advance, one may desire to discount investment credit allowances. Likewise, if tax considerations result in investment tax credit allowances being carried forward to future tax years, then such tax benefits to be received at later or distant time period(s) must be discounted.

FEASIBILITY OF THE INVESTMENT

To this point the profitability of a given investment has been considered. Now a decision can be made as to whether the investment would yield a rate of return sufficient to return a profit to the business. Deliberately omitted has been any concern or discussion pertaining to investment financing. Analyses of the financing options for an investment and its profitability are separate and distinct.

Financing and the associated cash flow characteristics of a given investment fall under the general category of feasibility analysis. For a given investment, the amount financed outside of the business can range from 0 to 100 percent. Most of the time, however, the amount falls at some midpoint. Rarely would 100 percent of the investment be obtained from a financial institution without other collateral being assigned to the lender.

For many farmers the investment under consideration must not only be profitable, but must also be feasible. A completely feasible investment, often termed self-liquidating, is one in which the cash flow after taxes is adequate to meet the loan commitment of the investment. That is, the cash flow must always be a positive.

Assume that 100 percent financing can be obtained for investment B. That is, no down payment is required. Interest must be paid at 10 percent and the loan is a standard plan of amortization (equal payments). Amortizing a $1,000 loan over a six-year period at 10 percent interest amounts to a total annual payment of $229.60. Exhibit 19–5 shows the cash flow after payment for tax and loan servicing (principal plus interest). Note the positive cash flow for all years with the exception of the first two years. A negative cash flow must be accounted for in investment analysis. This negative cash flow must be made up from some other source. It is generally made up from the profits of the manager and his family, or it could be covered by additional short-term borrowing or from accumulated savings.

An additional table has been prepared to show the influence of alternative finance methods. For example, Exhibit 19–6 reflects the unpaid balance method (decreasing-payment method) of loan liquidation. It shows that negative cash flows can create important problems. Discussion thus far highlights the fact that repayment alternatives greatly influence the cash flows after taxes and loan liquidation. Cash flow problems usually do not arise when investments are profitable. Exceptions occur when the term of loan does not generally coincide with the economic life of the investment. Visualize the cash flow problems that would occur in financing investment B if, instead of a six-year term, loan repayment was limited to three years. This condition is shown in Exhibit 19–7. Note that negative cash flows are substantial for such a repayment schedule.

Negative cash flows, as shown by Exhibit 19–7, are not unusual for many agricultural investments, such as tractors, combines, etc., classified as intermediate-term assets. Often they are financed by relatively short-term loans (loans of two to four years), but their economic life may be seven to ten years. Likewise, sometimes major investments in land and buildings are financed by intermediate loans of five to ten years, but their

Exhibit 19–5. Cash flow and tax consequences when 100 percent of purchase price is financed (Investment B: $1,000 initial cost)

(1) Year	(2) Flow	(3) Amortized payment	(4) Interest	(5) Principal	(6) Unpaid principal balance	(7) Depreciation	(8) Interest plus depreciation	(9) Taxable income (after interest & depreciation) (col 2 − col 8)	(10) Change in taxes (20% × col 9)	(11) Cash flow after taxes (col 2 − col 10)	(12) Cash flow after tax & payment (col 11 − col 3)
	$	$	$	$	$	$	$	$	$	$	$
1	100	229.60	100.00	129.60	870.40	100	200.	−100.	−20.	120.	−109.60
2	200	229.60	87.04	142.56	727.84	100	187.04	12.96	2.59	197.41	−32.19
3	300	229.60	72.78	156.82	571.02	100	172.78	127.22	25.44	274.56	44.96
4	400	229.60	57.10	172.50	398.52	100	157.10	242.90	48.58	351.45	121.85
5	500	229.60	39.85	189.75	208.77	100	139.85	360.15	72.03	427.97	198.37
6	600	229.60	20.88	208.72	—	100	120.88	479.12	95.82	504.18	274.58

Exhibit 19–6. Payments associated with unpaid balance loan liquidation when purchase is 100 percent financed
(Investment B: $1,000 initial cost)

Year	Principal payment	Interest	Total payment	Unpaid balance	Net cash flow
	$	$	$	$	$
1	166.66	100	266.66	833.34	−166.66
2	166.66	83.33	249.99	666.68	− 49.99
3	166.66	66.67	233.33	500.02	66.67
4	166.66	50.00	216.66	333.36	183.34
5	166.66	33.34	200.00	166.70	300.00
6	166.66	16.67	16.71	.04	583.29

economic life justifies long-term loans. Under financing terms that require relatively small down payments, cash flow problems arise unless the investments are extremely profitable.

MUTUALLY EXCLUSIVE INVESTMENTS AND INVESTMENT QUIRKS

The previous discussion of example investments A and B implied that one or the other would be selected. A mutually exclusive investment, as previously defined, is one in which only one investment from two or more alternatives will be made.

When mutually exclusive investment opportunities exist, additional

Exhibit 19–7. Cash flow of investment B financed on a three-year amortized loan (8 percent interest)

Year	Annual payment	Cash flow after tax	Net cash flow after tax and loan repayment
1	388	100	−288
2	388	180	−208
3	388	260	−128
4	0	340	340
5	0	420	420
6	0	500	500

analysis may be required to insure that the most profitable alternative is selected. A second look is required for mutually exclusive investments when the economic life, the project type, or the costs are substantially different for each.

Different Lives

Assume investments F and G are mutually exclusive investments with lives of five and ten years, respectively. Each requires investment outlays of $5,000. Net annual cash flows of F and G are $3,500 and $2,000, respectively. Under the condition that investment F has a cash flow of $3,500 and no salvage value, computations for the benefit/cost ratio are:

$$\$3,500 \times 3.993 = \$13,975$$

$$\text{Benefit Cost Ratio} = \frac{\$13,975}{\$\ 5,000} = 2.80$$

Benefit-cost ratios of 2.80 for F and 2.68 for G result when benefits are discounted at 8 percent interest. Previous decision-making rules indicate that one should select investment F. But is this the right decision? A "yes" response requires that a very important condition exists. This condition is that at the end of the fifth year, when the economic life of investment F stops, there will be other investment opportunities that yield a rate of return of 8 percent (our original discount rate) or more.

Adjustment for Different Economic Lives

Two different methods exist for adjusting or standardizing investment differences so that fair comparisons and, in turn the right decision, can be made when the investments have different economic lives.

The procedures are (1) selecting a common economic life by assigning appropriate salvage values at a common terminal date or (2) treating investments as continuous replacement cycles, until economic lives coincide.

Common terminal period: In the previous examples (F and G), the appropriate terminal period would be at the end of year five when the life of investment F expires. Assume the salvage value of G is $3,000 at the end of year five. The present value of cash flows from G, using the discount rate of 8 percent, is $10,029. This results in a B/C ratio of 2.01. Hence by this criterion, investment F would be selected over G. The computation for G follows:

PV of cash flow ($2,000 × 3.99)	$ 7,986
PV of salvage value ($3,000 × .681)	2,043 $10,029

$$\text{B/C ratio: } \frac{10,029}{5000} = 2.01$$

Replacement cycle: This particular procedure is one in which replacements continue until a common terminal period is reached, as, for example, when alternative machines are available to perform the same job, but differ in durability and thus have different economic lives.

The F and G investments, although they differ in terms of value of annual cash flow, are good examples of the need for terminal dates. A common terminal date could be attained by purchasing another F at the end of year five. As a result, the F and G would expire or wear out at the same time period (end of year ten).

Assume that investment F can be purchased at $6,000 at the end of the fifth year (the additional $1,000 increase in the initial cost is the expected price increase of investment F). Computations of the benefit cost analysis when F is replaced at end of fifth year are:

$$\text{PV of benefits} = \$3,500 \times 6.710 = \$23,485$$

$$\text{PV of costs} = 5,000 + (6,000 \times .681) = \$9,086$$

$$\text{Benefit/cost ratio} = \frac{23,485}{9,086} = 2.58$$

When Costs or "Breed of Cat" Differ

Generally, "horse sense," at least in the real world, should prevent the kind of mistake to be discussed in this section. A decision maker (a very important and successful one, as reflected by net worth and other income measures) responded to an ad by a consulting firm in *BIG TOP* (a magazine to which all important managers subscribe). The consultant was given the job of selecting investment opportunities. The consultant in turn was "backstopped" by a number of line staff and computers. The computer analysis shows the internal rates return associated with investments H and I were 31 and 20 percent, respectively. But *no information on kinds of investments or costs was revealed.* The selection of investment H could be in error. A 31 percent return on an outlay of $10,000 is much different from a 20 percent return on an outlay of $100,000.

This kind of error can be prevented by considering only similar investments. A normally alert person does not usually consider the purchase of a disk or a farm as mutually exclusive investment alternatives. In short, the saying "birds of a feather flock together" has meaningful implications when selecting investment alternatives.

Added Costs and Added Returns

Normally, mutually exclusive investment opportunities differ in both costs and returns, even after investments of similar kinds are grouped. The appropriate question is whether added initial and/or operating costs are justified. To illustrate, let's say farms J and K are under purchase consideration. After careful analysis, it is determined that farm J, with a price of $200,000, has a benefit-cost ratio of 1.4 ($280,000/$200,000 = 1.4). On the other hand, farm K has a benefit-cost ratio of 1.3 and is priced at $150,000. Which farm should the broker be asked to purchase? Are the added costs of farm J justified? This analysis can be accomplished by evaluating farm L as an imaginary farm with a price of $50,000 (the added cost of farm J over K). The added earnings of farm L represent the difference in earnings between farms J and K. Exhibit 19–8 helps one to understand the technique of developing an imaginary investment, and then analyzing for profitability. If the imaginary investment proves to be profitable, then the more expensive investment is the appropriate choice over the less expensive alternative. The benefit-cost ratio of 1.7 for farm L shows that the most expensive and highest producing farm, farm J, should be purchased. The added benefits are large enough to warrant the higher cost (added cost of $50,000).

UNCERTAINTY AND RISK

This section deals with the means for taking risk and uncertainty into consideration when analyzing investment alternatives. There are significant differences between the concepts of risk and uncertainty. In layman's terms, the term *risk* implies that probabilities can be associated with deviations from the expected or point values of an outcome or situ-

Exhibit 19–8.

Farm	Cost	Benefits	B/C ratio
J	$200,000	$280,000	1.4
K	$150,000	$195,000	1.3
L	$ 50,000	$ 85,000	1.7

ation. The principle of risk is the basis of insurance. For example, probabilities can be computed for such events as accidents or fire loss to buildings and equipment.

The term *uncertainty* implies that the outcome is indeterminate—that is, not certain to occur. Estimates of probability cannot be attached to any deviation from expected outcomes that result from uncertainty. Government programs and activities that influence production and marketing are examples of uncertainties. The situation wherein a farmer who produces peanuts has the opportunity to buy another farm that has a peanut allotment highlights the inability to evaluate objectively the benefits of a peanut allotment. Whether the government will continue to maintain a peanut supply control program is an unknown; hence, it is considered an uncertainty. The probability of maintaining the program cannot be estimated.

From an individual manager's point of view, the deviations due to either risk or uncertainties are very similar, except when a deviation from the expected value can be covered by insurance. Suggestions of how to cope with or consider the effect of risk and uncertainty are limited to practical or appropriate methods under field conditions.

Alternative Outcomes

Our discussion of the data and procedures to use in developing the cash flow budget highlighted the fact that alternative budgets often are desirable. The alternative estimates (optimistic, best-guess estimate, and pessimistic) were suggested as appropriate for many investment analyses. This procedure provides the decision maker with a crude measure of the risk associated with a given investment. Consider the situation where two investments (with equal costs and economic life) have: (1) best-guess estimates that provide the same benefit-cost ratios, (2) ratios that differ slightly when optimistic cash flow estimates are used, and (3) a ratio for one investment falls to .5 while the other remains above a ratio of 1. The decision under these conditions would obviously be to select the investment whose benefit-cost ratio remains profitable regardless of conditions.

Breakeven

A breakeven cash flow estimate exists when discounted cash flows over the expected economic life result in a net present value of zero or a benefit-cost ratio of one. Should the internal rate of return approach be used, breakeven cash flow is one that provides a yield (rate of return) equal to that of the expected interest rate over the term of the investment.

A comparison of the breakeven cash flow estimate with the best-guess estimate provides a measure of risk associated with the investments. The comparison can be "eyeballed" or more formally made by computing the percentage decline in an estimate before a breakeven value is reached. For example, suppose the ultimate in a confinement finishing parlor for hogs is introduced. It costs $10,000 and has a life of ten years. Conferences with other producers as well as with the manufacturer's promoters indicate complete obsolescence at the end of the expected life. The construction makes the facility fireproof. Disposal of the structure appears to be a problem, but the manufacturer agrees to remove it for $1,000. The net cash flow expectation is $2,000 annually. Given a discount rate of 10 percent, the calculation of the breakeven annual cash flow is found by dividing present value of costs by present value of annuity (tabular value at 10 percent and ten years is 6.145) for the appropriate time period and interest rate. Computations for determining breakeven:

PV of initial outlay	$10,000
PV of salvage (1,000 × .36)	386
	$10,386

$$\frac{\$10,386}{6.145} = \$1,690$$

The annual cash flow could fall to $1,690 (breakeven value) and still provide the 10 percent return on investment. Note that the cost of the salvage operation was discounted and added to the initial cost outlay. Had the salvage value (net salvage value) been a positive value, then it (the $386) would have been subtracted from the initial cost.

Another way of looking at the breakeven value in terms of risk is that the difference of $310 is about 15 percent of the $2,000 expected cash flow. That is, the annual cash flow could fall 15 percent and still break even.

Suppose that by buying the swine confinement system wholesale (direct from factory), a 20 percent saving could be realized; the result would be a present value investment cost of $8,386. Under this condition, the breakeven value would fall to $1,365 ($8,386 ÷ 6.145 = $1,365) or the annual cash flow could be reduced to 68 percent of the originally estimated cash flow. Such computations for different investment alternatives provide the decision maker with a measure of the risks associated with the alternatives.

Varying the Discount Rate

Varying the discount rate among investment alternatives is a possible way of adjusting for different uncertainty levels of the investment. Varying the discount rate among years for a single investment to reflect uncertainty of cash flow is likewise a possibility. The shortcoming of this approach is the problem of and lack of guidance in selecting the relative change in discount rates to reflect different risks or uncertainties associated with investment opportunities.

SUMMARY

Sound decisions on capital investments require that decision makers evaluate the profit potential of numerous alternatives. In order to make this evaluation, management must determine the amount of capital required for each investment, forecast added benefits likely to occur, and use a realistic method to evaluate and select among the alternatives. This chapter addressed these concerns.

Attention was given to the need to consider the time value of money in evaluating investments. A number of analysis techniques (payback, accounting rate of return, and present worth) were discussed. The advantages of using present worth techniques in evaluating capital budgeting alternatives were shown. Present worth methods (benefit of cost, net present value, and internal rate of returns) are equally effective in determining the profitability of a given investment opportunity. However, when ranking several profitable alternatives, different rankings can occur. The benefit-cost ratio is an effective method to use in selecting and ranking investments.

APPLYING THE PRINCIPLES OF CHAPTER 19

1. What are the limitations of using the payback and average rate of return methods to evaluate investments?

2. Why is the benefit/ratio considered the best technique to rank investment alternatives?

3. What is investment feasibility?

4. Why must both investment profitability and feasibility be considered in evaluating an investment opportunity?

5. When investments differ in economic life, how can adjustments be made to standardize for the differences?

REFERENCES

Aplin, R. D., G. L. Cosler and C. P. Francis. *Capital Investment Analysis Using Discounted Cash Flow,* 2nd ed. Columbus, Ohio: Grid Inc., 1977.

Bierman, H., Jr. and S. Smidt. *The Capital Budgeting Decision.* New York, N.Y.: Macmillan Co., 1960.

Johnson, R. L. *Financial Decision Making.* Pacific Palisades, Calif.: Goodyear Publishing Co., 1973.

Quirin, C. D. *The Capital Expenditure Decision.* Homewood, Ill.: Richard D. Irwin Inc., 1967.

Weston, J. F. and E. F. Brighan. *Managerial Finance,* 5th ed. Hinsdale, Ill.: The Dryden Press, 1975.

Part 7

Taxes and Insurance

Insurance

20

- Considerations in planning an insurance program
- Development of priorities for insurance needs
- Kinds of insurance available and coverage under each

Insurance is a method of safeguarding against losses incurred by a contingent event such as fire, theft, or storm. Farmers have a variety of insurance needs because of the nature of their business. "Rules of thumb" with respect to insurance are suspect since individuals vary considerably in their willingness (because of personality or psychic characteristics) and their financial ability to assume risk. Consequently, how much and what kinds of insurance a farmer should carry are difficult to specify. Individual and family goals must be considered to make appropriate decisions about an insurance program.

To meet family goals, farmers select from alternative business organizations the one most likely to realize these goals successfully. An individual should take care to identify various adverse events that could cause hardships for the business or jeopardize its survival. An insurance program should be tailor-made to cover those risks that could affect the efficiency of the farm business, the survival of the farming operations, and the attainment of family goals.

A good way to plan and start an insurance program is to consider the following questions:

1. What are the chances of any particular loss occurring?

2. How great will the loss be if it does occur?

3. How can insurance be used for protection from these losses and what are the costs?

PRIORITY LISTING OF INSURANCE NEEDS

Several kinds of insurance are so important that it is useless to single out the one most important risk. It is helpful, though, to set up a classification by relative importance. The following classification would hold true on many farms, although farm and family circumstances could change the ranking.

The most important types of insurance for most farmers include fire insurance on all major farm property, liability insurance on road vehicles, life insurance on the farmer, and comprehensive public liability insurance.

Next in importance are health and accident insurance for the family, employer's liability and/or workmen's compensation insurance, life insurance on the farmer's wife, and crop insurance.

Less important than those above are comprehensive, collision, and medical payment insurance on the auto and truck; extended coverage (other than wind) on farm property, and life insurance on the children.

PROPERTY INSURANCE

Fire and Extended Coverage

Fire and wind insurance on farm buildings, machinery, livestock, and building contents is one of the most important parts of a farmer's insurance program. Basic fire insurance covers damage to insured property resulting from fire or lightning.

The devastation of a fire is not debatable. In rural areas, the consequences of fire are acute because timely fire control measures and modern fire fighting equipment are often lacking.

In general, fire insurance is considered a "best buy" when costs of insurance are weighed against the consequences of a fire. Besides the insurance covering losses from fire or lightning, many companies, by endorsement, will extend coverage to losses due to riot, explosion, hail, windstorm, aircraft, and vehicles.

Cost: Fire insurance rates (cost per $100 coverage) vary by geographical areas. Insurance costs basically reflect history of losses and physical characteristics of property. Most companies, therefore, "rate" the property and consider such characteristics as whether building(s) have approved lightning rods and approved roofs. Also, lower rates can be expected if the area is served by organized fire protection services.

The cost of fire insurance is expressed in dollars per $100 coverage. If one has property that qualifies for a "superior rating," insurance costs may be reduced by as much as 30 percent.

Another problem tangential to insuring buildings is that of determining appropriate values. Buildings, by and large, are rather permanent in nature. Therefore, markets for used buildings are practically nonexistent and afford little help. Also, and more significant, are the technological changes in agricultural production. Accompanying changes in production techniques has been the rapid obsolescence of production durables (intermediate assets); buildings are a case in point. As a result, the practice of affixing insurable value by determining replacement cost less depreciation (wear and tear as the result of time) may be misleading. Overinsuring may result.

Rather than insuring for a value that would replicate the original, one is wise to insure for an amount that would permit functional replacement. As an illustration, note the impracticality of insuring an "old horse barn" for replacement value when it is used for machine and baled hay storage.

Insuring Machinery

One can buy several types of policies to insure equipment. Because insurance laws vary from state to state, the provisions of the policy should be checked with a competent local agent. The three most important coverages are discussed below.

Farm fire and extended coverage: Basic fire insurance, which protects from losses caused by fire and lightning, can be written not only on farm machinery, but also on buildings, farm products, livestock, and other personal property. Most fire policies carry the extended coverage endorsement at extra cost to protect against such losses as those from hail, windstorm, explosion and riots, and others mentioned above. Endorsements also can be added to most policies to cover machinery involved in collision or overturn.

Theft: Theft of or damage to major pieces of equipment, such as a tractor or combine, can place a farmer in a financial strait both in terms of immediate loss and, perhaps, in terms of foregone earnings. Although theft is somewhat rare, it does occur. Events such as an overturn and fire, particularly during harvest, are more likely. Some companies do not write insurance for theft only, but provide extended coverage insurance that covers losses due to theft, vandalism, overturn, windstorm, and fire.

Farm equipment floater policy: This policy is especially tailored for coverage of farm machinery and is often written as an addition or floater to other coverage. For instance, the farm equipment floater could be part of the combination farm owner policy discussed in the next section. The floater can be purchased in blanket or specific form. The blanket form is written for a set amount and covers all items in the machinery inventory. The specific form is written with a specified dollar value for each itemized piece of equipment. Insurance for machinery is a "best buy" for all farmers who have a considerable amount of their total capital tied up in machinery, but is considerably more important to the custom operator whose machinery is at numerous geographical locations, often with limited protection from theft and vandalism.

Kinds of Companies Offering Insurance

The two basic kinds of companies in the insurance business today are stock and mutual. The stock company is a corporation organized and operated as any other business corporation. Insurance coverage is provided at a guaranteed cost and no additional assessments are made.

Mutual companies, which are owned by policyholders, issue either (1) assessable or (2) nonassessable policies. Under an assessable policy the company can require policyholders to pay additional premiums to cover losses and expenses. Thus the cost to the insured may vary from year to year and in any given year be very high or very low. On the average, rates for coverage by mutual companies are generally lower than for stock companies. Nonassessable policies usually require higher premiums because losses cannot be made up by special assessment.

One should shop for insurance. A study of several companies showed that insurance costs vary considerably among companies. Savings of 15 to 20 percent could be realized.

Farmers who have a considerable amount of personal property may find that by insuring under a blanket policy, costs can be reduced by 25 to 30 percent as opposed to insuring individual risk items.

Blanket or Farm Owner's Policies

This kind of package provides fire and extended coverage along with coverage for other perils. Additional coverages, of course, come at an additional cost, but at a lesser amount than if one insured for the specific loss. This type of policy, as one might expect by name, insures against losses from theft and vehicle overturn, and losses to livestock, poultry, farm implements, machinery, grain, hay, straw, feed, silage, fodder, and some portable buildings.

To obtain lower insurance rates per $100 coverage, there is usually a coinsurance clause. For illustrative purposes, assume a farmer wishes to insure property valued at $30,000. Under the coinsurance clause, a farmer receives lower rates if he agrees to insure the premises for a value of 80 to 90 percent (the percentage varies by company). The farmer who takes out a policy for $24,000 (an assumed 80 percent coinsurance clause) is compensated for losses at 100 percent of 80 percent. On the other hand, if the policy is written for a value of $20,000, the farmer is compensated for two-thirds of every loss ($20,000/$30,000). In essence, the farmer is the coinsurer; and in the example, he stands one-third of each loss. Losses under the blanket policy are compensated at a rate of 100 percent of market value; however, some companies require that each item insured must be so named in the policy.

If a farmer qualifies for the combination farm owner policy and wants the protection offered, he can generally save money.

COMPREHENSIVE LIABILITY INSURANCE

Liability insurance provides payment for personal injuries and property damage to third persons to whom the farmer is legally liable. It is designed to protect farmers against lawsuits from members of the general public. Medical payments are made to injured persons regardless of legal liability. Although most policies exclude coverage for injured employees, such coverage can be obtained by endorsement.

Protection is extended only to property described in the policy. The property or "premises" are normally defined as all farms or residences maintained by the farmer and his family. The insured is defined as a farmer, his wife, dependent relatives, and other persons under 21 years of age in the farmer's care. The policy covers actions or incidents of the insured and employees under his direction, but excludes intentional injuries inflicted by them.

LIABILITY INSURANCE FOR EMPLOYEES AND WORKMEN'S COMPENSATION

Every farm employer has a responsibility to see that employees are free from physical harm in the performance of their duties. The rules that determine liability for an employee's injuries fall into two distinct categories, depending on whether they are covered by workmen's compensation insurance. A farmer's responsibility to keep employees free from harm is similar to his responsibility to business visitors.

Protection from liability resulting from injuries to employees can be obtained, usually by endorsement, with the comprehensive liability policy. The workmen's compensation, however, *guarantees* compensation to an employee for injuries arising out of employment. No litigation is involved. Furthermore, workmen's compensation does not have the disadvantage of liability insurance that judgment might exceed the insured limits of the policy.

An employer has a responsibility to employees, both to warn them of hidden dangers and to inspect the premises to locate dangerous conditions. When employees suffer injuries, one is liable if (1) one failed to inform the employee of the known hidden danger which caused the injuries or (2) one, not knowing of the presence of such a danger, could have discovered it by virtue of a reasonable inspection.

Under present law, it may not be sufficient to warn employees of hidden dangers. Although this warning is evidence that the employee assumes the risk of injury, the employee must also realize and understand the prospective danger if the employer is to avoid liability.

CROP INSURANCE

The new crop insurance program, administered by the USDA's Federal Crop Insurance Corporation (FCIC), is a partnership among the federal government, the farmer, and the private insurance industry. It eliminates many of the problems of the old crop insurance law and permits easy access and service for farmer policyholders locally, where some 20,000 private agents and federal offices will service insurance policies.

In 1981, the insurance covered 28 crops in 1,926 counties in 39 states. Coverage will expand to another 250 counties each year for the next 5 years. In time, all commercial crops will be covered by insurance.

How the Insurance Works

Once you are insured, you are guaranteed a certain amount of production—in bushels or pounds—per acre. You can select from three levels of coverage—60, 65, or 75 percent of the average crop yield calculated for your farm or area. Yield can be determined by county/area averages or by "proven" yields. For example, if your average corn yield per acre is set at 100 bushels and you select the 50 percent production option, FCIC will pay you for anything you produce that is less than 50 bushels per acre. If you select the 65 percent option, you'll be paid for anything less than 65 bushels per acre. For the 75 percent option, you will be paid for anything less than 75 bushels of corn per acre.

The all-risk insurance covers all losses caused by natural conditions beyond your control, but the insurance does not protect anyone from the consequences of mismanagement.

You can also select in advance how much money per bushel or pound you will receive from FCIC when you produce less than your insured guaranteed option as the result of a natural disaster. Before the planting season, FCIC will establish three price levels. The highest of those levels will be based on an estimate of what the market price will become harvest time. The other two levels will be lesser amounts. For corn grown in 1981, production could be valued at $2.70, $2.00, or $1.70 per bushel. Other crops have different price levels.

Let's look at an example. Let's say your average annual yield of corn is set at 100 bushels per acre. You select the 65 percent guaranteed yield option. You also select the $2.70 per bushel payment level.

Drought hits your farm, and your overall yield drops to 20 bushels per acre. Since your guaranteed insurance production is 65 percent of 100 bushels—65 bushels—and your actual production is 20 bushels, you have an insured loss of 45 bushels, and FCIC will pay you $2.70 × 45 bushels per acre ($121.50) for the number of acres you have insured. What's more, you still have your 20 bushels per acre to sell at the current market price.

The new all-risk FCIC insurance program protects you not only against loss in quantity of production, but also against loss in quality as well.

In addition, crop insurance can be used as collateral for loans. It aids the farmer in borrowing for crop inputs because the banker knows that the farmer's investment is insured. The farmer can assign insurance benefits directly to the lender through a "collateral assignment," which the lender can obtain with the farmer's consent through the local FCIC office. In the event that a loss occurs, the FCIC makes the check payable to the lender and the farmer jointly.

LIFE INSURANCE

Almost any family faces financial problems if the primary breadwinner dies. Hence, there is need to hedge against such difficulties. Levels of financial protection needs are influenced by such factors as family size, age of dependents, and the desired living standard that the farm operator wishes to assure his dependents. Funds may also be needed for estate settlement and taxes.

A Sample of Selected Farmers' Insurance Decisions

A recent study of New York dairy farmers showed that a majority of them relied on an insurance agent to select the type of policy—quite a vote of confidence.

When farmers were asked the reasons they purchased life insurance, 69 percent stated family protection. Another 25 percent cited debt protection, but this response could be translated as family protection. Respondents could give more than one reason for purchase; however, only 22 percent mentioned investment as a purpose of their life coverage.

Although the primary reason that farmers purchased life insurance was financial protection, about 70 percent of the annual premiums were expended for policies with cash values, policies that have both investment and protection features.

Types of Insurance Policies

There are four basic kinds of life insurance one may consider: (1) term, (2) whole life, (3) limited payment, and (4) endowment.

Term: Term insurance gives protection only. It is available for a specified number of years such as five, ten, fifteen, or to age 65. Unless a borrower documents adequate insurance protection, lenders often require that adequate insurance back their loans. This insurance, often referred to as credit life, is invariably one form of term insurance. When a loan is made and secured by a fixed asset such as land, the policy is one with declining coverage that corresponds to the loan balance outstanding—thus the name declining term or mortgage insurance. Term insurance provides for protection only; generally, there is no savings or cash value feature.

Whole life: Whole or ordinary life has both the savings and cash value features. Premiums must be paid for the insured person's lifetime. As with any life insurance policy, the premium depends on the age of the insured at the time the policy is purchased.

Limited pay life: For limited pay life insurance, the insured pays a premium for a specified number of years, at which time the policy is paid up and the insured may exercise settlement options. The insured may take paid up insurance or cash in the policy for its accumulated cash value. The cash value of a limited pay policy increases faster than whole life because the premiums for an expected lifetime are squeezed into the specified number of years for which one pays premiums.

Endowment: Endowment insurance pays the insured the face value of the policy after a specified number of premium payments (e.g., ten, twenty, thirty years). The insurance protection is then ended with the payment of the lump sum accumulated over time.

HEALTH AND ACCIDENT INSURANCE

Hospitalization and Surgical

Prices for medical services have led the inflationary spiral in recent years. Sickness can be considered a major budget item and can spell financial disaster to many families. It is not uncommon for medical expenses for a family of four to average over $500 per year.

Insurance for hospitalization and surgical expenses and major medical policies are ways of hedging against sickness. Hospital insurance provides for costs incurred for hospital room and board, operating room fees, anesthesia, ambulance service, X-rays, laboratory tests, and drugs.

Policies usually have a maximum payment limitation for itemized expense categories. For example, limits are defined by surgery specification as well as room and board rates.

Major Medical

Major medical insurance generally covers a specified percentage (80 percent, for example) of all qualified expenses in excess of a deductible amount, subject to maximum benefits. Most policies have maximum payment limitations specified similar to hospitalization insurance. For example, a detailed study of a "representative" major medical policy of $10,000 with a $500 deductible clause showed payment limitations specified for all cost categories; for example, a $1,050 limit for surgical services.

To meet a large medical bill, one could use: (1) major medical, (2) a combination of major medical and hospitalization insurance, or (3) a combination of hospitalization or major medical and income protection.

Income Protection/Disability Insurance

Work absenteeism or a recovery period is usually associated with large medical bills. Therefore, income protection insurance may well assist in meeting the unexpected large financial outlay and economic consequence of extended sickness. Although income protection insurance may be an excellent way to supplement income for medical expenses, its primary use, as the name implies, is to assure an income level if sickness of considerable duration occurs.

Let's look at two extreme situations for illustrative purposes. Assume a highly mechanized crop-livestock farm in which the owner-operator (farmer #1) provides most of the labor. His labor is supplemented with some summer assistance provided by a son in college. He has 300 acres of cropland, farrows 100 sows twice a year, and fattens 200 feeder cattle. An extended sickness could jeopardize the entire farm business as it now exists. Therefore, some consideration should be given to an income protection policy.

On the other hand, let's look at the situation of a relatively small farmer in terms of acreage and dollar business. The farm consists of 160 acres of land and a dairy herd of 40 cows. There are four boys in the family ranging in age from 8 to 16 years. Also, the neighborhood is noted for its willingness to assist farmers in times of sickness and need under adverse situations.

This particular farmer's need for disability insurance obviously differs from the first farmer's. These examples highlight the fact that an insurance program is individualistic in nature and depends on an individual's aversion to risk and financial ability to withstand adverse events.

When buying any insurance, the buyer should read the entire policy and discuss coverages and exemptions with the agent. The farmer should determine these basic facts about disability insurance:

1. Whether the policy is noncancelable
2. How disability is defined
3. Whether there is an average earnings clause
4. Whether occupational disability is covered

Not all policies have the same definition for disability. Policies vary with respect to whether one must be home and confined to be disabled and whether one must be ruled unable to work in any occupation. Also, whether one can materially participate in management and still be considered totally disabled should be ascertained.

Some policies have the average earnings clause which states, in effect, that in the event of disability, payments would be based on the average earnings during a stated period prior to the disability. Because in farming incomes may vary considerably, it may be best to shop around to find a policy without such a clause.

INSURANCE POLICY COMPARISON

When the consumer finally decides to buy life insurance, he usually purchases a whole life policy. The big question probably boils down to determining from which company to buy. The consumer may have heard that there are no significant price differences among reputable companies so he is as well off to buy from one company as any other. Thus, the consumer surrenders to the better salesman, not knowing whether he got a good deal or not.

Actually, differences in cost do exist among companies and knowing how to compare these costs may save money. The purpose of this section is to help compare costs of whole life policies from different companies and compare costs of different types of policies within specific companies.

Two initial pieces of information are needed: (1) appropriate mathematical tables and (2) a schedule of premium rates and projected cash values. A consumer has several alternatives for using his money. With mathematical tables to provide the time value of money, the consumer can calculate the value of insurance premiums had they been used some other way, such as savings deposits at 5 percent interest.

The return for using the insurance premiums in some other way is the opportunity cost. For most of us, the best alternative to buying insurance for saving is to place the amount of the premium in a savings account. However, different time schedules are involved for premium payments, insurance benefits, savings deposits and interest payments. For the best comparison, costs and benefits must be based on the same time period. To do so requires a procedure to move all costs and benefits either to some future time period, to the present, or to an annual basis taking appropriate account of the time value of money (interest cost).

Future Costs and Benefits

The first method is taking all annual costs (premiums) and benefits to a future time period. Exhibit 20–1 provides the information and procedure necessary for determining the future value of $1 each year for a given number of years under various interest rates. Multiply the annual premium by this figure to determine the future value of $1 each year for a given number of years, assuming a 5 percent interest rate.

Exhibit 20–1.

Company	Premium (1)	Amount of annuity of $1[1] (2)	Opportunity cost (3) (col. 1 × col. 2)	Projected cash value[2] (4)	Cost (40 years) (5) (col. 3 − col. 4)
A	$135.00	120.80	16,308.00	5,660	10,648.00
B	180.20	120.80	21,768.16	12,716	9,052.16
C	172.00	120.80	20,777.60	11,913	8,864.60
D	240.00	120.80	28,992.00	16,167	12,825.00
E	136.80	120.80	16,525.44	7,904	8,621.44

[1]Tabular value of 120.80 comes from an amount of annuity of table $\left[\dfrac{(1+i)^n - 1}{i} \right]$

[2]Remember, the projected cash value is not the guaranteed cash value. The projected cash value estimate has been influenced by the past growth and earnings of the company. Likewise, it is affected by the expected earnings and growth in the future. These facts suggest the importance of dealing with reliable and established companies.

As an example, suppose a 25-year-old person finds that the annual premium for a $10,000 whole life policy is $170. Assuming retirement at 65, the annual payment would be $170 for 40 years. An annuity table shows that one dollar invested each year at 5 percent interest for 40 years will be worth $120.80. Thus, 120.80 × $170 = $20,536 opportunity cost.

To estimate the cost of being insured for 40 years, take the company's total projected cash value of the policy at age 65, and subtract it from the opportunity cost of the premium. The guaranteed cash value on a policy can't be used for this calculation unless it is a nonparticipating policy (a stock company policy), i.e., total future cash value of a participating company will be composed of guaranteed cash value plus dividend accumulation.

Suppose in the example above, the cash value of the policy at age 65 was found to be $11,420. This would result in a cost for protection of $9,116 for 40 years ($20,536.00 minus $11,420.00).

The above procedure can be followed to arrive at a basis for comparing costs of insurance among several companies. To illustrate the varied results, five companies were selected at random and the above procedure was applied. The results listed in Exhibit 20–1 were calculated for a $10,000 whole life policy and for a consumer of age 25 who assumes a five percent opportunity cost for the money and plans to retire at age 65.

All other things being equal, the rational insurance buyer would select insurance Company E because of lower cost. Over a period of 40 years, Company E's policy is $4,203.56 cheaper than that of the most expensive company (Company D).

The same technique can be applied to determine the relative costs of different types of insurance within or among companies. For example, what is the cost of term insurance compared to a whole life policy?

A nonparticipating company was selected for the cost comparison between its ordinary life and term policies. The ordinary life premium for a 25-year-old was $126.50 for a $10,000 policy; it had a cash value at age 65 of $6,060. On the other hand, the same company had a term 65 policy with an annual premium of $86.10. The difference in premium, therefore, would be $40.40 per year.

The appropriate cost comparison is to compare the cash value of the ordinary life policy at age 65 with the accumulated future value of the $40.40 savings deposited each year for 40 years.

Assuming a 5 percent interest rate, the accumulated savings of $40.40 each year would be worth $4,880.32 at the end of a 40-year period. With this particular company, the ordinary life policy is the best buy, saving $1,169.68 at the end of 40 years. However, at a 6 percent interest rate, the term insurance is the best buy. The future value of accumulated savings would be $6,232.30 as opposed to the cash value of $6,050.00 for the ordinary life policy.[1]

Present Value of Costs and Benefits

Probably the most common method of analyzing investment alternatives differing in costs, benefits, and investment life is finding the present value (discounting) of all benefits and costs. Given the cost and benefit data from our five companies, an appropriate analysis is to find the present value of the flow of premiums over 40 years and the projected cash value 40 years from now. Note that an annuity table to find the present value of fund flows can be used only when the annual dollar values are equal.

Once the present values of all costs and benefits are obtained, the

---

[1]Many salesmen use the cash value aspect of a policy as a selling point. To the author, this is a fallacious position. One cannot have the cake and eat it too. Once one borrows on an insurance policy, the insurance coverage is reduced. Assume that a loan of $2,000 is secured from a $10,000 nonparticipating policy and that the next week the individual dies. The $2,000 must be paid back before the face amount of the policy is received, so the beneficiary receives only $8,000. On the other hand, an individual with a term policy has no borrowing privileges. However, the beneficiary would receive the $10,000 face amount of the policy plus any amount the policy holder had placed in savings, as shown in the discussion regarding premium differentials above.

present value of benefits is subtracted from the present value of costs for analysis purposes (commonly known as net present value techniques).

To determine the cost of protection and because premium costs exceed benefits (cash value), benefits are subtracted from costs to give a net cost estimate. The results of this technique are shown in column 8 of Exhibit 20–2.

Annual Basis

Comparing on an annual basis may be the most plausible and comprehensible of the three techniques for those who have not analyzed investments and figured the time value of money. The time value of money (opportunity cost) can be considered, yet both premiums and benefits are on an annual basis.

Premiums and cash values are converted to an annual basis by using an amortization table to amortize the present value of benefits over the 40 years. At 5 percent interest rate the present value of the cash value of Company A ($803.72) is equivalent to $78.86 on an annual basis.

The net cost is then found by subtracting the annual benefits from the premium payments ($135 minus $48.86). Column 10 of Exhibit 20–2 gives net costs of insurance computed by this method. Note that all three techniques give the same company ranking when comparing and determining the least cost for protection. That is to say, companies ranked E, C, B, A, D, in terms of lowest to highest cost, regardless of analysis technique used.

Exhibit 20–2.

Company	Annual premium (1)	Projected cash value (2)	Present value of $1[1] (3)	Amortization factor[2] (4)	Present value of annuity of $1[3] (5)
A	$135.00	5,660	.1420	.0583	17.159
B	180.20	12,716	.1420	.0583	17.159
C	172.00	11,913	.1420	.0583	17.159
D	240.00	16,167	.1420	.0583	17.159
E	136.80	7,904	.1420	.0583	17.159

[1]Tabular value of .1420 comes from present value of $1 (PV) table $[(1+i)^{-n}]$ at the intersection of 5 percent and year 40.

[2]Tabular value of 0.583 comes from an amortization table at the intersection of 5 percent and year 40.

[3]Tabular value of 17.159 comes from present value of annuity table at the intersection of 5 percent and year 40.

Selecting an Interest Rate

One should consider the various investment alternatives when selecting the interest rate for the above comparisons and also realize that the interest rate may vary for different people. Those who have no savings program should use zero interest.

If saving money is difficult, choose a low interest rate. However, persons who have no trouble saving voluntarily and have a knack for making good investments may choose a higher rate, say 6 or 7 percent.

The higher the interest rate selected, the smaller the total cost of policies with lower annual premiums. On the other hand, the lower the interest rate, the more attractive the higher annual premium policies will be.

One should recognize that the savings is not being suggested as a substitute for insurance, but rather that the consumer use a few simple calculations as an aid in getting the most for the money.

SUMMARY

Individual and family goals must be considered for appropriate planning and decision making in developing an insurance program. The cost of providing 100 percent protection from unexpected losses is not economically feasible, and is for most farmers an impossibility.

A good way to plan and start an insurance program is to consider the following questions:

1. What are the chances of any particular loss occurring?
2. How great will the loss be if it does occur?

Exhibit 20–2. (cont'd.)

Present value of premium (6) (col. 5 × col. 1)	Present value of cash value (7) (col. 3 × col. 2)	Net cost (8) (col. 6 − col. 7)	Amortized value of PV benefits (9) (col. 4 × col. 7)	Annual net cost (10) (col. 1 − col. 9)
2,316.46	803.72	1,512.74	46.86	88.14
3,092.05	1,805.67	1,286.38	105.27	74.93
2,951.35	1,691.65	1,259.70	98.62	73.38
4,118.16	2,295.71	1,822.45	133.84	106.16
2,347.35	1,122.37	1,224.98	65.43	71.37

3. How can insurance be used for protection from those losses and what are the costs?

A priority listing of insurance needs is developed in terms of importance:

Most Important—Fire insurance on all major farm property, liability insurance on vehicles on the raod, life insurance on the manager's life, comprehensive public liability insurance.

Important—Health and accident insurance for the family, employer's liability or workmen's compensation insurance, life insurance on the manager's wife, and crop insurance.

Less Important—Comprehensive, collision, and medical payment insurance on the auto and truck, extended coverage (other than wind) on farm property, and life insurance on the children.

The chapter discussed the kinds of insurance available and the perils that each covers. In addition, techniques of computing least cost life insurance alternatives were covered.

APPLYING THE PRINCIPLES OF CHAPTER 20

1. Specify the insurance needs of a young farmer.

2. How might the insurance needs of a young farmer differ from those of an older, established farmer?

3. How can savings be realized in buying insurance?

4. Under what conditions is the employer liable for an employee's injury?

5. Which life insurance policies have a savings in addition to protection features?

REFERENCES

Bailey, W. R. and L. A. Jones. "Economic Considerations In Crop Insurance," USDA FRS Bulletin No. 447, 1970.

Belth, J. M. "Life Insurance Price Measurement," Reprint Series No. 66, Bureau of Business Research, Indiana University, 1969.

Federal Crop Insurance Corporation, annual reports.

Jones, A. J. and E. I. Reinsel. "Insurance Facts for Farmers," USDA Farmers Bulletin No. 447, 1970.

Nelson, A. G., W. F. Lee and W. G. Murray. *Agricultural Finance,* 6th ed. Iowa State University Press, 1973.

Osburn, D. D. "How to Shop for Life Insurance," *Science and Technology Guide.* University of Missouri, Extension Division, 1972.

Income Tax Management

- Use of tax management to avoid, not evade, taxes
- Cash method versus accrual method of tax reporting
- Income leveling strategies
  Activities to increase income
  Activities to decrease income
  Investment credit
  Income averaging
- Special tax situations
  Change in form of business
  Major business expansion
  Improvement in labor management practices
  Obtaining use of major equipment items
  Sale of a capital item
  Planning for retirement
  Weighing farm versus off-farm investment
  Estate planning

21

Income tax management, or taxmanship, is *the management of income, expenses, and capital in a manner that will result in minimum tax obligation without reduction in profitability.* It includes calculating tax due and filing returns in a manner to meet all tax responsibilities at the least cost in time and money to the manager of the business.

Through tax management, the farm manager tries to keep income tax liability as low as the law allows. Tax management is tax avoidance, *not* tax evasion. A fundamental understanding of income tax law is essential if the farm manager is to keep the proper accounts and make intelligent decisions in tax as well as other areas of management. The goal of tax management is to maximize after-tax income, thereby increasing the dollars available for family living and increasing new worth.

Management of taxable income can help the taxpayer even out the tax load while making use of all exemptions. The taxpayer who expects an extremely low income should tax manage, just as should taxpayers with high or variable incomes.

Each taxpayer has a certain amount of tax-free income. For example, the standard deduction for a single taxpayer is $3,300, but it is $5,400 for a couple filing a joint return. This is income not subject to federal tax. The taxpayer should thus try to bring income up to this tax-free level.

METHOD OF TAX REPORTING

Farmers may keep records and report their income on either the cash or accrual method. They make their choice when they file their first farm tax return. Having made the choice, they are not allowed to change without written consent from the Internal Revenue Service, by which they must apply in writing within the first 180 days of the tax year affected. A business must be able to justify the change. Permission to change is not automatic.

A farmer on the cash method reports when income in cash or its equivalent is received and when expenses are paid. A farmer on the accrual basis reports income in the year it is earned, even though not actually received, and reports expenses when incurred, even if not paid. On the accrual basis, an inventory must be kept of livestock, crops, feed, and supplies. An increase in the value of these items is included as income and a decrease as a reduction in income for tax purposes.

To illustrate the difference between cash and accrual reporting, assume that a farmer buys $100 worth of feed on December 15, but does not use the feed until January. If he is on the cash basis he can pay for the feed in December and lower his current taxable income by $100 or pay for it in January and reduce his next year's taxable income by $100. If he is on the accrual basis, the December purchase will not affect his current taxable income because the feed will appear in his inventory at year's end. If he pays for it in December, the expense will be offset by the addition to inventory. If he does not pay for it in December, the $100 will be added to accounts payable. Thus on the accrual basis, purchase of the feed will not affect taxable income until the year it is used. Income is treated similarly. If a sale of grain is made in December, but payment is not available until January, the accrual method farmer reports the income in December and adds the amount to accounts receivable. The cash basis farmer makes no report until the cash is received in January.

Advantages of the Cash Method

Most farmers use the cash method of accounting and reporting. The cash method offers these advantages:

1. Fewer records need to be kept, and the problem of maintaining inventories is largely avoided.

2. An aggressive farmer who is continually investing in and building up the business pays less tax currently because the increase in his inventories is not recognized. He thus postpones payment of tax until business property is liquidated.

3. Under the cash method, there are greater opportunities to even out income from year to year and to avoid high tax brackets in years of unusually high production or prices.

4. Sales of raised dairy or breeding livestock result in less tax if the cash method is used. This is because these animals have a zero basis when sold, while under the accrual method, the last inventory value is the cost basis for determining gain. The cash basis farmer can, in effect, convert more ordinary income to capital gain through raising dairy or breeding livestock than can the accrual basis farmer, who has less gain to report when such livestock is sold.

5. Upon death of a farmer using the cash basis, unsold livestock, crops, and other farm commodities pass to his estate free of income tax because the estate takes the property with a tax basis of fair market value at death. The accrual basis farmer has already included these items as income year by year.

The accrual method may have advantages in some unusual situations. For example, a crop farmer who sometimes holds crops for sale into the following year will automatically avoid the problem of reporting income from two crops in one year on the accrual basis. For most farmers, however, cash basis accounting offers significant tax advantages, assuming they practice taxmanship.

WHEN TO USE TAX MANAGEMENT STRATEGIES

Each taxpayer has an income pattern which can be defined as "normal." This income pattern could be viewed as the tax bracket of the taxpayer for the past three to five years. The taxpayer who has had a steady increase in income may be gradually moving into higher tax brackets. On the other hand, the trend could be downward or the income level rather static. At any rate, a look back over several years helps to determine a pattern. It is costly in terms of after-tax dollars to fluctuate among different tax brackets. Thus, in a given year, a taxpayer who is up or down from a typical range should select methods of tax management to help come as close to the normal pattern as possible.

The consequences of wide taxable income fluctuations can be illustrated for two different couples that had the same taxable income over a 2-year period. Bob and Ann had taxable income in consecutive years of $0 and $40,000. Joe and Jane had the same total, $40,000, but received $20,000 each year. Based upon the 1984 tax tables their taxes would be:

	Taxes paid by:	
Year	Bob and Ann	Joe and Jane
1	$ 0	$2,461
2	7,858	2,461
Total tax paid	$7,858	$4,922

It is often possible to reduce the income fluctuation and increase after-tax income by using some of the tax management techniques discussed below.

Make a Tax Estimate

A good farm manager will be aware of taxes all twelve months so that day-to-day decisions result in the greatest tax advantage consistent with maximum after-tax income. Exercising the most appropriate tax management options requires a manager to know the probable tax status of the business.

The tax estimate is the tool used to determine the expected tax liability. It is based on what has happened to date in an accounting year and on an estimate of what will happen for the remainder of the year. If the farm records are complete and up-to-date, it is relatively easy to follow a format for the tax estimate. One should assemble the following information: ordinary farm receipts, receipts from the sale of resale items and their tax cost, capital gain sales, capital sales that do not qualify for capital gain, nonfarm income, farm expenses, depreciation records, capital purchases, list of personal exemptions and deductions, federal gas and oil tax refund due, investment credit information, social security information, self-employment retirement programs, and tax tables. By carefully following an organized format, the taxpayer can estimate taxes due for the current year very well.

If it looks as if the income tax estimate will fall below the "tax free income" or vary from the normal pattern, the manager can consider the various techniques of taxmanship. If the estimate looks normal, at least the taxpayer knows it and knows, further, the dollar value of the tax liability to plan for in the cash flow budget.

INCOME LEVELING STRATEGIES

What are some methods available to the manager for reducing income tax variability? Particular attention should be devoted to sales and purchases to insure that taxable income is sufficient to cover or use all personal exemptions and deductions allowed. Any income credit not used in a given taxable year is lost.

Activities to Increase Income

Tax management strategies should only be employed if they are consistent with other good farm management decisions. Regular farm management techniques should be brought to bear on tax management decisions. For example, managers can use the partial budget technique to see if holding a pen of market animals an extra week or two from one tax year to another is a profitable decision. Once that is decided, the tax ramifications should be considered. One could easily lose $100 of profit to save $60 of taxes; such is not the purpose of tax management.

Some methods to increase income in the present year could be:

1. Sell marketable grain, livestock, etc., before December 31.
2. Postpone expenditures and investments until after January 1.
3. Work with suppliers to pay bills after January 1.
4. Forego "expense method" depreciation.
5. Do some off-farm or custom work.

Activities to Decrease Income

The manager who wishes to accelerate expenses should make sure all purchases are bona fide purchases. A bona fide purchase is one in which prices and quantities are stated in the transaction. A "deposit" to be applied to future expenses is not a deductible item.

Some methods to delay income or speed up expenses to maintain an "even" level of taxable income could be:

1. Use deferred sales contracts.
2. Make advance purchases of feed and fertilizer (must be firm and have an advantage).

3. Postpone some sales until next year.

4. Use allowed "expense method" depreciation.

5. Purchase needed machinery, equipment, etc., before end of the year to get investment credit and some depreciation.

6. Use "income averaging" if taxable income is $3,000 or more above 120 percent of average taxable income (as discussed below) for the past four years.

Select Appropriate Depreciation Techniques

The cost of machinery, equipment, farm buildings, and other property with a useful life of more than one year is a capital expenditure. Such items may not be treated as deductible expenses in the year of purchase. However, a business is entitled to deduct, as depreciation, a reasonable allowance for the exhaustion, wear and tear, and obsolescence of property (capital items) used in a business or held for the production of income.

Depreciation must be taken in the year it is sustained. To insure complete and accurate reporting, use a form which furnishes (1) a record of depreciable assets, (2) depreciation allowance, and (3) information required to determine the "adjusted basis" of depreciable assets if they are sold or traded. The *tax basis* (amount to be depreciated) for determining annual depreciation allowance is the same as the basis one would use to determine capital gain if the property were sold. Usually, the cost of property is its basis. If the capital item was obtained by a cash or credit transaction and a trade-in, the basis is book value of the trade-in plus "boot" paid. Basis is never determined by replacement cost or current list price.

Depreciable property must have a limited and determinable life. Land is never depreciable because its useful life is indefinite, but fences on the land are. There is no average useful life that is recognized as applicable to all farm items.

The Economic Recovery Act of 1981 turned things topsy turvy as far as depreciation is concerned. The Act eliminated the 20 percent additional first-year depreciation option and replaced it with a new provision called the "expense method depreciation" (EMD). EMD allows a taxpayer to directly deduct up to $10,000 per year of investment in tangible personal property (e.g., tools, machines, equipment).

The 1981 Act also significantly altered the methods allowed for depleting the cost of capital expenditures. For assets placed in service after 1980, the method for determining depreciation (called Accelerated Cost Recovery System, ACRS) is greatly simplified. In most cases, the writeoff period is shorter than was previously allowed. Note, however, that a farmer desiring to minimize depreciation allowances may use the "New Straight Line" depreciation techniques (see Chapter 4).

The farmer's problem in tax management is to decide when and how to use EMD and/or ACRS, and in what combinations. The decision affects both taxable income and the amount of investment tax credit that can be taken.

Expense method depreciation: The EMD provision was designed primarily to help small businesses. The EMD allows treating personal property placed in service in 1984 and 1985 as an expense, up to $7,500. The amount that can be directly expensed increases to $10,000 in 1986. The provision applies to both new and used property. However, if old property is traded in, only the cash boot paid is eligible for EMD. Further, expensed property is not eligible for investment tax credit.

An example showing the effects of EMD on taxable income is presented in the next section.

Regular depreciation: The 1981 Act established one primary depreciation method: The Accelerated Cost Recovery System. ACRS, sometimes referred to as "10–5–3 depreciation," simplified most depreciation computations; you simply go to the tables supplied in the Farmer's Tax Guide. The ACRS method, which applies to new and used property, has four basic depreciation categories:

3 years: Autos, light trucks, tools, and some equipment with less than 4 years expected life. Hogs for breeding.

5 years: Most farm machinery, equipment, grain bins, drainage tile and fences, but no other land improvements. Cattle (beef and dairy) for breeding. Horses, breeding or work. Single-purpose structures (confinement hog barns, poultry houses, greenhouses, some dairy barns).

10 years: Some farm buildings, but mostly nonfarm property, e.g., railroad cars and other real property with useful life under 12.5 years.

15 years: Farm buildings that normally have a useful life of more than 12.5 years.

Exhibits 21–1 and 21–2 summarize the depreciation percentages allowed on depreciable property for the periods January 1, 1981, through December 31, 1984, and after January 1, 1985. Under ACRS, a "half-year convention" is applicable for the year of acquisition. The half-year convention results in a taxpayer receiving only a half-year depreciation in year 1 regardless of the time of acquisition. Thus, a farmer buying a $30,000 tractor in December would obtain the same tax benefit as his neighbor who paid $30,000 in January of the same year.

Exhibit 21–1. Annual depreciation deductions for property placed in service after December 31, 1980, and before January 1, 1985

Recovery year	Type of property		
	3 year	5 year	10 year
	Percent		
1	25	15	8
2	38	22	14
3	37	21	12
4	—	21	10
5	—	21	10
6	—	—	10
7	—	—	9
8	—	—	9
9	—	—	9
10	—	—	9

An Example Applying the Depreciation Options

The depreciation decisions a manager makes in any given year are influenced by (1) the tax bracket he/she expects to be in this year and (2) the tax bracket he/she expects to be in in future years. Taxes paid in previous years may also influence the decision if there are credits from prior years or if some years were unusually low income years.

For illustrative purposes we will consider the tax situations of farm-

Exhibit 21–2. Annual depreciation deductions for property placed in service in 1985.

Recovery year	Type of property		
	3 year	5 year	10 year
	Percent		
1	29	18	9
2	47	33	19
3	24	25	16
4	—	16	14
5	—	8	12
6	—	—	10
7	—	—	8
8	—	—	6
9	—	—	4
10	—	—	2

ers Jones and Smith. Assume both have been averaging about $21,000 in taxable income. That would be the 22 percent marginal tax bracket for years after 1985.

Now, suppose Jones is expecting to have an unusually high income ($45,800) in the current year and Smith expects a lower than average ($11,900) income year. Also suppose both are considering the purchase of a $10,000 piece of machinery. How might they use the depreciation options to influence taxes paid? (Assume they expect taxable income to return to near $21,000 in the next 2 years.)

Exhibit 21–3 looks at two options that are open to Jones and Smith. There are also some "in-between" options.

- Option A: Take the maximum depreciation allowed under EMD and ACRS this year. Take allowed investment tax credit.
- Option B: Use ACRS only. Take allowed investment tax credit.

Exhibit 21–3. Example of depreciation options under the 1981 Tax Act for a "high income" and a "low income" taxpayer; $10,000 investment

Year	Projected taxable income	Taxes to be paid if $10,000 investment is not made	Treatment of the investment for tax purposes under two depreciation options		Taxes paid under each depreciation option if $10,000 investment is made	
			Option A	Option B	Option A	Option B
			High income Farmer Jones			
1	$45,800	$9,772	EMD = $10,000 ACRS = 0 ITC = 0	EMD = $0 ACRS = 1,800 ITC = 1,000	$6,472	$8,178
2	21,000	2,673	EMD = 0 ACRS = 0	EMD = 0 ACRS = 3,300	2,673	2,047
3	21,000	2,673	EMD = 0 ACRS = 0	EMD = 0 ACRS = 2,500	2,673	2,191
			Low income Farmer Smith			
1	11,900	1,085	EMD = $10,000 ACRS = 0 ITC = 0	EMD = 0 ACRS = 1,800 ITC = 1,000	0	0
2	21,000	2,673	EMD = 0 ACRS = 0	EMD = 0 ACRS = 3,300	2,673	1,880
3	21,000	2,673	EMD = 0 ACRS = 0	EMD = 0 ACRS = 2,500	2,673	2,191

Because this is a $10,000 depreciable item, the entire amount can be written off as an expense in year one under option A. There would be no eligible investment tax credit under option A.

The tax effects of the decision to spend $10,000 for a depreciable asset are somewhat different for Jones and Smith. Although taxes paid would be reduced in both cases, option A has the most benefit for Jones, but option B gives Smith the greatest benefit. Jones could reduce expected taxes by $3,300 over the three years, with all the savings realized in the first year. Farmer Smith could realize $2,360 in tax savings over three years, but the first year savings is only $1,085.

The reader will recognize that there are other factors that will ultimately influence a decision like this one faced by Jones and Smith. Both must also look at projected cash flows, the opportunity cost of capital used for this item versus another use, the source of the funds, and the costs and benefits of leasing versus ownership.

Investment Credit

In 1975 the investment tax credit on purchases of qualified property was increased from 7 to 10 percent. Also, the limit on used property eligible for the credit was increased from $50,000 to $100,000. These increases were extended through 1980 by the Tax Reform Act of 1976.

The amount of investment credit that can be used to reduce taxes is generally limited to $25,000 plus one-half of the tax over that amount, with a three-year carryback and seven-year carryover of any credits exceeding the limitation. Under prior law the credit earned in the current year had to be used first before any carryback or carryover could be applied. As a result of these limitations, some taxpayers were unable to get full benefit from investment credit otherwise allowable. The new law reduces the risk of losing benefit from credit carryovers by changing the order in which the credits are absorbed. For taxable years beginning after 1975, taxpayers will be allowed to apply unused credits from earlier years before having to use current year credits.

To qualify for investment credit, property must be depreciable, have a useful life of at least three years, be tangible personal property or other tangible property, and be placed in service during the year purchased. Generally, if property is depreciable (except for general-purpose buildings), it is eligible for investment credit. Livestock (except horses) is also eligible. For property to qualify under other tangible property, the property must be used as an integral part of production, etc., or constitute a research or storage facility.

If the useful life of the property is seven years or more, 100 percent of the investment qualifies; if it has five to seven years of useful life, two thirds qualifies; and if three to five years, one-third of the investment qualifies. On property with less than three years useful life, there is no credit.

To supplement the above rules regarding investment credit, the interested reader should consult the Farmers Tax Guide, IRS publication 225, and other IRS publications.

From a tax management standpoint, the important thing to remember is that investment credit reduces a person's tax bill by the amount of the credit. One should be aware of this when planning eligible expenditures, so that he/she may reduce the tax bill in the year the investment is made.

Income Averaging

Income averaging, instituted in 1964 and liberalized in 1969, is designed to ease the income tax burden to taxpayers whose incomes fluctuate widely from year to year. Income averaging is not a substitute for year-round tax management. The latter will benefit many farmers whose incomes are not great enough and whose incomes do not fluctuate widely enough to benefit materially from income averaging. Good tax strategy dictates that the farm manager first make an effort to erase widely fluctuating income through year-end tax management, then resort to income averaging if it is needed.

Although income averaging is somewhat complicated, a general understanding of its application may be gained from the following simplified example (see Exhibit 21–4). These points will help to illustrate the method:

1. Income for the four years prior to the current year is averaged. This is called the base period.

2. In the current year, only income in excess of 120 percent of this "base period average" is eligible for averaging.

3. Averaging is not available at all unless current income exceeds base period average income by $3,000.

Pay Family Members a Salary

A farmer or rancher who has children who work on the farm should consider paying them a reasonable wage. It is a means of reducing the income of the farm business, which is likely to be in a higher tax bracket than the child. The children have their own money for spending on items of their choice or for saving for some future use and pay little or no taxes.

If the family business happens to be incorporated then there is a definite advantage in paying both husband and wife a salary. By having

Exhibit 21-4. Income averaging: $22,00 current year taxable income

Steps	Example	
1. Taxable income for the previous four years is averaged.	$\dfrac{\$8,000 + 12,000 + 9,000 + 11,000 = \$10,000}{4}$	
2. Multiply average by 120 percent to get non-averageable income.	$\$10,000 \times 120\% = \$12,000$	
3. Subtract nonaverageable income from current income. The remainder, as in this case, must exceed $3,000 to be subject to averaging.	$\$22,000 - 12,000 = \$10,000$	
4. Add one-fifth of averageable income to non-averageable income.	$\$12,000 + 2,000 = \$14,000$	
5. Compute tax as follows:		
A— Tax on $14,000		$2,760
B— Less tax on $12,000		2,260
Difference equals tax attributable to one-fifth of averageable income		$ 500
C— $500 × 5 = tax on all averageable income		$2,500
D— Add tax on $12,000 (non-averageable income)		$2,260
E— Total tax equals sum of C + D		$4,760

both on the payroll you qualify for a special deduction for a two-wage family. A married couple filing a joint return can take a deduction on their joint return equal to 10 percent of the first $30,000 earned income from the lower earning spouse, up to a maximum $3,000.

Incorporate?

Reducing income taxes is only one consideration in the decision to incorporate. However, the 1981 Tax Act does give small corporations (taxable income less than $50,000) a tax break. The federal tax rates are as follows:

Taxable income	Marginal tax rate
$0 to 25,000	15%
$25,000–50,000	18%
$50,000–75,000	30%
$75,000–100,000	40%
Over $100,000	46%

Individuals with a $50,000 taxable income are in the 38 percent marginal tax bracket.

As mentioned in Chapter 14, there are numerous other advantages and disadvantages that must be considered in the incorporation decision.

SPECIAL TAX SITUATIONS

Discussion thus far highlights the importance of utilizing tax management strategies to minimize annual income deviation from the income trend. A number of activities which can affect an individual or firm's tax bracket and which may have significant tax implications have been identified. Some examples for a farm/ranch business are:

A change in form of business: If a child is entering the business, a sole proprietorship may be changed to a partnership or corporation. The tax advantages and disadvantages of various forms of business organization must then be weighed. (See Chapter 14.)

A major business expansion: Enlarging the business usually entails sizable capital investments in both depreciable and nondepreciable property. It is important to know how fast these investments can be recovered, what the effect on cash flow will be, and whether capital gain can be created from future disposition of the acquired items. Investment credit implications and depreciation may also be significant.

An improvement in labor management practices: Increased efficiency in use of farm labor can often be attained with better labor management practices. Improved fringe benefits and an ownership share in the business may be considered for key employees. Tax considerations will influence the form that such compensation takes.

Obtaining the use of major equipment items: It is sometimes possible to lease or rent large pieces of equipment as an alternative to outright purchase. It may be tax advantageous to rent, rather than buy, a large machine or to lease on a long-term basis rather than purchase outright.

Sale of a capital item: The disposition of farm land or a herd of dairy or breeding animals certainly requires attention to the tax impact before the sale is consummated. Planning can often also reduce the tax bite when standing timber, a gravel or coal deposit, or dirt is sold.

Planning for retirement: Farmers looking ahead to retirement can sometimes increase their retirement income and decrease current taxes by planning to postpone income until retirement years. This may be done directly through investing in approved retirement plans or indirectly by using current income to build a larger business which will be disposed of at retirement.

Weighing farm versus off-farm investments: Successful farmers with money to invest weigh the advantages and disadvantages of investing in more farm property—including land—against investments in common stock, nonfarm real estate, and many other alternative investments. The tax position of the income from and the growth in these alternative investments must be a major part of the decision to invest.

Estate planning: An important objective of estate planning for many farm owners is to arrange for ownership of the farm to pass to the next generation. Income taxes and estate taxes have a direct bearing on transfers of farm property. Even where there is no younger generation to take over, income tax is an important consideration in disposing of farm property for estate planning purposes.

SUMMARY

Income tax management or taxmanship is the managing of income, expenses, and capital in a manner that will result in minimum tax obligation consistent with the objective of maximum after-tax income. Taxmanship offers returns when annual taxable income fluctuates or deviates from the "normal" income trend of the business.

Particular attention is devoted to identifying means of leveling income. Some tax management strategies a manager might use to reduce taxable income are:

1. Use deferred sales contracts.

2. Make advance purchases of feed and fertilizer.

3. Postpone some sales until the next year.

4. Use "expense method" depreciation.

5. Purchase needed machinery, equipment, etc., before the end of the year to get investment credit and some depreciation.

6. Use "income averaging" if taxable income is $3,000 or more above 120 percent of the past four-year average taxable income.

Some methods to increase income in a tax year are:

1. Sell marketable grain, livestock, etc., before December 31.

2. Postpone expenditures and investments until after January 1.

3. Work with suppliers to pay bills after January 1.

4. Forego "expense method" depreciation.

5. Use straight line depreciation.

6. Do some off-farm or custom work.

APPLYING THE PRINCIPLES OF CHAPTER 21

1. What are the advantages of "normalizing" taxable income?

2. What special situations are likely to provide the opportunity for large dividends to taxmanship?

3. What are some advantages of the cash accounting for tax reporting?

4. Why is income averaging not considered an "approved" income tax management practice?

5. How do the different depreciation techniques influence taxable income?

6. What activities can be used to increase taxable income?

7. What activities can be used to decrease taxable income?

REFERENCES

Durst, Ron, *et. al. The Economic Recovery Tax Act of 1981*, U.S. Department of Agriculture, ERS/NED, Staff Report AGES 810908, September 1981.

Farmer's Tax Guide, Publication 225, 1981 Edition, Department of the Treasury, Internal Revenue Service, November 1981.

Fundamentals of Tax Preparation, Publication 796, Department of the Treasury, 1981.

Harl, Neil E. "The Economic Recovery Tax Act of 1981," in *Agri-Finance Magazine,* Century Communications, Inc., Skokie, Ill., October 1981.

Income Tax Management for Farmers, North Central Regional Publication No. 2, University of Missouri, Revised.

Smith, Robert S. "Taxmanship in Farm Management Decision Making," Agricultural Economics Information Bulletin 25, Cornell University, Ithaca, New York.

Appendix

Mathematical Tables

Table 1
FUTURE VALUE AT COMPOUND INTEREST
$$FV = (1 + i)^n$$

YEAR	4%	5%	6%	7%	8%	9%	10%	11%	12%
1	1.0400	1.0500	1.0600	1.0700	1.0800	1.0900	1.1000	1.1100	1.1200
2	1.0816	1.1025	1.1236	1.1449	1.1664	1.1881	1.2100	1.2321	1.2544
3	1.1248	1.1576	1.1910	1.2250	1.2597	1.2950	1.3310	1.3676	1.4049
4	1.1698	1.2155	1.2624	1.3107	1.3604	1.4115	1.4641	1.5180	1.5735
5	1.2166	1.2762	1.3382	1.4025	1.4693	1.5386	1.6105	1.6850	1.7623
6	1.2653	1.3400	1.4185	1.5007	1.5868	1.6771	1.7715	1.8704	1.9738
7	1.3159	1.4071	1.5036	1.6058	1.7138	1.8280	1.9487	2.0761	2.2106
8	1.3685	1.4774	1.5938	1.7181	1.8509	1.9925	2.1435	2.3045	2.4759
9	1.4233	1.5513	1.6894	1.8384	1.9990	2.1718	2.3579	2.5580	2.7730
10	1.4802	1.6288	1.7908	1.9671	2.1589	2.3673	2.5937	2.8394	3.1058
11	1.5394	1.7103	1.8982	2.1048	2.3316	2.5804	2.8531	3.1517	3.4785
12	1.6010	1.7958	2.0121	2.2521	2.5181	2.8126	3.1384	3.4984	3.8959
13	1.6650	1.8856	2.1329	2.4098	2.7196	3.0658	3.4522	3.8832	4.3634
14	1.7316	1.9799	2.2609	2.5785	2.9371	3.3417	3.7974	4.3104	4.8871
15	1.8009	2.0789	2.3965	2.7590	3.1721	3.6424	4.1772	4.7845	5.4735
16	1.8729	2.1828	2.5403	2.9521	3.4259	3.9703	4.5949	5.3108	6.1303
17	1.9479	2.2920	2.6927	3.1588	3.7000	4.3276	5.0544	5.8950	6.8660
18	2.0258	2.4066	2.8543	3.3799	3.9960	4.7171	5.5599	6.5435	7.6899
19	2.1068	2.5269	3.0255	3.6165	4.3157	5.1416	6.1159	7.2633	8.6127
20	2.1911	2.6532	3.2071	3.8696	4.6609	5.6044	6.7274	8.0623	9.6462
25	2.6658	3.3863	4.2918	5.4274	6.8484	8.6230	10.8347	13.5854	17.0000
30	3.2433	4.3219	5.7434	7.6122	10.0626	13.2676	17.4494	22.8922	29.9599
35	3.9460	5.5160	7.6860	10.6765	14.7853	20.4139	28.1024	38.5748	52.7996
40	4.8010	7.0399	10.2857	14.9744	21.7245	31.4094	45.2592	65.0008	93.0509

Table 1 (cont'd.)
FUTURE VALUE AT COMPOUND INTEREST
$$FV = (1 + i)^n$$

13%	14%	15%	16%	17%	18%	19%	20%
1.1300	1.1400	1.1500	1.1600	1.1700	1.1800	1.1900	1.2000
1.2769	1.2996	1.3225	1.3456	1.3689	1.3924	1.4161	1.4400
1.4428	1.4815	1.5208	1.5608	1.6016	1.6430	1.6851	1.7280
1.6304	1.6889	1.7490	1.8106	1.8738	1.9387	2.0053	2.0736
1.8424	1.9254	2.0113	2.1003	2.1924	2.2877	2.3863	2.4883
2.0819	2.1949	2.3130	2.4363	2.5651	2.6995	2.8397	2.9859
2.3526	2.5022	2.6600	2.8262	3.0012	3.1854	3.3793	3.5831
2.6584	2.8525	3.0590	3.2784	3.5114	3.7588	4.0213	4.2998
3.0040	3.2519	3.5178	3.8029	4.1084	4.4354	4.7854	5.1597
3.3945	3.7072	4.0455	4.4114	4.8068	5.2338	5.6946	6.1917
3.8358	4.2262	4.6523	5.1172	5.6239	6.1759	6.7766	7.4300
4.3345	4.8179	5.3502	5.9360	6.5800	7.2875	8.0642	8.9161
4.8980	5.4924	6.1527	6.8857	7.6986	8.5993	9.5964	10.6993
5.5347	6.2613	7.0757	7.9875	9.0074	10.1472	11.4197	12.8391
6.2542	7.1379	8.1370	9.2655	10.5387	11.9737	13.5895	15.4070
7.0673	8.1372	9.3576	10.7480	12.3303	14.1290	16.1715	18.4884
7.9860	9.2764	10.7612	12.4676	14.4264	16.6722	19.2441	22.1861
9.0242	10.5751	12.3754	14.4625	16.8789	19.6732	22.9005	26.6233
10.1974	12.0556	14.2317	16.7765	19.7483	23.2144	27.2516	31.9479
11.5230	13.7434	16.3665	19.4607	23.1055	27.3930	32.4294	38.3375
21.2305	26.4619	32.9189	40.8742	50.6578	62.6686	77.3880	95.3962
39.1158	50.9501	66.2117	85.8498	111.0646	143.3706	184.6752	237.3762
72.0685	98.1001	133.1755	180.3140	243.5034	327.9972	440.7005	590.6681
132.7815	188.8834	267.8635	378.7211	533.8686	750.3782	1051.6674	1469.7713

Table 2
PRESENT VALUE OF 1
$$PV = 1/(1 + i)^n$$

YEAR	4%	5%	6%	7%	8%	9%	10%	11%
1	0.9615	0.9523	0.9433	0.9345	0.9259	0.9174	0.9090	0.9009
2	0.9245	0.9070	0.8899	0.8734	0.8573	0.8416	0.8264	0.8116
3	0.8889	0.8638	0.8396	0.8163	0.7938	0.7721	0.7513	0.7311
4	0.8548	0.8227	0.7920	0.7629	0.7350	0.7084	0.6830	0.6587
5	0.8219	0.7835	0.7472	0.7130	0.6805	0.6499	0.6209	0.5934
6	0.7903	0.7462	0.7049	0.6663	0.6301	0.5962	0.5644	0.5346
7	0.7599	0.7106	0.6650	0.6227	0.5834	0.5470	0.5131	0.4817
8	0.7306	0.6768	0.6274	0.5820	0.5402	0.5018	0.4665	0.4339
9	0.7025	0.6446	0.5918	0.5439	0.5002	0.4604	0.4240	0.3909
10	0.6755	0.6139	0.5583	0.5083	0.4631	0.4224	0.3855	0.3521
11	0.6495	0.5846	0.5267	0.4751	0.4288	0.3875	0.3509	0.3172
12	0.6245	0.5568	0.4969	0.4440	0.3971	0.3555	0.3186	0.2858
13	0.6005	0.5303	0.4688	0.4150	0.3676	0.3262	0.2896	0.2575
14	0.5774	0.5050	0.4423	0.3878	0.3404	0.2992	0.2633	0.2319
15	0.5552	0.4810	0.4172	0.3624	0.3152	0.2745	0.2393	0.2090
16	0.5339	0.4581	0.3936	0.3387	0.2918	0.2518	0.2176	0.1882
17	0.5133	0.4362	0.3713	0.3166	0.2702	0.2310	0.1978	0.1696
18	0.4936	0.4155	0.3503	0.2959	0.2502	0.2119	0.1798	0.1528
19	0.4746	0.3957	0.3305	0.2765	0.2317	0.1944	0.1635	0.1376
20	0.4563	0.3768	0.3118	0.2584	0.2145	0.1784	0.1486	0.1240
25	0.3751	0.2953	0.2329	0.1842	0.1460	0.1159	0.0922	0.0736
30	0.3083	0.2313	0.1741	0.1314	0.0993	0.0753	0.0573	0.0436
35	0.2534	0.1812	0.1301	0.0936	0.0676	0.0489	0.0355	0.0259
40	0.2082	0.1420	0.0972	0.0668	0.0460	0.0318	0.0220	0.0153

Table 2 (cont'd.)
PRESENT VALUE OF 1
$$PV = 1/(1 + i)^n$$

12%	13%	14%	15%	16%	17%	18%	19%	20%
0.8928	0.8849	0.8771	0.8695	0.8620	0.8547	0.8474	0.8403	0.8333
0.7971	0.7831	0.7694	0.7561	0.7431	0.7305	0.7181	0.7061	0.6944
0.7117	0.6930	0.6749	0.6575	0.6406	0.6243	0.6086	0.5934	0.5787
0.6355	0.6133	0.5920	0.5717	0.5522	0.5336	0.5157	0.4986	0.4822
0.5674	0.5427	0.5193	0.4971	0.4761	0.4561	0.4371	0.4190	0.4018
0.5066	0.4803	0.4555	0.4323	0.4104	0.3898	0.3704	0.3521	0.3348
0.4523	0.4250	0.3996	0.3759	0.3538	0.3331	0.3139	0.2959	0.2790
0.4038	0.3761	0.3505	0.3269	0.3050	0.2847	0.2660	0.2486	0.2325
0.3606	0.3328	0.3075	0.2842	0.2629	0.2434	0.2254	0.2089	0.1938
0.3219	0.2945	0.2697	0.2471	0.2266	0.2080	0.1910	0.1756	0.1615
0.2874	0.2606	0.2366	0.2149	0.1954	0.1778	0.1619	0.1475	0.1345
0.2566	0.2307	0.2075	0.1869	0.1684	0.1519	0.1372	0.1240	0.1121
0.2291	0.2042	0.1820	0.1625	0.1452	0.1298	0.1162	0.1042	0.0934
0.2046	0.1806	0.1597	0.1413	0.1251	0.1110	0.0985	0.0875	0.0778
0.1826	0.1598	0.1400	0.1228	0.1079	0.0948	0.0835	0.0735	0.0649
0.1631	0.1414	0.1228	0.1068	0.0930	0.0811	0.0707	0.0618	0.0540
0.1456	0.1252	0.1077	0.0929	0.0802	0.0693	0.0599	0.0519	0.0450
0.1300	0.1108	0.0946	0.0808	0.0691	0.0592	0.0508	0.0436	0.0375
0.1161	0.0980	0.0829	0.0702	0.0596	0.0506	0.0430	0.0366	0.0313
0.1036	0.0867	0.0728	0.0611	0.0513	0.0432	0.0365	0.0308	0.0260
0.0588	0.0471	0.0378	0.0303	0.0244	0.0197	0.0159	0.0129	0.0104
0.0333	0.0255	0.0196	0.0151	0.0116	0.0090	0.0069	0.0054	0.0042
0.0189	0.0138	0.0101	0.0075	0.0055	0.0041	0.0030	0.0022	0.0016
0.0107	0.0075	0.0052	0.0037	0.0026	0.0018	0.0013	0.0009	0.0006

Table 3
ANNUAL PAYMENT PER $1 OF LOAN AT GIVEN INTEREST RATES
AND MATURITIES (AMORTIZATION TABLE)

YEAR	4%	5%	6%	7%	8%	9%	10%	11%
1	1.0400	1.0500	1.0600	1.0700	1.0800	1.0900	1.1000	1.1100
2	.5301	.5378	.5454	.5530	.5607	.5684	.5761	.5839
3	.3603	.3672	.3741	.3810	.3880	.3950	.4021	.4092
4	.2754	.2820	.2885	.2952	.3019	.3086	.3154	.3223
5	.2246	.2309	.2373	.2438	.2504	.2570	.2637	.2705
6	.1907	.1970	.2033	.2097	.2163	.2229	.2296	.2363
7	.1666	.1728	.1791	.1855	.1920	.1986	.2054	.2122
8	.1485	.1547	.1610	.1674	.1740	.1806	.1874	.1943
9	.1344	.1406	.1470	.1534	.1600	.1667	.1736	.1806
10	.1232	.1295	.1358	.1423	.1490	.1558	.1627	.1698
11	.1141	.1203	.1267	.1333	.1400	.1469	.1539	.1611
12	.1065	.1128	.1192	.1259	.1326	.1396	.1467	.1540
13	.1001	.1064	.1129	.1196	.1265	.1335	.1407	.1481
14	.0946	.1010	.1075	.1143	.1212	.1284	.1357	.1432
15	.0899	.0963	.1029	.1097	.1168	.1240	.1314	.1390
16	.0858	.0922	.0989	.1058	.1129	.1203	.1278	.1355
17	.0821	.0886	.0954	.1024	.1096	.1170	.1246	.1324
18	.0789	.0855	.0923	.0994	.1067	.1142	.1219	.1298
19	.0761	.0827	.0896	.0967	.1041	.1117	.1195	.1275
20	.0735	.0802	.0871	.0943	.1018	.1095	.1174	.1255
25	.0640	.0709	.0782	.0858	.0936	.1018	.1101	.1187
30	.0578	.0650	.0726	.0805	.0888	.0973	.1060	.1150
35	.0535	.0610	.0689	.0772	.0858	.0946	.1036	.1129
40	.0505	.0505	.0664	.0750	.0838	.0929	.1022	.1117

Table 3 (cont'd.)
ANNUAL PAYMENT PER $1 OF LOAN AT GIVEN INTEREST RATES
AND MATURITIES (AMORTIZATION TABLE)

12%	13%	14%	15%	16%	17%	18%	19%	20%
1.1200	1.1300	1.1400	1.1500	1.1600	1.1700	1.1800	1.1900	1.2000
.5916	.5994	.6072	.6151	.6229	.6308	.6387	.6466	.6545
.4163	.4235	.4307	.4379	.4452	.4525	.4599	.4673	.4747
.3292	.3361	.3432	.3502	.3573	.3645	.3717	.3789	.3862
.2774	.2843	.2912	.2983	.3054	.3125	.3197	.3270	.3343
.2432	.2501	.2571	.2642	.2713	.2786	.2859	.2932	.3007
.2191	.2261	.2331	.2403	.2476	.2549	.2623	.2698	.2774
.2013	.2083	.2155	.2228	.2302	.2376	.2452	.2528	.2606
.1876	.1948	.2021	.2095	.2170	.2246	.2323	.2401	.2480
.1769	.1842	.1917	.1992	.2069	.2146	.2225	.2304	.2385
.1684	.1758	.1833	.1910	.1988	.2067	.2147	.2228	.2311
.1614	.1689	.1766	.1844	.1924	.2004	.2086	.2168	.2252
.1556	.1633	.1711	.1791	.1871	.1953	.2036	.2121	.2206
.1508	.1586	.1666	.1746	.1828	.1912	.1996	.2082	.2168
.1468	.1547	.1628	.1710	.1793	.1878	.1964	.2050	.2138
.1433	.1514	.1596	.1679	.1764	.1850	.1937	.2025	.2114
.1404	.1486	.1569	.1653	.1739	.1826	.1914	.2004	.2094
.1379	.1462	.1546	.1631	.1718	.1807	.1896	.1986	.2078
.1357	.1441	.1526	.1613	.1701	.1790	.1881	.1972	.2064
.1338	.1423	.1509	.1597	.1686	.1776	.1862	.1960	.2053
.1275	.1364	.1454	.1546	.1640	.1734	.1829	.1924	.2021
.1241	.1334	.1428	.1523	.1618	.1715	.1812	.1910	.2008
.1223	.1318	.1414	.1511	.1608	.1707	.1805	.1904	.2003
.1213	.1309	.1407	.1505	.1604	.1703	.1802	.1901	.2001

Table 4
PRESENT VALUE OF ANNUITY OF $1

YEAR	4%	5%	6%	7%	8%	9%	10%	11%
1	.9615	.9524	.9434	.9346	.9259	.9174	.9091	.9009
2	1.8861	1.8594	1.8334	1.8080	1.7833	1.7591	1.7355	1.7125
3	2.7751	2.7232	2.6730	2.6243	2.5771	2.5313	2.4868	2.4437
4	3.6299	3.5459	3.4651	3.3872	3.3121	3.2397	3.1699	3.1024
5	4.4518	4.3295	4.2124	4.1002	3.9927	3.8896	3.7908	3.6959
6	5.2421	5.0757	4.9173	4.7665	4.6229	4.4859	4.3553	4.2305
7	6.0020	5.7864	5.5824	5.3893	5.2064	5.0329	4.8684	4.7122
8	6.7327	6.4632	6.2098	5.9713	5.7466	5.5348	5.3349	5.1461
9	7.4353	7.1078	6.8017	6.5152	6.2469	5.9952	5.7590	5.5370
10	8.1109	7.7217	7.3601	7.0236	6.7101	6.4177	6.1446	5.8892
11	8.7605	8.3064	7.8869	7.4987	7.1390	6.8052	6.4951	6.2065
12	9.3851	8.8632	8.3838	7.9427	7.5361	7.1607	6.8137	6.4924
13	9.9856	9.3936	8.8527	8.3576	7.9038	7.4869	7.1034	6.7499
14	10.5631	9.8986	9.2950	8.7455	8.2442	7.7862	7.3667	6.9819
15	11.1184	10.3797	9.7122	9.1079	8.5595	8.0607	7.6061	7.1909
16	11.6523	10.8378	10.1059	9.4467	8.8514	8.3126	7.8237	7.3792
17	12.1657	11.2741	10.4773	9.7632	9.1216	8.5436	8.0216	7.5488
18	12.6593	11.6896	10.8276	10.0591	9.3719	8.7556	8.2014	7.7016
19	13.1339	12.0853	11.1581	10.3356	9.6036	8.9501	8.3649	7.8393
20	13.5903	12.4622	11.4699	10.5940	9.8181	9.1285	8.5135	7.9633
25	15.6221	14.0939	12.7834	11.6536	10.6748	9.8226	9.0770	8.4217
30	17.2920	15.3724	13.7648	12.4090	11.2578	10.2736	9.4269	8.6938
35	18.6646	16.3742	14.4982	12.9477	11.6546	10.5668	9.6442	8.8552
40	19.7928	17.1591	15.0463	13.3317	11.9246	10.7574	9.7790	8.9511

Table 4 (cont'd.)
PRESENT VALUE OF ANNUITY OF $1

12%	13%	14%	15%	16%	17%	18%	19%	20%
.8929	.8850	.8772	.8696	.8621	.8547	.8475	.8403	.8333
1.6901	1.6681	1.6467	1.6257	1.6052	1.5852	1.5656	1.5465	1.5278
2.4018	2.3611	2.3216	2.2832	2.2459	2.2096	2.1743	2.1399	2.1065
3.0373	2.9745	2.9137	2.8549	2.7982	2.7432	2.6901	2.6386	2.5887
3.6048	3.5172	3.4331	3.3522	3.2743	3.1993	3.1272	3.0576	2.9906
4.1114	3.9975	3.8887	3.7845	3.6847	3.5892	3.4976	3.4098	3.3255
4.5638	4.4226	4.2883	4.1604	4.0386	3.9224	3.8115	3.7057	3.6046
4.9676	4.7988	4.6389	4.4873	4.3436	4.2072	4.0776	3.9544	3.8372
5.3282	5.1317	4.9464	4.7716	4.6065	4.4506	4.3030	4.1633	4.0310
5.6502	5.4262	5.2161	5.0188	4.8332	4.6586	4.4941	4.3389	4.1925
5.9377	5.6869	5.4527	5.2337	5.0286	4.8364	4.6560	4.4865	4.3271
6.1944	5.9176	5.6603	5.4206	5.1971	4.9884	4.7932	4.6105	4.4392
6.4235	6.1218	5.8424	5.5831	5.3423	5.1183	4.9095	4.7147	4.5327
6.6282	6.3025	6.0021	5.7245	5.4675	5.2293	5.0081	4.8023	4.6106
6.8109	6.4624	6.1422	5.8474	5.5754	5.3242	5.0916	4.8759	4.6755
6.9740	6.6039	6.2651	5.9542	5.6685	5.4053	5.1624	4.9377	4.7296
7.1196	6.7291	6.3729	6.0472	5.7487	5.4746	5.2223	4.9897	4.7746
7.2497	6.8399	6.5504	6.1280	5.8178	5.5339	5.2732	5.0333	4.8122
7.3658	6.9380	6.6231	6.1982	5.8774	5.5845	5.3162	5.0700	4.8435
7.4694	7.0248	6.6869	6.2593	5.9288	5.6278	5.3527	5.1009	4.8696
7.8431	7.3300	6.8729	6.4641	6.0971	5.7662	5.4669	5.1951	4.9476
8.0552	7.4956	7.0027	6.5660	6.1772	5.8294	5.5168	5.2346	4.9789
8.1755	7.5856	7.0700	6.6166	6.2153	5.8582	5.5386	5.2512	4.9915
8.2438	7.6344	7.1050	6.6418	6.2335	5.8713	5.5481	5.2581	4.9966

Index

Index